GOVERNANCE WITHOUT GOVERNMENT: ORDER AND CHANGE IN WORLD POLITICS

Cambridge Studies in International Relations is a joint initiative of Cambridge University Press and the British International Studies Association (BISA). The series will include a wide range of material, from undergraduate textbooks and surveys to research-based monographs and collaborative volumes. The aim of the series is to publish the best new scholarship in International Studies from Europe, North America and the rest of the world.

D0168860

CAMBRIDGE STUDIES IN INTERNATIONAL RELATIONS

GOVERNANCE WITHOUT GOVERNMENT: ORDER AND CHANGE IN WORLD POLITICS

edited by

JAMES N. ROSENAU
Director, Institute for Transnational Studies and Professor of International Relations and Political Science, University of Southern California

and

ERNST-OTTO CZEMPIEL
Professor of International Relations, University of Frankfurt, and Co-Director, Frankfurt Peace Research Institute

CAMBRIDGE
UNIVERSITY PRESS

Published by the Press Syndicate of the University of Cambridge
The Pitt Building, Trumpington Street, Cambridge CB2 1RP
40 West 20th Street, New York, NY 10011–4211, USA
10 Stamford Road, Oakleigh, Melbourne 3166, Australia

First published 1992
Reprinted 1993

Printed in Great Britain by The Athenaeum Press Ltd, Newcastle upon Tyne

A catalogue record for this book is available from the British Library

Library of Congress cataloguing in publication data

Governance without government: order and change in world politics /
edited by James N. Rosenau and Ernst-Otto Czempiel.
    p.   cm. – (Cambridge studies in international relations: 20)
Includes index.
ISBN 0 521 40531 9 (hardback)
1. International organization.   2. International relations.
I. Rosenau, James N.   II. Czempiel, Ernst-Otto, 1927– .
III. Series.
JX1954.G68   1992
341.2–dc20   91–22168 CIP

ISBN 0 521 40531 9 hardback
ISBN 0 521 40578 5 paperback

WD

CONTENTS

NOTES ON CONTRIBUTORS

Thomas J. BIERSTEKER is Professor of International Relations at the University of Southern California. He has written extensively on foreign investment in the developing world, has strong interests in international relations theory and international political economy, and is currently working on developing country debt, structural adjustment, and the relationship between economic and political liberalization.

James A. CAPORASO is Professor of Political Science at the University of Washington. The editor of *Comparative Political Studies* since 1974, his work has been distinguished by efforts to achieve theoretical coherence among political and economic dynamics as well as those that transgress the boundaries between domestic and international politics.

Linda CORNETT is a graduate student at the University of Washington, where she is working toward completion of her Ph.D. Her major interests include international political economy and political theory.

Robert W. COX is Professor of Political Science at York University in Canada. A former official of the International Labor Organization, his research focuses on theoretical problems in the field of international economy and international organization.

Ernst-Otto CZEMPIEL is Professor of International Relations at the University of Frankfurt. The Co-Director of the Frankfurt Peace Research Institute, his research program includes a concern with the dynamics of U.S. foreign policy as well as the general challenge of theorizing about world politics.

K. J. HOLSTI is Professor of Political Science at the University of British Columbia. His research interests concentrate on the theory and practice of international war and order, and presently he is examining the sources of conflict in the Third World.

James N. ROSENAU is Director of the Institute for Transnational Studies and Professor of International Relations and Political Science at the University of Southern California. His research program combines theoretical and empirical inquiries into various facets of the boundaries that divide national and international political systems.

Janice E. THOMSON is Assistant Professor of Political Science at the University of Washington. Her research focuses on the organization of violence, state-building, and the political economy of sovereignty.

Oran R. YOUNG is affiliated with the Institute of Arctic Studies at Dartmouth College and is also a senior fellow at the Center for Northern Studies in Wolcott, Vermont. His theoretical work probes the nature of international institutions, which he traces empirically through research into the resource and environmental problems of world politics.

Mark W. ZACHER is Professor of Political Science and Director of the Institute of International Relations at the University of British Columbia. His research focuses on the political development of international regimes. His past and present studies encompass regimes in security and economic issue-areas as well as broader trends in international order.

PREFACE

It is no accident that the chapters in this book are coordinated around the common theme of international governance. For this is the second of a projected three volumes designed to promote theoretical inquiry into the dynamics of world politics. It follows logically from the first volume, *Global Changes and Theoretical Challenges: Approaches to World Politics for the 1990s* (Lexington Books, 1989), which we co-edited and which was cast at a much higher level of abstraction than the present work as a means of identifying specific problem areas worthy of theoretical exploration. This expectation proved more sound than we anticipated: during the last session of the workshop that resulted in the initial volume, it was suggested that the next step was to probe systems of rule in world politics. The present volume is a direct consequence of that suggestion and the wide agreement it evoked among those present.

What follows logically, however, is not always easily implemented. The contributors to this volume met a number of times to discuss their perspectives on international governance and to evolve shared understandings of the key concepts inherent in the subject. These meetings extended across four years in a variety of settings and, consequently, drafts of the chapters were subjected to intense evaluations as they went through several iterations.

Throughout the long history of the project, our goal was not so much that of developing a common framework for the analysis of international governance as it was to make sure that we were not working at cross purposes. From the outset it seemed clear that the subject was too unexplored, too controversial, and too discursive to lead to a single formulation and consensual definitions. A grasp of how governance occurs in world politics is challenging enough for the individual scholar, so that achieving an integrated perspective among ten scholars, all of whom have developed intellectual identities of their own, seemed highly unlikely. As a result, we opted to delineate both the boundaries and the dynamics with which meaningful inquiry would have to contend, while at the same time recognizing that each of us would pursue different paths within this common overall context. While the conceptual problems and methodological obstacles encountered in this process are summarized in Chapter 1, the results for each contributor are presented in the remaining chapters.

Needless to say, of course, we do not view the ensuing collection as the last word on matters pertaining to international governance. The subject is too vast and unexplored to allow for a definitive statement. Rather, we hope that our mode of breaking into the problems of governance in the absence of a final authority serves to stimulate further inquiry and eventual convergence around common foci of inquiry.

During the long gestation period that preceded the publication of this volume our work has been ably facilitated by five associates of the Institute for Transnational Studies at the University of Southern California. E. Martha Decker helped greatly in the planning of a 1990 conference in Ojai, California, R. B. A. DiMuccio made crucial suggestions during the period when the chapters underwent their last round of editing, and Christine Kralovansky, Donald F. Hansen, Jr., and Tricia E. Pobjoy assisted ably in preparing the index. We are grateful to all of them for their invaluable assistance. In addition, it is a pleasure to acknowledge the early inputs of two colleagues, John Gerard Ruggie and Stephen D. Krasner, whose other obligations prevented them from translating their conceptions of international governance into a written contribution to this book. We are also indebted to the School of International Relations of the University of Southern California and the Esther A. and Joseph Klingenstein Fund, as well as to our respective universities, for the financial support that enabled us to meet together on five separate occasions.

None of the foregoing, however, is responsible for the final product. This book is rather the fruit of a continuous collaboration and the editors are pleased to express their appreciation to our colleagues for both their contributions and their commitment to the lengthy process whereby we have finally converged in print.

J.N.R.
E.-O.C.

1 GOVERNANCE, ORDER, AND CHANGE IN WORLD POLITICS

James N. Rosenau

At a time when hegemons are declining, when boundaries (and the walls that seal them) are disappearing, when the squares of the world's cities are crowded with citizens challenging authorities, when military alliances are losing their viability – to mention but a few of the myriad changes that are transforming world politics – the prospects for global order and governance have become a transcendent issue. As the scope of the transformation widens and as its pace intensifies, the more urgent do questions about the nature of order and governance become. Change means the attrition of established patterns, the lessening of order, and the faltering of governance, until such time as new patterns can form and get embedded in the routines of world politics. Such is the situation today. One senses that the course of history is at a turning point, a juncture where the opportunities for movement toward peaceful cooperation, expanded human rights, and higher standards of living are hardly less conspicuous than the prospects for intensified group conflicts, deteriorating social systems, and worsening environmental conditions. Either set of arrangements – and possibly both – could evolve as leaders and publics get accustomed to the heady realization that some control over the future has been regained as a consequence of all the changes.

The goal of the collaborative project that resulted in the ensuing chapters is precisely that of seizing upon this time of change as a chance to clarify the nature of global order and the processes through which governance occurs on a worldwide scale. We do not seek to anticipate the specific forms of order and governance that are likely to emerge out of the rubble of the Cold War or the military conflict in the Persian Gulf. It may be years before the outlines of such an order evolve. But the present dynamics of change and statics of continuity are so arresting as to highlight a number of crucial questions that will surely frame our grasp of what lies ahead. What do we mean by governance on a global scale? How can it operate without government? If governance connotes a system of rule, and if it is not sustained by an organized government, who makes and implements the rules? Does the prevailing global order

1

depend on the nature and extensiveness of governance? Indeed, to what does global order refer? What forms can it take? Is global order a mental construct, an ideational image of how things work? Is it an implicit and largely unrecognized complex of norms that limits and shapes the conduct of international actors? Or does it consist of patterns and regularities that are empirically discernible? Can extensive, disorderly conflict be considered a form of order? Or is order founded on normative considerations that stress cooperation and preclude the notion of a conflict-ridden and chaotic order? Can there be global order during a period of rapid change? And how is order to be distinguished from stability and the interests and material conditions on which it rests?

There is no lack of attention to these questions in the international relations (IR) literature.[1] Unlike the ensuing essays, however, most prior attempts to delineate global order have not been propelled by a world undergoing change in the fundamental arrangements through which the course of events unfolds. Our advantage is the perplexity induced by recent developments, an awe that enables us to pose questions that might not otherwise get asked and to identify alternative lines of development that might not otherwise get explored.

The questions proved easier to ask than to answer, however. We met to discuss them on five separate occasions over the course of four years and each time we found the answers elusive, partly because our collective focus on the concepts of order, governance, institutions, and polyarchy varied from meeting to meeting and partly because we encountered nuances of difference among ourselves as to the essential scope and content of these key concepts. Some of these nuances remain. A careful reading of the several chapters will reveal we preferred to allow for different emphases rather than straining to converge around a watered down consensual formulation.

But it is important not to be misled by the nuanced differences. We may differ somewhat in our use of concepts and terminology, but we are concerned about the same problems. We share a view of the central issues that confront analysts who seek to develop an understanding of the emergent structures of world politics. Most notably, we agree that in a world where authority is undergoing continuous relocation – both outward toward supranational entities and inward toward subnational

---

[1] For two comprehensive inquiries into the nature of international order, see Hedley Bull, *The Anarchical Society: A Study of Order in World Politics* (New York: Columbia University Press, 1977), and Lynn H. Miller, *Global Order: Values and Power in International Politics* (Boulder, CO: Westview Press, 1990).

groups – it becomes increasingly imperative to probe how governance can occur in the absence of government.

Given both our differences and shared conceptions, the task of this introductory chapter follows. It seeks to highlight the range of meanings encompassed by our collective concerns and to indicate how the various chapters fit together into a coherent whole.

GOVERNANCE AND ORDER

To presume the presence of governance without government is to conceive of functions that have to be performed in any viable human system irrespective of whether the system has evolved organizations and institutions explicitly charged with performing them. Among the many necessary functions, for example, are the needs wherein any system has to cope with external challenges, to prevent conflicts among its members or factions from tearing it irretrievably apart, to procure resources necessary to its preservation and well-being, and to frame goals and policies designed to achieve them. Whether the systems are local or global in scope, these functional needs are ever present if a system is to persist intact through time.

Activities designed to service a system's functional necessities are readily self-evident in the operations of governments which, normally, either evolve constitutions to regulate their conduct domestically or sign treaties to guide their performance internationally. During the present period of rapid and extensive global change, however, the constitutions of national governments and their treaties have been undermined by the demands and greater coherence of ethnic and other subgroups, the globalization of economies, the advent of broad social movements, the shrinking of political distances by microelectronic technologies, and the mushrooming of global interdependencies fostered by currency crises, environmental pollution, terrorism, the drug trade, AIDS, and a host of other transnational issues that are crowding the global agenda. These centralizing and decentralizing dynamics have undermined constitutions and treaties in the sense that they have contributed to the shifts in the loci of authority. Governments still operate and they are still sovereign in a number of ways; but, as noted above, some of their authority has been relocated toward subnational collectivities. Some of the functions of governance, in other words, are now being performed by activities that do not originate with governments.

What, then, is an appropriate way of formulating the concept of governance as it operates in world politics? Is it merely a synonym for international institutions and regimes? Can governance be effective in the absence of central authority? To what extent is the stability of a global order dependent on the presence of governance?

Such questions invite a lengthy disquisition on the nature of government and how sovereign national systems are so much more conducive to governmental operations than international systems that are not endowed with sovereign powers. And, indeed, the collapse of the Cold War and the many other changes that mark our time readily justify such a disquisition. Given the profound transformations in the nature and location of authority, legitimacy, and compliance, and given the emergent roles and structures of the modern state, transnational organizations, social movements, common markets, and political parties, the basis for extensive re-examinations of government and governance in an increasingly interdependent world is surely compelling. Obviously, however, this is not the occasion to undertake this task. Here we can only take note of possible meanings of governance in the emergent international context and how it is linked into the prevailing order and the prospects for change.[2]

As indicated by the title of this book, governance is not synonymous with government. Both refer to purposive behavior, to goal-oriented activities, to systems of rule; but government suggests activities that are backed by formal authority, by police powers to insure the implementation of duly constituted policies, whereas governance refers to activities backed by shared goals that may or may not derive from legal and formally prescribed responsibilities and that do not necessarily rely on police powers to overcome defiance and attain compliance. Governance, in other words, is a more encompassing phenomenon than government. It embraces governmental institutions, but it also subsumes informal, non-governmental mechanisms whereby those persons and organizations within its purview move ahead, satisfy their needs, and fulfill their wants.

Governance is thus a system of rule that is as dependent on intersubjective meanings as on formally sanctioned constitutions and charters. Put more emphatically, governance is a system of rule that works only if it is accepted by the majority (or, at least, by the most powerful of those it affects), whereas governments can function even in the face of widespread opposition to their policies. In this sense

---

[2] For another, more extensive and cogent inquiry into the meaning of the governance concept, see Lawrence S. Finkelstein, "What Is International Governance?," a paper presented at the Annual Meeting of the International Studies Association (Vancouver: March 21, 1991).

governance is always effective in performing the functions necessary to systemic persistence, else it is not conceived to exist (since instead of referring to ineffective governance, one speaks of anarchy or chaos). Governments, on the other hand, can be quite ineffective without being regarded as non-existent (they are viewed simply as "weak"). Thus it is possible to conceive of governance without government – of regulatory mechanisms in a sphere of activity which function effectively even though they are not endowed with formal authority.

Nor is it far-fetched to derive from this line of reasoning a plausible scenario marked by government without governance. Indeed, if one ponders all the deeply divided countries whose politics are paralyzed and stalemated, it can readily be concluded that the world is populated with more than a few formal authorities who lack the regulatory mechanisms to function effectively, that is, with governments without governance. One might even argue, given all the noxious policies governments pursue, that governance without government is in some ways preferable to governments that are capable of governance. As one exasperated analyst has succinctly and tellingly observed, "Governance has been usurped by governments."[3]

To suggest that governance is always effective is to posit a close link between governance and order. It might even be said that governance is order plus intentionality. Global order consists of those routinized arrangements through which world politics gets from one moment in time to the next. Some of the arrangements are fundamental (such as the dispersion of power among key actors, the hierarchical differences among them, the rules which bound their interactions, and the premises they share about the role of force, diplomacy, cooperation, and conflict) and some are quite routinized (such as trade, postal, and passport procedures). But irrespective of whether they are fundamental or routinized, not all of the arrangements are the result of self-conscious efforts on the part of those who sustain them. Some of the arrangements derive, rather, from the aggregation of individual decisions that are designed to serve immediate subsystem concerns but that cumulate to system-wide orderly arrangements. The setting of prices in a market place exemplifies a self-regulating aggregation that facilitates order: sellers are concerned with receiving the highest possible amount for their goods and buyers seek to pay the lowest possible amount, but the result of their individual bargains is normally a stable and orderly system-wide market for the commodity. Similarly, individual members of Amnesty International work on specific cases of illegal

[3] Rajhi Kothari, "On Human Governance," *Alternatives*, 12 (1987), p. 277.

imprisonment and torture, but the collective sum of their efforts makes a substantial contribution to that dimension of global order through which a modicum of human rights is preserved. Or consider the example of the flight of East Germans to the West in the fall of 1989: as participants in the Cold War order they previously acquiesced in the prohibition against movement across the East–West border, but that consensus unraveled with the decision of each family to flee to West Germany and, within only weeks, the cumulative impact of these decisions hastened an end to that system of governance and initiated a new one that is still very much in the process of formation.

On the other hand, some of the arrangements underlying a global order spring from activities that are self-consciously designed to maintain the order. Most markets have created rules and officials charged with monitoring and preventing unfair practices; Amnesty International has an executive committee that assigns cases to individuals and issues periodic reports on overall patterns in the human rights field; during the Cold War East Germany had officials and laws that relied on police powers to insure the continuance of the consensus that kept East Germans from emigrating, just as the subsequent breakdown of that consensus was facilitated by West German, Hungarian, and other authorities who sought to encourage the emergence of a new order. And it is here, in those dimensions of order suffused with intentionality, that its close links to governance are most readily discernible.

While examples help to clarify the concept of governance and how it is more encompassing than that of government, they obviously do not guarantee the resolution of conceptual ambiguity. The distinction between governance and government and the links between governance and order are not self-evident. In some languages (German for one), in fact, there is no readily identifiable word that signifies governance. The notion of intersubjective systems of rule not backed by legal and constitutional authority is too improbable an aspect of political processes in the cultures that employ these languages to have allowed for convergence around a simplified, single-word designation of the concept. But even those whose language includes such a designation can easily encounter difficulty in using the concept. A host of diverse (but not incompatible) nuances attach to the use of "governance" in English. As indicated above, some formulations conceive of governance in functional terms, that is, in terms of the tasks that have to be performed to sustain the routinized arrangements of the prevailing order and that may or may not be performed by governments. For other observers governance is linked to the capacity to regulate the arrangements so that they remain routinized. For still others governance is associated with occasions when power is exercised independently of the authority of government. Some distinguish governance as a mode of allocating values while viewing government as operating the mechanisms through which the allocation is accomplished. In some instances governance is equated with the emergence of rule-like systems and problem-solving devices.[4]

Notwithstanding the various shades of meaning attached to the concept, there is one dimension of governance about which all of the ensuing chapters fully agree. It is that while a focus on "governance without government" does not require the exclusion of national or subnational governments from the analysis, it does necessitate inquiry that presumes the absence of some overarching governmental authority at the international level. Put differently, the concept of governance without government is especially conducive to the study of world politics inasmuch as centralized authority is conspicuously absent from this domain of human affairs even though it is equally obvious that a modicum of order, of routinized arrangements, is normally present in the conduct of global life. Given an order that lacks a centralized authority with the capacity to enforce decisions on a global scale, it follows that a prime task of inquiry is that of probing the extent to which the functions normally associated with governance are performed in world politics without the institutions of government.

Many students of world politics are inclined to use the term "anarchy" to designate the absence of a centralized authority in world politics. For them anarchy has neither good nor bad connotations. Nor does it necessarily imply that the prevailing global order is marked by pervasive disarray and commotion. Rather, "anarchy" is employed simply as a descriptive term for the lack of a centralized authority that stands over national governments and has the capacity, including the use of force if necessary, to direct their conduct. For some analysts, however, anarchy implies a lack of patterned rule, a tendency for actors to go their own separate ways without regard for common principles, norms, rules, and procedures. Such an implication seems highly questionable. As one observer puts it, noting the authority that attached

---

[4] For an inquiry that identifies sixteen different types of situations in which governance operates as a system of rule, see James N. Rosenau, "Governance without Government: Systems of Rule in World Politics" (Los Angeles: Institute for Transnational Studies, University of Southern California, November 1987). An extended critique of this essay is developed in Richard K. Ashley, "Imposing International Purpose: Notes on a Problematic of Governance," in Ernst-Otto Czempiel and James N. Rosenau, eds., *Global Changes and Theoretical Challenges: Approaches to World Politics for the 1990s* (Lexington, MA: Lexington Books, 1989), ch. 13.

to many treaties, international legal precedents, and international organizations, "the international system (in spite of its lack of an overarching regime or world government) is several steps beyond anarchy."[5]

In sum, governance and order are clearly interactive phenomena. As intentional activities designed to regularize the arrangements which sustain world affairs, governance obviously shapes the nature of the prevailing global order. It could not do so, however, if the patterns constituting the order did not facilitate governance. Thus order is both a precondition and a consequence of government. Neither comes first and each helps explain the other. There can be no governance without order and there can be no order without governance (unless periods of disorder are regarded as forms of order).

GOVERNANCE, REGIMES, AND INSTITUTIONS

Some might wonder whether the foregoing delineation of governance is any different from the concept of international regimes that is presently very much in vogue in the study of world politics.[6] Like governance, regimes are conceived as arrangements – "as sets of implicit or explicit principles, norms, rules, and decision-making procedures around which actors' expectations converge"[7] – for sustaining and regulating activities across national boundaries. Like governance, they encompass governmental and non-governmental actors who intersubjectively concur that cooperation on behalf of their shared interests justifies acceptance of the principles, norms, rules, and procedures that differentiate and give coherence to their regimes. In effect, therefore, since they operate in the absence of any central authorities, regimes can readily be described as forms of governance without government. Are they not, then, the equivalent of what has been identified here as the governance that is inherent in a global order? No, they are not. Despite the similarities between the two concepts, they are far from identical. The widely accepted definition of the characteristics of regimes quoted above has an added phrase which summarizes the prime difference: the principles, norms, rules, and procedures of any regime are defined as converging "in a given area of international relations,"[8] or what has also been called an "issue-area." As used in this

---

[5] Robert C. North, *War, Peace, Survival: Global Politics and Conceptual Synthesis* (Boulder, CO: Westview Press, 1990), p. 136.

[6] See, for example, Stephen D. Krasner, ed., *International Regimes* (Ithaca, NY: Cornell University Press, 1983).

[7] *Ibid.*, p. 2.   [8] *Ibid.*, p. 2.

8

volume, on the other hand, governance in a global order is not confined to a single sphere of endeavor. It refers to the arrangements that prevail in the lacunae between regimes and, perhaps more importantly, to the principles, norms, rules, and procedures that come into play when two or more regimes overlap, conflict, or otherwise require arrangements that facilitate accommodation among the competing interests. In the case of the Cold War, for example, governance involved according a greater priority to the arms control regime than to, say, issues involving the free movement of people, with the result that Soviet–American arms control negotiations, unlike those over trade matters, were never interrupted by questions pertaining to the emigration of Jews from the U.S.S.R.

Again, in short, the governance inherent in a global order is the more encompassing concept. As one regime theorist puts it, "International orders are broad framework arrangements governing the activities of all (or almost all) the members of international society over a wide range of specific issues," whereas "international regimes, by contrast, are more specialized arrangements that pertain to well-defined activities, resources, or geographical areas and often involve only some subset of the members of international society. Thus, we speak of the international regimes for whaling, the conservation of polar bears, the use of the electromagnetic spectrum, and human activities in Antarctica."[9]

The author of this formulation posits the governance of international orders and regimes as different subcategories of international institutions. Such an additional conceptual layer, however, seems more optional than necessary. Institutions connote the presence of authoritative principles, norms, rules, and procedures, thereby running the risk of obscuring the informal, non-authoritative dimensions that are so essential to the functioning of international orders and regimes.

ANALYTIC ORDER VERSUS NORMATIVE ORDER

The dynamics of global transformations are especially conducive to clarifying the distinction between "order" as an analytic concept and "order" as a normative precept. For change fosters uncertainty, and the more dynamic the change processes, the more extensive the uncertainty as people become apprehensive over the loss of the pre-change stability and fearful that the change might result in institutions

[9] Oran R. Young, *International Cooperation: Building Regimes for Natural Resources and the Environment* (Ithaca, NY: Cornell University Press, 1989), p. 13.

and conditions less satisfying than those which prevailed earlier. Thus the transforming dynamics are bound to focus concern around the desirability of the emergent global arrangements vis-à-vis those they are replacing. That is, normative concerns are bound to intensify as questions about global order – about the fundamental arrangements for coping with conflicts and moving towards goals – surface in the political arena. But, clearly, there is a huge difference between empirically tracing the underlying arrangements and analyzing their potential consequences on the one hand and judging the pros and cons of the arrangements on the other. The empirically discerned order may cry out for judgment and the normative order may cry out for accurate description, and both intellectual exercises can be pervaded by difficulties as the line dividing them can be obscure and variable. Nevertheless, the line is important and international relations analysts need to be ever-mindful of when they cross it. To be insensitive to the distinctions between normative judgments and empirical observations is to run the risk of either clouding sound analysis with preferred outcomes or confounding preferred outcomes with empirically faulty recommendations. Perhaps no degree of sensitivity can prevent some confusion along these lines – as observation is in some respects a normative enterprise – but surely it is the case that confusion can be kept to a minimum if we relentlessly monitor our tendency to allow the wish to be the father of our thoughts or the empirical assertion to be the source of our judgments.[10]

The problem of differentiating between empirical and normative orders can be nicely illustrated by the question of whether global arrangements marked by a high degree of disorder are to be considered a form of order. If by an "empirical order" is meant the arrangements through which global affairs move through time, then obviously a vast array of diverse arrangements can qualify as forms of order. History records, for example, years of hegemonic order in which a single country dominated world politics, eras of power balances in which countries formed alliances to offset each other's strengths, decades of bipolar rivalries in which two countries vie for world leadership, and periods of polyarchy in which many countries competed for global

---

[10] A good case in point here is the World Order Models Project (WOMP), which is considered by some analysts to have transgressed the line between empirical and normative orders. While seeking to advance specific normative views of global order, it is argued, WOMP embeds the reasoning on behalf of order in a rationalist, scientific context that implies objectivity but that is heavily value-laden. For an indication of the WOMP approach, see the essays in Saul H. Mendlovitz, ed., *On the Creation of a Just World Order* (New York: Free Press, 1975).

influence. Indeed, one observer has identified eight possible forms of order that may evolve in the future.[11]

Whatever its particular form, any global order can be located on a continuum which differentiates between those founded on cooperation and cohesion at one extreme and those sustained by conflict and disarray – i.e., disorder – at the other. Viewed in this way, much of the twentieth century, its hot and cold wars and ideological competitions, can be treated as every bit an international order as the relatively stable and peaceful conditions that prevailed under the Concert of Europe during parts of the nineteenth century. In other words, it is possible to conceive of any moment of history as an international order, no matter how undesirable it may be.

But many analysts are uncomfortable with this formulation. They associate order with minimal degrees of stability and coherence, so that periods of international history marked by war, exploitation, and a host of other noxious practices are viewed as disorderly arrangements – as "chaos" or "entropy," or anything but forms of order. For them, order has a positive, normative connotation even as they may concede that too much stability and coherence can be expressive of stagnant arrangements that allow for little or no progress.

The distinction between empirical and normative orders is also manifest whenever analysis focuses on policy questions, on promoting or preventing new global arrangements. Those who link forms of systemic order with policy goals necessarily work with images of normative orders. They may strive to recommend only actions founded on empirically sound assessments, but by turning from the assessments to recommendations they necessarily move into the realm of norms, of orders that are constructed or reinforced so as to enhance or thwart the establishment of specific values. To be concerned about the protection or advancement of human rights, for example, is to become enmeshed in problems of normative order as one focuses on the ways in which the prevailing global arrangements impact on individuals and how their freedom to speak, organize, and worship is or might be curtailed by the practices and institutions through which their lives are governed.

LAYERS OF EMPIRICAL ORDER

While the normative dimensions of global order are pervasive and unavoidable, it is nonetheless possible to tease out and separately analyse the empirical dimensions. By being mindful that observations

[11] Bull, *The Anarchical Society*, pp. 248–56.

can subtly slip into judgments, one can describe activities and anticipate outcomes without recourse to approving or disapproving the former or applauding or regretting the latter. Or at least it is possible to be more rather than less successful at suspending or postponing judgment. Just as the normative theorist is ever ready to characterize the desirable and undesirable qualities inherent in an activity, outcome, or institution, so is the empirical theorist ever alert to what the activity, outcome, or institution encompasses or portends, irrespective of its desirability. Indeed, it can well be argued that the more normative evaluations and recommendations are rooted in sound empirical estimates, the more are they likely to be incisive and effective. For policy goals to be realizable as well as emotionally satisfying, that is, they must be minimally in touch with the empirical circumstances in which any efforts to implement them are undertaken. Appreciation of these circumstances is likely to elude actors who do not pause to distinguish between the empirical and normative orders they seek to understand and affect.

But this is not to imply that tracing and anticipating the empirical dimensions of global order are easily accomplished. Sorting the empirical from the normative is only the first of several important steps. Next is the equally difficult task of delineating empirical orders at several levels, of comprehending the extraordinary complexity of human affairs and peeling off the layers of order that sustain it. Quite aside from normative considerations, there is no coherent set of arrangements whereby global politics gets from one day to the next. Rather, the patterns that constitute the order of an international relationship, a geographic region, or all of world politics recur at diverse sites, at different rates, and in various forms. Each pattern shapes and is shaped by the others so that together they comprise an organic whole – an order that with varying degrees of success and failure copes with challenges, manages change, and endures until such time as its foundations are no longer consistent with the needs, wants, capacities, and practices of people.

It follows that the prevailing global order, whatever it may be in any period, consists of a more extensive diversity of sites, rates of change, and configurations of structure than any international order. Here the global order – also referred to as "world politics" – is conceived as all-encompassing, as embracing every region, country, international relationship, social movement, and private organization that engages in activities across national boundaries. The purposes and scope of these activities may be limited to particular issues, dyadic concerns, or regional controversies – indeed, few activities undertaken on the world stage are intended to have worldwide consequences – but as such they are nonetheless a part of the prevailing global order. That is, the activities at the diverse sites may be quite unrelated to each other and their repercussions may not extend beyond the particular regions or relationships in which they occur; yet, they are an expression of the prevailing global order in the sense that the very narrowness of their scope is among the arrangements through which world politics gets from one moment in history to the next.

Stated in still another way, a central characteristic of the prevailing global order is the degree of connectedness or disconnectedness among the system's actors that marks its diverse arrangements. In earlier centuries, for example, transportation and communications technologies were such as to isolate various components of the global system from each other, with the result that the prevailing order was sustained by highly decentralized arrangements for moving through time. The European part of these earlier orders was, to be sure, dominant, but its dominance did not become global in scope until the middle of the nineteenth century.[12] Yet, what happened in other parts of the world prior to the opening of the Far East to Western ways in the mid-1800s was surely part of the global order even if the attention of politicians and historians focused mainly on Europe. As technology reduced geographic and social distances, the prevailing order can be said to have become progressively more centralized, with the repercussions of activities in one part of the world reaching ever more widely to other parts. Today, with transportational and communications technologies more dynamic than ever, with the problems of the Third World more salient than ever, and with the globalization of national economies more thoroughgoing than ever, the prevailing order probably involves more connectedness than it ever has before (even as it also continues to be the case that the arrangements which sustain the present order allow for disconnected activities that are localized in their scope and impact). Thus it is, for example, that the present global order includes an Islamic order as well as a Western order, two components that function side by side in an uneasy, distant, and friction-filled relationship which is as often marked by separate, unconnected activities as by coordinated efforts at accommodation.

In short, global order is conceived here to be a single set of arrangements even through these are not causally linked into a single coherent

---

12 For a cogent discussion of the role of Europe in the global order of earlier centuries, see William H. McNeil, *The Rise of the West: A History of the Human Community* (Chicago: University of Chicago Press, 1963).

array of patterns. The organic whole that comprises the present or future global order is organic only in the sense that its diverse actors are all claimants upon the same earthbound resources and all of them must cope with the same environmental conditions, noxious and polluted as these may be.

The numerous patterns that sustain global order can be conceived as unfolding at three basic levels of activity: (1) at the ideational or inter-subjective level of what people dimly sense, incisively perceive, or otherwise understand are the arrangements through which their affairs are handled; (2) at the behavioral or objective level of what people regularly and routinely do, often unknowingly, to maintain the pre-vailing global arrangements; and (3) at the aggregate or political level where governance occurs and rule-oriented institutions and regimes enact and implement the policies inherent in the ideational and behavioral patterns. The first involves the mental sets, belief systems, shared values, and any other attitudinal or perceptual screens through which the events of world politics pass before evoking reactions or inactions. As such, the ideational level is most manifest in the recurrent themes of speeches, editorials, books, and any other media through which those who participate in international relations give voice to their understanding of how the world is ordered. Except during trans-formative periods when uncertainty about the evolving structures of global order is high, the recurrent themes that are expressive of order at the ideational level tend to be widely shared among allies and adver-saries alike, forming an intersubjective consensus that locks all concerned into the same premises about the nature of the underlying arrangements for the conduct of global affairs. From this perspective alone, the Cold War was nothing more than a set of globally accepted assumptions that the U.S. and the Soviet Union were caught up in a hostile, competitive, and ideological contest for influence and power.

The second level of activity that sustains any global order consists not of what actors think or perceive, but of what they do in a regular and patterned way to give behavioral expression to their ideational under-standings. They threaten, negotiate, arm, concede, or otherwise engage in a whole range of recurrent behaviors that are so salient as to shape and reinforce the prevailing conceptions of the underlying global order.[13] During the height of the Cold War, for example, repeated

---

[13] For example, the World Event/Interaction Category System (WEIS), a content analytic scheme for creating events data bases, consists of 63 major types of action that states can undertake in world politics. An initial WEIS analysis of 5,550 events yielded an intriguing set of recurrent patterns depicting the extent of conflict and cooperation that prevailed on a global scale in 1966. Cf. Charles A. McClelland and Gary D.

demands by the superpowers that their allies support their policies became part and parcel of the existing order (even as subsequently a growing resistance to these demands were, in retrospect, clear signals that the order was beginning to come apart).

The third level of activity involves the more formal and organized dimension of the prevailing order. Those institutions and regimes that the diverse actors in the system fashion – such as Bretton Woods, the Council for Mutual Economic Assistance (COMECON), and the United Nations – as a means of pursuing their ideational and behavioral inclinations are obviously constituent elements that shape the arrangements through which global politics moves through time.

It should be stressed that, whatever may be the degree of orderliness that marks global affairs at any period in history, it is a product of activity at all three of these levels. This is plainly evident in the analysis of the Concert of Europe in Chapter 2, and it is perhaps even more manifest in the period of the Cold War: without officials and publics in both the East and West intersubjectively sharing the premise that both sides were locked in aggressive competition to prevail over the other, the Cold War could not have endured for more than four decades. Nor could it have persisted without the regularized behavior of officials and publics that articulated, intentionally or otherwise, the premise of aggressive competition. And, obviously, the competition could not have been sustained without the North Atlantic Treaty Organization (NATO), the Warsaw Pact, and the many other institutional arrangements that gave expression and direction to the ideational consensuses and the behavioral routines of people on both sides of the so-called Iron Curtain (itself a symbol of the boundaries imposed by the prevailing order). Once the course of events began to undermine the premises and patterns at the ideational, behavioral, and institutional levels, however, the Cold War quickly unraveled, with developments at each level reinforcing change at the other two and thus hastening the end of the period and the start of a transition into the new, post-Cold War era of the present. Note again that activities at all three levels were necessary components of the transformation. Without a growing perception shared by East Europeans that their conduct could not be controlled by the Soviets, a termination of the Cold War could not have occurred. Nor could it have dwindled down without new behavior patterns whereby

Hoggard, "Conflict Patterns in the Interactions among Nations," in James N. Rosenau, ed., *International Politics and Foreign Policy: A Reader in Research and Theory* (New York: Free Press, rev. edn., 1969), pp. 711–24.

people demanded change by converging in city squares and atop the Berlin Wall (itself a symbol of the obsolescence of Cold War boundaries). Likewise, the advent of a post-Cold War order could not have occurred without the policy initiatives of the major powers and their alliance systems that facilitated the replacement of the rigid premises of aggressive competition with a less structured search for new power relationships.

For analysts who have occasion to probe deep into the origins of global order, this three-dimensional formulation might seem insufficient. It fails to distinguish between the sources and practices of empirical orders, they might argue, adding that it also does not specify whether a global order is the regularized activities of world politics or the outcomes of these activities. During the Cold War, they might ask, which patterns constituted the global order of that period? Was it the arms race, deterrence policies, the espionage networks, the competition for influence in the Third World, and the rhetoric of antithetical ideologies? Or was it the consequences of these activities – the Cuban missile crisis, the deadlocked Summit meetings, the closed borders, the ban against technological transfers, the wariness of hostile publics, etc.? Or was it the deep attitudinal structures of suspicion and hostility that led publics and elites alike to engage in such activities and foster such outcomes?

On the grounds that the diverse ideational sources, behavioral patterns, and political institutions of any global order are interactive – that each is a source, an activity, and an outcome relative to the other two – efforts to answer such questions need not be undertaken. It is enough to stress that each dimension is a necessary but not a sufficient determinant of the prevailing order. Only those concerned with narratively tracing its evolution and decline through time need to specify temporal sequences of causation. For those with analytic rather than narrative concerns, it suffices to focus on the interactive nature of ideational, behavioral, and institutional dynamics and to treat their temporal priority as simply a chicken-and-egg problem for which there is no clear-cut solution.

This avoidance of specific causal sequences, however, should not be interpreted as minimizing the strength of the multidirectional interactions among the three sets of dynamics. There can be no gainsaying, for example, the large degree to which inertia and transaction costs sustain an order long after material conditions change and exert pressure for ideational, behavioral, and institutional transformations. But once the dynamics of change so strongly challenge the ideational bases of the prevailing order as to result in altered attitudes and orientations, the behavioral and institutional dimensions of that order will surely be weakened and eventually shattered. Contrariwise, if the behavioral and institutional bases of a new order are spurred into place despite the inertia of old habits, the ideational perspectives will be under strong pressure to fall into line accordingly. In short, world politics, no less than any other domain of human affairs, are marked by a strong tendency to fit beliefs to behavior, and vice versa, and thus it would be erroneous to equate an interactive perspective with the absence of powerful causal dynamics. It is precisely because the multi-directionality of the causal flows can be so strong that an interactive perspective seems preferable to attempting to locate them in temporal sequences.

Once again the Cold War is illustrative. At least with hindsight, one can readily discern how the patterned behavior of, say, the arms race facilitated the institutionalized practices of alliance systems and Summit meetings, how these institutional arrangements exerted pressure for intersubjective ideational consensuses, how the shared mental sets reflected in the consensuses influenced the arms race and stimulated institutionalized efforts at arms control, all of which further reinforced the systems of thought that distinguished the Cold War from its predecessor and successor as a form of global order. From an inter-active perspective, in short, a global order is indivisible. It is both idea and practice, stimulus and outcome, premise and institution. Whatever contributes to the expected and regularized ways in which events happen – the tangling of adversaries, the bargaining of allies, the surfacing of issues, the waning of controversies – is a constituent part of the order that prevails in world politics during a recognizable period of history. Indeed, it is this order that makes the period recognizable.

Viewed as an interactive set of dynamics, moreover, any of the several dimensions of global order can serve as a point of entry for analysts interested in assessing the viability of a particular order. One may be especially concerned with the ideational soil in which an order flourishes, but it will not be long before such a focus leads one to test and exemplify the dominant ideas through the behaviour and insti-tutions that give concrete expression to the order. To be sure, analysts are not precluded from specializing in one or another of the dimen-sions, but in so doing they will hardly be able to ignore the relevance of the other dimensions.

Viewing the ideational, behavioral, and institutional dimensions of global order as so interactive as to inhibit the tracing of causal sequences poses a noteworthy methodological problem. Such a

17

conception challenges the framing of hypotheses that systematically link independent and dependent variables. This scientific procedure deflects attention away from the interactive dynamics of global order by presuming that certain phenomena (the independent variables) are prior in time to those they systematically affect (the dependent variables). While such may be the case in a short-term context, it may not hold in a stretched-out time perspective that encompasses the interactive nature of the variables and that thus treats the new values for the dependent variables as systematic stimuli to changes in the original independent variables. In other words, the essential dynamics of any global order are, in effect, both independent and dependent variables in the endless processes whereby the patterns that constitute the order are maintained.

Three possible solutions to this problem are available. One is to confine analysis to limited short-term hypotheses that focus on linear rather than interactive relationships. Analysts can, for example, hypothesize about the impact of particular ideational premises on specific behavioral patterns, consigning to subsequent hypotheses the question of how the latter feed back and affect the former. A second solution is to focus empirically on critical situations, or "hard" cases, as a means of advancing theoretical perspectives. If hypothesized expectations survive the test of the "hard" case – the complex circumstance that encompasses so many variables as seemingly to defy testing – it becomes reasonable to conclude that other, more clear-cut cases will have also been explained. Several chapters in this volume use one or another form of the hard-case procedure to test the theoretical propositions they develop.

A third solution to the methodological problems of probing global orders, and one that may especially lend itself to the stretched-out perspective of some of the ensuing chapters, is that of eschewing the scientific procedure of designating independent and dependent variables, replacing it with a method that maintains a sensitivity to the interactive complexity of global order by relentlessly estimating how a shift in one set of dynamics may affect each of the other two sets and feed back as a stimulus to reinforcing or further shifting the original change. This procedure is, admittedly, ungainly and subject to grievous error (since the presumption of multiple causality may encourage unrestrained, hasty, and possibly faulty attributions of consequence), but the alternatives of avoiding causal inquiry or confining it to short-term sequences are surely even more inappropriate if comprehension of the nature of global order is to be enlarged.

ORDER AND CHANGE

If ideational, behavioral, and institutional patterns inter-actively sustain established global orders, what causes them to change? It is not enough simply to respond that alterations in these patterns give rise to corresponding transformations of the prevailing order. Not only is such an answer self-evident and tautological, but it also ignores the key question of what underlies changes in the ideational, behavioral, and institutional dynamics. To be sure, once an order is in place, these dynamics operate as sources in the sense that they interactively feed on each other to maintain the order. But, obviously, there are even deeper sources that either prevent the transformation of the dynamic patterns or foster their breakdown and the emergence of a new order.

Nor do questions about the links between change and order end with the identification of deeper sources that underlie the ideational, behavioral, and institutional patterns. One is also impelled to ask whether the change reflects a decay or a reconstitution of the old order? Whether the transformations are so fundamental as to lead to a new order or whether they are of only limited scope such that some dimensions of the older order remain intact? Does the emergence of a new global order constitute systemic change or change within the system? Is there a difference between changes in the behavioral patterns of actors and changes in the distribution of power among them? Is there likely to be a substantial time lag between changes in, say, the ideational dimension and those that occur at the behavioral and institutional levels? Can periods of intense and pervasive conflict persist across long stretches of time, or are the underpinnings of order bound to break down if the conflict becomes too intense and too pervasive? Is order a cyclical phenomenon such that periods of extensive conflict that foster disorder and chaos are merely transitional moments in history that are soon followed by the establishment of new, more orderly arrangements? Can new global orders be created through political will and imagination, or is their emergence more the result of dynamic technologies, altered socioeconomic conditions, and transformed psychological perspectives that lie beyond human control?

There are, of course, no final answers to such questions. Much depends on how order and change are conceptualized.[14] The more the

---

[14] For extensive efforts to conceptualize the concept of change, see Robert Gilpin, *War and Change in World Politics* (Cambridge: Cambridge University Press, 1981); James N. Rosenau, "Global Transformations: Notes for a Workshop on Change in the International System," *Emerging Issues*, Occasional Paper No. 1 (Cambridge, MA: American Academy of Arts and Sciences, November 1989); and John Gerard Ruggie,

nature of global order is elaborately specified in terms which encompass ideational, behavioral, and institutional phenomena, the greater is the likelihood that the delineation of a collapsed order and the emergence of a new one will be confined to those rare circumstances when the transformative dynamics are viewed as expressive of fundamental decay rather than limited reconstitution, as systemic changes rather than within-system changes, as occurring across long stretches of time rather than precipitously, as too complex to be subject to the political will of a single generation. Furthermore, however order and change may be defined, each transition from an old to a new order may result from a different mix of ideational, behavioral, and institutional dynamics as well as a different combination of underlying technological, socioeconomic, and psychological conditions. Every global order, in other words, flourishes or fails in a specific historical context that cannot be ignored and that even the most elaborate formulation of the order concept must take into account.

One way to develop tentative insights, if not answers, into the foregoing questions is to raise them in the context of the unfolding international scene: why did the postwar, Cold War order come to an end? Yes, the underlying premises of aggressive competition and ideological rivalry were revealed to be mental images rather than objective realities and, as such, they collapsed as quickly as it took for the Berlin Wall to be pulled apart and transgressed; but why did the collapse occur in 1989 rather than 1979, 1969, or 1959? Indeed, why did the Cold War not persist until 1999 or into the next century? Posed in another way, assuming the events of 1989 were only the final, most dramatic stage in a longer process of systemic collapse, when did the end of the Cold War begin? With the advent of Solidarity in Poland? With the election of Ronald Reagan? With the death of Leonid Brezhnev? With the mass production of VCRs and the orbiting of television satellites in space?

Phrasing the problem of the relationship between order and change in these terms calls attention to the crucial importance of material

"Continuity and Transformation in the World Polity: Toward a Neorealist Synthesis," *World Politics*, 35 (January 1983), pp. 261–85. Compilations of essays on the subject can be found in Czempiel and Rosenau, eds., *Global Changes and Theoretical Challenges*; Ole R. Holsti, Randolph M. Siverson, and Alexander L. George, eds., *Change in the International System* (Boulder, CO: Westview Press, 1980); and Barry Buzan and R. J. Barry Jones, eds., *Change and the Study of International Relations: The Evaded Dimension* (New York: St. Martin's Press, 1981).

interests and conditions as exogenous sources of the life and death of global orders. As has been outlined elsewhere,[15] there are a great variety of material conditions that can shape the rules through which governance without government is sustained and order thereby maintained. Contrariwise, a transformation of the material conditions can foster a breakdown, or at least a restructuring, of the prevailing order. If, for example, an order is ensconced in widening economic discrepancies among its actors, the pressures for change and a new order are likely to be extensive and unremitting. Similarly, if the distribution of resources among an order's key actors should, for any one of a number of reasons, undergo substantial alteration, then corresponding changes in the prevailing hierarchical arrangements are likely to occur so that they remain consistent with the order's material underpinnings. To a large extent this is what happened when the Cold War came to an end. While the advent of the Reagan and Gorbachev administrations doubtless contributed to the end of that order, perhaps even more fundamental was the bankruptcy of the Soviet economy and the widespread realization in the communist world that the premises of its ideology were profoundly flawed. Events culminated in 1989 rather than in earlier decades because it took that long for the disparity between the tenets of the ideology and the reality of the standard of living to become undeniable. One of the prime changes, in other words, involved the material conditions on which one party to the Cold War based its competition. The protests of Polish workers and the westward flight of East Germans of diverse occupations were in part responses to prolonged political repression, but no less central to their actions was a culmination of despair over their economic plight and the loss of hope that it could improve.

Another material condition that underwent a transformation undermining of the ideational, behavioral, and institutional foundations of the Cold War order involved the analytic competence of individuals on both sides of the ideological divide. Aided by expanding educational opportunities and the proliferation of VCRs, global television, computers, and many other products of the microelectronic revolution, citizens everywhere became increasingly adept at explicating scenarios of the macroeconomic, social, and political circumstances in which their lives were located. Accordingly, they became more aware of how, when, and where they could contribute to the aggregation of demands

---

[15] Cf. Rosenau, "Governance without Government."

that served their interests.[16] Thus is was not sheer coincidence that the Cold War order came to an end in the public squares of Eastern Europe and the Soviet Union. That order had been founded, in part, on the ideational presumption that the masses accepted the necessity of aggressive superpower competition, that they would compliantly conduct themselves in accordance with the behavioral implications of this mental set, and that they would support, or at least not contest, the military, economic, and political institutions through which the Cold War was waged. The enlarged capacity of people to discern the growing inappropriateness of these arrangements in an ever more interdependent world thus altered one of the prime material conditions, the level of human skills, from which the postwar order derived much of its strength.

Still another exogenous interest that changed enough to hasten the decline of the Cold War order was the advent of public issues with which the existing arrangements were ill-designed to cope. As previously noted, the dynamics of polluted environments, currency crises, terrorist attacks, AIDS, and the drug trade post challenges that have transgressed the boundaries of national competition and superpower rivalry, that require cooperation rather than conflict for amelioration to occur, and that thereby heighten the need for new ideational, behavioral, and institutional patterns to supplement, if not to replace, those through which global order was maintained in the immediate decades after World War II. Viewed in this way, the 1986 accident at Chernobyl nuclear power plant becomes a symbol of the beginning, possibly even the next-to-last stage, of the end of the Cold War.

SYSTEM CHANGE VERSUS WITHIN-SYSTEM CHANGE

Having delineated global order as the routinized arrangements through which world affairs are conducted, and having suggested how an order breaks down and gets replaced, the question remains of whether the emergent, successor order rests on new systemic foundations or whether it derives from the reconstitution of the existing system. The ensuing chapters shed considerable light on this issue, but it may be useful to anticipate these responses by outlining an answer to a prior question: on what grounds should the emergent order be treated

---

[16] For a development of this thesis, see Chapter 10 below. Extensive data supporting the notion of a skill revolution among citizens can be found in James N. Rosenau, *Turbulence in World Politics: A Theory of Change and Continuity* (Princeton, NJ: Princeton University Press, 1990), esp. ch. 13.

as either wholly original or as a reconstituted version of its predecessor? Put more specifically, should the end of the Cold War be viewed as systemic change toward a new order, or are these bases for treating this development as within-system change of the old order?

Much depends, of course, on how the characteristics of the global system are perceived and identified. If they are conceived in broad terms which stress the continuing competence and dominance of states and their anarchical system which accords them sovereignty and equality, then the end of the Cold War and the replacement of its super-power rivalry with a more dispersed, less militaristic competition among many states can be seen as merely a new form of the existing order. Rearranged relationships, altered hierarchies, and new patterns of interaction, to be sure, but still the same old state system with the same old arrangements for conducting and managing its affairs. The post-Cold War changes are surely profound and extensive, and their consequences are surely bound to be enormous for decades to come, but in this interpretation they are nonetheless only within-system changes.[17] If, on the other hand, emphasis is placed on the diminished competence of states, the globalization of national economies, the fragmentation of societies into ethnic, religious, nationality, linguistic, and political subgroups, the advent of transnational issues that foster the creation of transnational authorities, and the greater readiness of citizenries to coalesce in public squares, then the end of the Cold War and the emergent arrangements for maintaining global life are likely to be viewed as the bases for a wholly new order. States are still active and important, to be sure, but their participation in the processes of world politics is nevertheless of a different, less dominating kind, thereby leading to the interpretation that fundamental systemic change has occurred.[18]

Is there clear-cut evidence indicating support for one of these perspectives and rejection of the other? No, not yet; or at least the matter still seems open-ended. Many of the present global arrangements appear too unsettled in the aftermath of the collapse of the Soviet empire to warrant one or the other perspective. To repeat, moreover, much depends on how the key concepts are defined, thus enabling

---

[17] For an elaborate formulation that supports the permanence of the state system – summarized by "the conclusion that the territorial map [of a world of states] has been frozen into its present shape once and for all" (p. 67) – and that thus allows for only within-system change, see James Mayall, *Nationalism and International Society* (Cambridge: Cambridge University Press, 1990), esp. ch. 4 ("Nationalism and the International Order").

[18] For an extensive presentation of this perspective, see Rosenau, *Turbulence in World Politics*, ch. 10.

different analysts to offer different interpretations as they accord greater or lesser weight to the post-Cold War competence of states, the strength of transnational issues, the power of sub-group dynamics, and the changing skills of citizens.

The fact that the evidence on the scope of the transformations currently at work in world politics remains murky highlights a central feature of the processes whereby a global order undergoes either systemic or within-system change: namely, that both kinds of change are so fundamental that neither unfolds rapidly. The last stages of an old order may transpire as quickly as it takes for the Berlin Wall and East European communist regimes to crumble, but the processes whereby new arrangements come into being and fall into place are much more halting and cumbersome. Why? Because to some large extent the ideational, behavioral, and institutional foundations of an order are rooted in habits – in standardized, routinized, and repetitive ways of responding to events – and habits are not readily replaced. They can come apart rapidly when confronted with unmistakable indications of their disutility, but piecing together new routines and attitudes appropriate to the new, unfamiliar circumstances is quite a different matter. It takes time for confidence in the changes to develop, for sorting out the opportunities and dangers inherent in the changes, for a repertoire of diverse responses to evolve, and, indeed, for predispositions and actions to be repeated enough to be patterned.

If it is the case, moreover, that the prevailing order of world politics is a "human contrivance" (to borrow a phrase that has been used to characterize the Concert of Europe), and if its intersubjective foundations must today be global in scope, then the pace at which a new or reconstituted order emerges is bound to be slow. The Concert of Europe was contrived by just a few persons, whereas the presently emerging "contrivances" must extend across millions upon millions of people,[19] some of which are likely to lag behind others in the quickness with which they come to share in the intersubjective bases of new global structures. Viewed as a process of habit and consensus formation, in short, a new or reconstituted global order may well take decades to mature.

[19] Early in the 1990 controversy over the unification of Germany, for example, Soviet Foreign Minister Eduard Shevardnadze proposed that the matter be decided by a referendum in which all the peoples of Europe, East and West, would vote. While the proposal never went any further, it is suggestive of the scale on which the new or reconstituted order may be fashioned.

SPECIFIC APPLICATIONS

Each of the chapters that follow explores an important aspect of global order, change, and governance in the context of the foregoing considerations and mindful of the opportunities for insight offered by the dynamics of change presently at work in world politics. In Chapter 2, K. J. Holsti seeks to develop perspective on the current scene by probing the origins, operations, and consequences of the system of governance that prevailed among the great powers in nineteenth-century Europe. In a direct challenge to hegemonic stability theory, which argues that order in international relations is established and sustained by a single hegemon, Holsti demonstrates that "multipower stewardship" can flourish in world politics. His analysis shows how the shared experience of the Napoleonic drama provided a strong impetus among elites in Prussia, Russia, Great Britain, and Austria-Hungary to avert the replay of a hegemonic war against France and avoid the liberal, populist revolutions and strife which further interstate warring would likely provoke. As a result, Holsti's chapter highlights how the convergence of specified governing tasks, institutions, and decision-making rules, authoritative decisions, and coercive capacity gave rise to a system of governance that exerted a positive, independent causal effect on great power relations in the nineteenth century.

Mark W. Zacher uses historical comparison in Chapter 3 to construct an analysis of the "decay" of the "Westphalian temple," by which he means the system of states that has conditioned the structure and functioning of world politics since the seventeenth century. Zacher argues that the growth of institutions, regimes, interdependence, and regulatory ventures constitutes compelling confirmation of emerging systems of governance in contemporary world politics. States are becoming increasingly enmeshed in a network of collaborative arrangements and regimes that are casting international politics in a very different mold from the one that has existed in recent centuries. As states increasingly demonstrate their willingness to trade autonomy off for other values, Zacher contends, assumptions about world politics that cling to the centrality of the sovereign state are becoming less and less credible.

In Chapter 4 Thomas J. Biersteker explores the study of governance in world politics by seeking to explain why a neoclassical convergence has recently emerged among underdeveloped countries. He focuses on the new and similar foreign and domestic policies through which Third World countries are participating in the international political economy as a basis for reflection on the relationships among different forms of

25

order in international relations (i.e., order as a system of ideas; order as behavioral convergence; or order as purposive governance), and as a means of clarifying the relative explanatory importance of factors lying at different levels of analysis. Biersteker's central proposition is that while behavioral convergence is likely to facilitate purposive governance in the international political economy, a degree of ideational convergence – often brought about by systemic shocks – tends to precede behavioral convergence in the causal chain. At the same time, in the final analysis, the triumph of neoclassical economics in the developing world is seen as the result of a complex interplay among levels and types of order in world politics.

Like Biersteker, Robert W. Cox is especially concerned with the ideational dimension of governance, what he regards as the "intersubjective" foundation of world politics. To probe this dimension, however, Cox looks to the past. In Chapter 5 he pursues his approach to governance without government by examining the writings of Ibn Khaldun, a fourteenth-century Islamic philosopher, as a vehicle for delineating a framework for the deconstruction of the ontological constructs of the "passing present." Cox's thesis is consistent with the other chapters in this volume in that one of its main goals is to shape an analytical framework which will allow an understanding of orders, institutions, and structures as transhistorical, phenomenological products that achieve a "material" status precisely because of their intersubjective pervasiveness. On the other hand, Cox's chapter deviates from the others in that it seeks to outline a non-positivist methodology for detecting change in world order. In so doing, the chapter provides a basis for action geared toward structural change in world politics, a practical knowledge to serve as a guide for political activity. What the Islamic philosophy of Khaldun contributes in this regard is the notion that analysts must become conscious of the conditioning of the historical period within which they operate, and at the same time pursue moral principles within the realm of the feasible.

The institutional dimensions of governance without government serve as the focus of Chapter 6, where Oran R. Young assesses the independent causal effect, or "effectiveness," of international institutions in world politics. The theme of Young's chapter concerns the role of social institutions in shaping both the behavior of individual members of international society and the collective behavior resulting from their interactions. In what sense is the behavior of states responsive to the dictates of international institutions? Under what circumstances does their behavior contribute to the implementation of the implicit and explicit requirements of international regimes? According to Young, an international institution is "effective" to the extent that its operations can be shown to impel actors to behave differently than they would have behaved in the absence of the institution or under the influence of a significantly different institution. This causal nexus is best established, Young argues, by looking at "hard cases" – those situations that are unfavorable to the operation of social institutions. He identifies several critical variables that go a long way toward explaining the relative effectiveness of institutions across a range of cases.

Janice E. Thomson assesses in Chapter 7 the usefulness of "state-building theory" – the general proposition that what does and does not get regulated at the international level is a function of the will of strong states – as a framework for understanding the emergence of international regulation. The state-building framework is tested through a comparative analysis of the nature of international regulatory ventures concerning such issues as terrorism, mercenarism, and the trade of alcohol, arms, and illicit drugs. Through this testing, the value of state-building theory is shown to be nebulous. It does not provide a definitive answer as to what does or does not get regulated at the international level or why. On the other hand, whereas the power of a state is not fully determinative of the emergence and nature of international regulation, Thomson shows that to some degree the powerful do generate the legitimacy and form international regulations will take. One might be inclined to view governance of this type as resulting from the gradual growth of Western practices, but it seems that norms in world politics stem more from the unintended consequences of a long history of state-building. In short, Thomson concludes that international regulation is a political rather than a moral phenomenon.

Linda Cornett and James A. Caporaso explore in Chapter 8 contending approaches to governance without government by looking at the revival of tendencies toward European integration in the middle and late 1980s. The opportunities created by the "EC 1992" program, coupled with the uncertainty and complexity stemming from the upheavals in Eastern Europe and the Soviet Union, are seen to lend "particular urgency" to inquiries about governance in international relations. Cornett and Caporaso place integration in Europe within the discourse on international order by comparing the explanatory value of several contrasting theoretical perspectives: neorealism, neoliberal institutionalism, functionalism, and neofunctionalism. While each perspective, they argue, offers a different explanation of the key dynamics behind the development of the European Community in the 1980s, only together do they capture the complexities and contradictions of governance systems in Europe. In their discussion of the

27

points of intersection and divergence among the diverse theories, they outline the foundations of a more sophisticated understanding of the strengths and weaknesses of competing views of governance without government.

Ernst-Otto Czempiel's essay (Chapter 9) is rooted in a liberal tradition that views global democratization as an overall positive basis for ideational, behavioral, and purposive convergence. Based on the proposition that liberal states do not tend to go to war with one another, Czempiel posits that the interactions of a global society consisting predominantly of states erected on the Western model will result in a peaceful system of governance. It is through this set of lenses that Czempiel analyzes the erosion of the Cold War order and offers projections and prescriptions for future orders in world politics.

Chapter 10 departs from the widely held assumption that global order and change are macro-level phenomena and explores the role of micro-level actors in the unfolding of governance without government. Can there be profound transformations in the nature of global governance, my chapter asks, without alterations in the orientations of citizens? Posed more directly, to what extent can we say that order and order transformations are the consequences of micro-level changes? These questions have both empirical and theoretical dimensions. At the empirical level, the chapter suggests the growth of interdependence and the "skill revolution" that has accompanied the microelectronic revolution have rendered citizens and their circumstances very different from earlier eras. At a theoretical level, it highlights how the increase in the intellectual and cathetic capabilities of individuals throughout the world has contributed to the transformations occurring at the global level. While the enhancement of micro skills are not seen as determining the exact nature and direction of macro order and change, it is argued that students of world politics need to recognize that people are adapting rather than remaining constant and that micro- and macro-level developments are thus interactive in the processes of governance without government.

Taken together, the chapters that follow affirm an observation made by Inis Claude to the effect that the world has less governance than most states, more than some, and probably less than it needs.[20] The contributors agree that systems of governance operate at the global level, that they can be founded on deeply entrenched beliefs, habits,

---

[20] I have been unable to find the exact quote, though memory tells me it is somewhere in Inis L. Claude, Jr., *Swords into Plowshares: The Problems and Progress of International Organization* (New York: Random House, 3rd edn., revised, 1964).

and institutions even as they are also ever susceptible to change, and that they can provide the bases for cooperation and collective benefits in world politics. Perhaps even more important, for a discipline that has long been rooted in the premise that governance is bounded by the prerogatives of sovereign powers, the chapters highlight the challenging proposition that there is much to be learned about the nature, scope, and limits of governance in a context where the actions of states, their sovereignties and their governments, are not preconditions of how events unfold.

2 GOVERNANCE WITHOUT GOVERNMENT: POLYARCHY IN NINETEENTH-CENTURY EUROPEAN INTERNATIONAL POLITICS

K. J. Holsti

In his now classic analysis of international politics, Kenneth Waltz argues that communities and systems of states are organized around one of two fundamental principles: hierarchy and anarchy.[1] These are ideal types, and he would probably allow that systems may combine elements of both. Yet, for a parsimonious theory of international politics, it is necessary to start with simplifying assumptions and from them to infer important qualities of the relationship between actors. Hierarchies are characterized by divisions of labor, specialization, and authority structures. Within states, for example, governments possess legitimate authority and maintain a monopoly of power to compel obedience. Anarchies have the opposite characteristics: there is no authority to command, the units copy each other's multiple tasks (there is no division of labor), and there is no presumption of obedience. States must therefore bargain with each other to defend and achieve their objectives and purposes. War is the ultimate arbiter of conflicts of interest, and, in the final analysis, self-help is the only reliable strategy for survival.

In anarchy, there is no governance. Outcomes of conflicts are determined by the relative power positions of the actors rather than by the application of law or some other regulatory device by a legitimate authority. Change in international relationships is achieved either by persuasion, coercive threats, or armed force. There are no institutional or procedural counterparts of the executive, legislative, or judicial functions within a hierarchical system.

Hedley Bull has argued that the stark dichotomization of organizing principles between hierarchy and anarchy oversimplifies and thus

---

[1] Kenneth N. Waltz, *Theory of International Politics* (Reading, MA: Addison-Wesley, 1979).

cannot adequately characterize the international system or explain its dynamics.[2] There is a fundamental distinction, he suggests, between a system of states and a society of states. While both are structurally anarchies, at the process level there are substantial and critical differences between them. In a society of states, governments fashion norms, "rules of the game," institutions, and procedures that produce certain collective outcomes, especially order, stability, and the preservation of the states system. In a society of states, the members "conceive themselves to be bound by a common set of rules in their relations with one another, and share in the working of common institutions."[3] These ingredients are lacking in mere systems of states, where the only distinguishing feature is the interaction – usually war – between separate political units. The Vandals and Romans were part of an international system, but not of a society of states.

Order implies limits on behavior. In a society of states, these limitations are spelled out in international law, the conventions of diplomacy, the balance of power, and even in war, when it is used to enforce community norms. There are entrance requirements (the qualifications of statehood) in a society of states that are not found in systems of states, and frequently the members develop institutions and procedures to manage or resolve conflicts among themselves. The system is not one of pure self-help. The weak and the disadvantaged can rely on a number of international customs, norms, institutions, and practices to bolster their security. The doctrine of sovereignty is one of the most important bases of state security, and its significance is accentuated and sustained in many ways in international practice and convention. Unlike economic markets (Waltz's favorite analogue for an international system), where firms are constantly the object of successful predation or bankruptcy, states have an impressive record of survival and endurance. Not counting voluntary integration into larger entities (the unification of Italy and Germany), only a handful of states has succumbed to permanent conquest in the last 185 years, while in the same period about 150 new states have been born. In terms of endurance, the state is far safer than is a typical business firm. Part of the explanation for the survival of states resides in the norms of the society of states, and in the institutions of governance they create to sustain statehood and reduce the incidence of war.

[2] Hedley Bull, *The Anarchical Society: A Study of Order in World Politics* (New York: Columbia University Press, 1977).
[3] *Ibid.*, p. 13.

WHAT IS GOVERNANCE?

In Waltz's scheme, there is but a single device for management or governance of the system: balances of power. It is not the contrivance of agents in the sense that specific policy-makers design them and adapt their policies to make certain that they are maintained. Balances, rather, are the automatic consequence of the interactions of functionally similar units operating in an anarchy. Bull does not attach such automaticity to management systems. His rules, conventions, and institutions are human contrivances rather than law-like regularities deriving from first principles. Yet, Bull is not interested in their origins; he focuses primarily on their consequences, which are order, stability, and the perpetuation of the society of states.

This study examines the origins, operations, and consequences of the governance system found in nineteenth-century Europe. A system of international governance was created by specific individuals in 1814–15. The system developed, changed, oscillated between effectiveness and immobility, and ultimately collapsed. It had certain characteristics commonly associated with both hierarchical and anarchical systems. Nineteenth-century Europe was a *mixed* system.

This imperfect system of governance was operated by five great powers. It was therefore a polyarchy. Contrary to hegemonic stability theory, which argues that international regimes grow and flourish under the benevolent auspices of a single hegemon, the evidence from nineteenth-century Europe overwhelmingly supports the existence of multipower stewardship.

For some purposes it may be suitable to conceive of governance in a very loose sense. Hidden hands, habits, patterned behavior, and cultural mores, among other things, can be conceived as governors. I prefer to establish stricter and narrower indicators of the concept. Some of them derive explicitly from Waltz's analysis of the principles underlying hierarchical systems. These include authority and legitimacy. They may be observed in anarchical systems as well, as the case of the Concert of Europe will illustrate. Foucault's definition of governance indicates the outcomes of decisions: to govern is "to structure the possible fields of actions of others."[4] What we examine in the context of Europe's diplomatic relations in the nineteenth century is evidence of (1) authority; (2) a set of specified governance tasks; (3) institutions and

---

[4] Michel Foucault, "The Subject and Power," in Hubert Dreyfus and Paul Rabinow, eds., *Beyond Structuralism and Hermeneutics* (Chicago: University of Chicago Press, 1982), p. 21.

decision-making rules; and (4) authoritative decisions, actions, and coercive capacity (limiting fields of action). As guides to the inquiry, these elements of governance are transformed into four questions. Who governs? Governance for what purposes? How do the governors govern? What happens when the governors govern (impact)?

WHO ARE THE GOVERNORS? POLYCENTRISM AND POLYARCHY

We do not yet possess an adequate conceptualization of hegemony, although Wallerstein's rendering comes close to the common-sense meaning of the term: "Hegemony . . . refers to that situation in which the ongoing rivalry between the so-called 'great powers' is so unbalanced that one power is truly *primus inter pares*; that is, one power can largely impose its rules and its wishes (at the least by effective veto power) [on the others]."[5] Unfortunately, Wallerstein then goes on to say that this imposition of rules and wishes can extend into the economic, political, military, diplomatic, and even cultural areas – all simultaneously. Hegemony is therefore all-embracing.

Other recent renderings of the concept have suggested sectoral hegemonies, particularly in the economic domain. Most of the hegemonic stability literature refers to international trade, investment, and finance, for example. Yet, Keohane argues that economic hegemony derives from or is sustained ultimately by a preponderance of material resources: "a hegemonic state must possess enough military power to be able to protect the international political economy that it dominates."[6] Another approach employs the very loose Gramscian sense of hegemony. This suggests "blocs" of thought, culture, and modes of production that transcend national boundaries and even world regions. The Gramscian rendering of hegemony has been ably employed by Robert Cox.[7]

None of these conceptualizations of hegemony fits well with the patterns of governance described and analyzed below. Wallerstein's is far too broad. How can one think of a single European hegemon in nineteenth-century Europe when Great Britain dominated North

---

[5] Immanuel Wallerstein, *The Politics of the World-Economy* (Cambridge: Cambridge University Press, 1984), pp. 38–9.
[6] Robert O. Keohane, *After Hegemony: Cooperation and Discord in the World Political Economy* (Princeton, NJ: Princeton University Press, 1984), p. 32.
[7] In his "Social Forces, States and World Orders: Beyond International Relations Theory," in Robert O. Keohane, ed., *Neorealism and its Critics* (New York: Columbia University Press, 1986).

American, Latin American, and South Asian, but not European, trade; when France and Germany dominated the arts and culture; when Russia was by far the greatest military power of the immediate post-1815 period; and when Austria dominated much of the diplomatic landscape for the first thirty years after the Congress of Vienna? Hegemonic stability theory, implying a form of governance, is inappropriate because throughout most of the nineteenth century economic strength did *not* translate to diplomatic strength, and because most of the war-threatening situations of the century had little or nothing to do with commercial problems. The peacemakers of 1815, 1856, 1878, and other select dates were largely indifferent to commercial questions, as was befitting their class origins, their training, and their interests. Cox's formulations are useful for examining the spread and ultimate domination of various civilization forms, but for the narrower concerns of governance in international politics – meaning determination of outcomes on questions of war and peace – they are too broad although not irrelevant. Contrary to hegemonic stability and other recent characterizations of European international politics in the nineteenth century,[8] there was no single hegemon in continental Europe between the Napoleonic and Great Wars. The system of governance was created by a five-power coalition, defined by it, and operated in terms of its members' interests.

The distribution of power in Europe throughout the nineteenth century was polycentric. The five great powers fashioned the settlements of 1814–15 (France was formally admitted to the club only in 1818, but its representative, Talleyrand, was instrumental in arranging the bargains that made up the settlements). From a military point of view Russia, not Great Britain, was the power to be concerned with in the immediate postwar period. Most of the other members of the coalition regarded France as a potential hegemon and fashioned the territorial settlement specifically to prevent that from occurring. Great Britain remained part of the system of coalition governance until 1822, then for the rest of the century wavered between periodic involvement in and indifference toward continental matters.[9] It was a world power, in Modelski's sense of a global trading nation,[10] but it never sought to become, nor was it perceived as, a hegemon in Europe. When it *was*

---

[8] For example, Robert Gilpin, *War and Change in World Politics* (Cambridge: Cambridge University Press, 1981).

[9] Cf. Paul Schroeder, *Austria, Great Britain, and the Crimean War: The Destruction of the European Concert* (Ithaca, NY, and London: Cornell University Press, 1972), p. 401.

[10] George Modelski, "The Long Cycle of Global Politics and the Nation-State," *Comparative Studies in Society and History*, 20 (1978), pp. 214–35.

involved in continental matters, security considerations predominated over commercial concerns. Castlereagh, the drafter of the 1814–15 settlements, argued vigorously that political considerations had to override economic hopes.[11] Not infrequently throughout the nineteenth century, Great Britain made major commercial concessions for the sake of political-security gains.

The order that was fashioned in 1814–15 and reaffirmed on numerous occasions was designed explicitly to prevent a recurrence of hegemony-seeking. The fundamental principle underlying it was a territorial balance of power that would prevent French – or any other power's – ascendancy in Europe. But there was much more to it. It was also a balance of status, rights, deference, obligations, and satisfaction.[12] This fact is inconsistent with any notion of single power hegemony. Many of the serious crises of the second half of the nineteenth century arose when one of the governors challenged the status, rights, and honor of the others. The crises surrounding the unification of Italy in the 1850s, for example, developed more because of Napoleon III's failure to consult the fellow members of the Concert than because of the territorial adjustments he and Cavour made at Austria's expense.

The great powers that led the grand coalition against Napoleon arrogated for themselves the right to create the postwar order and system of governance. It was to be governance by the great powers, but for all of Europe. While Tsar Alexander I had visions and hopes of creating a universal confederation of states based on nationality and constitutional orders (he was acquainted with the plans of the Abbé de Saint Pierre, Rousseau, and Kant), the exigencies of war demanded entitlements to those who had led the coalition. At a wartime conference in Chatillon (February 1814), the allied representatives declared that they did not come to the conference as mere envoys of the four courts "but as men entitled to treat for Peace with France in the name of Europe, which is but a single entity."[13] The Treaty of Chaumont (1814) subsequently sealed the agreement of the four coalition partners to create a peace *for all of Europe* and included a commitment to protect Europe for twenty years against any renewed French aggression. A secret article of the first Peace of Paris (June 1814) appropriated for the victors the right to establish the "relations from whence a system of real

[11] Christopher Bartlett, "Britain and the European Balance, 1815–48," in Alan Sked, ed., *Europe's Balance of Power* (London: Macmillan, 1979), p. 147.
[12] Paul W. Schroeder, "The Nineteenth Century System: Balance of Power or Political Equilibrium?," *Review of International Studies*, 15 (April 1989), pp. 143–4.
[13] Quoted from the declaration in G. A. Chevallaz, *The Congress of Vienna and Europe* (Oxford: Pergamon Press, 1964), p. 123.

and permanent balance of power in Europe [would be] derived, [and] will be regulated at [the forthcoming Congress of Vienna] upon the principles determined by the Allied Powers amongst themselves."[14] While one decision-making committee at the Vienna Congress included Spain, Sweden, and several other states of significance, the main decisions relative to the territorial redistributions underlying the new equilibrium of power were made through bargains struck by representatives of the five great powers. Metternich's secretary, Friedrich Gentz, described the 1814–15 settlements as

> uniting the sum total of states in a federation under the direction of the major powers . . . The second-, third-, and fourth-rate states submit in silence and without any previous stipulation to the decisions jointly taken by the preponderant powers; and Europe seems to form finally a great political family, united under the auspices of an areopagus of its own creation.[15]

Gentz overstated the case for federation, but he was not far from the mark in characterizing the relationship, between the great powers on the one hand and the smaller states on the other: the system was to be governed solely by the five great powers. Alexander continued to champion the cause of the small states, insisting at Aix-la-Chapelle in 1818 that the congresses incorporate all the states of Europe. But like so many of his liberal projects, this one came to nought.

The governors of the system were self-selected. Their legitimacy was based on little other than leadership of the anti-Napoleon coalition, the entitlements that task brought, and their status as great powers. The system thus rested initially on weak foundations of legitimacy, but over the years the small powers came increasingly, if not happily, to the conclusion that the Concert exercised significant constraints over their fields of action. The leaders of the Concert, for most of the succeeding century, came to feel the same restraints on their foreign policy behavior. The governors created the system on (1) an ideational consensus – a desire to avoid a replay of the Napoleonic drama, hegemony, and pan-European war; (2) a previous pattern of collaboration that had developed during the coalition wars against Napoleon; and (3) agreement that institutions, if not organizations, were necessary to carry out the tasks of governance.

---

[14] Quoted in Charles K. Webster, *The Congress of Vienna* (London: Bell, 1934), p. 45.
[15] Quoted in Hans J. Morgenthau, *Politics among Nations* (New York: Knopf, 1948), pp. 436–7.

GOVERNANCE FOR WHAT? THE TASKS

From the beginning, this "areopagus" could not agree on all of its purposes. The Tsar initially wanted to construct a system that would transcend the unbridled anarchy of the eighteenth century. He wanted to place all international relationships on a basis of self-abnegation for the common good.[16] The task of an international organization or arrangement would be to reinforce the principles of nationality and constitutionalism within states and to secure perpetual peace between states through a confederal structure. Even his original draft of the document that was to emerge as the Holy Alliance retained liberal principles and sought to define the *modus operandi* of states committed to the European good. Metternich's alterations to the draft transformed the document into a "meaningless nothing," a statement of innocuous principles.[17] It was only after repeated rejection of his liberal ideas, several poor diplomatic experiences, and Metternich's importunings that the Tsar ultimately espoused the cause of allied collaboration to quell liberal-national revolutions throughout Europe.

The Troppau Declaration (1818) outlined the great problem to be handled by the polyarchy. It was revolution. For Metternich, the ultimate cause of war was revolution, and in a convoluted set of mental gymnastics he was able to convince himself, the Tsar, and others that any revolution, anywhere in Europe, was a threat to the 1814–15 settlements. The task of the governors, therefore, was to root out revolutionary conspiracies and to intervene – collectively if possible, but unilaterally if necessary – to quell any disturbances. Metternich was less concerned with the territorial balance of power or with French revisionism than he was with liberal and nationalist ideas.

Castlereagh, the main architect of the 1814–15 settlements, had other priorities for the postwar coalition. His inability to persuade Metternich to accept a more limited task of policing the peace against external aggression eventually led him and his successor, Canning, to abandon the Congress system and to revert to strategies of national primacy and selective involvement in European affairs. In Castlereagh's view, the sole purpose of the new European "Government" (his term, used in 1815) was to guarantee the terms of the Treaty of Vienna. This meant, in practice, preventing a French war of revenge or the restoration of a

---

[16] H. G. Schenk, *The Aftermath of the Napoleonic Wars* (London: Kegan Paul, 1946), chs. 1–2; Warren F. Kuehl, *Seeking World Order* (Nashville, TN: Vanderbilt University Press, 1969), pp. 13–15.

[17] Schenk, *The Aftermath of the Napoleonic Wars*, pp. 37–9; Paul W. Schroeder, *Metternich's Diplomacy at its Zenith, 1820–1823* (Austin, TX: University of Texas Press, 1962), p. 6.

Bonaparte regime. Castlereagh did not support Metternich's crusade against revolution, arguing that only those revolutions that threatened to destroy the terms of the Final Act of Vienna would be a cause of common concern and potential joint action.

Disagreement over the main tasks of the polyarchy resulted in the withdrawal of Great Britain from the Congress system, Austria's unilateral interventions against the Neapolitan and Piedmontese rebellions (1820 and 1821), and France's intervention in Spain (1823). By the time the Congress of Verona broke up in 1822, it seemed that the areopagus had dissolved. There was no unanimity on the *casus foederis* and on the primary threat(s) to the system, and therefore no wish to arrange further grandiose meetings of heads of state (congresses) to publicize these great power differences.

But the system, if not the congresses, survived. Some of its other essential tasks, on which there was implicit consensus if not specific treaty obligations, remained more or less intact for the remainder of the century. Two are of particular note: (1) to prevent any hegemony on the continent and (2) to avoid a pan-European war. It was not so much that war was abhorred, but that it contained too many revolutionary possibilities. Nationalism and liberalism (termed Jacobinism by conservatives) were seen as the causes of Napoleon's onslaughts on Europe, and it was commonly feared that another war would lead to their victory. The twin specters of revolution and war drove the peacemakers to maintain a system of governance for Europe, even after the system of congresses collapsed. All rejected the alternative of returning to the laissez-faire, predatory international politics of the eighteenth century.[18] The European statesmen in 1814–16 "had learned that eighteenth-century poker led to Russian roulette and decided to play contract bridge instead."[19]

HOW TO GOVERN: INSTITUTIONS AND PROCEDURES

The most significant procedural innovation of the governors was the establishment of the Congress system. Article VI of the Quadruple Alliance (November 1815) committed the signatories to hold periodic conferences or congresses "for the purpose of consulting upon their interests, or for the consideration of measures . . . which shall be considered the most salutary for the purposes and prosperity of

---

[18] Kalevi J. Holsti, *Peace and War: Armed Conflicts and International Order, 1648–1989* (Cambridge University Press, 1991), ch. 6.

[19] Schroeder, *Austria, Great Britain, and the Crimean War*, p. 404.

Nations and the maintenance of the Peace of Europe."[20] Over the next seven years, the heads of state or foreign ministers met formally four times (with Great Britain only as an observer during the last two). Throughout the remainder of the century, the powers were to meet together at eighteen different conferences and two further congresses. Less formally, they consulted constantly through bilateral diplomacy, royal summits, personal correspondence among the "monarchs' international," and through numerous multilateral meetings of Concert ambassadors in various capitals. Consultation *prior* to taking major foreign policy actions had become the norm by the 1830s.

The areopagus of Europe had no formal organization, but it remained an institution (in the sense of agreed procedures, norms, and the creation of collective outcomes) for governance right up to the outbreak of the Great War. In the early years, when the anti-revolution and peacemaking purposes were on the top of the international agenda, Castlereagh could write that the meetings of the governors were somewhat less fractious than those of the cabinet in London.[21] After 1822, this was no longer the case, but throughout the century the procedures of haggling and bargaining in conferences and congresses usually led to an outcome that had substantial authority and legitimacy. Treaties that emerged from conferences or congresses, for example, became the "law of Europe" and were considered binding on all states.

HOW TO GOVERN: NORMS, DECISIONS, RULES, AND THE DEFINITION OF LIMITS

The peacemakers of 1814–15 established an order for Europe. Its underlying theory was a territorial balance or equilibrium of power, one that would hem in France to prevent any replay of the French revolutionary and Napoleonic dramas. The list of territorial adjustments is long and detailed; it need not concern us. Its result, however, was to create a system of special spheres of influence that left no area of Europe a vacuum that could cause competitive expansion. Russia made major gains in Poland and the Balkans. Austria emerged as the dominant power in the German Confederation and in Italy, thereby filling a potential vacuum. Prussia was rewarded with important territories on the Rhine, thus creating one of several counterweights to France. Belgium (formerly the Austrian Netherlands) was coupled to

---

[20] Quoted in Gordon Craig and Alexander George, *Force and Statecraft: Diplomatic Problems of our Times* (New York: Oxford University Press, 1983), p. 31.
[21] Schenk, *The Aftermath of the Napoleonic Wars*, p. 126.

Holland, thus hemming in France in the north. France was downsized to its 1792 frontiers – a matter of substantial grievance and revisionist agitation among significant sectors of the French political community in later years – but otherwise received a relatively generous peace. One of Castlereagh's main purposes in his negotiations with the Allies in 1814–15 was to insist on a lenient peace and immediate French assimilation into the great power system. He saw this policy as essential to prevent a French war of revenge. In fashioning the territorial equilibrium, Great Britain gave up a number of its wartime overseas conquests for the sake of the overall plan.

The great lacuna in the new order was the Ottoman Empire. It was not admitted to the governance system until 1856, and all of the troubles that had led to chronic conflict and war between St. Petersburg and Constantinople throughout the eighteenth century were not included in the agenda at Vienna. The failure to deal with the immensely complicated "Eastern Question" was to be a source of grievance, crisis, and war for the next ninety-nine years, and was a major factor in the collapse of the system in 1914.

The peacemakers approached the task of order-building with mechanistic rather than organic metaphors in the backs of their minds. They assumed that once the system of territorial balances and counterweights was in place, it would last permanently. Great care was taken, therefore, to contrive it scientifically and empirically. Based on the careful enumerations of the Statistics Committee at the Congress of Vienna, the planners allocated territories taking into consideration populations and strategic lines. New frontiers were to reflect defensibility and population concentrations. Considerations of nationality (so close to Alexander's early concerns) and economic rationality were notable mostly for their absence. The drafters anticipated conquest and war as the only likely methods of changing the system. Changes through population dynamics and economic development were not yet imagined. It was assumed that the polycentric features of power in Europe would last forever, and in fixed ratios.

Having constructed the postwar permanent order, composed of a territorial balance, a set of governors, and some rough notion of the tasks of governance, the powers had to develop some explicit or implicit decision-making rules. These were mostly unstated norms or assumptions underlying the congresses, conferences, and informal communications. They were not observed in all cases, to be sure, but when they were violated, crises usually resulted.

The fundamental procedural principle underlying the system of governance was that no power should attempt to settle a European

40

question (defined as altering the 1815 territorial arrangement or challenging the status and rights of any of the governors) by an independent and self-regulated initiative. All broad issues required collective responses. "European problems require European answers."[22]

The first subsidiary decision rule was that any power must consult the others before taking any decision or action that affected the honor, status, interests, or rights of others. The second was that no power could move against the interests of another without the implied or expressed consent of the collectivity. Metternich toiled for many months, for example, to obtain the approval of his peers before intervening in Naples in 1820. Indifference implied consent. A third rule was that one or more of the powers had a veto. This was implied in the refusal to agree to a conference or congress. Yet, in European crisis situations, there was the assumption that some form of collective decision-making had to take place. The fourth rule held that no power could be excluded from an international conference or congress.[23] Fifth, the small power enemy of a power could not be invited to a conference or congress.[24] Finally, only the great powers decided the great diplomatic questions of the time. Small states had rights to be protected, and their interests had to be taken into account in any critical situation. They could be heard (by invitation) but they had neither a vote nor a veto.

The substantive rules were equally restrictive. The settlements of 1814–15 implied a prohibition against waging war in Europe for territorial gain or promoting revolution or unrest within another power's territory or sphere of vital interest.[25] Direct challenges and provocations had to be avoided. In the offing of war, there must be Concert rather than unilateral solutions. Terribly sensitive to questions of honor and prestige, perhaps the fundamental norm of the system was to avoid threats or humiliations to each other.[26]

The final norm was the obligation to consider joint interests in decision-making and to share responsibility for the system as a whole. The documentation of the period makes frequent reference to "Europe." Whatever the diverging national interests of the individual players, they all recognized in rhetoric and decision calculations that there is a greater interest, a common good, and an obligation to do

---

[22] Richard B. Elrod, "The Concert of Europe: A Fresh Look at an International System," *World Politics*, 28 (1976), p. 164.

[23] Schroeder, *Austria, Great Britain, and the Crimean War*, p. 405.

[24] Elrod, "The Concert of Europe," pp. 163–6.

[25] Schroeder, *Austria, Great Britain, and the Crimean War*, p. 405.

[26] *Ibid.*

things that are consistent with the peace or "repose" of Europe. Treaties are replete with such references (e.g., the 1830 treaty resolving the Belgian question), as is the diplomatic correspondence. The Tsar spoke of his European "family," Castlereagh expounded on the virtues of "European government," and Metternich talked about his "European home." Collective outcomes of conferences and congresses were regarded as the "law of Europe," thus creating new benchmarks against which to measure foreign policy claims and actions of individual states. The "law of Europe" was continually invoked to restrict new claims and foreign policy adventures by individual states. It became just one of many forms of ensuring conformity of both small states and the powers. It is never easy to gauge the exact significance of notions of common destiny or common obligations, but they were conspicuously included in the diplomatic discourses and messages of nineteenth-century Europe and help distinguish it from a mere system of states.

Few of these procedural or substantive norms were incorporated into treaty form; their force was moral and prudential rather than legal. But everyone knew that to violate them would incur a variety of costs, including European war. In 1877, for example, Russia and Great Britain came close to war because the Tsar had imposed a peace treaty on the Ottoman Empire that not only threatened British interests, but contravened some aspects of the "law of Europe" as it had been spelled out in the Congress of Paris (1856). The powers at the Congress of Berlin (1878) compelled Russia – a victor in war – to revise the Treaty of San Stefano (1876) to make it conform to their conceptions of equilibrium in the Balkans.

Given these procedural and substantive norms, how do we characterize the nineteenth-century system of governance? It is easy to slip into sentimentality and to suggest, as some have done, that the Concert system was the germ of a world government (e.g., that it radically altered the principle of anarchy), and was therefore a truly significant departure from all past practices. Jervis has taken the opposite position, arguing that probably after 1822 and certainly after 1856 the system was transformed from a concert into a classical balance of power system.[27] In spare game-theoretic terms, he outlines the essential differences between them. In terms of payoff structures, choices, and the allocation of gains and losses, the systems are fundamentally different. For reasons of explicating different types of systems, Jervis' analysis is

---

[27] Robert Jervis, "From Balance to Concert: A Study of International Security Cooperation," *World Politics*, 38 (October 1985), pp. 58–79.

important. But it lacks in historical detail and nuances, and fails to acknowledge the mixed properties of concert and balance of power that persisted throughout the century and the important linkages between them. Concert and balance are not opposites, but are complementary. In the minds of the peacemakers in 1814–15, the Concert could not work unless there was a balance, defined in territorial terms.

The system of governance and structures of conflict did not change from one type to another at a specific date, but featured complex combinations of egoistic and altruistic behaviors throughout the period. In some periods the former predominated, in others the latter. There were numerous situations perceived and structured in zero-sum terms, and in violation of established rights and statuses. These included the Russian drive to dominate and ultimately to eliminate the Ottoman Empire; the French and British commitment to prop it up as a counterweight; and France's role in fomenting the unification of Italy against Austria's vital interests. Some notable statesmen frequently violated community norms. Metternich, for all his European outlook, seldom sacrificed national advantages for the common welfare.[28] Bismarck was for the most part contemptuous of notions of self-abnegation for some supposed community interest.[29] Napoleon III, despite his rhetorical devotion to the 1814–15 settlements and European order, flouted its conventions on numerous occasions, most notably in Italy.

But throughout the century we also see numerous acts of almost heroic national self-abnegation, often in defiance of strong domestic pressures. Illustrations include the British relinquishment of colonial conquests for the sake of constructing the overall balance in the Treaty of Vienna; Guizot's moderate policies and abandonment of the French revisionist cause;[30] Alexander's feelings of loyalty toward the unity of the powers, and his and Nicholas I's sacrifice or tempering of Russian ambitions in Greece and elsewhere in the Balkans for the greater good of Europe, all despite immense pressure to take aggrandizing actions from nationalist and military elements in the Tsar's court;[31] and the collaborative undertakings vis-à-vis Africa concluded at the Berlin Conference (1885). These were not expedients or costs assumed for the

---

[28] Schroeder, *Metternich's Diplomacy at its Zenith*, pp. 251–2.
[29] W. N. Medlicott, *Bismarck, Gladstone, and the Concert of Europe* (London: Athlone Press, 1956); R. B. Mowat, *The Concert of Europe* (London: Macmillan, 1930), p. 57.
[30] Roger Bullen, "France and Europe, 1815–1848: The Problem of Defeat and Recovery," in Sked, ed., *Europe's Balance of Power*, pp. 143–4.
[31] Matthew Anderson, "Russia and the Eastern Question, 1821–41," in Sked, ed., *Europe's Balance of Power*, pp. 92–7.

sake of temporary diplomatic alignments. They expressed, rather, a commitment to the common good of Europe.

Before attempting a periodization of the Concert's effectiveness, we need to estimate the extent of a governance system's authority. This is done by examining the consequences of its decisions and actions.

THE OUTCOMES OF GOVERNANCE: DECISIONS, ACTIONS, AND COMPLIANCE

Institutions and organizations may exist, but if their work does not result in decisions (allocation of values, establishment of rules, and the like) and compliance, or if they are imposed solely by coercion and violence, there is government but no governance. To establish the existence of a system of governance, then, we need to look beyond norms, rules, procedures, and institutions and examine also the outputs and responses. Compliance without coercion indicates legitimate authority. Yet, as in the domestic realm, the possibility of coercion may also be in the background. A system of governance must have some capacity to enforce decisions in the case of non-compliance, but it cannot rely solely on coercion and force. What did the Concert decide? What were the responses to its decisions and actions? What did it do in the event of non-compliance?

The agendas of the various conferences and congresses were taken up primarily with questions that could lead to war and to validating or vetoing changes to the order established in 1814–15. But there were numerous items of lesser import as well. Morgenthau[32] lists the following questions that were raised at the Congress of Aix-la-Chapelle (1818): the claims of certain German princes against the abuses of their new sovereigns; the petition of the Elector of Hesse to exchange his title for that of King (rejected); a request by Napoleon's mother for the release of her son (rejected); the claims of Bavaria and the House of Hochberg to the succession in Baden; a dispute between the Duke of Oldenburg and Count Bentninck about the lordship of Knupen-haussen; the situation of the Jews in Prussia and Austria; the rank of diplomatic representatives (firmly established); the slave trade (ultimately prohibited); the suppression of the Barbary pirates (development of a common policy); and the question of the Spanish colonies (no action). We see here acts of governance. Some conflicts or disputes were authoritatively settled. The conference participants created new

---

[32] Morgenthau, *Politics among Nations*, p. 441.

regimes and rules. Other problems were put on the back burner or not pressed because of resistance from one or more of the powers.

Throughout the nineteenth century, the powers made the following *types* of decisions, most of which brought compliance without attending coercion:

1 *Declarations announcing new norms or clarifying old ones.* Illustration: the rules announced at Troppau and Laibach defining the conditions under which military intervention by the powers would be justified (in this case, against liberal-national revolutions).

2 *Validation of projects and policies having consequences for the system.* Illustrations: the Concert's approval of Metternich's intervention against Naples (1820); the creation of Belgium through treaty by the Concert powers (1831); the alterations of the Congress of Berlin to the Treaty of San Stefano (1876) terminating in the Russo-Ottoman war, bringing its terms in line with the interests of all the powers;[33] and the collective recognition of Bulgaria, Romania, Serbia, and Montenegro as new states.

3 *Prevention of, or pre-preempting unilateral actions.* Illustrations: preventing a Russian intervention in Spain, 1822–3; preventing a Russian attack on Turkey, 1822 and 1853 (the latter ultimately unsuccessful); preventing war between Belgium and Luxembourg (1839) and several possible wars between Belgium and Holland; preventing war between Greece and Turkey over Crete (1869 and 1886); and intervention in the Levant (1860) to protect Christian minorities, after which there was a lengthy period of peace.[34]

4 *Creation of new statuses and positions/incumbents.* Illustrations: the creation and recognition of Belgium as a sovereign state (1830–1); neutralization of the Aaland Islands (1856); resolving the succession problem in Denmark (1852); admitting the Ottoman Empire into the Concert (1856); and selecting a king for Greece (1862).

5 *Creation of international regimes.* Illustrations: elimination of the slave trade; creating rules for navigation on the Danube (seemingly insignificant, this arrangement formally put to an

---

[33] Mihailo Stojanovic, *The Great Powers and the Balkans, 1875–1878* (Cambridge: Cambridge University Press, 1939).

[34] For a full catalogue of Concert decisions and actions that had war-preventing characteristics, see Charles Dupuis, *Le Principe de l'équilibre et le Concert Européen* (Paris: Librairie Academique, 1909), esp. p. 504.

end the eighteenth-century view that trade was a zero-sum game); regimes governing trade and military transit through the Turkish straits (frequently amended until 1922).

6 *Introduction of conflict-resolving mechanisms and institutions.* Before, during, and after crises, the powers developed a number of devices and contrivances to "obviate the misunderstandings and disputes which might in future arise," for "diminishing occasions of conflict," to "remove suspicion," and to create a "means adapted for the prevention of conflicts."[35] These included the establishment of neutral buffer states (Luxembourg, 1867); neutral zones and demilitarized areas (the Black Sea, 1856 [subsequently repudiated by Russia, 1870], and the Ionian Islands, 1863); limiting the transfer of arms to various conflict areas (Africa, the Brussels Act of 1890); delimiting spheres of influence; and agreements of mutual self-abnegation in conflict areas. This included, for example, the 1827 multilateral agreement regarding Greece "not to seek . . . any augmentation of territory, any exclusive influence, or any commercial advantage . . . which those of every other Nation may not equally obtain."[36] There were, finally, various undertakings (the Treaty of Paris, 1856, and the General Act of the Conference of Berlin, 1885), to resort to mediation prior to using force to settle disputes.

In these and other cases, the powers agreed on means to avoid going to war among themselves; not infrequently, they dictated to the smaller states the conditions they thought necessary to maintain their harmony.

7 *Acts of coercion.* If most of the decisions and actions of the governance system were ultimately accepted by those immediately involved, occasionally the decisions of the Concert required coercive measures. The authority of the system did not always go unchallenged. The Ottoman Empire was the target of numerous joint measures of the powers, particularly after the Congress of Berlin (1878). Most frequently they were collective acts of diplomacy and persuasion, but throughout the century single or joint naval flotillas representing the Concert displayed and used force to bring about changes in the

---

[35] All the quotations are from Paul Gordon Lauren, "Crisis Prevention in Nineteenth Century Diplomacy," in Alexander George, ed., *Managing U.S.–Soviet Rivalry: Problems of Crisis Prevention* (Boulder, CO: Westview Press, 1983), p. 37.
[36] *Ibid.*, p. 47.

foreign and domestic policies of the Porte. In 1905, for example, a combined fleet, without German participation, occupied Mitylene (Lesvos) as a means of compelling the Sultan to accept a series of Austrian-initiated reforms of the gendarmerie and fiscal systems of Macedonia.

The history of the period is not without its numerous challenges to the system's norms and decisions. The authority and legitimacy of the Concert were always qualified. Between the unilateral French intervention in Spain in 1823 and Austria-Hungary's annexation of Bosnia in 1908, there were many breakdowns and several wars. The reminders of continued anarchy, self-help, and security dilemmas were seldom in the distant background. Yet, as Decazes wrote about the overall influence of the Concert on international politics, "Europe has learned that the authority of its councils is decisive."[37] The more blatant transgressions against the conventions of the governance system were exactly the ones that led to the most dangerous crises and to war. Numerous other situations were prevented from escalating to that point precisely because the conventions were followed and the decisions and actions of the governors were authoritative.

GOVERNANCE: DID IT MAKE A DIFFERENCE?

Skeptics, like the historian W. N. Medlicott, have argued that the Concert operated only because a variety of background conditions predisposed the powers to behave as if they were constrained: "As long as Europe remembered the horrors of the Napoleonic wars it remained, for the most part, at peace, and therefore in concert; but it was peace that maintained the Concert, and not the Concert that maintained peace."[38] The opposite view is that the Concert was a necessary condition for the relative peace that pervaded the continent in the nineteenth century. It is, of course, impossible to provide an authoritative causal analysis that would settle the cause–consequence issue. But just the enumeration of governance norms and decisions – particularly in the realm of conflict prevention or management – suggests that the record of war incidence in the nineteenth century would have been much higher in the absence of the polyarchy. The peacemakers of 1814–15 were determined to create something new and to improve upon the record of the eighteenth century. To some extent, they succeeded.

[37] Quoted in Mowat, *The Concert of Europe*, p. 32.
[38] Medlicott, *Bismarck, Gladstone, and the Concert of Europe*, p. 18.

47

One way to proceed would be to compare the record of great power war and predation in the two centuries. In the century between the Utrecht settlements (1713–15) and the Congress of Vienna, there were thirty-three bilateral and multilateral European wars involving some or all of the eleven powers of the period (aside from the usual ones, we would have to include Spain, Sweden, Denmark, Holland, and Saxony). For the 1815–1914 period, there were seventeen European wars involving one or more of the eight powers (including Spain and Sweden). A figure of the probabilities of initial war involvement per year per power (number of European wars divided by number of powers, divided by 100 years) should tell us something about the relative war-proneness of the two centuries. For 1715–1814, the figure is .030. For the succeeding period, the figure declines to .021. The probabilities of war participation for any power declined by 30 percent. A change of this magnitude is not likely to be random. While explanations for the change, other than those of the Concert's effectiveness, have to be entertained, the exclusion of the Concert as part of the explanation would be a signal error.

If one compares the complexity of problems in the two centuries, the significance of the Concert system of governance is further underlined. In the nineteenth century, there were important ideological cleavages between the powers. In contrast, dynastic principles and practices provided eighteenth-century Europe with political homogeneity. (The religious issues of the previous century had been resolved through the Thirty Years War and did not constitute a source of conflict between Utrecht and Vienna.) The nineteenth century was characterized by the erosion and ultimate collapse of two European empires and the emergence of many new nation-states (see below). In contrast, the eighteenth century saw the consolidation of dynastic states. In the nineteenth century, the Ottoman Empire and its weakness were a chronic source of international rivalry and conflict. Throughout most of the eighteenth century, the "sick man of Europe" was only beginning to display symptoms of infirmity. Given the nature and complexity of the international agenda in the nineteenth century compared to previous periods, we would be justified in expecting more, not fewer, wars. But the reverse was the case.

Unlike their eighteenth-century predecessors, the peacemakers of 1814–15 and their successors learned some important lessons about the consequences of pan-European wars. They therefore built or fashioned institutions and developed norms and conventions that were designed to move beyond the rudimentary "hidden hand" of the eighteenth-century balance of power. We have called it a system of governance. While not undermining the principle of anarchy and the persistence of security dilemmas, it effectively "restricted the field of action" of both small and great powers, prevented many violations of its norms, "smothered" egoistic behavior by reference to group wishes, and thereby significantly reduced the incidence of war. At least until 1854, "in repeated plays of the Prisoner's Dilemma . . . each state cooperated in the expectation that the others would do the same. Multilateral and self-restrained methods of handling their problems were preferred to the more common unilateral and less restrained methods."[39] The Concert did many other things as well, none of them perfectly. Its decisions and actions were sometimes ignored, resisted, or challenged. But more often problems were solved short of war. Having withdrawn from the Congress system in 1822, Canning rejoiced in a new freedom of action: "every nation for itself and God for us all!"[40] But while Great Britain could briefly withdraw into relative isolation and ignore or forget the European interest, the others could and did not. They were now constrained by devices of their own making. The breaching of those constraints usually led to war; their observance maintained peace.

Throughout the ninety-nine years of general peace in Europe after the Vienna settlements, there were a number of crises that, in other circumstances, probably would have led to war. There are more than a few "hard cases" (Oran Young's term in his contribution to this volume), situations "in which the circumstances at hand are distinctly unfavorable to the operation of social institutions as determinants of social outcomes." We have already cited the unprecedented case, in 1878, of the Concert compelling a victorious power (Russia) to revise a peace treaty to make it accord with the desires of the other powers. An almost certain bilateral war was averted by this means. In the 1820s Concert pressures on Russia and the Ottoman Empire brought the independence of Greece and a limitation of Russian ambitions in the Balkans. Throughout the nineteenth century, the powers' collective support for the Ottoman Empire (e.g., against Mehment Pasha of Egypt) slowed down its collapse and unilateral partition by, for example, Russia. The list of wars between small powers that were prevented by concerted diplomacy is also impressive. As suggested, many of them would have gone to the battlefield in the eighteenth century. While it is undoubtedly the case that the territorial balance of power constructed in 1814–15 was a necessary condition for the Concert

---

[39] Jervis, "From Balance to Concert," p. 59.
[40] Quoted in Roy Bridge, "Allied Diplomacy in Peacetime: The Failure of the Congress 'System'", in Sked, ed., *Europe's Balance of Power*, p. 53.

to operate, it is also true that the powers, with the possible exception of the 1856–75 period, were collectively committed to maintaining its main outlines. Balance and Concert went hand in hand, and the two made a significant difference on the incidence of war, particularly great power war, throughout the nineteenth century.

THE BREAKDOWN OF THE SYSTEM OF GOVERNANCE

If there have been debates about the effectiveness and impact of the Concert, there has also been a lack of consensus on when it broke down and why. Jervis and Schroeder use 1854 as the watershed. But Napoleon III wrote Queen Victoria in 1863 that the Vienna order was *on the verge* of breaking down.[41] Some have proposed that the Franco-Prussian war sealed the fate of the Concert – the Concert did nothing to prevent it – and still others suggest that at least some of its norms and conventions lasted right up to the Great War. A careful study would probably reveal that the governance system waxed and waned after 1854, but never died out entirely. Gladstone attempted to revive a form of concerted diplomacy in the late 1870s, but without much success. Yet the "monarchs' international" played a role in diffusing a war scare in 1875, the Congress of Berlin (1878) created virtually a new regime for the Balkans – filling the great lacuna of the Vienna settlements – and the Conference of Berlin (1885) was instrumental in developing rules of the game governing expansion and competition in Africa. The Concert, minus Germany, played a major role as pacifier and reform agent for the Balkans until about 1906, and a conference of its ambassadors in London played a collective, though ultimately unsuccessful, role in the Balkan wars of 1912 and 1913. Yet, it remained dormant during the years of the Italian and German wars of unification, and was either ineffective or immobilized during the Algeciras crisis (1906) and when Austria annexed Bosnia in 1908. Its greatest failure, of course, was in July 1914 when, despite pleas for a conference or congress, mobilizations went ahead. Table 1 offers a rough periodization of the Concert's effectiveness. Three of the criteria or indicators of a governance system are used: (1) employment of institutions (norm observance, consultation, frequency of decisions and actions, for example); (2) ideational consensus on tasks of governance; (3) authority and legitimacy of collective outcomes. The judgments are indicative of impressions rather than precise measures.

---

[41] Augustus Oakes and R. B. Mowat, *The Great European Treaties of the Nineteenth Century* (Oxford: Clarendon Press, 1918), p. 225.

Table 1. *Periodization of the Concert of Europe*

	1815–22	1823–56	1857–75	1876–1914
Institutional use	high	high	low	medium
Ideational consensus	high	medium	low	low
Authority of outcomes	high	high	low	medium

Although the Concert appeared to be more effective as a governance system in the post-1875 period than during the 1860s and early 1870s, its effectiveness as the guardian of the Vienna order was rendered increasingly problematical as fundamental structural and attitudinal changes were undermining the order's foundations. Rather than single out most of the usual explanations for Europe's descent to war in 1914 – secret diplomacy, inflexible alliances, the cult of the offensive,[42] mobilization procedures, and Germany's irresponsible support of Austria-Hungary are the usual culprits – I prefer to emphasize three more fundamental factors. The first includes major structural changes in the system. The second refers to technological innovations as they applied to estimations of the balance of power and war preparation. The third emphasizes changing attitudes toward war among high-level decision-makers.

The Concert system was constructed and developed by leaders of states that had many similar characteristics. Most fundamental was that all were historic states that had been major actors in European diplomatic relations since at least the middle of the seventeenth century. While some were or became republics and others retained dynastic regimes, all had undergone a common set of historical experiences and the socializing effects of diplomacy, war, and peacemaking. The order created in 1814–15 assumed the integrity and continued existence of the governors. Indeed, the system was designed specifically to sustain a society of states led by five capable and similarly socialized leaders.

Throughout the nineteenth century the main issue that generated war was the effort to create nation-states based on ethnic/religious/language divisions and particularisms.[43] The process of state-creation

---

[42] Stephen Van Evera, "The Cult of the Offensive and the Origins of the First World War," in Stephen E. Miller, ed., *Military Strategy and the Origins of the First World War* (Princeton, NJ: Princeton University Press, 1985), pp. 58–107; Thomas J. Christiansen and Jack Snyder, "Chain Gangs and Passed Bucks: Predicting Alliance Patterns in Multi-Polarity," *International Organization*, 42 (Spring 1990), pp. 137–68.
[43] Holsti, *Peace and War*, ch. 7.

was necessarily at the expense of some of the historic states, in particular the Ottoman Empire, Austria, and France. Starting with the liberation of Greece from the Ottoman Empire in the 1820s, continuing with the unification of Italy (at the expense of Austria) and Germany (at the expense of Austria and France), and finally with the blossoming of states in the Balkans, again at the expense of the Ottoman and Austrian Empires, the whole process eroded the foundations of the post-Napoleonic order. Instead of five great historic states, managing a system totalling about eleven powers-that-mattered (excluding the few remaining German principalities), by the turn of the century two historic empires were on the verge of collapse and the number of new states, all flexing their nationalist muscles, had increased by nine (Norway, Romania, Bulgaria, Serbia, Greece, Montenegro, Bosnia-Herzegovina, Albania, and Italy), for a total of twenty or more states-that-mattered. Almost all the new states were born through violence and among the first things they did upon achieving independence was to go to war against their neighbors and/or to threaten the historic states of Europe. They had no commitment to the order created in 1814–15 and understood little of its substantive or procedural norms. In their struggles for independence and subsequent territorial land-grabs, they cumulatively threatened the system as a whole.

The order created by Metternich, Talleyrand, Alexander, Stein, and Castlereagh had been designed in part to repress nationalism. Reflecting changing attitudes, by the 1830s one of the tasks of the Concert was to help bring forth new states with a minimum of violence (Greece, Belgium), or to sanction changes they could not prevent (the unifications of Italy and Germany). But by the end of the century the birth of new states and their resulting expansionism threatened not just interests, but the very existence of two of the historic states. In perhaps its greatest signal failure, the Concert after about 1910 did nothing collectively to prevent the collapse of the Ottoman and Austro-Hungarian Empires.[44]

The great transformation of political organization from the historic-empire format to the nation-state format was fundamentally inconsistent with the assumptions upon which the Concert system of governance was founded. The purpose of the system was to protect its members. Balkan nationalism's aim was to destroy at least two of them.

This transformation did not represent, in Waltz's sense, a change of system structure. For Waltz, a state is a state. States only differ in their

---

[44] Schroeder, "The Nineteenth Century System," p. 146.

capacities to carry out tasks. But I would argue that the essential properties and numbers of states in a system are important structural variables, even when anarchy is held constant. Changes from empires to nation-states (and vice versa) are likely to explain a great deal of the variation in war incidence in an international system.[45]

The second transformation was technological. The order constructed in 1814–15 was a *territorial* equilibrium of power, providing each participant (except defeated France) with some net gains. In those days, the main index of national power was territory, not armaments. Armaments levels and numbers of troops in 1815 and subsequently varied substantially, and yet European policy-makers regarded the continent in terms of a stable and enduring equilibrium. Russia had by far the largest army, and Great Britain sustained naval supremacy throughout the century. The differentials of armed might were not, however, a matter of great concern beyond some sentiments of envy, and did not suggest threats to the balance of power. Increments of military capabilities seldom caused crises of significantly raised perceptions of threat.

The applications of technology to the art of war changed all of this. Weapons and transportation innovations in the second half of the century placed a premium on mobility, speed of mobilization, and pre-preemptive attack. This was an era of the cult of the offensive, when many thought that decisive battles would determine the outcome of war. Military strength now became the measure of the balance of power, and any increment was perceived as threatening to the equilibrium. Arms racing gave the appearance of rapid changes in relative power and generated fears of lagging behind. Before the 1860s, approximately, only territorial conquests and challenges to honor, rights, and status threatened the order. The Concert frequently prevented both types of challenge. After the 1860s, in contrast, power could be changed unilaterally without reference to the concerns of the other powers. Industrial dynamics replaced territory as the main metric of power analysis.

The launching of a new dreadnought brought visible increments of security or insecurity; railways, military mobilization times, and the numbers of troops that could be transported rapidly to the front were all variables that could be manipulated to create an increasing sense of superiority or inferiority. The Peloponnesian complex was the result:

[45] K. J. Holsti, *The States System and War* (Department of Political Science, the Maharaja Sayajirao University of Baroda, Baroda, India: The Ford Foundation Lectures in International Relations Studies, 1989).

governments began considering the necessity of going to war to avoid being left behind.[46]

Thus, a state could pose a threat to the order without making a single territorial demand or rectification, or without challenging the rights and status of others. The bounds of legitimacy, which in 1814–15 had been defined in territorial, norm, and status terms, were now no longer obvious. No one could claim that the launching of a naval vessel or the building of a railway somehow contravened the territorial balance of power or the norms of the Concert constructed at Vienna. Yet, even small increments of military power created perceptions of imbalance. By the late nineteenth century it was competitive arms dynamics rather than territorial conquest that became the great threat to the system.

In the first forty years after the Vienna settlements, the time available for handling crises or problems was extensive. The Greek "question" was on the agenda for almost eight years before the battle of Navarino (1828). The Russian actions that gave rise to the conflict ending in the Crimean War took place many months before the first shot was fired. There was no sense that military actions had to be taken immediately in order to avoid catastrophe. There was time for diplomacy and conferences. But by the end of the century, there were strong pressures to act *before* diplomacy had a chance. Inaction could provide the adversary with an advantage that might mean the difference between victory and defeat.

The structural and technological changes were accompanied by an intellectual revolution. Conceptions of, and attitudes toward, war in the first half of the century reflected the Clausewitzian notion of carefully calibrated use of force for specific foreign policy purposes. War was conducted in a framework of moral ideas, specific purposes, and assumed limits. The peacemakers of 1814–15 understood that a return to war of the Napoleonic variety posed the threat of pan-European revolution. The ideas about and ideals of war after Vienna were distinctly of the pre-1792 variety.

In contrast to the views of war propagated during the latter part of the nineteenth century by the peace societies, liberals, and pacifists, another view developed in tandem. Its roots were in the ideas of Hegel, Treitschke, Darwin, and others. The new philosophers of war and peace did not view armed conflict as an evil, an avoidable consequence of diplomatic breakdowns, a social disease, or a tragic mistake. It was, rather, an inevitable and constructive consequence of the eternal struggle between nations and civilizations. Assaulted by growing

---

[46] Holsti, *Peace and War*, ch. 7.

materialism, class warfare, secularism, and the decline of the sense of honor and duty in domestic social relations, adherents of this perspective on war saw in it a number of redeeming and positive features. These included social cohesion and group solidarity, patriotism, sacrifice, and national rejuvenation. For the new philosophers of war, it was a moral good, as much an agent of historical progress as commerce and science were for liberals.[47]

These ideas clashed with and subverted the older Clausewitzian notions of war. War did not need a defined political purpose to justify it; it could be justified in its broad social consequences. The problem for the diplomat, then, was no longer to find ways to avoid war – the fundamental assumption underlying the Concert system of governance – but to prepare the way and to choose the appropriate time for it. International relations were no longer viewed as the adjustments between states and the management of conflicts, but as a struggle between civilizations.

These sorts of views were commonly found in the highest levels of government, particularly among the military leadership in Berlin, St. Petersburg, and Vienna. When the crises of the early twentieth century began to unfold, "the service leaders . . . forced the issues, and everywhere [except Great Britain] politicians willingly surrendered a large amount of political responsibility to them."[48]

Militarist attitudes accompanied the structural and technological changes of the late nineteenth century. They were attitudes that fundamentally undermined the assumptions, norms, and practices of the Concert system of governance. There were other sources of the breakdown (alliance inflexibility after the Franco-Prussian war, colonial competition, and the like), but the system-wide structural, technological, and attitudinal changes in the latter part of the nineteenth century were fundamental. Good intentions, established habits, and well-founded institutions, no matter how seemingly permanent and effective, may not survive major alterations in political forms, technology, and philosophy.

CONCLUSION

The series of questions examined here provides strong evidence for the argument that there are half-way houses between systems

---

[47] *Ibid.*; Richard Rosecrance, *Action and Reaction in World Politics* (Boston, MA: Little, Brown & Co., 1963), pp. 163–5.
[48] Brian Bond, *War and Society in Europe, 1870–1970* (Leicester: University of Leicester Press, 1983).

of governance based on principles of anarchy and those based on hier-archy. There are alternatives to pure self-help systems, on the one hand, and command systems on the other. Nineteenth-century international politics combined anarchical features and behaviors with those commonly found in loose systems of governance featuring norms, institutions, and authority structures that modify, constrain, and direct egoistic behavior.

The analysis also challenges those versions of hegemonic stability theory that have extended beyond the economic domain. Great Britain's position as a world power did not translate into continental hegemony. The governance system in nineteenth-century Europe was a polyarchy, not a hegemony. The five powers drafted the outlines of an international order and some of its institutional features. Through practice, those were amended and extended, used, and abused during the rest of the century. The fundamental purpose of the order was to prevent the rise of a hegemon, and in this task the powers succeeded for almost a century. No single power "laid down the law" (to use Vattel's definition of hegemony) for the continent. Laying down the law was a collective endeavor, with mixed results. In other tasks, the polyarchy developed regimes, prevented wars, allocated rewards after wars, developed conflict resolution mechanisms, and prevented or validated changes to the 1815 order.

History rarely repeats itself exactly, but in the post-Cold War environment, we see certain similarities with the nineteenth-century system. There is a broad consensus – as revealed in numerous state-ments by the leaders of the great powers and in the justification rhetoric surrounding the imposition of economic sanctions against Iraq – that some form of new order must be created, although there is scant agreement on its outlines and details beyond norms elaborated in the Charter of the United Nations. There is an assumption that the center-piece of that order will be the explicit or implicit collaboration of the great powers. This does not mean unanimity, for even in the moments of greatest solidarity among the European powers during the nine-teenth century, ambitions, claims, and expectations clashed. But tempering the pursuit of unilateral gains and advantages there was the recognition of a larger interest. The idea of a global community interest has been articulated by many, in particular by Mikhail Gorbachev and, during the Iraq crisis, by George Bush, James Baker, and some Euro-pean leaders. The idea remains in primitive form, and unilateral actions that are scarcely consistent with it remain on the diplomatic agenda. One cannot expect sudden transformations of world politics. Yet the practices of multilateralism, partial self-abnegation for long-range mutual benefits, and broad consultations prior to the making of decisions having regional or global repercussions have become established norms.

For some, this type of governance no doubt smacks of a northern domination of the south, but others will see it as a necessary condition for the United Nations to work as it was originally intended. We can perhaps learn something about international governance today – its shape, assumptions, prerequisites, and weaknesses – by examining the nineteenth-century experience. While alert to false historical analogies, there still may be things to be learned from the experience of earlier eras.

3 THE DECAYING PILLARS OF THE WESTPHALIAN TEMPLE: IMPLICATIONS FOR INTERNATIONAL ORDER AND GOVERNANCE[1]

Mark W. Zacher

> Everything in the world has changed except our thinking.
> Albert Einstein

> We playwrights who have to cram a whole human life or an entire historical era into a two-hour play, can scarcely understand this rapidity [of change] ourselves. And if it gives us trouble, think of the trouble it must give political scientists who have less experience with the realm of the improbable.
> President Vaclav Havel of Czechoslovakia,
> Address to U.S. Congress, February 1990

International relations scholars are one of the most conservative groups of social scientists in the world in the sense that we are very skeptical, if not cynical, about the possibility of fundamental change in the parameters of our area of study. In fact, we generally believe that illusions concerning the possibility of major change can wreak greater havoc in the world than a realistic acceptance of the rather nasty nature of international politics. The basic reality that we feel we must accept is a system of states that are subject to minimal international governance and that go to war regularly to realize various goals. In the present era our long-held and justifiable cynicism concerning the possibility for change in the traditional interstate system could blind us to a significant transformation in global politics.

Increasingly, academic experts and policy-makers are observing explicitly or implicitly that the international system might be in the midst of some fundamental political changes. However, it is important to note that this is certainly not the first time that they have projected

[1] I would like to thank the following for research assistance and comments: Tim Carter, Deepa Khosla, Paul Samson, and Willy Wong. I would like to thank the following for their comments: David Armstrong, Eva Busza, Barry Buzan, Raymond Cohen, Claire Cutler, Yale Ferguson, Robert Jackson, Brian Job, Masaru Kohno, Richard Mathew, Sasson Sofer, Michael Webb, Steve Weber, as well as other contributors to this volume.

fundamental changes in international politics. One need only think back to the end of World War I, "the war to end all wars," and the expectations of some statesmen and scholars of the time. However, there are grounds now for thinking that there are significant changes occurring in the growth of international cooperation or regimes – and consequently in the strength of governance in the international system. It is a process whose roots can be traced back at least to the beginning of the industrial revolution, but it has only been since 1945 that it has accelerated so as to have a marked effect on the international order – "order" here referring to the corpus of regimes or governing arrangements in the international system.

The traditional international system has often been referred to as the Westphalian system after the Treaty of Westphalia of 1648 which recognized the state as the supreme or sovereign power within its boundaries and put to rest the church's transnational claims to political authority. States' mutual respect for each other's sovereignty is generally regarded as the constitutive principle of the system. Other key principles that are derivative of state sovereignty are nonintervention in each other's internal affairs (at least with respect to religious practices), consent as the basis of obligation to comply with international laws, and diplomatic immunity.[2] However, nonintervention has never really been a strong dimension of the system since states have tried to influence internal political developments in other states quite frequently (e.g., the Holy Alliance). Also, it is important to stress that war for the purpose of territorial revision was accepted and frequent. At best what states sought to do in the traditional system was to preserve the existence of most other states (although not their borders) and to prevent the dominance of any single state through either the operation of the very flexible balance of power system or a great power concert. Cooperation to protect each other's sovereignty and manage wars varied a great deal and was strongest in the half-century after the Napoleonic wars. Also, within the Westphalian system until very recently, economic, social and environmental interdependencies were not intense enough to necessitate high levels of coordination. A

---

[2] The Westphalian system is discussed in: Leo Gross, "The Peace of Westphalia, 1648–1948," in Richard A. Falk and Wolfram F. Hanrieder, eds., *International Law and Organization* (Philadelphia, PA: Lippincott, 1968), pp. 45–67; Lynn H. Miller, *Global Order: Values and Power in International Politics* (Boulder, CO: Westview Press, 1990), chs. 2–3; F. H. Hinsley, *The Pursuit of Peace* (Cambridge: Cambridge University Press, 1963), esp. chs. 8–11; Martin Wright, *Systems of States* (Atlantic Heights, NJ: Humanities Press, 1977); James Mayall, *Nationalism and International Society* (Cambridge: Cambridge University Press, 1990); and the contribution of K. J. Holsti in this volume.

significant proliferation in international organizations and laws did not really begin until the twentieth century.

In looking back at this traditional system, states' respect for each other's sovereignty most of the time and the existence of a very modest corpus of international regimes deserve highlighting and recognition. Because of their existence the character of the international system is much better captured by Hedley Bull's concept of "the anarchical society" than it is by Kenneth Waltz's notion of "anarchy."[3] However, it is equally important to stress that states had a very high degree of autonomy in their international relations in that they accepted very few international obligations in either conventional or customary law. In other words, not only were states sovereign, but they also maintained a high degree of policy autonomy by not enmeshing themselves in a large number of international regimes – and especially not in a regime that restricted their ability to use military force.

From a purely legal perspective states still have the sovereign right not to be bound by an international accord supported by most or even all of their fellow states. However, in practice they are becoming increasingly *enmeshed* in a network of interdependencies and regulatory/collaborative arrangements from which exit is generally not a feasible option. This portrayal accords with the judgment of Harold Jacobson that "States entangled in webs of international organizations is the proper simile to describe the contemporary global political system."[4] Basically, it is no longer accurate to conceptualize states as having their traditional degree of autonomy because of the network of formal and informal regimes in which they are becoming increasingly involved, and this process of enmeshment is likely to progress (albeit in fits and starts) throughout the coming century. It is also no longer valid to describe the international system in terms of billiard balls colliding unless one envisages the billiard balls as being attached by strings of resin that constrain their movement in any direction. The system, like the process of historical change, might be viewed as "sticky."

Several observations should be stressed at this point concerning the changing international order. First, there are significant differences among groups of states as to the speed at which they are involved in this process of historical change. It is largely the developed industrialized world in which the process is most noticeable, although with time

---

[3] Hedley Bull, *The Anarchical Society: A Study of Order in World Politics* (New York: Columbia University Press, 1977); and Kenneth N. Waltz, *Theory of International Politics* (Reading, MA: Addison-Wesley, 1979).

[4] Harold K. Jacobson, *Networks of Interdependence: International Organizations and the Global Political System* (New York: Knopf, 2nd edn., 1984), p. 516.

it is likely to draw in the Third World. The involvement of the socialist or formerly socialist states is also likely to be uneven for some time. Second, it is a long-term process which is likely to have periods of rapid progress and occasional times of reversal. Connected to this it is important to understand that there will continue to be a great deal of conflict in the world. It is just that it will increasingly occur and be resolved within a growing body of explicit and implicit regimes. Lastly, as will be elaborated on below, progress toward greater collaboration in security, economic, environmental, and social fields depends on one development – the continued reluctance of great powers to embark on war with each other because of the costs of nuclear war. If this breaks down because of technological or political developments, the general projections of this chapter are unlikely to hold.

In analyzing the process of international political change that has been developing quite rapidly in the post-1945 period and is likely to continue, it is important to understand what conditions sustained the two central features of the traditional Westphalian system.[5] As noted above, one feature is the central legal ordering principle – namely, states' obligation to respect each other's sovereignty. The other is the central behavioral pattern (although it can take on legal characteristics), and that is a high level of state autonomy in domestic and foreign affairs. Another way of phrasing this latter feature is the existence of a very low level of governance or a modest body of regimes in the international system.

The central conditions or pillars that have sustained the principle of reciprocal respect for sovereignty are: (1) the desire of rulers to prevent incursions on their own powers; (2) the absence of a transnational ideology that seriously competes with states for people's political loyalties; (3) an historical memory (and/or perceived likelihood) of overlapping political authorities and competing political loyalties leading to massive violence and disorder; (4) a common set of values that engender an element of respect for other states and their rulers; and (5) states' provision to their citizens of important values such as protection of life and economic welfare. While there has, of course, been some decay in these pillars of sovereignty, the decay does not appear to be so serious as to threaten seriously the centrality of states in world politics.

---

[5] For insightful analyses of the transformation from the medieval to the Westphalian system and of present changes, see John Gerard Ruggie, "Continuity and Transformation in the World Polity: Toward a Neorealist System," in Robert O. Keohane, ed., *Neorealism and its Critics* (New York: Columbia University Press, 1986), pp. 131–57, and "'Finding our Feet' in Territoriality: International Transformation in the Making," (mimeo, 1990).

Related to (and in part overlapping with) the conditions that sustain state sovereignty are those that sustain a high degree of state autonomy in domestic and especially foreign affairs – or a low level of international governance. It is clear to anyone who studies the development of the modern interstate system that states have sought to evade international constraints on their behavior, but that they have found themselves increasingly pressured or motivated to enter into a variety of international regimes or governing arrangements. In other words, the pillars of state autonomy in the traditional Westphalian international system have eroded in the past and appear to be in a continual process of decay – albeit at varying speeds and to varying degrees. There are six key pillars or conditions supportive of a high level of state autonomy on which this study will focus.[6] The first three concern interdependencies among states whereas the latter three are important largely because they affect the strength of the first three pillars. The pillars are:

1   A cost/benefit ratio for the use of force (especially by the great powers) that makes the costs of periodic resort to war appear quite tolerable, makes strong regimes to control resort to war unnecessary, and promotes a high degree of economic autarky.

2   Low physical externalities among states that cause little transboundary damage and therefore do not require international collaboration to control them.

3   Low levels of economic interdependence that do not require strong international collaboration to manage their effects – and that can be ruptured by war without serious economic losses. (A desire to avoid ruptures of economic relations can, of course, be an incentive for a war-prevention regime.)

4   Low information flows that limit the growth in economic interdependence and promote cultural distinctiveness.

5   A predominance of authoritarian or non-democratic governments that limit the flow of information and people and that are not morally or politically constrained in using force against other states.

6   A high degree of cultural, political, and economic heterogeneity among states that makes the coordination of policies

---

6 The pillars of state sovereignty and state autonomy that are identified represent simply the author's judgments of supportive conditions. Observations on individual pillars can be found in numerous readings, but they are not listed in any particular source.

difficult because the differences sustain a nationalist commitment to autonomy, promote varied interests, and hinder
communication.

As is evident from a review of these pillars, some of them are closely
interrelated. Also, key points that should be stated here are that the
pillars differ in importance and there have been (and are likely to be)
quite distinct differences in the degree of their decay. Of all the pillars
the first one relating to the cost/benefit ratio of the use of military force
is the most important, and it is precisely in this pillar that some of the
most serious decay appears to be occurring. The decay in this military
pillar tends to spread to other pillars. The second pillar, little damage
from negative externalities (e.g., pollution), is like the first in that both
concern extensive physical harm to individuals and their property. The
third pillar relating to low levels of economic interdependence is
multifaceted and is difficult to summarize easily. It is as a result of
change in this pillar that possibilities for realizing mutual gains largely
arise. Decay in the last three pillars (low information flows, the predominance of authoritarian governments, and cultural heterogeneity)
can spawn regulatory regimes in their own issue areas, but their
transformations are important largely because of their impacts on
international accords relating to the first three pillars – the central areas
of international interdependence. A final point concerning these pillars
is that change in them is for the most part technology-driven. With
perhaps the exception of the pillar of the predominance of authoritarian
governments, the recent rapid changes in the other pillars are largely
products of the technological revolution of the twentieth century.

In positing that a certain transformation is occurring in the strength
of international governance or the body of international regimes and
attributing it to changes in certain international conditions, it is clear
that the analysis falls within a basically liberal theoretical mold. First, a
number of factors other than the distribution of power are viewed as
affecting modal patterns of interstate interactions – in particular, the
destructiveness of capabilities, the nature of international interactions,
and the pattern of state characteristics. Second, it is posited that while
states seek autonomy, they are, in fact, willing to trade off autonomy
against other goals such as the preservation of life, economic welfare,
and even ethical values under certain circumstances. States' ranking of
preferences can change as international conditions evolve, and hence
general policy priorities must be seen as endogenous to any theory of
international relations. Third, in keeping with the previous point, the
international system is seen as moving from the high level of anarchy
that previously existed to one in which reasonably important regimes

exist in a large number of international issue-areas and states are increasingly constrained in their competitive behavior.

An additional point should be made about the ongoing international transformation and the theoretical orientation that underlies it. Many liberal theorists see the declining importance of states as the major actor in international politics as central to their predictions of system change, and for the most part they attribute their reduced importance to growing international transactions. This is certainly central to functionalist theorists and James N. Rosenau's recent book *Turbulence in World Politics*.[7] However, this chapter does not posit that the present international transformation is undermining the centrality of states; rather, it involves the enmeshment of states in a network of explicit and implicit international regimes and interdependencies that are increasingly constraining their autonomy. Non-state actors such as multinational corporations and banks may increase in importance, but there are few signs that they are edging states from center stage. Perhaps this could occur in the long term;[8] but it is unlikely in the first half of the twenty-first century. The position adopted here is perfectly compatible with John Herz's views on the "new territoriality" or Janice Thomson and Stephen Krasner's critique of international transactions leading to a significant weakening of the state as the central actor in international relations.[9] However, this chapter projects a willingness of states to

---

[7] David Mitrany, *A Working Peace System* (Chicago: Quadrangle Books, 1966); Ernst B. Haas, *Beyond the Nation-State: Functionalism and International Organization* (Stanford, CA: Stanford University Press, 1964); A. J. R. Groom and Paul Taylor, eds., *Functionalism: Theory and Practice in International Relations* (New York: Crane, Russak, 1975); James N. Rosenau, *Turbulence in World Politics: A Theory of Change and Continuity* (Princeton, NJ: Princeton University Press, 1990). Also see C. R. Mitchell, "World Society as Cobweb: States, Actors and Systemic Processes," in Michael Banks, ed., *Conflict in World Society: A New Perspective on International Relations* (New York: St. Martin's Press, 1948), pp. 59–77; and Robert O. Keohane and Joseph S. Nye, *Power and Interdependence: World Politics in Transition* (Boston, MA: Little, Brown & Co., 1977), esp. ch. 2. A paper that posits that we have always overestimated the centrality of the state and that its importance is declining is Yale H. Ferguson and Richard W. Mansbach, "Between Celebration and Despair: Constructive Suggestions for Future International Theory" (mimeo, 1990).

[8] The possibility of this long-term trend is suggested in Ruggie, "'Finding our Feet' in Territoriality."

[9] John H. Herz, "The Territorial State Revisited: Reflections on the Future of the Nation-State," in James N. Rosenau, ed., *International Politics and Foreign Policy: A Reader in Research and Theory* (New York: Free Press, rev. edn., 1969), pp. 76–89; Janice E. Thomson and Stephen D. Krasner, "Global Transactions and the Consolidation of Sovereignty," in Ernst-Otto Czempiel and James N. Rosenau, eds., *Global Changes and Theoretical Challenges: Approaches to World Politics for the 1990s* (Lexington, MA: Lexington Books, 1989), pp. 195–220. Herz actually projects some possibilities for collaboration among states that are very close to those presented in this paper.

sacrifice autonomy over time that the previous authors would probably not accept.

The first short section of this chapter provides some information on the growth of international collaboration and some observations by scholars of present trends. The next section and its six subsections discuss the decay that has been occurring in the six pillars of the Westphalian system of highly autonomous states, and analyzes why and how this decay is promoting and might promote greater collaboration or stronger regimes. The conclusion comments briefly on the various trends.

SOME DATA AND COMMENTS ON THE GROWTH OF INTERNATIONAL COLLABORATION

One manifestation of the growth of collaboration and regulation in the international system is the increase in the number of international organizations – most of which prescribe a variety of regulatory arrangements for their members. In 1909 there were 37 conventional intergovernmental organizations (IGOs) and 176 non-governmental organizations (NGOs); in 1951 the respective figures were 123 and 832; and in 1986 they were 337 and 4,649.[10] There is also a striking increase in the number of congresses and conferences that these organizations sponsor. Between 1838 and 1860 there were 2 to 3 a year; in the decade after 1900 there were about 100 per year; in the decade after 1910 there were about 200 per year; and in the 1970s there were more than 3,000.[11]

Concerning this growth in international organizations and their activities, Inis Claude remarks that it "suggests that statesmen are now more willing to emphasize collective rather than merely unilateral approaches to a wide range of issues."[12] He also notes that "Their growth in the past half-century, in both quantitative and qualitative terms, has been a major phenomenon of the international system. They have not transformed the system, but they have become indispensable

---

[10] *Yearbook of International Organizations, 1986/87* (Munich: K. G. Saur, 1988), Table 2. If one includes "non-conventional" international organizations, the numbers are higher. J. David Singer and Michael Wallace found an exponential growth in international organizations from the beginning of the nineteenth century through the 1960s: "Intergovernmental Organization and the Preservation of Peace, 1816–1964," *International Organization*, 24 (Summer 1970), pp. 520–47.

[11] Ithiel de Sola Pool, *Technologies without Boundaries: On Telecommunications in a Global Age* (Cambridge, MA: Harvard University Press, 1990), p. 71.

[12] Inis L. Claude, *States and the Global System: Politics, Law and Organization* (London: Macmillan, 1988), p. 117.

to states – and, in serving states, they have contributed to the manageability of the system constituted by states."[13] Claude's reservation that their growth has not transformed the system may not be completely accurate in that international organizations have been crucial to the steady growth of regulatory regimes.

There has also been a marked increase in the number of international treaties in force in the postwar period. One study indicates that there were 6,351 bilateral treaties that entered into force in the decade 1946–55; 10,456 treaties in the period 1956–65; and 14,061 treaties in the period 1966–75. It is noted that multilateral treaties, which are also listed but not specifically counted, are approximately 10 percent of the number of bilateral treaties. An interesting figure that indicates the growing importance of international organizations is that in the first decade international organizations were parties to 623 treaties with states or other organizations; in the second decade they were parties to 1,051 treaties; and in the third decade they were parties to 2,303 treaties. It is also clear that the large majority of the treaties concerned international economic issues of various types.[14]

A recognition that we are in the midst of some basic transformations in the direction of greater collaboration in the international system is apparent in the writings of many observers of the international scene. In a recent issue of *Foreign Affairs* both Stanley Hoffmann and William McNeill remark that while the world is not ready for world government, it seems to be going in the direction of a half-way house. Hoffmann foresees the possible emergence of "polycentric steering" whereby the major powers would coordinate policies in a wide range of fields,[15] and McNeill comments on the likely emergence of greater "[p]iecemeal coordination and negotiation among existing states and transnational organizations, private as well as public."[16] A belief that significant changes in the international system are going on and must be encouraged is no longer the preserve of the starry-eyed idealist. As the military defense specialist Carl Kaysen notes: "To seek a different system with a more secure and a more humane basis for order is no

13 *Ibid.*, p. 132.
14 Peter H. Rohn, *World Treaty Index: Volume I* (Santa Barbara, CA: ABC-Clio Information Services, 2nd edn., 1984), pp. 6–9, 694, 702–3. Bilateral treaties are counted twice in the charts so I have divided by two to get the number of treaties. Data on 800 multilateral treaties are described in M. J. Bowman and J. J. Harris, *Multilateral Treaties: Index and Current Status* (London: Butterworths, 1984).
15 Stanley Hoffmann, "A New World and its Troubles," *Foreign Affairs*, 69 (Fall 1990), pp. 120–1.
16 William H. McNeill, "Winds of Change," *Foreign Affairs*, 69 (Fall 1990), p. 170.

longer the pursuit of an illusion, but a necessary effort toward a necessary goal."[17]

F. H. Hinsley writes that "It was from about the 1620s that men began to recognize that Europe contained a multiplicity of states."[18] This was, of course, several decades before the 1648 Peace of Westphalia. It is quite possible that in the future scholars may say that it was around 1990 that a good number of observers of the international system began to recognize that a network of formal and informal international regimes was developing to a point where states' enmeshment in them marked the advent of quite a different type of international order. First and foremost in this transformation have been new attitudes toward the use of force and the collaboration (particularly among the great powers) to prevent it, and secondarily there are the growing interdependencies in economic, social, and environmental areas and the arrangements that are developing to manage them. What is occurring in the world is not a serious demise of states as the central actors in the system (although certain transnational actors are achieving greater prominence) but rather their acceptance that they have to work together in controlling a variety of interdependencies.

PILLARS OF STATE AUTONOMY IN THE WESTPHALIAN SYSTEM

Cost/benefit ratio of war

While the traditional Westphalian system did have an element of order that was based on states' mutual recognition of each other's sovereignty, there was never a strong feeling in Europe that wars were or should be illegitimate. War for purposes of territorial aggrandizement or a desire to change foreign governments was quite common – "a perfectly legitimate instrument of national policy."[19] This situation has begun to change in the twentieth century, and in recent decades (especially the late 1980s) there has been an increasing recognition that the probability of war (particularly among the great powers) has been

---

[17] Carl Kaysen, "Is War Obsolete?," International Security, 14 (Spring 1990), p. 63.

[18] Hinsley, The Pursuit of Peace, p. 157.

[19] Hans J. Morgenthau, "The Danger of Thinking Conventionally about Nuclear Weapons," in Carlo Schaerf, Brian Holden Reid, and David Carlton, eds., New Technologies and the Arms Race (New York: St. Martin's Press, 1989), p. 255. See also Ian Clark, The Hierarchy of States: Reform and Resistance in the International Order (Cambridge: Cambridge University Press, 1989), p. 103; Kalevi J. Holsti, Peace and War: Armed Conflicts and International Order, 1648–1989 (Cambridge: Cambridge University Press, 1991).

greatly reduced. The key reasons are the destructiveness of nuclear weapons and to a lesser extent other factors such as the fragility of modern technological civilization, the higher priority assigned to economic welfare, the high costs of military occupation in the age of the nation-state, and liberal democratic inhibitions. Whether and when different Third World areas might be pulled into the "no-war zone' is viewed as problematic.

Of all the changes that are occurring in the international system today, the one that is affecting and will affect the political order more than any other is the distribution of extremely destructive nuclear weapons among the great powers – and increasingly non-great powers as well. Not only is the distribution of capabilities a fundamental feature of the international structure, but the destructiveness of those capabilities is as well. It is impossible to explain what has been occurring in international security politics without an understanding of the exponential increase in the destructiveness (and delivery capability) of weaponry. As Steve Weber notes, it is the "spread" of nuclear weapons rather than their mere existence that has constituted a structural change.[20] A comparable observation is made by Robert Jervis when he comments: "As Bernard Brodie, Thomas Schelling, and many others have noted, what is significant about nuclear weapons is not 'overkill' but 'mutual kill.'"[21] The great powers' possession of extremely destructive retaliatory capabilities has become a central structural feature of the international system that has affected basic patterns of interstate relations (i.e., mutual deterrence), and the understanding that nuclear weapons have had this fundamental effect constitutes "a critical intellectual breakthrough" in the contemporary study of international relations.[22]

The present situation of mutual deterrence among the great powers is the culmination of a long process of less frequent and more destructive wars among the great powers that has occurred between the sixteenth century and the mid-twentieth century.[23] We have now gone

20 Steve Weber, "Realism, Detente and Nuclear Weapons," *International Organization*, 44 (Winter 1990), pp. 55 and *passim*.
21 Robert Jervis, "The Political Effects of Nuclear Weapons," *International Security*, 13 (Fall 1988), p. 83.
22 Patrick Morgan, "On Strategic Arms Control and International Security," in Edward Kolodziej and Patrick Morgan, eds., *Security and Arms Control* (New York: Greenwood Press, 1989), p. 302. Some very good essays relevant to this subject are in Charles W. Kegley, ed., *The Long Postwar Peace: Contending Explanations and Approaches* (New York: Harper/Collins, 1990).
23 Jack S. Levy, *War in the Modern Great Power System* (Lexington, MA: University Press of Kentucky, 1983), pp. 130–6.

forty-five years without a great power war, and the chances of one in the near future are very remote. This unprecedented development in great power relations has occurred in the eyes of the great majority of observers because of the advent of nuclear weaponry. As K. J. Holsti remarks: "An actor cannot use such weapons in the Clausewitzian instrumental sense of war . . . To say that any political value is worth national self-immolation and probably the destruction of modern civilization makes no sense."[24] At another point he comments that "The greatest threat to the security of the modern industrial state is not a particular adversary but nuclear war and perhaps even some forms of conventional war."[25] He also notes that there "have been numerous Soviet–American crises, any one of which would probably have led to war in earlier eras."[26] John Mearsheimer makes a comparable judgment of the significance of nuclear weapons when he writes that they "seem to be in almost everybody's bad book but the fact is that they are a powerful force for peace. Deterrence is most likely to hold when the costs and risks of going to war are unambiguously stark."[27]

It is particularly important to give special attention to the views of Kenneth Waltz since no one has had as much influence on contemporary thinking that the distribution of power is the dominant influence on the quality of international relations.[28] Yet in 1990 he wrote:

> because so much explosive power comes in such small packages, the invulnerability of a sufficient number of warheads is easy to achieve and the delivery of fairly large numbers of warheads impossible to thwart, both now and as far into the future as anyone can see. The absolute quality of nuclear weapons sharply sets a nuclear world off from a conventional one.[29]

---

[24] Holsti, *Peace and War*, p. 287.

[25] *Ibid.*, p. 333.   [26] *Ibid.*, p. 305.

[27] John Mearsheimer, "Why We Will Soon Miss the Cold War," *Atlantic Monthly*, 266, 2 (August 1990), p. 37. Comparable judgments on the importance of nuclear weapons for maintaining peace can be found in: Kaysen, "Is War Obsolete?," p. 61; John Lewis Gaddis, *The Long Peace: Inquiries into the History of the Cold War* (London: Oxford University Press, 1987), p. 277; Barry Buzan, "Economic Structure and International Security: The Limits of the Liberal Case," *International Organization*, 38 (Autumn 1984), p. 606; Morgenthau, "The Danger of Thinking Conventionally about Nuclear Weapons," pp. 255–6; Emanuel Adler, "Seasons of Peace: Progress in Postwar International Security," in Emanuel Adler and Beverly Crawford, eds., *Progress in Postwar International Relations* (New York: Columbia University Press, 1991), pp. 128–73.

[28] Waltz, *Theory of International Politics*.

[29] Kenneth N. Waltz, "Nuclear Myths and Political Realities," *American Political Science Review*, 84 (September 1990), p. 732.

Waltz, in fact, goes a bit further than it is prudent to go when he states that "In a nuclear world any state will be deterred by another state's second-strike capability."[30] He has little confidence in the ability of any great power to design an effective defensive system that will neutralize a second-strike capability and thinks that any attempt to build one is destabilizing.[31] Waltz also believes that the outcome of the launching of a conventional war among nuclear powers could even be worse than one that starts nuclear because of the likely use of nuclear weapons by the losing side in a moment of desperation. And therefore such wars are improbable.[32] In conclusion he notes that "Although the possibility of war remains, nuclear weapons have drastically reduced the probability of its being fought by the states that have them . . . waging war has more and more become the privilege of poor and weak states."[33] A more articulate case for the inclusion of the destructiveness of military capabilities in defining the international structure and for a profound transformation in that structure would be difficult to find. Joseph Nye has recently written that "If our analyses are cast solely in terms of the power transitions of the past, we will overlook what is new about the future."[34] Waltz is, in fact, straying from his traditional sparse view of the international structure in which only the distribution of capabilities varies. And he is stressing (at least implicitly) the importance of an additional feature of the international structure – the changing destructiveness of those capabilities.

While the existence of nuclear weapons is the major reason for the absence of great power war and even a possible decline of war in the Third World (a matter to be discussed below), there are other factors that have discouraged states from resorting to war. Apart from and prior to the advent of nuclear weapons the process of industrialization was increasing the destructiveness of weaponry and consequently the impact of war on society.[35] Related to this is the fact that modern industrial societies are more "fragile" in the sense that the destruction of particular facilities (particularly infrastructure industries) can wreak much greater damage and social havoc than was the case in the past.

---

[30] *Ibid.*, p. 737.   [31] *Ibid.*, pp. 742–3.
[32] *Ibid.*, p. 739.   [33] *Ibid.*, p. 744.
[34] Joseph S. Nye, *Bound to Lead: The Changing Nature of American Power* (New York: Basic Books, 1990), p. 21.
[35] John Mueller, "The Essential Irrelevance of Nuclear Weapons," *International Security*, 13 (Fall 1988), p. 78 and *passim*; Evan Luard, *War in the International Society* (New Haven, CT: Yale University Press, 1986), p. 271. For an evaluation that the destructiveness of non-nuclear weapons is not great enough to prevent conventional war, see Jervis, "The Political Effects of Nuclear Weapons," pp. 84–7; and Trevor N. Dupuy, *The Evolution of Weapons and Warfare* (Indianapolis, IN: Bobbs-Merrill, 1980).

Beyond these purely military factors it has also been posited that the process of "modernization" is having effects on people's values that affect their proclivity to support war – in particular, their attachment to economic welfare and their moral inhibitions concerning the use of force.[36] Connected to the process of modernization are the spread of democracy and an increase in economic interdependence – important pillars for a more peaceful system which will be discussed in other sections.

A final factor that influences the cost/benefit ratio of waging war is the extent to which states have become nation-states with socially and politically cohesive populations. The costs of conquering and, even more, of occupying and exploiting such states can be very high.[37] However, there are many states where such integration has not occurred. Pertinent to the effect of integration and its effect in different parts of the world Holsti notes that "In the industrial world the process is largely completed, and it may not be accidental that the mutual relations of the states comprising it have become predictably peaceful." However, he points out that in the Third World cohesion is not as great, and thus the incentives for going to war are likely to remain.[38]

Civil conflicts, traditional national acquisitiveness, a continued willingness to take risks despite the destructiveness of weapons,[39] the persistence of traditional international security "cultures,"[40] religious fundamentalism in some areas, an attachment to autonomy,[41] and an absence of adequate institutions to manage peaceful change[42] all make one pause about any assertion that we have reached or are approaching a watershed in states' thinking about the utility of waging war. However, it is still quite possible that we have reached such a point with respect to relations among the great powers. Even in the case of the Third World states there are some reasons for guarded optimism. Outside of the Middle East there do not seem to be serious possibilities of international war.[43] Of great importance is that boundaries have achieved a legitimacy that they did not have in the past. Third World states have been for the most part strong backers of existing boundaries,

---

[36] Mueller, "The Essential Irrelevance of Nuclear Weapons"; James L. Ray, "The Abolition of Slavery and the End of International War," *International Organization*, 43 (Summer 1989), pp. 405–40; Jervis, "The Political Effects of Nuclear Weapons," p. 89.

[37] Kaysen, "Is War Obsolete?," pp. 53 and 58.

[38] Holsti, *Peace and War*, p. 323. John Herz makes a comparable point in "The Territorial State Revisited," pp. 83–4 and 88–9.

[39] Luard, *War in the International Society*, p. 396.

[40] Kaysen, "Is War Obsolete?," p. 62.

[41] Clark, *The Hierarchy of States*, p. 220.

[42] Holsti, *Peace and War*, p. 343.   [43] *Ibid.*, p. 304.

and the consensus against the Iraqi invasion of Kuwait is reflective of this consensus.[44] These countries are also very absorbed with economic development, and few are willing to contemplate the costs attendant on waging a war. In important ways international competition really has shifted from the battlefield to the economic front.[45] It also seems that the great powers are anxious to promote stability in the Third World in order to prevent circumstances that might exacerbate their relations, to promote circumstances conducive to stable economic relations, and to discourage the acquisition of nuclear, chemical, and bacteriological weapons (which could be used against them by states or terrorists). It is, however, important not to be too sanguine about a dramatic decrease in war in the Third World. Conflicts over economic resources (especially under the pressure of population growth), tensions over religious and ideological differences, the uneven spread in nuclear weapons, and a loss of American hegemony in the international security system could all possibly lead to wars in the Third World (sometimes involving the great powers). On the other hand, they are likely to be infrequent given a variety of countervailing pressures.

The strong commitment of the great powers to avoid war with each other and the increasing proclivity of the great powers and most developing countries to prevent wars in the Third World has had, and will have, important impacts on explicit and implicit collaboration in the security field. The great powers, and more particularly the super-powers, have developed a variety of general rules and guidelines to avoid nuclear war.[46] They include:

1 Do not threaten the second-strike capability of the other side (i.e., support mutual deterrence) and, in fact, seek to enhance it.

---

[44] Mark W. Zacher, *International Conflicts and Collective Security, 1946–1977: The United Nations, Organization of American States, Organization of African Unity, and Arab League* (New York: Praeger, 1979), esp. chs. 4 and 5; Holsti, *Peace and War*, pp. 307–11. While Holsti finds that territorial wars still occur regularly (albeit at a reduced rate), he does indicate that both international normative constraints and a decrease in the import-ance of territory for international power is reducing the probability of wars over territory. Third World states' commitment to territorial boundaries as well as juridical sovereignty is also a strong message in Robert H. Jackson, *Quasi-States: Sovereignty, International Relations and the Third World* (Cambridge: Cambridge University Press, 1991), and "Quasi-States, Dual Regimes, and Neoclassical Theory: International Jurisprudence and the Third World," *International Organization*, 41 (Autumn 1987), pp. 519–50.

[45] Richard Rosecrance, *The Rise of the Trading State: Commerce and Conquest in the Modern World* (New York: Basic Books, 1986).

[46] The best overview of these is in Gaddis, *The Long Peace*, pp. 235–8. Also see Gordon Craig and Alexander George, *Force and Statecraft: Diplomatic Problems of our Times* (New York: Oxford University Press, 1983).

72

2 Use nuclear weapons only as a last resort when one's territory or that of one's core allies are threatened.

3 Avoid direct military conflict with the forces of other great powers.

4 Do not militarily threaten the core allies of other great powers.

5 Do not undermine the political leadership of other great powers.

6 Do not undermine the ability of other great powers to monitor major military activities.

7 Convey understandings of policies in crisis situations to the other side so as to avoid incidents that could lead to conflicts.

8 Prevent allies from undertaking actions (particularly against allies of the other side) that could drag one into a great power war.

Unquestionably the dramatic transformation in Soviet foreign policy in recent years, which has laid the groundwork for greatly increased security collaboration, would not have taken place if the Soviets had not come to realize the prospect of a Western attack in the nuclear era was virtually nil.[47] As Weber notes, for the first time in history security is not a scarce commodity among the great powers.[48] This may be a slight overstatement in that uncertainties do remain – if only because of the prospects of technological change. However, the basic message is correct. Another related issue concerning the Soviet Union is whether that country as well as the international security system can absorb the possible breakup of the Soviet federation without intense instability and a war. Given the fact that the Russian Republic does not fear a military attack from another great power and that the Western nations are not likely to try to exploit short-term advantages at the cost of long-term stability, the world is probably now safe for the dissolution of that vast multicultural empire.

A key issue for the study of the transformation of the world order is whether nuclear deterrence now gives the great powers a degree of security independence such that security collaboration is not particularly important. To an extent this is true since it is extremely difficult to

---

[47] Steve Weber, "Cooperation and Interdependence," *Daedalus*, 120 (Winter 1991), pp. 183–201, and Steve Weber, "Security after 1989: The Future with Nuclear Weapons," in Patrick Garrity, ed., *The Future of Nuclear Weapons* (New York: Plenum Press, 1991).

[48] Weber, "Security after 1989." John Herz makes a comparable point when he states that "the security dilemma can at least be attenuated through scientific-technological progress that 'modernizes' mankind and thus frees it from scarcity": "The Territorial State Revisited," p. 87.

undermine great powers' second-strike capability. But in a larger sense it is important for them to manage weapons systems and troop deployments as well as the international political scene so that no great power perceives a possible threat. Waltz notes that despite a high degree of security independence the great powers still have incentives for arms control to improve general political relations and to secure economic gains.[49] The great powers are likely to have a strong interest in promoting stability in most areas of the world so that local conflicts do not draw them into confrontations with each other, do not create incentives for nuclear proliferation, and do not undermine stable economic relations (including access to resources). It is also very important to stress that the high degree of security possessed by the major powers greatly facilitates collaboration in non-security areas since there is no longer a fear that differences in economic gains will be translated into military advantage.[50]

A dimension of modern warfare that has grown in importance because of the destructiveness of modern weaponry and the fragility of parts of our modern technological civilization is terrorism by non-state actors. It has already evoked some international collaborative and regulatory ventures, and much stronger regimes could develop in the future. Concerning the seriousness of the terrorist threat Albert Carnasale has commented that he does not greatly fear great power war in the next several decades but that he is not so sanguine about terrorism. He said that international security specialists should ask themselves every day what they will wish they had proposed to control terrorism twenty to thirty years from now.[51] An indication of the potential scope of the problem is presented in the statement of a former U.S. official: "To produce about the same number of deaths within a square mile, it would take about 32 million grams of fragmentation cluster bomb material; 3,200,000 grams of mustard gas; 800,000 grams of nerve gas; 5,000 grams of material in a crude nuclear fission weapon; 80 grams of botulinal toxin type A; or only 8 grams of anthrax spores."[52] In other words the range of destructive devices as well as the range of

---

[49] Waltz, "Nuclear Myths and Political Realities," p. 741. Weber probably overstates the degree of independence and the lack of need for arms control in "Cooperation and Interdependence."

[50] This discussion draws heavily on three articles by Steve Weber: "Cooperation and Interdependence"; "Security after 1989"; and "Realism, Detente and Nuclear Weapons," *International Organization*, 44 (Winter 1990), pp. 55–82.

[51] Session of the Pacific Northwest Colloquium on International Security, University of Washington, November 10, 1989.

[52] Louis Giuffrida, "Dealing with the Consequences of Terrorism – We Are Not Yet Where We Must Be," *Terrorism*, 10 (November 1987), p. 73.

targets is very large, and the international control problems are vast indeed.[53]

Most of the global regulatory approaches to terrorism have concerned hijacking of planes and ships since they threaten the business and government elites of virtually all countries.[54] However, with regard to acts committed in the territories of a particular state or the actual destruction of planes and ships international differences with regard to the "causes" at issue usually block global accords. There has been a great deal of sharing of information among the Western powers on activities of terrorists or suspected terrorists over the years, and now the Soviets and Eastern European states are being brought into the process. An indication of this new collaborative relationship is an agreement in 1990 (initiated by the major Western powers, the U.S.S.R., and Czechoslovakia which is the main manufacturer of the explosive semtex) to establish a "finger-printing" scheme for semtex that will allow them to trace any users.[55] International police, military and legal collaboration to deal with terrorism is likely to expand considerably in the future if the above-cited comment of Carnasale is correct. If there is a major successful act of nuclear, chemical, or bacteriological terrorism, there will be a quantum leap in cooperation. The symbolism of international *police* collaboration will also have an impact on people's nascent sense of an international community.

If the world, in the words of Emanuel Adler, is in the process of a transition from "a season of general stability" to "a season of common security,"[56] the implications for the scope and strength of international governance will be profound. Not only will greater collaboration emerge in the security sphere, but it will be facilitated in a variety of other areas as well. Realists are unquestionably correct in their understanding of the centrality of security concerns to all facets of international relations, but they are wrong with respect to their conception of states' unwillingness to compromise their autonomy in some significant ways in order to prevent the killing of a large percentage of their populations.

[53] Paul Levanthal and Yonah Alexander, *Nuclear Terrorism* (Washington, DC: Pergamon-Brassey's, 1986); Paul Levanthal and Yonah Alexander, *Preventing Nuclear Terrorism* (Lexington, MA: D. C. Heath, 1987); Louis R. Beres, *Terrorism and Global Security* (Boulder, CO: Westview Press, 1987).

[54] James P. Wootten, "Terrorism: U.S. Policy Options," in Y. Alexander and H. Foxman, eds., *The 1988–1989 Annual on Terrorism* (Deventer, Netherlands: Kluwer, 1990), pp. 203–18.

[55] Roger Hill and Ronald Purver, eds., *The Guide to Canadian Policies on Arms Control, Disarmament, Defence and Conflict Resolution, 1990* (Ottawa: Canadian Institute for International Peace and Security, 1990), p. 346.

[56] "Seasons of Peace." Adler defines these terms in his paper.

International physical externalities

While modern military technology is the most serious common enemy that threatens the lives and welfare of humankind today, a number of international physical externalities have developed that are also serious common enemies for all or most humans. Such externalities refer to activities within states that have negative side-effects on the populations of other countries. The most serious externalities result from the effects of national economic activities on the health and welfare of people in other countries, and generally fall under the rubric "environmental damage." Another concerns the spread of diseases across state borders as a result of the movement of people.[57]

In recent decades there has been a variety of types of environmental harm that have elicited international interest – particularly, marine pollution and acid rain. They have evoked a variety of forms of international collaboration, but it would be difficult to conceive of them as involving unusual degrees of cooperation.[58] Also, most of the regimes are concentrated in certain regions of the world and involve a small number of countries. Since the mid-1980s two problems have emerged that are seen as affecting the entire planet (albeit in different degrees) – the ozone problem and the climate change or global warming problem. They have a much greater potential for evoking important forms of collaboration than have previous environmental problems.

Ozone is a gas that exists in the upper atmosphere, and it is important to human life because it screens out a great deal of ultraviolet radiation from the sun. A decrease in the ozone layer would increase the incidence of skin cancer and glaucoma. Since the mid-1970s it has been increasingly realized among scientists that the use of chlorofluorocarbons (CFCs) as aerosols, refrigerants, and constituents in insulation was reducing the ozone layer. This was highlighted by the discovery of a hole in the ozone layer over Antarctica in 1985. In 1985 states formulated the Vienna Convention on the Protection of the Ozone Layer, which only spelled out general goals, and then in 1987 they adopted the Montreal Protocol which established specific targets. (It was revised and strengthened in 1989.) The major long-run obstacle to reduction in CFC emissions is the reluctance of the developing countries to pay higher prices for the substitutes that are presently

---

[57] For a comparable list, see Rosenau, *Turbulence in World Politics*, pp. 94 and 106.
[58] For a review of the problems and international responses, see Lynton K. Caldwell, *International Environmental Policy: Emergence and Responses* (Durham, NC: Duke University Press, 1990); R. Michael M'Gonigle and Mark W. Zacher, *Pollution, Politics, and International Law: Tankers at Sea* (Berkeley, CA: University of California Press, 1979).

being developed. The developed nations have already begun to provide financial assistance to the developing countries to help them switch to substitutes, and a great deal more assistance will probably have to be offered in the future. However, given the fact that the magnitude of the additional expenditures for substitutes is not huge and that the health problems from ozone depletion fall on all countries relatively equally, a more effective regime and a decrease in CFC emissions should occur in the next several decades. Of course, given the eighty-year life cycle of CFCs our past "sins" will create problems for some time.[59]

The much larger environmental problem that has descended on us recently is the warming of the earth as a result of the emission of "greenhouse gases" which reduce the escape of radiation from the earth's atmosphere. The main gases are carbon dioxide, methane, nitrous oxide, and CFCs. The biggest problem is carbon dioxide which comes largely from the burning of fossil fuels. A development that exacerbates the problem is deforestation (especially the tropical rain forests) because forests absorb carbon dioxide in the air. There have been several large international conferences on the problem, and there has been a major study by experts from around the world sponsored by the World Meteorological Organization and the UN Environment Program (the Intergovernmental Panel on Climate Change which reported in 1990).[60] There are also plans to approve a framework treaty and possibly some specific protocols at the 1992 United Nations Conference on the Environment and Development. However, the immediate prospects for significant progress are not good because there is still quite a bit of uncertainty about the impacts, because the effects are likely to fall in quite different ways on the world's states, and because the economic costs (e.g., reduction in the use of fossil fuels and curtailing deforestation) are large. The common enemy of global warming is not commonly harmful to all states and the costs of contributing to its solution are quite different for countries at different levels of development. In fact, it is not at all clear that increases in temperature over the

---

[59] Mark Crawford, "Landmark Ozone Treaty Negotiated," *Science* (Sept. 25, 1987), p. 1557; *The Economist* (June 16, 1990), pp. 18–20; Peter Morrisette, "The Evolution of Policy Responses to Stratospheric Ozone Depletion," *Natural Resources Journal*, 29 (Summer 1989), pp. 793–820; Peter M. Haas, "Ozone Alone, No CFCs: Ecological Epistemic Communities and the Stratospheric Ozone Depletion," *International Organization* (forthcoming).

[60] There are many parts of the report of the Intergovernment Panel on Climate Change (IPCC) which are published jointly by WMO and UNEP. The most relevant one for this article is "Policymakers' Summary of the Formulation of Response Strategies" (June 1990).

coming century (1.5–3 degrees C) are going to have overall negative impacts on northern countries like the Soviet Union, Canada, and the United States.

In the long run it is, however, quite likely that major forms of cooperation will have to occur to control the emissions of greenhouse gases. States are going to be concerned not only about the environmental and hence economic effects on themselves but also the political repercussions that will occur if they do not support significant control efforts. Strong resentment will develop among those states that are significantly harmed by global warming (many of the most seriously harmed probably being in the Third World) and those who are not harmed or are actually helped. Apart from major steps toward international cooperation to control global warming that will probably have to develop in the twenty-first century, the global character of the problem will probably have a major impact on people's growing perception of the common plight of humankind on "spaceship earth." Despite the fact that environmental interdependencies are going to generate a lot of conflicts, the long-term outcome of these interdependencies will probably be greater coordination of national economic policies and a greater sense of global interconnectedness.[61]

In a speech in 1988 the Soviet foreign minister Eduard Shevardnadze commented that the environmental threat constituted "a second front fast approaching and gaining an urgency equal to that of the nuclear and space threat."[62] Jessica Tuchman Mathews has also written that "Environmental strains that transcend national borders are already beginning to break down the sacred boundaries of national sovereignty."[63] The Shevardnadze comment is certainly an overstatement, and the Mathews comment, while strictly speaking not inaccurate, is probably too optimistic in its projection of the short-term emergence of environmental regimes that will impose significant constraints on state behavior. The ozone problem will be resolved in the

---

[61] Eugene B. Skolnikoff, "The Policy Gridlock on Global Warming," *Foreign Policy*, 79 (Summer 1990), pp. 77–93; David Wirth, "Climate Chaos," *Foreign Policy*, 75 (Autumn 1989), pp. 1–20; Michael Grubb, "The Greenhouse Effect: Negotiating Targets," *International Affairs*, 66 (1990), pp. 67–89; Michael Grubb, *The Greenhouse Effect: Negotiating Targets* (London: Royal Institute of International Affairs, 1989); Dean Edwin Abrahamson, ed., *The Challenge of Global Warming* (Washington, DC: Island Press, 1989); Richard E. Benedick *et al.*, *Greenhouse Warming: Negotiating a Global Regime* (Washington, DC: World Resources Institute, 1991). The latter publication has some excellent discussions of possible accords.

[62] Quoted in Jim McNeill, "The Greening of International Relations," *International Journal*, 45 (Winter 1989/90), p. 34.

[63] Jessica Tuchman Mathews, "Redefining Security," *Foreign Affairs*, 68 (Spring 1989), p. 162.

next decade or two in the sense that CFCs will be seldom used (although the harmful effects of past CFC emissions will be felt for most of the twenty-first century). However, the regime will not constitute a major breakthrough in the strength of the international order. In the case of global warming an effective regime would constitute a reasonably dramatic step toward stronger international governance since it would demand an unprecedented degree of coordination of national development strategies and significant financial transfers from the wealthy to the poor nations. However, the regime is likely to develop gradually over coming decades, and it is certainly possible (although not likely) that there will be little international cooperation. On the basis of existing evidence one must judge that cooperation on international environmental problems will grow significantly in the late twentieth and early twenty-first centuries and will add to states' enmeshment in a network of international regulatory/collaborative arrangements.

While the development of environmental damages across state boundaries is the most important international externality that might engender significant international cooperation, another externality has led to international cooperation since at least the beginning of this century, and that is the spread of diseases resulting from the flow of international commerce and travellers. The major manifestation of this cooperation is the International Sanitary Regulations which are now regularly revised by the World Health Organization (WHO). However, these regulations which seek to prevent the transmission of diseases across state boundaries have not seriously constrained states' behavior, and neither the rules nor internationally funded ventures to eradicate diseases in particular parts of the world have required large financial resources.[64]

The problem of the international transmission of diseases may now be achieving a level of seriousness that will demand much greater cooperation as a result of the emergence of AIDS in the late 1970s. Since that time the number of individuals in the world who are HIV positive has risen to around 5 million, and over a twenty-year period almost of all these individuals contract AIDS and die. Presently about a half of the 5 million victims are in Africa, and of the remaining probably around two-thirds are in the United States. Present projections are that if an effective vaccine is not developed, the number of people who are HIV

---

[64] Fraser Brockington, *World Health* (Edinburgh: Churchill Livingstone, 3rd edn., 1975); W. Hobson, *World Health and History* (Bristol: John Wright, 1963); Norman Howard-Jones, "The World Health Organization in Historical Perspective," *Perspectives in Biology and Medicine*, 24 (1981), pp. 467–82; David M. Leive, *International Regulatory Regimes: Volume II* (Lexington, MA: Lexington Books, 1976), pp. 15–152.

positive will quadruple to 20 million by the year 2000. At the moment international cooperation through the World Health Organization is taking the form of the sharing of information on the nature of the disease, methods of preventing its spread, and scientific research endeavors. However, if medical science does not produce a preventative vaccine and a cure in the next decade, demands are likely to develop that international travellers carry certificates that indicate that they are not infected by the virus. Also, it is quite possible that an organization such as WHO could develop an international technical assistance and certification operation that assisted and vetted blood-testing laboratories throughout the world. The world could, in fact, see within a decade or two a highly developed international control system for testing people and controlling the travel of individuals who are HIV positive. On the other hand, this is not a strategy that is favored by the great majority of medical experts who see education in preventative techniques as the most productive strategy to follow. The advice of these experts may, however, not be followed if the publics and politicians in many states become extremely worried about the international spread of the virus. Regardless of the particular forms of international cooperation that occur, the spread of AIDS could reinforce many people's image of the interdependence of nations.[65]

International economic interdependence

The post-1945 era has seen marked increases in both international economic ties and regulatory/collaborative arrangements to manage them. "At least among the developed liberal countries interdependent ties since 1945 have come to be accepted as a fundamental and unchangeable feature" of international relations,[66] and "Few governments are willing to argue any longer for the benefits of economic closure."[67] Increased international economic ties exist at many levels involving trade, foreign investment (including global firms), and finance, and they are promoted by a growing acceptance of

---

[65] J. Chin and J. Mann, "Global Surveillance and Forecasting of AIDS," *Bulletin of the World Health Organization*, 67 (1989), pp. 1–7; J. Chin, P. A. Sato, and J. M. Mann, "Projections of HIV Infections and AIDS Cases to the Year 2000," *Bulletin of the World Health Organization*, 68 (1990), pp. 1–22; Jon Tinker, ed., *AIDS in the Third World* (London: Panos Institute, 1989), esp. chs. 7–9; Steve Connor and Sharon Kingman, *The Search for the Virus: The Scientific Discovery of AIDS and the Quest for a Cure* (London: Penguin, 1988).

[66] Rosecrance, *The Rise of the Trading State*, p. 141.

[67] Miles Kahler, "The International Political Economy," *Foreign Affairs*, 69 (Fall 1990), p. 148.

Table 1. *Trend in world exports,*
1960–87 (in 1985 U.S. constant $)

	Billion $
1960	441.6
1965	615.0
1970	940.6
1975	1,232.5
1980	1,649.1
1985	1,808.1
1987	1,930.8

Note: computed by dividing world exports in current dollars by the export unit value for that year and multiplying by 100.
Sources: IMF, *International Financial Statistics* (1980 and 1989).

liberal economic policies. One impact of these trends is that states are losing their degree of autonomy in managing their domestic and international economic policies because of both the intensity of the interdependencies and the development of explicit and implicit regimes. Robert Cox notes that "Globalization transforms the bases of state authority from within and produces a multilevel post-Westphalian world order in which the state remains important but only as one among several levels of authority."[68] What he is referring to is the emergence of a variety of transnational and intergovernmental arrangements or institutions that are assuming varying degrees of control over different international transactions.

International trade is the transaction that most people associate with economic interdependence, and while its centrality may have been overstressed, it is undoubtedly very important. From 1835 to 1968 (excluding 1920–45) trade increased on average by 55 percent each decade.[69] In the postwar years it has also grown steadily at a higher rate than world output in every five-year period.[70] According to Table 1, trade more than doubled in the 1960s for the market economies, and

---

[68] Robert W. Cox, "Globalization, Multilateralism and Social Choice," *Work in Progress* (published by United Nations University), 13 (July 1990), p. 2.

[69] Peter J. Katzenstein, "International Interdependence: Some Long-Term Trends and Recent Changes," *International Organization*, 29 (Autumn 1975), p. 1024.

[70] Michael C. Webb and Stephen D. Krasner, "Hegemonic Stability Theory: An Empirical Assessment," *Review of International Studies*, 15 (1989), p. 192.

almost doubled in the 1970s. It just went up by around 10 percent between 1980 and 1987, but according to International Monetary Fund (IMF) estimates there was a dramatic increase in trade in the last years of the decade. This projection is, in fact, reflected in the figures for the ratio of total exports to the total gross domestic products of the market economies. It was in the 9–10 percent range in the 1960s, rose dramatically to over 17 per cent in 1980, and then after dropping a couple of percentage points in the mid-1980s rose to around 17 percent by 1989.[71] There are marked differences in this ratio among different countries. While the percentage figure for the United States is presently comparatively rather low (at about the same level as Japan), its climb upward has been dramatic. Henry Wallich has written that "Very few major economies can have gone through so substantial a process of 'opening' as the United States . . . for the US exports and imports both were about 4 percent in the early 1930s; by 1984 . . . they had risen to 10 and 12 percent."[72] The above trend is also reflected in the import content of total supplies of finished manufactured goods for the developed market economies. In 1913 it stood at 8 percent, dropped to 4 percent in 1937, and then rose to 6 percent in 1963, 11 percent in 1971, and 22 percent in 1985.[73]

The trends cited above cannot continue at the same rate, but it is quite likely that they will move upward to a degree. Of course, the pattern may become more regionalized which would tend to decrease the likelihood of strong global regimes, but at least through 1986 there was not a trend toward greater regional concentration.[74] A remarkable aspect of

[71] Maurice D. Levi, *International Finance: The Markets and Financial Management of Multinational Business* (New York: McGraw-Hill, 1990), p. 3. For figures on exports plus imports as a percentage of national output for the seven largest market economies from 1840 to 1987, see Webb and Krasner, "Hegemonic Stability Theory," p. 192. It is true that for a number of the countries it took until the 1970s to reach the figures they had reached just before World War I. Comparable trend data for the last century and a half can be found in: Thompson and Krasner, "Global Transactions and the Consolidation of Sovereignty," p. 199.

[72] Henry C. Wallich, "U.S. Monetary Policy in an Interdependent World," *Essays in International Finance* (Number 157) (Princeton, NJ: Department of Economics, Princeton University, September 1985), p. 33. For figures on the largest economies see Levi, *International Finance*, p. 4.

[73] The 1899–1957 data is from Alfred Maizels, *Industrial Growth and World Trade* (Cambridge: Cambridge University Press, 1963), p. 136. The 1963–71 data is from R. A. Batchelor, R. L. Major, and A. D. Morgan, *Industrialization and the Basis for Trade* (Cambridge: Cambridge University Press, 1980), p. 38. The 1985 data is from Michael Toen, "Removing the Barriers to International Trade," *OECD Observer*, no. 149 (December 1987–January 1988). p. 16. I am grateful to Michael Webb for providing this data.

[74] Webb and Krasner, "Hegemonic Stability Theory," pp. 192–3.

the increase in trade over the last couple of decades is that it has occurred at the same time that states have violated at least in spirit many General Agreement on Tariffs and Trade (GATT) norms and rules. Voluntary export restraints (VERs) have multiplied; countertrade has increased considerably; and organized trade among branches of global corporations has climbed to levels far above what it was even a decade ago – one estimate being a third of all trade.[75] Many of these developments have, of course, occurred because tariffs have dropped to negligible levels and the use of many non-tariff barriers (NTBs) have been constrained by GATT codes. It is, however, important to stress that the expansion of trade that was described above could only have developed if overall states were pursuing a policy of lowering trade barriers. A degree of interstate management of trade does not have all of the bad connotations that it once did in that states are committed to exploiting comparative advantage while at the same time trying to avoid serious instability in their balance of payments. Also, the increased role of multinational corporations in the world economy and specially in the trade area has been seen as an important prop to trade liberalization.[76] Small states have always accepted the need to trade a good percentage of their outputs, but now even large states realize that they would pay a cost in standard of living if they pursued autarchic policies.[77] In a world where managed trade is more important, there may be more violations of global GATT rules, but they still provide an important framework within which states formulate their trade policies. Compliance is far from perfect, but at the same time states realize that they must not diverge too far if they want access to the markets of other member states.[78]

Perhaps the most dramatic increases in international economic interdependence have occurred in the financial sector. In the words of Henry Wallich "interdependence has made progress in financial

[75] *The Business Implications of Globalization* (Ottawa: Investment Canada, Government of Canada, May 1990), p. 14; Michael Stewart, *The Age of Interdependence* (Cambridge, MA: MIT Press, 1984), p. 22. On trade trends see the annual publication of the GATT entitled *International Trade*.

[76] Helen V. Milner, *Resisting Protectionism: Global Industries and the Politics of International Trade* (Princeton, NJ: Princeton University Press, 1988); Robert W. Cox, *Power, Production, and World Order: Social Forces in the Making of History* (New York: Columbia University Press, 1987), esp. chs. 7 and 8; Stephen R. Gill and David Law, "Global Hegemony and the Structural Power of Capital," *International Studies Quarterly*, 33 (December 1989), pp. 475–99.

[77] Rosecrance, *The Rise of the Trading State*, pp. 140–4.

[78] A very good source of information on trade policies and negotiations is the annual publication of the GATT entitled *International Trade*.

Table 2. *Trend in deposit banks'*
foreign liabilities, 1963–1988 (in
1985 U.S. constant $)

	Billion $
1963	134.7
1968	277.7
1973	931.5
1978	1,876.6
1983	2,683.6
1988	4,821.5

Note: computed by dividing deposit
banks' foreign liabilities in current
dollars for a year by the 1985 CPI for
that year and multiplying by 100.
Sources: IMF, *International Financial
Statistics* (1980 and 1989).

markets at a rate far eclipsing that in the real [i.e., trade] sector."[79] The
key indicators of integration of national financial markets are the
convergence in interest rates or yields and the absolute and relative
increases in volumes of lending across borders.[80] According to both
Wallich and Richard Cooper, there has been considerable movement
toward integration, but complete integration is still some distance off.[81]
Facilitated by modern telecommunications the international financial
market "is a global market place that never sleeps."[82] The changes that
have occurred are dramatized in an evaluation by *The Economist*: "The
ease with which savings have since [the early 1980s] been able to scour
the globe for the highest returns (and the lowest cost) lies at the heart of
the reforms that have swept through the world's financial markets.
That ease has set at loggerheads, governments, borrowers and financial
centers which ten years ago gave each other barely a thought."[83]

The extent of the increase in foreign lending by banks is recorded in
Table 2. In constant dollars the amount increased sevenfold from a base
of $135 billion between 1963 and 1973; trebled between 1973 and 1983,

[79] Wallich, "U.S. Monetary Policy in an Interdependent World," p. 35. Also see Kahler,
"The International Political Economy," p. 145.
[80] Richard N. Cooper, *Economic Policy in an Interdependent World* (Cambridge, MA: MIT
Press, 1986), p. 138.
[81] *Ibid.*, pp. 35–6; Wallich, "U.S. Monetary Policy in an Interdependent World," pp. 137–
44.
[82] Stewart, *The Age of Interdependence*, p. 26.
[83] "A Survey of International Financial Markets," *The Economist* (July 21, 1990), p. 7.

Table 3. *Trends in volume of direct investment abroad, 1970–88 (in millions of SDRs)*

	Million SDRs
1970	12,166
1975	20,723
1980	37,452
1985	61,466
1988	109,425

Note: "Direct investment refers to investment that is made to acquire a lasting interest in an enterprise operating in an economy other than that of the investor, the investor's purpose being to have an effective voice in the management of the enterprise" (IMF, *Balance of Payments Manual* [1977], p. 136). A minimum 25% ownership interest is said to constitute direct investment.
Sources: IMF, *Balance of Payments Statistics Yearbook* (1970–6, 1983, 1989).

and then almost doubled between 1983 and 1988 – reaching a figure of $4,822 billion.[84] Another aspect of the growth of financial markets is that the daily foreign exchange market alone is worth $600 billion.[85]

The tremendous increase in financial flows in recent decades has been matched by comparable trends in foreign investment. In the case of direct foreign investment there has been a steady increase – with the most notable change in recent decades being the increase in non-American investment. The global volume trebled in the decade 1970–80 and then trebled again from 1980 to 1988 (Table 3).[86] One of the most striking features of recent years is the growth of multinational

---

[84] For additional trend data, see Webb and Krasner, "Hegemonic Stability Theory," p. 191; and Thompson and Krasner, "Global Transactions and the Consolidation of Sovereignty," pp. 201–3. The latter article, while noting significant increases in recent decades, does stress that international banking has been quite important in other eras.
[85] "A Survey of International Financial Markets," p. 7.
[86] Thompson and Krasner ("Global Transactions and the Consolidation of Sovereignty," p. 201) show that foreign investment as a percentage of GNP for the Western industrial countries was much greater before World War I. However, it should be noted that this was the heyday of the colonial era. Their percentage changes between 1970 and 1981 differ from the IMF figures which include all market economies. The IMF records a remarkable increase over the last two decades. *The Economist* notes that annual

Table 4. *Trends in volume of portfolio investment abroad, 1980–8 (in millions of SDRs)*

	Million SDRs
1980	2,646
1982	60,159
1984	53,515
1986	158,734
1988	156,816

Note: "The category for portfolio investment . . . covers long-term bonds and corporate equities other than those included in the categories for direct investment and reserves" (IMF, *Balance of Payments Manual* [1977], p. 142).
Sources: IMF, *Balance of Payments Statistics Yearbook* (1983, and 1989). No figures are available before 1980

corporations that produce goods with parts supplied by branches from around the world. One writer has observed that the 1980s was "the decade in which the global factory came into its own."[87] The 1980s also witnessed a truly phenomenal sixtyfold increase in the volume of portfolio investment abroad from SDR 2,640 to SDR 156,816 from 1980 to 1988 (Table 4).

The present volume of foreign investment constitutes "the greater stake that countries have in each other's well-being" and "represents a much more permanent stake in the economic welfare of the host nation than exports to that market could ever be."[88] It is clear that a rupture of international ties would lead to much more serious losses for investors than traders. There has been a marked increase in the amount of foreign direct investment in all industrialized countries except Japan in recent years. In the case of Japan foreigners only own 1 percent of all assets, whereas for the United States the figure is 9 percent, for the United

global direct foreign investment was ten times greater for the last three years of the 1980s than it was for the first three years of the 1970s. *The Economist* (December 22, 1990), p. 44.
[87] Kahler, "The International Political Economy," p. 147; Kenichi Ohmae, *The Borderless World: Power and Strategy in the Interlinked Economy* (New York: Harper Business, 1990); Michael Porter, *The Competitive Advantage of Nations* (New York: Free Press, 1990).
[88] Rosecrance, *The Rise of the Trading State*, pp. 146–7.

Kingdom – 14 percent, West Germany – 17 percent, and for France still higher.[89]

It is unquestionably the case that the world has witnessed and is still witnessing a remarkable increase in international economic interdependence. There are, of course, possibilities of a reversal in present global trends and an increase in regional as opposed to interregional linkages, but as long as there are no major wars, there will probably not be any radical shifts. More interesting are the forms of collaboration that are developing and might develop to manage international economic interdependencies. In the case of trade it is first noteworthy that there is a large and growing body of international private trade law to govern transactions among private parties.[90] Of greater contemporary importance the GATT has been central to the development of a global intergovernmental regime that has reduced trade barriers. And despite the recent breakup of the Uruguay Round negotiations an accord is likely to develop and bring services and intellectual property issues into the regime. The degree of states' involvement in the global regime is likely to vary, but an overall commitment by the major economic powers to maintain a reasonable degree of openness is likely to persist.[91]

In the case of foreign investment, progress toward an international regime has largely taken the form of some rather general Organization for Economic Cooperation and Development (OECD) accords linking the developed market economies (apart from traditional law on expropriation),[92] but the likely GATT agreements on services certainly will move into the terrain of states' treatment of foreign investment. Given differences in states' policies toward foreign investment (including their competition for it) regulatory regimes are likely to remain general and involve groups of economically similar states, but on the other hand there does seem to be a broader international commitment to the

---

[89] *The Economist* (June 23, 1990), p. 67.

[90] Norbert Horn and Clyve M. Schmitthoff, eds., *The Transnational Law of International Commercial Transactions* (Deventer, Netherlands; Kluwer, 1982); Clyve M. Schmitthoff, "Unification of the Law of International Trade," *Journal of Business Law* (1968), pp. 105–19; H. J. Herman and C. Kaufman, "The Law of International Business Transactions," *Harvard Journal of International Law*, 19 (Winter 1978).

[91] Sidney Golt, *The GATT Negotiations, 1986–90: Origins, Issues and Prospects* (London: British-North American Committee, 1988); J. Michael Finger and Andrzez Olechowski, eds., *The Uruguay Round: A Handbook on the Multilateral Trade Negotiations* (Washington, DC: World Bank, 1987); Gilbert R. Winham, "The Prenegotiation Phase of the Uruguay Round," *International Journal*, 44 (Spring 1989), pp. 280–303.

[92] Charles Lipson, *Standing Guard: Protecting Foreign Capital in the Nineteenth and Twentieth Centuries* (Berkeley, CA: University of California Press, 1985); Bart S. Fischer, *Regulating the Multinational Enterprise: National and International Challenges* (New York: Praeger, 1983); John M. Kline, *International Codes and Multinational Business* (New York: Quorum, 1985).

facilitation of investment flows than there was in the past. In the case of financial flows one marked and quite important development has been an accord within the Bank for International Settlements on capital adequacy requirements for international banks, and in general there is considerable international monitoring and coordination of policies in this area – if only to give states' more control of their own banks.[93] There has, of course, also been a range of international coordination with regard to macroeconomic policies whose importance has varied in recent decades. Of great significance there has been a movement toward coordination of those policies that have traditionally been regarded as most central to state autonomy – namely, fiscal and monetary, and this has occurred significantly because of the integration of national capital markets. This wideranging coordination has involved a broad range of international organizations such as the IMF, the Bank for International Settlements, the OECD, and the Group of 7.[94]

An important issue is whether the state is going to lose significant control of international economic transactions and hence decline as the central actor in international relations. In a recent article on the subject *The Economist* projected that states were losing some control over international economic flows, but that it was by no means disappearing as the most important political actor. "Nothing else can govern whole societies without toppling, one way, into the intranationalist error of tribalism or, the other way, into the supranationalist sterility of rule by bureaucrats."[95] This points to the fact that the regimes governing international economic relations will largely be interstate – if only for the fact that enforcement powers still lie largely in the hands of states.

93 Ethan B. Kapstein, "Resolving the Regulators' Dilemma: International Coordination of Banking Regulations," *International Organization*, 43 (Spring 1989), pp. 323–47. International financial integration and general pressures for coordination are addressed in Jeffrey A. Frieden, "Invested Interests: The Politics of National Economic Policies in a World of Global Finance" (mimeo, January 1991).

94 Michael C. Webb, "International Power, Economic Structures, and International Coordination of Macroeconomic Adjustment Policies" (paper presented at the American Political Science Association Meeting, San Francisco, August 29–September 2, 1990); Robert D. Putnam and Nicholas Bayne, *Hanging Together: Cooperation and Conflict in the Seven-Power Summits* (London: Sage Publications, 1987); Michael Artis and Sylvia Ostry, *International Economic Policy Coordination* (London: Routledge and Kegan Paul, 1986). The rationale for this coordination was earlier discussed in Richard N. Cooper, *The Economics of Interdependence: Economic Policy in the Atlantic Community* (New York: McGraw-Hill, 1968). Of general relevance to international economic collaboration is John Gerard Ruggie, "International Regimes, Transactions, and Change: Embedded Liberalism in the Postwar Economic Order," in Stephen D. Krasner, ed., *International Regimes* (Ithaca, NY: Cornell University Press, 1983), pp. 195–232.

95 "The State of the Nation-State," *The Economist* (December 22, 1990), p. 46 (and pp. 43–5).

Information flows

The increase in the rapidity of communications has been highlighted by the comment of Isaac Azimov that it took five months for Queen Isabella to learn of Columbus' voyage; two weeks for Europe to learn of President Lincoln's assassination; and 1.3 seconds for the world to witness Neil Armstrong's first step on the moon.[96] The increase in the speed and volume of information flows since the mid-nineteenth century (and especially in the last several decades) is truly stupendous. Given these trends and their impacts it is easy to agree with the historian William McNeill that "one can argue that the central disturber of our age is the communications revolution."[97]

The following are some figures that indicate some of the dramatic changes that have taken place. The number of telephones in the world has increased from around 70 million to 600 million between 1950 and the mid-1980s.[98] The number of international telephone calls increased sixfold in the 1980s and is expected to increase fivefold in the 1990s. Most calls originate in the developed world, but the increases in the Third World are much more striking. Between 1980 and 1988 the number of international calls from the United States went up from 198,880 to 685,673 million and for Germany from 248,000 to 600,352 million; however, for Thailand it went from 873 to 12,643 million, for Singapore from 3,530 to 43,672 million, and for China from 1,075 to 45,030 million.[99] There was also a fivefold increase in the number of high frequency transmitters between 1955 and 1980 – a high percentage of which are used for international broadcasting.[100]

One important effect of the telecommunications revolution is that it has made it possible for states to monitor each other's military activities in a much more thorough manner, and this has both decreased the possibility of surprise attack and greatly improved states' perception of other countries' capabilities and behavior. The consequences have been greater stability overall and a greater willingness to enter into agreements. In fact, John Lewis Gaddis has written that "the

---

96 Cited in *The Business Implications of Globalization*, p. 36.
97 McNeill, "Winds of Change," p. 168.
98 *Telephone Statistics of the World* (New York: AT&T, various issues); Thomas L. McPhail and Brenda McPhail, "The International Politics of Telecommunications: Resolving the North–South Dilemma," *International Journal*, 42 (Spring 1987), p. 290.
99 *Yearbook of Public Telecommunication Statistics*: Chronological series, 1979–88 (Geneva: ITU, 1990); Greg Staple, *The Global Telecommunication Traffic Boom* (London: International Institute for Communications, 1990).
100 Hamid Mowlana, *Global Information and World Communication* (New York: Longman, 1986), p. 59.

'reconnaissance revolution' . . . may well rival in importance the 'nuclear revolution'."[101]

The effects of the communications revolution have also been crucial for the expansion of international business. Perhaps the most dramatic effects (as previously noted) have been in the area of international capital. To quote *The Economist*'s survey of financial markets: "In no more than a decade the power of the computer has transformed the nature of capital."[102] Also, it has had a dramatic effect on the globalization of firms; at least a third of all international telecommunications today are between branches of the same corporation.[103] Pertinent to this trend *The Economist* wrote: "What Mr. Marshall McLuhan called the 'global village' modern businessmen may prefer to see as 'the global office suite.' Information technology's ability to overcome distance enables companies to work more closely together in a variety of ways."[104] The expansion of international communications encourages the growth of economic transactions and the creation of international organizations and regimes to manage them.

Communications are also having impacts on the autonomy of the state and even people's cultural and political identification. Today it is very difficult for governments to monitor and control communications since they are voluminous and virtually instantaneous.[105] In the past Soviet bloc states tried to isolate their populations through a variety of methods, including jamming radio broadcasts, but their efforts were not very effective. In the 1960s one sixth of the Soviet population was listening to Western short-wave broadcasts. As Ithiel de Sola Pool noted: "No country can impose censorship without knowing that short-wave broadcasting will penetrate it."[106] The situation today is that "The direct-dial telephone, the videocassette, the short-wave radio, and the personal computer all will facilitate a rising degree of cross-penetration of every political system."[107] What is happening is that the values of the center of the communications network – the West – are permeating throughout the world because "A phenomenon that goes hand in hand

[101] Gaddis, *The Long Peace*, p. 228.
[102] "A Survey of International Financial Markets," p. 12.
[103] Jonathan Galloway, "INTELSAT's Markets and the New Competitors," *International Journal*, 42 (Spring 1987), p. 26.
[104] *The Economist* (June 16, 1990), p. 15.
[105] David E. S. Blatherwick, *The International Politics of Telecommunications* (Berkeley, CA: Institute of International Studies, University of California, 1987), ch. 1. On the increasing porosity of political jurisdictions, see Rosenau, *Turbulence in World Politics*, pp. 351–2.
[106] Pool, *Technologies without Boundaries*, pp. 79 and 210.
[107] Charles William Maynes, "Coping With The '90s," *Foreign Policy*, no. 74 (Spring 1989), p. 53.

with communications is cultural diffusion."[108] As Ronald Dore has written: "the emergent 'world culture' [of the urban middle classes] is perceived as Western culture. And by and large that perception is correct."[109] What is unclear is whether communications flows are undermining the control and autonomy of the state in fundamental ways by altering the political allegiances of the population or putting important economic and cultural activities outside the control of the state.[110] The increases in telecommunications are almost certainly having influences along these lines, but there is little chance that most countries will seriously curtail communications flows because of the likely economic losses. If they do, they will find out, as did those countries that restricted printing 400 years ago, that they will "pay a considerable price in productivity for doing so; they will lose out to competing countries that allow free use of any information."[111]

While the growth of international telecommunications capabilities and volume have largely influenced the evolution of the international order through their effects on security regimes, economic interdependencies and accords, and the ability of states to control their borders, there have also been a good number of collaborative/regulatory arrangements to manage the varied dimensions of international telecommunications. They include the management of the radio frequency spectrum (largely through the International Telecommunications Union [ITU]), the establishment of technical standards for interconnectivity (through the ITU and the International Standards Organization), and the regulation of prices and market shares (through the ITU, the International Telecommunications Satellite Organization [INTELSAT], and the informal network of state telecommunications administrations). The latter area of international regulation has been weakened as a result of movement toward deregulation in a good number of developed countries, but there is a good chance of coordination of more liberal policies in the long run.[112]

---

[108] Andrew Scott, *The Dynamics of Interdependence* (Chapel Hill, NC: University of North Carolina Press, 1982), p. 163.

[109] Ronald Dore, "Unity and Diversity in Contemporary World Culture," in Hedley Bull and Adam Watson, eds., *The Expansion of International Society* (Oxford: Clarendon Press, 1984), p. 423.

[110] Blatherwick, *The International Politics of Telecommunications*, p. 8.

[111] Pool, *Technologies Without Boundaries*, p. 13.

[112] G. A. Codding and A. M. Rutkowski, *The International Telecommunication Union in a Changing World* (Dedham, MA: Artech House, 1982); James Savage, *The Politics of International Telecommunication Regulation* (Boulder, CO: Westview Press, 1989); Jonathan D. Aronson and Peter F. Cowhey, *When Nations Talk: International Trade in Telecommunications Services* (Cambridge, MA: Ballinger, 1988).

Table 5. *Trends in the growth of democratic government, 1973–90*

	Free				Partly free				Not free				Total no. of states
	Popul'n	% of world Popul'n	No. of states	% of world states	Popul'n	% of world Popul'n	No. of states	% of world states	Popul'n	% of world Popul'n	No. of states	% of world states	
1973	1,029m	32.0	44	29.1	721m	21.0	38	25.1	1,583m	47.0	69	45.6	151
1981	1,613m	35.9	51	31.4	971m	21.6	53	32.7	1,912m	42.5	58	35.8	162
1990	2,034m	38.9	61	36.5	1,144m	21.9	44	26.3	2,056m	39.3	62	37.0	167

Notes:

1 The Freedom House classifications are based on a numeric scale, so there are some countries that are ranked very close but are in different categories.

2 Population figures include territories as well as states.

3 The January 1990 figures do not include the movements of Czechoslovakia, The German Democratic Republic, and Panama from "not free" to "partly free."

Sources: January–February issues of *Freedom-at-Issue* (1973, 1981, 1990). The annual surveys of Freedom House were written by Raymond Gastil.

Spread of democracy

Before addressing the international significance of the demise of authoritarian governments and the rise of democratic ones, it is important to ask whether the world is witnessing a steady expansion of democracy. One of the baldest assertions is that by Francis Fukuyama who declared "an unabashed victory of economic and political liberalism."[113] His analysis was widely and fiercely criticized, but his general assertions are supported in varying degrees by a number of scholars. Dankwart Rustow declares that "A tide of democratic change is sweeping the world."[114] Larry Diamond, Juan Linz, and Seymour Martin Lipset in the preface to a four-volume series on democracy write that the 1980s saw an "unprecedented growth of international concern for human rights . . . including the right to choose democratically the government under which one lives." They then go on to note: "The growth of democratic norms throughout the world is strikingly evident in the degree to which authoritarian regimes find it necessary to wrap themselves in the rhetoric and constitutional trappings of democracy."[115] George Modelski sees the growth of democracies as one of the most important trends in the world political system and notes that "from the Dutch Republic onward, there has been a progressive growth – via a massive learning-diffusion process – of an increasingly weighty community of democracies."[116]

The only attempt to trace trends toward and away from democracy in recent decades is the annual classification done by Freedom House. It ranks states on a variety of continua relating to freedom of expression and the openness of elections, and then classifies them as "free, partly free, and not free." Table 5 indicates that in 1973, 29.1 percent of all states were "free" and 25.1 percent were "partly free." By 1990 the figures had gone up to 36.5 percent and 26.3 percent. This is not a huge increase, but it does not register most of the changes in Eastern Europe. And, of course, if the former socialist bloc does move clearly into the democratic camp, it will have some marked effects on the figures. Some of the most significant recent changes have been in Latin America, and according to Diamond and Linz there are "reasons for

[113] Francis Fukuyama, "The End of History?," *National Interest*, 16 (Summer 1989), p. 3.
[114] Dankwart A. Rustow, "Democracy: A Global Revolution?," *Foreign Affairs*, 69 (Fall 1990), p. 73.
[115] Larry Diamond, Juan Linz, and Seymour Martin Lipset, *Democracy in Developing Countries*, I: *Persistence, Future, and Renewal* (Boulder, CO: Lynne Reinner, 1988), pp. ix and x.
[116] George Modelski, "Democratization," forthcoming in *Routledge Encyclopedia of Government and Politics*.

cautious optimism about the prospects for the new democracies."[117] The short-term prospects for Africa and the Middle East are not good, but there are grounds for a little more optimism in parts of Asia.

The importance of the growth of democracy for the transformation of the international order is based on a number of considerations. First, democracies tend to favor liberal capitalism and are hence inclined to support the growth of international economic ties. Second, they are predisposed to support the free flow of information and people among states, and this not only facilitates international economic ties, but also promotes transnational organizations and a certain homogenization in values and habits. Of course, some of the most important organizations for the purpose of this analysis are those such as Amnesty International that are concerned with the promotion of human rights. Third, there have been some nascent movements toward the formation of human rights regimes based on liberal democratic values, and this trend is likely to grow gradually.[118] Lastly, and of great importance, democracies do not tend to go to war with each other.[119]

The evidence is very clear that over the past 200 years democracies have not gone to war with each other. In the words of Michael Doyle, "liberal states have indeed established a separate peace – but only among themselves."[120] The basic reasons cited for this pattern are that in democracies those who bear most of the burden of war make the

[117] Larry Diamond and Juan Linz, "Introduction," in Larry Diamond, Juan Linz, and Seymour Martin Lipset, *Democracy in Developing Countries*, IV: *Latin America* (Boulder, CO: Lynne Reinner, 1989), p. 52; Howard J. Wiarda, *The Democratic Revolution in Latin America* (New York: Holmes and Meier, 1990). An optimistic view of recent global trends toward democracy is "New Democracies," *The Economist* (December 22, 1990), pp. 75–6.

[118] R. J. Vincent, *Human Rights and International Relations* (Cambridge: Cambridge University Press, 1986); Thomas Buergental, ed., *Human Rights, International Law and the Helsinki Accord* (Montclair, NJ: Hosmun/Universe Books, 1977); Jack Donnelly, "Recent Trends in UN Human Rights Activity: Description and Polemic," *International Organization*, 35 (Autumn 1981), pp. 633–56; Jack Donnelly, "International Human Rights: A Regime Analysis," *International Organization*, 40 (Summer 1986), pp. 599–642; David P. Forsythe, *The Internationalization of Human Rights* (Lexington, MA: Lexington Books, 1991).

[119] Michael Doyle, "Liberalism and World Politics," *American Political Science Review*, 80 (December 1986), pp. 1155–62.

[120] *Ibid.*, p. 1156. Also see Steve Chan, "Mirror, Mirror, on the Wall . . . Are the Freer Countries More Pacific?," *Journal of Conflict Resolution*, 28 (December 1984), pp. 617–48; Zeev Maoz and Nasrin Abdoladli, "Regime Types and International Conflict, 1816–1976," *Journal of Conflict Resolution*, 29 (March 1989), pp. 3–35; R. J. Rummel, "Libertarianism and International Violence," *Journal of Conflict Resolution*, 27 (March 1983), pp. 27–71; R. J. Rummel, "Libertarian Propositions on Violence within and between Nations: A Test against Published Research Results," *Journal of Conflict Resolution*, 29 (1985), pp. 419–55; Melvin Small and J. David Singer, "The War Proneness of Democratic Regimes, 1916–1965," *Jerusalem Journal of International Relations*, 1 (Summer 1976), pp. 51–69.

decisions; democratic nations feel constrained not to use force to settle problems with those with similar values; and democratic states develop more open interdependent economic relations. John Mearsheimer challenges this view on the grounds that people in democratic states do not seem to be less sensitive to the costs of war and that they are just as prone to nationalistic and religious antagonisms as the populations of non-democratic countries. Yet he has to admit that the empirical record is that democracies do not fight each other.[121] If, as is quite possibly the case, democracy gradually but steadily spreads to more countries, the incidence of international violence and hence the quality of the international order are bound to change.

It is important to make the general point that changes in international behavior and order are rooted in part in the character and the functions of the political units. As Ian Clark comments: "International relations may be practised in a constant framework of inter-state relations but the states themselves are changing, yielding a new substance to their contacts." He then goes on to remark that "Paradoxically, theories of international order have suffered both from too much concentration on the state and from too little elaboration of its evolving nature."[122] Unquestionably the increasing responsibilities of states in assuring economic welfare and the democratic character of many of them are affecting the quality of international interactions, and these changes in interactions that are inspired by transformations in the state are likely to expand in the future.

Cultural/social heterogeneity

This is a pillar that most observers would judge remains an important support for the contemporary international system of highly autonomous states. There are considerable differences among the cultures of the states, and in fact the variations are greater for the most part than the pattern that existed in the European state system of the eighteenth century. However, it is valuable to look at some information concerning this issue in investigating the evolving world order.

There are differences of view as to whether a world culture at an elite or mass level has been emerging. Adda Bozeman, for example, thinks that the process of Westernization has been reversed and that there are

---

[121] Mearsheimer, "We Will Soon Miss the Cold War," pp. 46–7. The United States has, of course, supported the use of force against elected governments by its own nationals (e.g., Iran in 1953, Guatemala in 1954, Chile in 1973, and Nicaragua in the mid-1980s).

[122] Clark, The Hierarchy of States, pp. 211–12.

well-entrenched differences among nations.[123] Another study of Westernization has similarly concluded that "Humanity represents a disparate mosaic of sharply contrasting cultural identities. People are set within their separate language communities, their separateness often reinforced by a common religion and historic experience."[124] Before judging that these differences are likely to persist in approximately their present form, it is important to note that no culture owes more than about 10 percent of its total elements to its own inventions. All cultures are hybrids of many influences. What makes the present situation so unique is that most cultures' exposure to foreign influences has been so massive and rapid; and because of this some very hostile reactions are inevitable.[125]

Contrary to the viewpoint of the above-cited authorities, Ali Mazrui believes that there has been "a process of normative convergence" over recent centuries based on Western values – now strengthened by the Third World's economic dependence on Europe and America.[126] Robert Cox concurs with this perspective in his observation that the present process of globalization of production "continues a process of cultural homogenization – emanating from the centers of world power, spread by the world media, and sustained by a convergence in modes of thought and practices among business and political elites."[127] This perspective on present trends is backed by a number of prominent writers on international business who portray a world of increasingly homogenized tastes and the growing prominence of global corporations. Kenichi Ohmae's analysis of the spread of "the Californization of need" dramatizes the process that these writers are analyzing.[128] It is of particular importance to this analysis that Western moral and legal norms have become the basis of modern international law and are becoming increasingly accepted by non-Western states. On this point a recent study noted that

---

123 Adda Bozeman, "The International Order in a Multicultural World," in Bull and Watson, eds., *The Expansion of International Society*, pp. 389–406.
124 Theodore H. Von Laue, *The World Revolution of Westernization: The Twentieth Century in Global Perspective* (Oxford: Oxford University Press, 1987), p. 338. He also recognizes its negative implications for international cooperation (p. 8).
125 Pool, *Technologies without Boundaries*, p. 66.
126 Ali A. Mazrui, *A World Federation of Cultures: An African Perspective* (New York: Free Press, 1976), p. 437.
127 Cox, "Globalization, Multilateralism, and Social Choice," p. 2.
128 Ohmae, *The Borderless World*; Porter, *The Competitive Advantage of Nations*; Christopher Bartlett and Sumantra Ghoshal, *Managing across Borders: The Transnational Solution* (Boston, MA: Harvard Business School Press, 1989); Theodore Levitt, "The Globalization of Markets," *Harvard Business Review* (May–June 1983). Porter does think that it is important that multinationals maintain a national identity.

> In the evolution of global society, the centrality of Western Europe initially and of the United States during this century cannot be overemphasized. Virtually all of the norms that are now identified as essential ingredients of international law and global society have their roots in the jurisprudence of European scholars of international law and in the notions and patterns of acceptable behavior established by the more powerful Western European states.[129]

As is made clear in this study, the influence of the West has suffused not just interstate relations but national legal systems as well.

It is difficult to find data that are directly pertinent to the issue of the emergence of cultural homogenization. There are, however, some data that are relevant – some of the most interesting concerning the prominence of Western languages. English is the main language in forty-two states; French in twenty-eight states; and Spanish in nineteen states.[130] There are also indications that English is fast becoming the world language that a growing number of people recognize they must learn if they are going to succeed in their professions. According to a 1966 study 50 percent of the world's businessmen described English as their first language of business; and another 20 percent described it as their second language.[131] The figure would almost certainly be higher today. A very interesting figure is the language in which scientific articles are published. In the case of those indexed by *Chemical Abstracts*, 64.7 percent of the articles indexed in 1980 were in English; in 1984 the figure was 69.2 percent; and in 1987 the figure was 73 percent.[132] This shows how rapidly such trends can escalate.

It is very difficult to project the implications of the above information. It can, however, be conjectured that a greater homogenization of consumer and even popular cultural tastes, the growth of a common elite language, greater similarity in economic systems,[133] and a growing acceptance of Western political values will facilitate an increase in international economic interdependence and the coordination of policies in many international issue-areas. The world is still so heterogeneous that

---

129 Ethan A. Nadelmann, "Global Prohibition Regimes: The Evolution of Norms in International Society," *International Organization*, 44 (Autumn 1990), p. 484.

130 J. A. Laponce, "Language and Communication: The Rise of the Monolingual State," in Claudio Cioffi-Revilla *et al.*, eds., *Communication and Interaction in Global Politics* (Beverly Hills, CA: Sage Publications, 1987), p. 203; J. A. Laponce, *Languages and their Territories* (Toronto: University of Toronto Press, 1987), pp. 96–8. The figures are a bit lower for English and French if the designation "official unilingual" is used.

131 Cited in Laponce, *Languages and their Territories*, p. 80.

132 *Ibid.*, p. 72. The 1987 figures were provided by Laponce.

133 See the article by Thomas Biersteker in this volume.

a highly centralized form of international governance would be very inappropriate, but at the same time it is becoming sufficiently homogeneous (especially at elite levels among many countries) that higher levels of coordination are becoming more feasible.

CONCLUSION

It is risky at any time to say that a social or political system is in a process of fundamental change, but there are times that enough evidence exists to make such an assertion. For international relations scholars this appears to be a time when it is possible to judge that the world is in the process of a fundamental transformation from a system of highly autonomous states to one where states are increasingly enmeshed in a network of interdependencies and regimes. Both the patterns of governance in the international system and modal patterns of state interactions are undergoing marked changes, and more than anything it is changes in these factors that define system transformation. Traditional realist theories of international relations cannot account for the changes that are occurring. They are too tied to the notion that states will not trade-off their autonomy to achieve other values and to the idea that all important changes are rooted in changes in power distributions. Concomitantly, they cannot conceive of states moving toward quite important systems of governance. Overall they cannot explain some important dimensions of change in the contemporary international system.

At the heart of the ongoing international transformation is the fact that the cost of war for the great powers is becoming so great in the nuclear age that not only do they seek to avoid war with each other, but they also cooperate in a variety of ways to avoid inadvertently falling into a military conflict. Their greater sense of security also means that the great powers (and other states as well) increasingly feel that they can cooperate on a host of non-security matters because they are not as concerned as in the past about differences in rewards and hence power resulting from the collaboration. There is always the chance that revolutions in technology will change the relationship of mutual deterrence among the great powers, but there are no signs that this will occur. The major uncertainty in international security politics is whether a shift away from resort to war will percolate from the northern industrialized world into the Third World. There are certainly reasons for doubting that this will occur, but there are also very good reasons for thinking that it will. The great powers are concerned that Third World conflicts might draw them in, might create incentives for the spread of nuclear weapons, and might disrupt economic relations. Most developing countries, on the other hand, are absorbed with pursuing the modern god of economic development, are not anxious to be bullied by larger neighbors, and are committed to the sanctity of existing territorial boundaries. Developments with respect to the 1990–1 Gulf crisis provide some examples of these policy orientations. Perhaps the international tensions that are most likely to lead to war are competition for economic resources (exacerbated by population growth), and these will probably lead to occasional military conflicts between developed and developing countries as well as between Third World states. However, it is important to recognize that while wars will occur occasionally, an absence of great power "conflagrations" and a greatly reduced frequency of wars in the Third World would constitute a true revolution in international politics. To what extent there will be significant movement toward more stable security orders in the Third World in the near future will be influenced significantly by international deliberations in the wake of the Gulf war, and at this point it is very difficult to project developments in this area.

All indications are that international interdependencies in the economic and environmental realms will increase and that more and stronger regimes will be necessary to manage them. There may be a marked movement toward regional, as opposed to global, ties and regimes, and this could be a product of considerable tension among regional groupings. But reasonably strong networks of interdependencies and regimes are likely to exist at the global level as long as military violence does not reappear as a major feature of the international scene. International environmental problems require global planning, and the same is basically true of many international economic issues because of the growth of economic transactions. The patchwork pattern of regimes that is evolving does not give an appearance of well-organized governance, and it is not. But it does constrain state behavior in an increasing number of ways.

The other three pillars are relevant largely because of their effects on the decay of the other pillars and hence on states' ability to come to agreements in managing their many interdependencies. The growth in speed and volume of international telecommunications cannot be underestimated because of their impact on increased international linkages, greater homogeneity in practices and values, and broader and stronger regimes for telecommunications itself. The spread in democratic values and institutions facilitates international ties, reduces the likelihood of war, and provides a basis for human rights regimes. Finally, gradual movement toward greater homogeneity in cultural values and practices reduces somewhat states' incentives to build walls to protect state autonomy and facilitates coordination of policies. It is important to stress again that all of these changes will be uneven and gradual and will affect the quality of international relations over a very long period of time. The spread of democracy and the movement toward greater homogeneity in cultural and other values are going to be particularly slow in certain areas of the world and will be challenged outright by important forces at times. But long-term trends in these directions are still likely.

To return to a point that was made in the introduction to this chapter, the Westphalian temple in which the peoples of the West and increasingly the rest of the world have politically worshiped for over three centuries is not completely collapsing. States are still the central political actors in international relations, and in fact they are tremendously important to consolidating the evolving order that has been discussed above. Whether one calls the new international arrangements the latter Westphalian system or the post-Westphalian system makes little difference. The key is that states are becoming increasingly enmeshed in a network of collaborative arrangements or regimes that are creating a very different international political world than the one that has existed in recent centuries. In fact, the transformation in terms of changes in modal behavior among the major political entities is much more profound than that from the medieval to the modern era. It is a world that a very perceptive international political observer John Herz once described as the emergence of "neoterritoriality" – or a world in which sovereign states recognize their interests in mutual respect for each other's independence and in extensive cooperation. Concerning this possible world he wrote: "Neoterritoriality will function only if and when the danger of nuclear destruction and the interdependence of humans and their societies on the globe will have made nations and their leaders aware that the destiny awaiting us is now common to all."[134]

There is a final point concerning the forces that underlie the present transformation that should be made. The preceding analysis has stressed the importance of growing international interdependencies as well as technological, political, and cultural changes that promote the evolution of stronger regimes. There is, however, something else of relevance to ongoing changes that is growing very slowly and fitfully, and it concerns people's cognitive map of the world as well as an

[134] "The Territorial State Revisited," p. 89.

accompanying ethical/mythological system.[135] It is captured by Marshall McLuhan's phrase "the global village" or the oft-used term "spaceship Earth." It is a notion of a world in which people's fates are closely linked to each other and with the natural/physical world and in which they increasingly see each other as members of humankind. Both space travel and global ecological crises have certainly encouraged this image, and it was captured well by the writer Archibald McLeish when he reflected on the pictures from the 1968 Apollo mission: "To see the earth as we now see it, small and blue and beautiful in that eternal silence where it floats, is to see ourselves as riders on the earth together, brothers on that bright loveliness in the unending night – brothers who *see* now they are truly brothers."[136] One can naively overstate the development and significance of this cognitive image and its ethical overtones, but one can also mistakenly ignore in the name of realism an incipient but important trend in international society.

---

[135] John Ruggie has described this as the pervading "social episteme," and has analyzed its importance in the transition from the medieval to modern Westphalian system. "'Finding our Feet' in Territoriality." Also see Ruggie, "Continuity and Transformation in the World Polity."

[136] *Riders on the Earth: Essays and Recollections* (Boston, MA: Houghton Mifflin, 1978), p. xiv. On the psychological effects of astronauts of seeing the earth from outer space, see Frank White, *The Overview Effect* (Boston, MA: Houghton Mifflin, 1987).

4 THE "TRIUMPH" OF NEOCLASSICAL ECONOMICS IN THE DEVELOPING WORLD: POLICY CONVERGENCE AND BASES OF GOVERNANCE IN THE INTERNATIONAL ECONOMIC ORDER[1]

Thomas J. Biersteker

Order and governance in international relations are related to each other in a variety of complex ways.[2] Governance is essentially *purposive* and should be distinguished from order, which does not require conscious purpose or intention. Order can exist without governance, but governance requires some form of order. At least three different types of order can be distinguished.

At the most basic level, world order can be conceptualized as a cohesive system of ideas (or a world view) mutually or intersubjectively shared by a group of individuals, including those located in different communities across territorial boundaries. This cohesive system of ideas and normative values encompasses ideas about political and economic systems, conceptions of religion (and its role), ontological and epistemological assumptions, a sense of mission in the world, a conception of the scope of that world, practices of legitimation, and ways of ordering, creating, and forgetting history. In this sense, one could talk about an American liberal world order vision, a Soviet socialist world order conception, or an Islamic world order view. Different world orders coexist, at times with mutual incomprehension, and are interpenetrated by one another. Although they may be associated with a state actor at a given moment in time (i.e., the U.S., the Soviet Union, or Iran in the examples cited above) and rely on that state actor for their extension, their presence or absence as world orders are

---

[1] I would like to thank Katrina Burgess, James N. Rosenau, and especially John Odell, for their helpful comments and suggestions on an earlier version of this chapter. I would also like to acknowledge the constructive advice I received from my discussions with each of the other contributors included in this volume.

[2] See the introductory discussion of this issue by James Rosenau in Chapter 1 of this volume.

not limited to, or exclusively contained within, any particular state. Aspects of the basic ideas of American liberalism have existed within communities in both the Soviet Union and Iran, even at the height of greatest interstate conflict between the U.S. and those countries.

A second form of order is that which emerges as a result of a degree of convergence across territorial boundaries at a given point in time. There might be a convergence on goals (such as modernity), on economic or political systems (such as market economies or democratic institutions), or on tastes and consumption preferences. This type of order (defined in terms of the presence of regularity or similar patterning) can be facilitated by the presence of a regime, but it does not require one. Indeed, as I will consider below, it may even facilitate the formation of a regime. As a form of order it may be identified as patterned regularity, or the convergence of policy and practices across state entities. It may be random, or it may be explained by a combination of factors, and it is probably temporary (as are virtually all forms of order).

Third and finally, order may be purposive or "governed" to some degree.[3] A governed order does not require a unitary institution or authority (that is, it can exist within "anarchy" as that concept is ordinarily defined rather narrowly in the neorealist tradition). Regimes provide the best examples of different institutionalized, governed world orders. We can talk about order in the international financial regime in general, or on a more narrowly defined issue and time period, such as the order that has governed the post-1982 debt regime, or the Paris Club negotiation regime.

There are therefore simultaneously *many* different world orders we can talk about. There is no single, unitary world order awaiting discovery, free from a particular standpoint or interest. Different world orders simultaneously coexist and overlap with one another with varying degrees of accommodation and contradiction.

In this chapter I will distinguish between these three different types of world order that I perceive as transnational in scope: (1) world order conceptions, (2) the convergence of practices, and (3) institutionalized or "governed" regimes. None of them is reducible to being the

---

[3] It was this type of order, "purposive" order, with which Hedley Bull was most concerned in *The Anarchical Society: A Study of Order in World Politics* (New York: Columbia University Press, 1977). His distinction between patterned regularity and purposive order in Chapter 1 (p. 4) is similar to the distinction between my second and third types of order. Robert O. Keohane makes a similar distinction between these two types of order in *After Hegemony: Cooperation and Discord in the World Political Economy* (Princeton, NJ: Princeton University Press, 1984), p. 51.

"natural" product of an international system *per se* (with the ontological implications of having a unitary standpoint). At the same time, they are related to each other in complex and interesting ways. When it does emerge, governance without government is related to (and even possibly built upon) the foundations of other forms of order, both patterned regularity and more fundamental world order conceptions.

My objective in this chapter is to try to explain the emergence of patterned regularity in foreign and domestic economic policy (the second form of order identified above) and reflect on the ways in which it might provide a basis for a change in an aspect of the governance of the international political economy. Patterned regularity is influenced by (and also influences) world order conceptions. Furthermore, just as I will examine the ways in which it may provide a basis for the formation of a more purposive order (regimes), it also can be influenced by the presence of partially formed prior regimes. Therefore, I will not devote exclusive attention to patterned regularity, but rather will attempt to use its emergence as an entry point for a discussion that considers the relationship between different forms of order and governance in international relations.

A limited degree of transnational convergence of foreign and domestic economic policies is likely to facilitate governance (or a change in the nature of governance) in the international political economy. That is, it is more difficult to form regimes or anticipate governance at the international level if the internal operating principles of actors are radically different.[4] The major international institutions that have dominated the international political economy since the end of World War II were founded on behalf of, and operate principally with, states with market economies. In order to obtain membership in these institutions, socialist economies have historically been required to make significant changes in their foreign and domestic economic policies, open themselves to the international economy, as well as alter their economic reporting schemes. Cooperation and the formation of effective regimes is more difficult when significant differences exist in

---

[4] Robert O. Keohane constructs his theory about the origins of cooperation from the experiences of countries which share common interests. It is for this reason that he focuses on relations among the advanced market-economy countries that "hold views about the proper operation of their economies that are relatively similar – at least in comparison with the differences that exist between them and most less developed countries, or the nonmarket planned economies." Keohane, *After Hegemony*, p. 6. He does not contend that cooperation cannot emerge in other arenas. However, he chose to focus first "on the area where common interests are greatest and where the benefits of international cooperation may be easiest to realize." *Ibid.*, p. 7.

the internal operating mechanisms of the principal actors involved. For example, it is significant that the only examples of formal, legal default on international loans in the post-1945 era have come from the socialist regimes in Cuba and North Korea.[5]

Therefore, the convergence of economic thinking and policy on a global scale could be viewed as a possible prerequisite for (or facilitator of) effective formal or informal governance of relations on the same scale. This is especially apparent today, as formerly socialist regimes continue to transform themselves into capitalist market economies and begin to join both the international financial institutions as well as apply to affiliate themselves with the European Community. In the process they are changing not only themselves, but are likely also to have an influence on the operations, and ultimately the governance, of the international political economy.

My substantive concern in this chapter is explaining the sudden and dramatic transformation of economic policy throughout the developing world between the 1970s and 1980s: the "triumph" of neoclassical economics.[6] It is a change that is reflected in both the domestic and foreign economic policies of developing countries. The 1960s and the 1970s were decades of economic nationalism, experimentation with state socialism, self-reliance, and an ever increased role for state economic intervention in the economy. Nationalization of foreign-owned enterprises reached an all-time high in the mid-1970s,[7] the Organization of Petroleum Exporting Countries (OPEC) fundamentally altered the traditional relationship between producer and consumer countries and at the same time provided a model emulated by virtually every other commodity producer organization. Negotiations for a "New International Economic Order" achieved unprecedented attention from the advanced industrial countries, and virtually every country of the developing world placed severe ownership restrictions

[5] Furthermore, even the study of international political economy (IPE) has tended to reflect the general idea that a limited degree of convergence in economic policy is a prerequisite for effective participation in the world economy. As long as the two blocs of East and West (i.e., of socialist and capitalist systems) co-existed, when one spoke of the international political economy, the subject matter was divided regionally into North–North, North–South, or East–West. In all cases, the central concern was with the North/West, the advanced industrial market economies of the OECD. The study of IPE has been dominated by an examination of their relations with each other (N/N), with the developing world (N/S), or with the socialist world (E/W).

[6] This is what John Gerard Ruggie in another context has called, "The resurgent ethos of liberal capitalism." John Gerard Ruggie, "International Regimes, Transactions, and Change: Embedded Liberalism in the Postwar Economic Order," *International Organization*, 36 (Spring 1982), p. 413.

[7] Stephen J. Kobrin, "Expropriation as an Attempt to Control Foreign Firms in LDCs: Trends from 1960 to 1979," *International Studies Quarterly*, 28 (September 1984).

on the operations of multinationals investing in their territories. Socialist self-reliance was introduced in many countries (particularly those emerging from colonial rule following armed struggle), and socialism of various shades defined the national development program of many countries. Comprehensive development planning was also a widespread and generally favored practice. The prevailing model of development throughout much of Latin America, Asia, and Africa was a variant of a statist, socially redistributive, inward oriented, import substitution industrialization. There were a few exceptions to this general description (Chile after 1973, and in certain respects, most notably in their shift from inward to outward oriented production, both Korea and Taiwan). However, the general description applies to the vast majority of developing countries during the period.

The 1980s, by contrast, have provided a nearly complete turnaround in economic policy. Virtually everywhere, developing countries began restructuring the nature of their intervention in the domestic economy,[8] liberalizing their domestic trade and investment regimes, privatizing state-owned enterprises,[9] and pursuing a variety of economic reforms more generally.[10] Foreign investment restrictions have been eased and new investment incentives established in historical bastions of economic nationalism such as India, Nigeria, and Brazil. With the exception of OPEC, producer commodity cartels are no longer a subject of concern, and the specific proposals of the New International Economic Order are rarely discussed any longer, even in the corridors of the United Nations. The very idea of socialist development is under increasing challenge, as the classic models for this alternative form of development in the Soviet orbit have all but disappeared. Even Mexico, long a paragon of economic nationalism and frontline opponent of U.S. imperialism, has joined the General Agreement on Tariffs and Trade (GATT) (in 1986), undertaken a dramatic economic opening (the apertura in 1987), and is currently (1991) talking about entering into a North American free trade zone with the United States and Canada. Comparable changes in economic policy are being undertaken on a global scale and cut across national boundaries, regional arenas, and previous ideological barriers. With the possible exceptions of Cuba and

8 Thomas J. Biersteker, "Reducing the Role of the State in the Economy: A Conceptual Exploration of IMF and World Bank Prescriptions," *International Studies Quarterly*, 34 (December 1990).
9 Raymond Vernon, *The Promise of Privatization* (New York: Council on Foreign Relations Books, 1988).
10 Joan Nelson, ed., *Economic Crisis and Policy Choice* (Princeton, NJ: Princeton University Press, 1990), ch. 1.

North Korea, one is hard pressed to identify countries in the world where the movement is currently in the other direction.[11]

In an effort to explain this change and assess its implications for both order and governance in the international political economy, I plan to proceed by considering in the first section the content of the change in direction in economic policy. In the second and third sections, I will address the questions of (and consider alternative explanations of) why this dramatic turnaround has taken place. Why has it happened at this time, why has it been so comprehensive (affecting so many countries), and why does it appear increasingly to be so deeply embedded (even irreversible) in so many instances? In the fourth section, I will consider what this alteration in foreign and domestic economic policy might mean for a country's position in, and ultimately for the very nature of, the international political economy. What does the change in national economic policy make possible, and at the same time, what might it prevent or make more difficult? In a concluding discussion, I will speculate about the relationship between different types of order and governance in international relations more generally.

THE "TRIUMPH" OF NEOCLASSICAL ECONOMIC POLICY IN THE DEVELOPING WORLD

The recent shift in economic policy in the developing countries is similar to, but more difficult to characterize than, the adoption of Keynesian policies in many countries during the postwar years. Keynes provided a general theory and published his principal ideas in a major single volume in 1936. In a recent book on the spread of Keynesian ideas, Peter Hall has described three major dimensions to Kenyesianism: a new set of concepts in macroeconomic analysis (the neoclassical synthesis); a rationale for more active government management of the economy; and a particular set of policy descriptions commonly termed "countercyclical demand management."[12] The shift in thinking I am interested in is neither as elegant nor as coherently focused as Keynesianism. Its core elements can be identified fairly clearly, however.

---

[11] Although virtually all countries are moving in the same direction, they are not pursuing identical policies, and the ultimate products of their economic reversal are not likely to be the same. As I will discuss below, different countries started the process at different points, and their movements (even in the same general direction) will interact with prior events and development experiences. What I hope to explain in this chapter is the reversal in policy direction and its possible implications for governance of the international political economy.

[12] Peter Hall, ed., *The Political Power of Economic Ideas* (Princeton, NJ: Princeton University Press, 1989), pp. 363-4.

107

At the most general level, the economic reforms being pursued throughout the developing world today include a reduction *and transformation* of state economic intervention (a reversal of a principal component of Keynesianism that took root in the postwar developing world), an increased reliance on market mechanisms, more frequent use of monetarist policy instruments, and a shift in public–private relations in the direction of greater support for (and increased reliance upon) the private sector. Countries are shifting away from import substitution industrialization policies in the direction of export promotion (whether or not it involves industrial products). The specific policy measures generally associated with economic stabilization are of less significance in this analysis, since they are ordinarily short-term measures designed principally to reverse acute balance of payments deficits by generating large trade surpluses in relatively short periods of time. Of greater interest and importance is the process of structural adjustment, involving the array of policy measures designed to promote longer term economic recovery, increase economic efficiency, improve resource allocation, and enhance the adaptability of developing country economies to changes in the world economy.

Structural adjustment is primarily directed toward the medium and longer term and ordinarily entails efforts to institutionalize elements of the economic policy measures introduced initially as part of shorter term stabilization efforts. In the most general terms, structural adjustment entails a reduction and redirection of state economic intervention in the economy,[13] in combination with an increased reliance on the market for the allocation of scarce resources and commodities. Specific policy measures common to most structural adjustment programs include an effort to institutionalize nominal devaluations of the currency in order to generate and sustain *real* exchange rate adjustment. In some instances, a routine currency auction system might be instituted; while in others, some active form of exchange rate management such as a crawling peg system might be introduced, following the initial devaluation undertaken during the stabilization period.[14] The unification of multiple exchange rates might also be undertaken as part of a structural adjustment effort. Each of these measures entails an institutionalization of exchange rate adjustment

---

[13] Biersteker, "Reducing the Role of the State," p. 488.

[14] Sebastian Edwards, "Structural Adjustment Policies in Highly Indebted Countries," in Jeffrey D. Sachs, ed., *Developing Country Debt and Economic Performance* (Chicago: University of Chicago Press, 1989), p. 193.

in an effort to "get the prices right" (i.e., market determined) externally.[15]

Another component to the majority of structural adjustment programs is the effort to engage in major fiscal policy reform. Ordinarily, this means that countries are reducing (or at least constraining) the rate of growth in government spending, reforming the tax structure, rationalizing expenditure, phasing out or reducing government subsidies, and improving the efficiency of public investment (scaling down and shifting the focus from manufacturing to infrastructure and social sectors).[16]

Trade liberalization has also become a central component of virtually every structural adjustment program. Exchange rate flexibility, the elimination of trade licensing systems, the introduction of export incentives, the replacement of quantitative restrictions (QRs) by tariffs, and the general lowering of tariff levels are all being pursued (depending to a large extent on the policy environment within which the reforms are attempted).

Financial reform is another component associated with the majority of structural adjustment programs. Constraining the rate of growth of the money supply is an objective of many programs,[17] but longer term financial reform ordinarily entails some institutionalized change as well. Liberalizing foreign exchange controls is a common policy objective, as is the effort to reduce or eliminate subsidized credit (either by removing or simplifying existing ceilings on interest rates and credit).[18] The provision of preferential rates of credit for preferred borrowers unable to service their debts following a major devaluation is also a part of the general financial restructuring involved in many structural adjustment programs.[19]

A variety of other policy reforms are also being pursued, depending on the particular country context. Specific measures can include reducing price controls, ending or reducing government subsidies, adjusting agricultural pricing policy (introducing new incentive

---

[15] The World Bank does not always include exchange rate adjustment among the conditions it requires for structural adjustment loans. The IMF usually takes the lead in this area, due to the historical division of labor between the two international financial institutions. However, "governments are usually expected to establish and maintain exchange rates that are competitive internationally." World Bank, *Adjustment Lending: An Evaluation of Ten Years of Experience*, Policy & Research Series, Number 1 (Washington, DC: World Bank, 1988), p. 59.

[16] *Ibid.*, pp. 38–41. Institutional reform of public sector management is also included in many World Bank adjustment efforts.

[17] This is obviously of central concern to monetarists in the creditor countries and within the international financial institutions.

[18] World Bank, *Adjustment Lending*, p. 47.   [19] *Ibid.*

schemes), eliminating state marketing boards, and limiting wage indexation. Privatization has also been routinely prescribed as a component of most World Bank sponsored structural adjustment programs, at least since the mid-1980s, but many countries are experimenting with privatization even without World Bank encouragement.

Like the spread of Keynesian policies, the recent reversal in economic policy in the developing world has not been gradual, evenly distributed, or uniform. The process is uneven in important respects.[20] Signing an agreement with the International Monetary Fund (IMF) or the World Bank in order to reschedule accumulated debts ordinarily entails acceptance of many of these policy reforms. However, many of these policy changes have been introduced in countries without a formal Fund or Bank agreement. What is even more striking (and ultimately more important) is the number of countries that have undertaken the far more difficult task of actually implementing the policy reforms. It is here, in the implementation of economic reforms, that state organizational factors intervene, where new coalitions have to be formed, and where political-economic discourse has been directly affected by the economic policy reform process. There is little question that a major change in macroeconomic policy has taken place.[21] What is less clear, however, is precisely why this particular change has taken place (the content of policy reform), why it has occurred during the last decade (its timing), and why it has been pursued so extensively and simultaneously in so many countries of the developing world (its scope and breadth).

EXPLANATIONS FOR THE CHANGE IN ECONOMIC POLICY THINKING

On first consideration, there are a number of plausible explanations for this dramatic change in economic policy.[22] First, it is possible that developing countries may have finally "seen the light" and accepted the superiority of the liberal economic ideas they resisted for decades. This could be best described as a variant of the "social learning" explanation briefly discussed (and largely dismissed) by

[20] John Odell, *U.S. International Monetary Policy: Markets, Power and Ideas as Sources of Change* (Princeton, NJ: Princeton University Press, 1982), p. 368, describes the uneven spread of Keynesian ideas. Hall, ed., *Political Power of Economic Ideas*, also provides extensive analysis of the phenomenon.

[21] John Williamson, *The Progress of Policy Reform in Latin America* (Washington, DC: Institute for International Economics, January 1990).

[22] It is "dramatic" by virtue of the fact that so many countries have moved so far in the same policy direction in a relatively short period of time.

Kahler.[23] Second, it is possible that the changes in economic policy simply reflect the power of international financial institutions (most notably, the IMF and the World Bank) that have enforced a new market orientation in the developing world. Their power was undoubtedly enhanced significantly after the onset of the 1981 global recession, the ensuing global debt crisis,[24] and the continuing debt overhang. Third, perhaps changes in the global market (such as the globalization of production and increased competition), along with the evident success of export-oriented development regimes have forced countries to engage in a fundamental rethinking of their economic policy. Or fourth, perhaps it is the exhaustion of prior models of accumulation (notably import substitution industrialization [ISI]),[25] and/or the collapse of socialism as an alternative model of development that has encouraged the recent policy transformation.

While any one of these explanations is no doubt at least partially correct and might be a useful place to begin, each of them is rather oversimplified and can be easily dismissed as a general explanation of the phenomenon.[26] In an effort to evaluate different explanations, I will begin by differentiating between four major varieties of explanation that have emerged in most of the discussion of this issue to date: systemic explanations, domestic interest explanations, international institutional explanations, and ideational explanations. Each of these should be considered as an idealized construction, designed to identify and differentiate between different explanations on the basis of their *principal* point of departure. In a later section I will present a more integrated explanation synthesizing core elements from several of them.

Systems level and systemic explanations

Systems level or systemic explanations would explain the change in developing country economic policy by first examining the ways in which changes in global economic conditions are likely to force

---

[23] Miles Kahler in Nelson, ed., *Economic Crisis and Policy Choice*, ch. 2.

[24] Manuel Pastor reflects on this issue in his book, *The International Monetary Fund and Latin America: Economic Stabilization and Class Conflict* (Boulder, CO: Westview Press, 1987).

[25] Alain Lipietz, "How Monetarism Has Choked Third World Industrialization," *New Left Review*, no. 145 (1984).

[26] Many scholarly explorations of this issue combine several explanations in some form. For example, Kahler combines systemic change with ideational influences and domestic politics in his explanation in Nelson, ed., *Economic Crisis and Policy Choice*.

changes within states.[27] That is, developments such as the globalization of production,[28] the general increase in economic competition, and/or growing concerns about the potential for protectionism (as regional trade groups in North America and East Asia develop as defensive responses to increased European integration) might on their own (or in some combination) change the environment of the international political economy in which all countries exist. Simply put, this new global economic environment might have forced developing countries to choose between joining the world economy or being marginalized from it.[29] Participation in the world economy was historically viewed rather benignly as "mutually beneficial" for the developing countries. Today it is increasingly viewed as "imperative" for them.[30]

A global shock, such as the petroleum price hikes of the 1970s or the deep recession of the early 1980s, might intensify and accelerate these general trends. Other system level arguments might include the exhaustion of prior models of accumulation on a global scale (e.g., the growing fiscal deficits produced by the failure of import substitution models of development and the increased unwillingness of transnational banks to provide any more credit in the early 1980s).[31] The political and economic liberalization sweeping Eastern and Central Europe in 1989 and 1990 might be another example of a system-wide shock, a point that will be developed more fully below.

This general argument might be viewed as an international political economy analog of Kenneth Waltz's idea that individual states become socialized into certain patterns of behavior in the international system.[32] In the particular instance of change being considered here, however, changes in the nature (rather than the structure) of economic

[27] This might be considered a variant of the second image reversed, see especially, Peter Gourevitch, "The Second Image Reversed: The International Sources of Domestic Politics," *International Organization*, 32 (Autumn 1978).

[28] Robert W. Cox, *Production, Power, and World Order: Social Forces in the Making of History* (New York: Columbia University Press, 1987), p. 244.

[29] Robert Gilpin attributes this general view to economic liberalism, which posits that "Inefficient actors are forced to adjust their behavior and to innovate or else face economic extinction," in *The Political Economy of International Relations* (Princeton, NJ: Princeton University Press, 1987), p. 67.

[30] Even scholars not typically associated with liberal internationalism have begun to express a variant of this view. See especially, Richard J. Barnett, "But What About Africa? On the Global Economy's Lost Continent," *Harper's Magazine* (May 1990).

[31] The contradictions contained within those prior models of accumulation may provide the basis for their change and transformation. The work of the French regulation school provides a good example of this kind of systemic argument about crises of capitalism. See especially, Alain Lipietz, *Mirages and Miracles: The Crises of Global Fordism* (London: Verso, New Left Books, 1987).

[32] Kenneth N. Waltz, *Theory of International Politics* (Reading, MA: Addison-Wesley, 1979).

conditions, i.e., the operation of basic market forces, appear to be producing the socialization of developing countries in the international political economy. Only the "fittest" are likely to survive in this new, increasingly competitive environment. States that adapt their economic policies to respond receptively (both flexibly and favorably) to these changing global conditions will do well, or at least have a better chance of doing well, in the increasingly competitive world economy. Those that do not adapt their policies will fare relatively more poorly (certainly in comparison to how well they would perform if they had adapted more receptively to global market changes).[33] Robert Cox has characterized this general phenomenon as the "internationalization of the state" or "the global process whereby national policies and practices have been adjusted to the exigencies of the world economy of international production."[34]

While many countries have historically been tempted at one point or another to pursue some form of autarky or relatively more inward-oriented development,[35] a systems level argument would examine the way they are eventually forced back into the fold (or self-destruct and become marginalized, as Argentina has experienced throughout the course of the twentieth century).[36] States, even in the developing world, are accorded an important degree of rationality in systems level explanations. It is assumed that they can discern the direction of change underway in the global economy and learn from the experiences of their past, as well as from each other.

Although it is possible to obtain a great many insights from examining systemic changes in the global economy, there are also problems using this level of explanation to describe the dramatic change that has taken place in the economic policy of developing countries in recent years. First, systems level explanations ordinarily do not specify which global developments or forces have actually *caused* the change. Is it caused by the globalization of production, the increase

---

[33] There is an important counterfactual assumption imbedded in the argument here, namely that the range of alternative policy responses is severely limited.

[34] Cox, *Production, Power, and World Order*, p. 253.

[35] This has been an important theoretical response to liberal economic policies ever since David Ricardo first extended Adam Smith's ideas about the operations of the market to the international arena. See especially Friedrich List, *Das nationale System der politischen Okonomie* (Tübingen: Mohr Verlag, 1959; 1st edn., 1841) and Mihail Manoilesco, *le Siècle du Corporatisme* (Paris: F. Alcan, 1934). These ideas reached their greatest influence in the post-World War II developing world during the 1950s in the form of the prescriptions of ECLA and later of UNCTAD. They also found important expression in the writings of dependency theorists in the 1960s and 1970s.

[36] Carlos Waisman, *Reversal of Development in Argentina* (Princeton, NJ: Princeton University Press, 1987).

in competition, the exhaustion of a mode of capitalist regulation, the prospect of increased protectionism, or the sudden shocks produced by oil price increases and global recession? Furthermore, should economic systems change (the globalization of production or increased competition) be given precedence over the effects of political systems change (the end of the Cold War)? Second, systems level explanations cannot answer the question of precisely *why* the change is taking place now. After all, it was possible to identify all of these global systemic changes (with the exception of the sudden shocks) as having been on the increase since the 1960s, possibly even earlier in some instances. They were certainly apparent during the 1970s, yet that decade was most assertively a period of radical statism and economic nationalism. The only way for system level arguments to explain the timing is to assert the presence of lags, combined with the gradual effects of the training of rational technocrats, or some kind of learning. Third, the argument as presented implies there is some natural evolution (or gradual progression) toward convergence in economic policy. How can we be sure, however, that the present convergence of policy thinking is not a temporary, momentary, or transitional phenomenon? Fourth and finally, systems explanations have relatively little to say about either the precise content or the direction of the shift in thinking.

Domestic interest explanations

Interest-based arguments have received an increasing amount of attention (and influence) during the 1980s as general sources of explanation for political behavior (e.g., rational choice explanations, formal theory, game theoretic models, etc.). If domestic interest explanations are used to explain the recent transformation in developing country economic thinking, one would begin by first examining the breakdown of the old development coalitions. The bureaucratic, authoritarian regimes of the past were increasingly unable to deliver the promise of development (on which their legitimacy was principally based). Therefore, new interests have increasingly come forward to challenge the prior bases of statist, redistributive, inward-oriented, authoritarian regimes.[37] There has, therefore, been an interest-driven demand for a major change in economic policy, derived at least in part

[37] Some of the early work on political transitions from authoritarian rule in Latin America produced arguments along these general lines. See especially the summary presented by Guillermo O'Donnell and Philippe C. Schmitter, *Transitions from Authoritarian Rule: Tentative Conclusions about Uncertain Democracies* (Baltimore, MD, and London: Johns Hopkins University Press, 1986).

from a populist rejection of statism,[38] and partially from the emergence of new economic elite interests dissatisfied with excessive state intervention in the economy. While principal business interests in the past may have sought state intervention in certain sectors (frequently in their efforts to stave off competitive challenges from multinational corporations), they are increasingly turning away from that general mode of articulation with the state. Local business elites have a great deal to gain from economic liberalization and are today more likely to demand a reduction of state intervention and more room for their own expansion.

Once again, as in the case of systems level explanations, there are a number of important insights from interest explanations, and they are especially useful for making assessments of the potential long-term institutionalization of the change in economic policy. However, while there may have been a general demand for *some* kind of change in economic policy, the specific type of policy change that has emerged (the "triumph" of neoclassical economics) has not in most instances emanated from civil society or from organized entities within it. There is a general paradox here, produced by the fact that much of the change is being driven by a politically insulated state, often in the face of strong opposition from many politically significant, entrenched interests.[39] Economic reform is often undertaken at the immediate, short-term expense of those well-established interests (the historical beneficiaries of state subsidies, overvalued exchange rates, high tariffs, and import licensing arrangements). It is being undertaken in the kind of states Robert Cox has characterized as "neomercantilist developmentalist states," those "not sustained in any coherent way by internal social forces."[40]

Thus it is difficult to identify the interest-based sources of the "demand" for this particular form of policy change in the developing world. While there are certainly some beneficiaries of the policy changes, they have not consistently organized themselves to obtain or pursue their material interests in a deliberate, rational manner.[41] Interest explanations appear more suited to explain the potential bases of opposition to economic reforms than account for the origins of support for them. The greatest explanatory power from interest approaches may ultimately come from their ability to evaluate the

---

[38] Hernando de Soto, *The Other Path* (New York: Harper & Row, 1989).
[39] Stephan Haggard makes this argument in "The Politics of Adjustment: Lessons from the IMF's Extended Fund Facility," *International Organization*, 39 (Summer 1985).
[40] Cox, *Production, Power, and World Order*, p. 230.
[41] James M. Cypher, *State and Capital in Mexico* (Boulder, CO: Westview Press, 1990).

construction of the new coalitions needed to sustain and institutionalize the economic reforms over the longer term.

In the final analysis, interest explanations have relatively little to say about the sudden and dramatic change of economic policy throughout the developing world.[42] There has certainly been no *demand* for the austerity that accompanies virtually all economic reform efforts, and yet virtually every country of the developing world has been moving in that direction, even if the movement is occasionally halting at times.

International institutional explanations

In many ways, both the IMF and the World Bank (IBRD) appear to have become suddenly far more effective during the 1980s than they have been in the recent past. They loom especially large in many of the poorest and most heavily indebted developing countries in Africa. The international financial institutions are involved in significant aspects of the economic policy-making process of most countries in the developing world today. The Bank and the Fund can use positive inducements to encourage policy change by rewarding those countries that implement and sustain economic reforms and punishing or sanctioning those that deviate (as both Peru and Brazil learned in the late 1980s). The global financial regime (and its particular manifestation in the post-1982 debt regime) have enhanced the role of the international financial institutions and made them the principal international representatives of the established order.[43]

An institutional explanation might focus on how the international financial institutions have used their time-tested, well-established (path-dependent) routines of conditional lending to ensure that borrowing countries make substantial changes in their economic policies. Scholars associated with the dependency tradition have frequently articulated one version of this general view.[44] From their

[42] This conclusion will, of course, vary from country to country. Interest-based explanations are likely to have greater utility in Latin American countries with a longer development of the institutions of civil society than in Africa, where the state has historically had relatively greater autonomy from civil society.

[43] The IMF in particular plays a critical role in the current financial regime. The presence of an agreement with the Fund is a prerequisite for Paris and London Club debt rescheduling agreements.

[44] See especially Cheryl Payer, *The Debt Trap* (New York and London: Monthly Review Press, 1974), for an early articulation of this view. For a more recent and more sophisticated version of the argument, see Pastor, *The International Monetary Fund and Latin America.*

standpoint, the IMF and the World Bank have *real* financial power, and they appear increasingly willing to use it to force changes in the economic policies of developing countries. From a dependency variant of the institutional approach, the developing countries would *never*, on their own volition, have embarked upon these particular reforms (or done so with such apparent "enthusiasm") if it were not for the coercive power of the international financial institutions. The economic reforms are likely to be viewed as having been forced on debt-dependent regimes against the wishes and the interests of the vast majority of their populations.

In spite of their increased visibility and their apparent ability to influence change in developing countries, the international financial institutions deny that they have much effective power and influence.[45] Many IMF and World Bank staff members describe themselves as frequently frustrated by "intransigent" governments in the developing world that sign agreements and fail to meet the performance criteria established at the time of initial agreement. Suspensions of formal agreements with the IMF are certainly not an unusual phenomenon.[46] However, individuals within powerful institutions rarely describe or recognize themselves as "powerful," and their realization (or denial) of it does not help us evaluate the significance of their intervention.

As the world economy has changed during the last two decades, both the IMF and the World Bank have added new programs, new adjustment facilities, and revised their thinking on a number of important issues.[47] In spite of these adjustments, however, there have been no substantial changes in some basic aspects of their operations. Both institutions still engage in conditional lending and make their resources available in exchange for commitments from recipient states about reforms in their economic policies. Furthermore, the core models from which their specific economic policy prescriptions are derived are essentially unaltered.[48] While both of the international financial

---

[45] The policy evaluation literature is full of references to the limits of their effectiveness. See especially the World Bank's *Adjustment Lending* and Morris Goldstein, *The Global Effects of Fund-Supported Adjustment Programs,* Occasional Paper No. 42 (Washington, DC: IMF, 1986).

[46] Stephan Haggard reported that out of a sample of thirty adjustment programs launched under the Fund's Extended Fund Facility (EFF), twenty-four were renegotiated, interrupted, or allowed to lapse "virtually all for noncompliance," in "The Politics of Adjustment," pp. 505–6.

[47] Kahler, in Nelson, ed., *Economic Crisis and Policy Crisis.*

[48] Lance Taylor argues that they are still based on Polak's 1957 model in *Varieties of Stabilization Experience* (Oxford: Oxford University Press, 1988).

institutions are increasingly aware that an understanding of domestic politics in developing countries is important for the effectiveness of their policy advice, there is no evidence that significant changes in their political analysis could explain their sudden effectiveness throughout the developing world. Moreover, there are some countries that have embarked on structural adjustment programs without the presence of a formal program endorsed by the IMF, suggesting that the presence of the international financial institutions may not even be a necessary condition for change.[49]

Thus, although the IMF and the World Bank are now playing a far more prominent role in the developing world (certainly in contrast to their role in the middle and late 1970s), it is not because they have changed their basic operating procedures to any significant degree. They have been pursuing the same arguments (and the same general prescriptions) for decades. It was only during the 1980s that they suddenly appeared to have become so much more effective. While there was little new in the internal operation of either the IMF or the World Bank that could readily explain their sudden influence in the 1980s, there was an important change in the World Bank administration in 1981, when A. W. Clausen succeeded Robert McNamara as President.[50] The appointment was made by President Carter in consultation with President-elect Ronald Reagan, an interaction that leads to a fourth possible explanation for the change in developing country policy: the role of ideas.

Ideational explanations

In many important respects, the major changes in developing country economic policy are parallel to, and closely followed important changes in, economic policy in the leading advanced industrial economies of the world: the United States, the United Kingdom, and Germany. Margaret Thatcher came to power in Great Britain in 1979, followed shortly thereafter by Ronald Reagan in the United States and Helmut Kohl in Germany. Although there is much debate about the long-term legacy of each of these political leaders, there is little doubt that they reversed decades of economic policy in their respective countries. Since the U.S. remains at least arguably hegemonic (at least

[49] Timothy M. Shaw and Rob Davies, "Adjustment without the IMF: The Political Economy of Liberalization in Zimbabwe," paper presented at the annual meeting of the International Studies Association, Washington, DC, April 1990.
[50] Robert Ayres, *Banking on the Poor* (Cambridge, MA: MIT Press, 1983).

118

in a Gramscian sense), changes within the United States might be expected to spread and reverberate throughout the rest of the world. Although he did not spend a great deal of time thinking about development issues, Ronald Reagan did address some of the issues at the last major global conference on development at Cancun in 1981, where he called for the developing world to get its house in order and allow the "magic of the market" to do its work.

However, one does not need to rely on assertions of major power ideological hegemony to illustrate the potential persuasive power of ideas. Within the scholarly community, neoclassical economic ideas have most certainly been around for a long time, but they clearly gained new force, visibility, and legitimacy in the late 1970s and early 1980s through a series of influential publications highly critical of much of the prevailing economic policy in the developing world. The influential National Bureau of Economic Research (NBER) studies on the advantages of liberal exchange regimes in the late 1970s provided a theoretical explanation for the emerging newly industrialized countries of East Asia.[51] The important Berg report on Africa in 1981,[52] studies of the urban bias in development,[53] and forceful rational choice critiques of the distorting effects of government policy intervention which appeared in the early 1980s[54] all contributed significantly to the critique of prevailing developing country economic policy. Economists like Peter Bauer turned many dependency arguments on their head with his polemical treatises on the importance of further integration with the world economy and his calls for a rethinking of basic development issues.[55]

At the same time, the new industrializing countries (the NICs) of East Asia were increasingly differentiating themselves from the rest of the "Third World" and were widely viewed as evidence of the virtues of turning away from import substitution industrialization, of reducing the role of the state in the economy, and of greater integration into the world economy more generally. They provided important international

[51] Anne O. Kreuger, *Liberalization Attempts and Consequences* (New York: National Bureau of Economic Research, 1978) and Jagdish N. Bhagwati, *Anatomy and Consequences of Exchange Control* (Cambridge, MA: Ballinger, 1978).

[52] World Bank, *Accelerated Development in Sub-Saharan Africa: An Agenda for Action* (The Berg Report), Report No. 3358 (Washington, DC: IBRD, 1981).

[53] Michael Lipton, *Why Poor People Stay Poor: Urban Bias in World Development* (Cambridge, MA: Harvard University Press, 1977).

[54] Robert Bates, *Markets and States in Tropical Africa* (Berkeley, CA: University of California Press, 1981), and Goran Hyden, *No Shortcuts to Progress* (Berkeley, CA: University of California Press, 1983).

[55] Peter Bauer, *Equality, the Third World, and Economic Delusion* (Cambridge, MA: Harvard University Press, 1981).

demonstration effects of the possibility of an alternative to prevailing economic policy.[56]

Ideas may come to play an important independent explanatory role by way of several different processes. There may be general contagion effects and international "policy emulation," as in the case of the NICs,[57] or a trickle-up process where ideas gain initial acceptance among academic economists who subsequently press their policy advice on the political leadership. The reception of ideas is likely to be contingent on the institutional configuration of the state, its prior policy experiences (and recent failings), as well as on their political viability (i.e., their ability to mobilize support among existing coalitions or their ability to forge new coalitions and hold them together).[58] Ideas can facilitate the formation of political coalitions of interest groups that might not otherwise have emerged (or seen their interests as overlapping) if they had never been articulated.

Like each of the previous explanations, ideational ones are initially quite plausible and appealing. Ideas are certainly important for an explanation of the *content* of the change in economic policy and there were a number of rather zealous advocates of "new" economic thinking during the early 1980s. However, ideas also need an enabling environment in which to take root and flourish. As Peter Hall has suggested, "Ideas have real power in the political world, [but] they do not acquire political force independently of the constellation of institutions and interests already present there."[59]

As suggested above, the basic ideas have been around for quite some time. Although many of the scholarly works cited above exhibited high academic standards, there is little evidence that it was the particular academic expression of the ideas in the late 1970s and early 1980s that was especially important in policy decision-making within developing countries. Developing country decision-makers are not likely to have

---

[56] The current economic policy transformation underway in Eastern and Central Europe further reinforces the idea that there are few alternatives available to developing countries, although it cannot be used to explain the initial change in developing country economic policy orientation in most instances. The recent European developments are more significant for an explanation of the current international pressures to liberalize political systems in the developing world.

[57] John Ikenberry calls this "policy bandwagoning" in his paper "The International Spread of Privatization Policies: Inducements, Learning, and 'Policy Bandwagoning'" (Center for International Studies, Princeton University, 1988).

[58] Margaret Weir and Theda Skocpol, "State Structures and the Possibilities for 'Keynesian' Responses to the Great Depression in Sweden, Britain, and the United States," in Peter B. Evans, Dietrich Rueschemeyer, and Theda Skocpol, eds., *Bringing the State Back In* (Cambridge: Cambridge University Press, 1985).

[59] Hall, ed., *Political Power of Economic Ideas*, p. 390.

read Peter Bauer and been persuaded about the need for policy change. Indeed, a World Bank publication like the 1981 Berg report was roundly criticized by state elites throughout Africa when it first appeared. However, those same elites might have been persuaded by the arguments articulated by local economists. Ideas that have the capacity to empower or enhance the position of nascent local allies (often preexisting, recessive advocates of a particular policy position or view) are likely to have greater influence and potential impact than those which are entirely imported.

Furthermore, the mechanisms for the transmission of ideas are not always clear. Although there were critical cadres of economists in some instances (such as the "Chicago boys" in Chile in the mid-1970s), in other countries there is less evidence of the presence of anything resembling an "epistemic community" capable of formulating programs and obtaining their acceptance within governments.[60] In many instances, state bureaucracies remained sharply divided, and particular policy choices emerged in the aftermath of an internal bureaucratic struggle over different alternatives.[61]

TOWARD AN INTEGRATED EXPLANATION

When considered separately, each of the preceding explanations is plausible up to a certain point, but none is sufficient when considered alone. Systems level explanations cannot readily explain why the change in economic policy took place in the 1980s, or why it has been so sudden and far-reaching. Domestic interest explanations cannot explain the particular content of the economic policy change, especially given the number of entrenched interests adversely affected

---

[60] Peter M. Haas elaborates on the idea of the potential influence of epistemic communities in his book, *Saving the Mediterranean: The Politics of International Environmental Cooperation* (New York: Columbia University Press, 1990). However, in a number of countries in the developing world, there is only fragmentary evidence of the presence or an influence group of Chicago, Manchester, or Austrian trained economists. For discussions of Nigeria, the Philippines, Ghana, and Mexico, see especially Thomas J. Biersteker, "Reaching Agreement with the IMF: The Nigerian Negotiations, 1983–1986," in Thomas J. Biersteker, ed., *International Financial Negotiations* (Boulder, CO: Westview Press, 1992); Penelope A. Walker, "Political Crisis and Debt Negotiations: The Case of the Philippines, 1983–1986," also in Biersteker, ed., *International Financial Negotiations*; E. Gyimah-Boadi, "Economic Recovery and Politics in the PNDC's Ghana" (Department of Political Science, University of Ghana, Legon, 1989); and Cypher, *State and Capital in Mexico*.

[61] Emanuel Adler, "Ideological 'Guerrillas' and the Quest for Technological Autonomy: Brazil's Domestic Computer Industry," *International Organization*, 40, 3 (Summer 1986). See also Thomas J. Biersteker, *Multinationals, the State, and Control of the Nigerian Economy* (Princeton, NJ: Princeton University Press, 1987), ch. 7.

by the economic reforms. International institutional explanations alone cannot explain why the IMF has suddenly become more influential or why countries without an IMF program are similarly engaged in economic reform efforts. Ideational explanations generally require additional factors such as an enabling environment that includes both institutions and interests.

The different explanations can, however, be combined into an integrated explanation that can explain both the timing and the content of the change in economic policy. At the most general level, systemic changes in the world economy have provided the foundation for the transformation in economic policy in the developing world. A consistent increase in the globalization of production, accompanied by increased competition, a slowing of the rate of growth, and a general drying up of financial resources have forced all developing countries to focus more intensely on their relationship with (and competitiveness within) the world economy. This provides a background for, but not a sufficient explanation of, the transformation of economic policy. It took a particular system-wide shock to prompt a major reversal in policy.

The global recession that afflicted the economies of the advanced industrial world between 1980 and 1983 provoked a depression throughout most of the developing world. It was a critical event, a shock that reverberated throughout Africa, Asia, and Latin America, with different manifestations in each region. In Africa, the recession triggered a collapse in commodity prices, followed by an unsustainable debt burden. In Latin America (and some parts of Africa and East Asia), the recession triggered the global debt crisis, followed by the lingering debt overhang. In the countries of East Asia, the recession increased competition, reduced the total volume of world trade, prompted some protectionism, and slowed growth appreciably. Because this system-wide shock was transmitted to different parts of the developing world through the different filtering mechanisms of their mode of integration with the world economy, it affected different countries in different ways and at different times.

Higher interest rates in the OECD countries triggered the debt crisis, first in Mexico and subsequently throughout the rest of Latin America. It was made a continent-wide (and eventually a global) phenomenon by the reactions of the transnational banks during 1983. Most of the countries of Africa were affected by the collapse in commodity prices, which accompanied the global slowdown. Non-oil commodity prices dropped precipitously in 1982 to levels not previously seen since the end of World War II. The general slowdown in global production

122

contributed to a glut in the supply of oil that hit the oil-exporting countries with a lag in 1985, when global petroleum prices plummeted. While the export-dependent NICs of East Asia had a relatively less difficult time with the economic slowdown, the total volume of world trade fell in real terms throughout the 1980s.[62]

The 1980s recession provoked a rethinking of the basis of economic policy throughout the developing world. In a great many countries there was a growing sense of failure, a belief that the policies of the past had failed in some way, and that something new should be considered. Each successive development decade provoked more cynicism, and there was serious disillusionment with the outcome of economic nationalism. Cartels (outside of OPEC) had proven disappointing, nationalized firms had become fiscal burdens for the state, indigenized enterprises yielded little effective managerial control, and national self-reliance proved virtually unattainable.[63] Thus, the direction of the dramatic change in policy was at least partially a product of a dialectical reaction against the economic policies of the past.[64] There was, therefore, a crucial opening for new ideas.

"New" statements of neoclassical economic ideas were plentiful in the early 1980s, largely built upon critiques of previous approaches to development. These ideas emanated from the centers of world power, the U.S. and the U.K., as well as from the powerful international financial institutions, the IMF and the World Bank. The NICs provided the successful role models for the international demonstration effects of these ideas.

Before they could be persuasive and eventually realized as economic policy practice, however, these ideas needed both interests and institutional bases of support in the developing world. The individuals who articulated the critiques of the policy failures of the past became the first interests (located principally within the state) for economic reform. In most instances, the "demand" for policy reversal came from techno-cratic entry points for new thinking (from economic policy epistemic communities) located within the state. Although these factions were present in small numbers before the early 1980s, the magnitude of the

---

[62] Michael Todaro, *Economic Development in the Third World* (New York and London: Longman, 1989), p. 369.
[63] Thomas J. Biersteker, "The Limits of State Power in the Contemporary World Economy," in Henry Shue and Peter G. Brown, eds., *Boundaries: National Autonomy and its Limits* (Tatawa, NJ: Rowman and Littlefield, 1981).
[64] This is akin to Albert O. Hirschman's idea of the importance of disappointment in the shifting involvements between public and private as considered in his *Shifting Involvements: Private Interest and Public Action* (Princeton, NJ: Princeton University Press, 1982).

economic crisis provided them with an opportunity to articulate an alternative set of policies.

These nascent interests were given crucial international institutional backing from the IMF and the World Bank. There was a pronounced increase in the willingness to use the Fund and the Bank to force changes in developing country economic policy during the early 1980s, especially· on the part of the government of the United States. In general terms, ideas backed with power (and a willingness or eagerness to use that power) are more likely to be influential.

Thus, it appears that systemic change, interests (recently mobilized) within the state, international institutions and ideas all played a role in explaining the dramatic change in developing country economic policy in the early 1980s. However, they did not play an equal role in the dramatic change in policy orientation. On reflection, three factors appear critical: (1) the deep economic shock of the early 1980s recession, (2) the fact that this system-wide shock coincided with an historical opening (the perceived failure of the policies of the past), and (3) the ascendance of an epistemic community within the state committed to neoclassical ideas and reinforced strongly by the actions of international institutions.

It is difficult to imagine the scope and magnitude of the changes in economic policy in the absence of the global economic shock which magnified the sense of failure of the past. If it were not for the debt and government fiscal crises confronting so many developing countries, along with the drying up of alternative sources of finance,[65] few countries of the developing world would voluntarily have embarked upon such sweeping and generally unpopular reforms. However, while the systemic shock may have been necessary for the global policy shift, it did not take place within a vacuum. The content and particular direction of the change (the content of the economic reforms) was critically influenced by the historical legacy of statist developmentalism and the presence of an articulated alternative to the past in an atmosphere of a perceived absence of other alternatives. The "new" economic thinking was articulated by a small, but critically placed

---

[65] Robert Kaufman and Stephan Haggard stress the importance of the presence (or absence) or access to international finance in their chapter, "The Politics of Stabilization and Structural Adjustment," in Sachs, ed., *Developing Country Debt and Economic Performance*. Robert Cox makes a similar argument about the importance of finance when he writes: "international finance is the preeminent agency of conformity to world-hegemonic order and the principal regulator of the political and productive organization of a hegemonic world economy." Cox, *Production, Power, and World Order*, p. 267.

Table 1. *Schematic summary of an integrated explanation for the "triumph" of neoclassical economics in the developing world*

Deep GLOBAL RECESSION (early 1980s)

in the midst of secular trends:
1. globalization of production
2. increase in competitive pressures
3. exhaustion of prior models (ISI)

combined with the effective introduction of

NEOCLASSICAL IDEAS

(initially articulated in the U.S. and U.K., strongly backed
by International INSTITUTIONS, the IMF and the IBRD)
invigorated and empowered

⇓

Nascent domestic INTERESTS (within the state)
who forced through (or forged) new coalitions which produced

Major CHANGE in ECONOMIC POLICY Direction

(whose sustainability is contingent on the extent to which it can
create new interests)

emergent epistemic community within the state, powerfully backed by the IMF and the World Bank.[66]

Although their articulation was necessary, the mere presence of the ideas by themselves was not sufficient to bring about the policy change. The ideas needed an enabling environment (the major external shock, the perceived failure of the past, domestic articulators, and international institutional backing) to have major effects. If they ultimately succeed and produce sustained, non-inflationary, economic growth in developing countries, the neoclassical ideas (along with the policies they provoked) should begin to create and mobilize their own interests. Interests therefore are not just potential sources of ideational change, they can also be the object (or creation) of ideational change. Table 1 provides a schematic summary of the integrated explanation elaborated above.

In the final analysis, domestic interest-based explanations appear to have provided surprisingly little to the explanation of the recent

---

[66] The influence of institutions like the IMF and the World Bank was enhanced by the conjuncture of systemic crisis and the historical legacy of past policy experiences (and the perception of their failure).

transformation of economic policy in the developing world.[67] Potential interests simultaneously exist within the state for a number of different policy directions. For example, advocates of state intervention remain within most developing countries to this day, but their ideas are recessive for the time being. They can be mobilized and might even become effective again, if given voice by external shocks, resources from external institutions (or other sources), or the "heavy hand" of historical experience (that is, by some future perception of the failure of the current round of economic policy reform). It is for this reason that another system-wide shock in the early 1990s could well bring about another reversal in policy direction, particularly if countries pursuing economic reforms cannot soon demonstrate significant economic accomplishments in performance terms.[68]

IMPLICATIONS OF THE "NEW" ORDER

Depth and sustainability

The depth and sustainability of the new direction in economic policy in the developing world is largely contingent on its success in economic performance terms. As suggested above, if they succeed in performance terms, the economic reforms should be able to create domestic interests dedicated to defending the programs. It is in this sense that interests can be the creation of ideational change. If the new policy directions do not succeed in performance terms (even marginally), they are not likely to be sustained over the medium to longer term.[69]

There is already some evidence that policy disappointments and failures are emerging in several critically placed African countries, especially those which have produced few or only limited successes to date. The military regimes that introduced the economic reforms in both Ghana and Nigeria have increasingly found themselves with a

---

[67] I do not mean to imply that interest-based explanations are "falsified" in some manner, but rather that they appear surprisingly limited in their explanatory contribution in this particular instance of economic policy change.

[68] Thus, the stakes for the international financial institutions and advocates of economic reform are *extremely* high at present.

[69] A good test of this hypothesis would be possible if economic policy reforms are sustained in countries where they have failed in performance terms. Nigeria should be an interesting test case to consider, especially if its economic performance does not improve appreciably before its transition from military rule in 1992.

narrowing of their political base.[70] Without any significant economic successes to their credit, the legitimacy of their rule is increasingly under challenge.

The future course in much of Latin America is also uncertain at present. The sheer magnitude of the region's debt overhang, combined with the continued absence of any significant debt relief, makes the situation in Brazil and Argentina relatively precarious.[71] The principal exception to the pattern appears to be Mexico, which has benefited from its proximity to the United States and the inflow of new investment into its northern border region (at least partially in anticipation of an expanded North American free trade zone). Mexico might be in a position to achieve some performance successes from its economic liberalization program. However, the Mexican state has yet to broaden the political coalition on behalf of economic policy reform much beyond the immediate beneficiaries located in some sectors of the business community.[72]

The situation in East Asia appears relatively more promising for the continuation of the economic reform measures. The successful NICs (Hong Kong, Singapore, South Korea, and Taiwan) have already benefited from the "new" models and begun to develop influential domestic coalitions for their continuation.[73] Major questions, however, remain about the "near-NICs" (such as Thailand and Malaysia). If the recession of the early 1990s worsens appreciably, and trade barriers begin to increase on a global scale, the depth and sustainability of their economic reform programs are likely to appear far less certain.

Thus, the apparent "convergence" in economic policy thinking in the developing world may prove to be a momentary, transitory, or even illusory phenomenon of the late 1980s. Much depends on whether the policy measures begin to yield some tangible successes in economic

---

[70] Gyimah-Boadi, "Economic Recovery and Politics in the PNDC's Ghana." See also, Thomas J. Biersteker, "The Relationship between Political and Economic Reforms: Structural Adjustment and the Political Transition in Nigeria," in Thomas J. Biersteker, ed., *Economic Crisis, Structural Adjustment, and the Political Transitions in Nigeria* (forthcoming).

[71] Andrew Hurrell, "Brazilian Foreign Policy under Collor," paper delivered at the Latin American Studies Center seminar, Oxford University, June 1990.

[72] Cypher, *State and Capital in Mexico*. A similar point was made by Professor Soledad Loaeza at the California–Mexico Project seminar, "The Right and the Shaping of Political Change in Mexico," School of International Relations, University of Southern California, October 24, 1990.

[73] Michael Shafer, *Sectors, States, and Social Forces: Towards a New Comparative Political Economy of Development* (Draft manuscript, Department of Political Science, Rutgers University, New Brunswick, NJ, 1990). See also Stephan Haggard, *Partners from the Periphery* (Ithaca, NY: Cornell University Press, 1990).

performance terms. If they do, they may be able to create the interests necessary for their long-term institutionalization. If they do not, the present economic order (by which I mean the convergence in economic policy across territorial boundaries) may prove to be ephemeral. Although many countries have been moving in the same direction (away from the statist, inward-oriented, economic nationalism of the 1970s), it is important to remember that they began at very different starting points, have achieved different successes to date, and may eventually end up in very different places.

Potential consequences

If the economic reforms prove to be more than an ephemeral phenomenon, it is possible to speculate about what they might make possible (as well as what they might at the same time proscribe or deny). How are different parts of the developing world likely to fit into a changing international political economy?

Current investment and trade patterns suggest a continuation of the emergence of three major trading regions: one based on the United States, one based on the European Community, and one based on Japan.[74] Countries on the immediate periphery of these regions could end up playing important roles as low-wage production sites for the three largest markets in the world. Countries on their periphery (the periphery of the periphery) are more likely to be marginalized from the emerging trade areas, due in part to their distance from, and the costs of transportation to, each of the three major economic powers, but also to their initial exclusion from the emerging trade areas.

Developing countries that continue the process of economic reform will have the potential to join in an expanded regionalized world political economy (following the recession of the early 1990s). In order to participate, however, they will have to maintain flexible payments regimes, as well as general openness to both trade and investment from other countries within the regions. The international trading system may not have been able to absorb many other new NICs after the major trade expansion of the 1970s,[75] but a few carefully selected countries may be accorded special status with the emerging trading communities. Trade access is likely to become an ever more important issue for

[74] Gilpin, *Political Economy of International Relations*, ch. 10, especially pp. 389–96.
[75] William Cline, "Can the East Asian Model of Development be Generalized?," in Charles Wilber, ed., *The Political Economy of Development and Underdevelopment* (New York: Random House, 1984).

128

developing countries. As long as the Cold War defined strategic allies in the developing world, non-economic factors played an important role in determining the principal beneficiaries of aid, finance, and investment. With the rapid diminution of the Cold War, the pursuit of economic policy reform is likely to loom ever larger as a criterion for major participation in the emerging international division of labor. "Strategically" placed countries such as Zaire, Egypt, and the Philippines that routinely escaped careful scrutiny of their economic policies during the height of the Cold War may find themselves in a very different position in the emerging world order.

Mexico is a likely candidate for such a role in the North American market, and the reforming countries of Central and Eastern Europe (with their skilled, relatively low-wage labor forces) are likely to play a similar role for the expanded European Community market after 1992. There may be some additional room for the NICs, especially if China continues its slow pace of reform and incorporation into the world economy after Hong Kong is absorbed in 1997.

Other countries, however, are likely to become increasingly marginalized. As Gilpin suggests, "The tendency toward greater regionalization means that large segments of the human race will undoubtedly be excluded from the world economy."[76] This is especially true for most of Africa, as well as for some of the smaller countries of South Asia and Latin America unable to penetrate any of the major regional markets. A few of the larger countries of the developing world may eventually go their own way and pursue other strategies. Thus in spite of the general convergence in the direction of policy during the last few years, we have probably not reached the "end of history."

The economic policy convergence throughout the developing world may facilitate (though not guarantee) trade access, as well as make it possible for certain developing countries to regain limited access to scarce international finance, as both Chile and Mexico have experienced in recent years. For formerly centrally planned economies, some elements of the economic policy convergence (such as the recognition of property rights and the greater reliance on the use of market mechanisms for allocative decisions) are minimal requirements for their membership in the international financial organizations. However, while economic policy convergence facilitates some developments, it simultaneously proscribes others. Major redistributive social welfare programs, infant industry protection, and a variety of forms of

---

[76] Gilpin, *Political Economy of International Relations*, p. 400.

economic nationalism (particularly controls on direct foreign investment) appear increasingly unlikely in the contemporary environment.[77]

CONCLUSIONS: ECONOMIC POLICY CONVERGENCE AND GOVERNANCE OF THE INTERNATIONAL POLITICAL ECONOMY

While it may not ensure the emergence of purposive order, the
"triumph" of neoclassical economic policy in the developing world
may facilitate an extension of the governance of the world economy to
countries and regions previously excluded from active participation. A
minimal degree of convergence of liberal economic policy and interests
may indeed be a prerequisite for the formation of a liberal international
economy.[78] Policy convergence provides a basis for membership in
international financial institutions, entry to expanded regional markets,
and, most significantly, access to scarce international finance.[79] Thus, it
is possible to argue that policy convergence, the second type of order
considered in the introduction of this chapter may well facilitate the
establishment of purposive order or governance.

At the same time, partially formed regimes, or purposive orders (the
third type of order considered in the introduction) may simultaneously
reinforce tendencies toward policy convergence. If international
regimes are formed that can create mutual expectations, reduce transaction costs, and provide access to finance and markets, they may also
increase the probability that the current policy convergence will
become more than an ephemeral, transitory phenomenon. The
"triumph" of neoclassical economics will not endure, however, unless
developing countries are able to demonstrate some tangible economic
successes to their largely skeptical populations. Liberalized domestic
trade and payments regimes will not become institutionalized unless
they begin to yield some material accomplishments. For this reason
alone, liberal internationalists should endeavor to provide generous
trade access and significant debt relief to developing countries undertaking significant reforms.

---

[77] It goes without saying that socialization of the means of production is out of the
question in the new order.
[78] Robert Gilpin speculates about this when he asks, "Can a liberal international
economy long survive if it is not composed primarily of liberal societies as defined in
the West, that is, societies with an emphasis on the price system, markets open to all,
and limited interventionism on the part of the state?," in his *Political Economy of
International Relations*, p. 393.
[79] Robert Keohane makes a similar argument when he suggests that, "free markets
depend on the prior establishment of property rights," in *After Hegemony*, p. 11.

Finally, if it begins to appear successful over the longer term, the current economic policy convergence should begin to produce domestic groups with a vested interest in institutionalizing liberalized policies. This has yet to happen in most developing countries, where the reforms are sustained either by authoritarian regimes or a patient public waiting to see what transitional regimes and/or fragile, unconsolidated democracies can deliver after years of failed economic policy. Ultimately, however, if they begin to yield tangible results, the current economic policies should begin to affect deeper, intersubjectively shared ideas about order, create perceptions of common interests, and facilitate the development of consensus around meaning, all essential for international collaboration and governance without government.

5 TOWARDS A POST-HEGEMONIC CONCEPTUALIZATION OF WORLD ORDER: REFLECTIONS ON THE RELEVANCY OF IBN KHALDUN[1]

Robert W. Cox

In the beginning was the Word.   John 1.1.

When there is a general change of conditions, it is as if the entire creation had changed and the whole world been altered, as if it were a new and repeated creation, a world brought into existence anew.

Ibn Khaldun, *Muqaddimah*

Ontology lies at the beginning of any enquiry. We cannot define a problem in global politics without presupposing a certain basic structure consisting of the significant kinds of entities involved and the form of significant relationships among them. We think, for example, about a system whose basic entities are states and of an hypothesized mechanism called the balance of power through which their relationships may be understood to constitute a certain kind of world order. From such ontological beginnings, complex theories have been built and specific cases – particular interstate relationships – can be examined. There is always an ontological starting point.

Any such ontological standpoint is open to question. All of the terms just used have ontological meanings: global politics, structure, system, states, balance of power, world order. I choose "global politics" deliberately to avoid certain ontological presuppositions inherent in other terms such as "international relations," which seems to equate nation with state and to define the field as limited to the interactions among states; or "world system," which has been given a specific meaning by certain writers, notably by Immanuel Wallerstein. "Global politics" is looser and broader as a starting point than these other terms, although the reader will soon see that even "politics" constitutes an

[1] I would like to thank the other authors whose work is included in this volume, particularly James Rosenau, Janice Thomson, and Oran Young, and also Ahmed Samatar, for critical comment on an earlier draft of this chapter, with the usual disclaimer that they bear no responsibility for the final product.

ontological limitation for me. My thinking would prefer something like "political economy."

Theory follows reality. It also precedes and shapes reality. That is to say, there is a real historical world in which things happen; and theory is made through reflection upon what has happened. The separation of theory from historical happenings is, however, only a way of thinking, because theory feeds back into the making of history by virtue of the way those who make history (and I am thinking about human collectivities, not just about prominent individuals) think about what they are doing. Their understanding of what the historical context allows them to do, prohibits them from doing, or requires them to do, and the way they formulate their purposes in acting, is the product of theory. There is a grand theory written by scholars in books; and there is a common-sense theory which average people use to explain to themselves and to others why they are doing what they do.

The ontologies that people work with derive from their historical experience and in turn become embedded in the world they construct. What is subjective in understanding becomes objective through action. This is the only way, for instance, in which we can understand the state as an objective reality. The state has no physical existence, like a building or a lamp-post; but it is nevertheless a real entity. It is a real entity because everyone acts as though it were; because we know that real people with guns and batons will enforce decisions attributed to this non-physical reality.

These embedded structures of thought and practice – the non-physical realities of political and social life – may persist over long periods of time, only to become problematic, to be called into question, when people confront new sets of problems that the old ontologies do not seem able to account for or cope with. In such periods, certainties about ontology give place to skepticism. As the European old regime passed its peak and entered into decline, Pyrrhonism, a revival of skepticism from the ancient world, became an intellectual fashion.[2] Now post-modernism, more attuned to a generation that disdains to seek models from the past, performs the function of disestablishing (or, in its terms, deconstructing) the heretofore accepted ontologies.

In the collective work that precedes the present book,[3] Richard Ashley argued that there is no indubitable Archimedean point, no

---

[2] Paul Hazard, *La Crise de la conscience européenne, 1680–1715* (Paris: A. Fayard, 1967). Trans. as *The European Mind, 1680–1715* (London: Hollis and Carter, 1953).

[3] Ernst-Otto Czempiel and James N. Rosenau, eds., *Global Changes and Theoretical Challenges: Approaches to World Politics for the 1990s* (Lexington, MA: Lexington Books, 1989).

single firm foundation, on which to build a science of global politics.[4] Every purported firm ground is to be doubted in the eyes of eternity. We are not, however, working with the eyes of eternity but with a myopia particular to the late twentieth century. Indeed, our perspectives may be strongly influenced by a sense of the invalidity of former certainties – those of the Cold War, or a bipolar structure of world power, of American hegemony. Our challenge is not to contribute to the construction of a universal and absolute knowledge, but to devise a fresh perspective useful for framing and working on the problems of the present.

There is a lingering absolutism in the very denial of the possibility of absolute knowledge – a regret, a striving to approximate something like it, to endow our practical wisdom with universality. As intellectuals and theorists, we are disposed to think of our task as that of *homo sapiens*, though we might be more effective were we to see our task as that of an adjunct to *homo faber*, the maker of history. To deconstruct the ontological constructs of the passing present is a first step towards a more pertinent but still relative knowledge. The task of clearing the ground should not become an obstacle to constructing a new perspective that can be useful even though it in turn will ultimately be open to critical reevaluation.

Homo faber is also *homo sapiens*. There is a cumulative as well as a disjunctive quality to history. Distinctive historical phases, with their historically specific ontologies, are not sealed off from one another as mutually incomprehensible or mutually irrelevant constructs.[5] Historical phases in our own current of civilisation are produced, one following the other, in a process of contradiction. The contradictions and conflicts that arise within any established structure create the opportunity for its transformation into a new structure. This is the simplest model of historical change. The successive phases of other currents of civilization can be understood by the human mind's capacity for analogy. The encounters and merging of civilizations can be understood by a combination of process and analogy. These capacities of thought make the historical process intelligible. Knowledge of history, not just of events but of the regularities or general

---

[4] Czempiel and Rosenau, *Global Changes and Theoretical Challenges*, pp. 257, 286. For a critique of post-modernism in world politics studies see Pauline Rosenau, "Once Again into the Fray: International Relations Confronts the Humanities," *Millennium. Journal of International Studies*, 19, 1 (Spring 1990), pp. 83–110.

[5] This point is well made by Joseph Femia, drawing upon the "absolute historicism" of Antonio Gramsci, in his article "An Historicist Critique of 'Revisionist' Methods for Studying the History of Ideas," *History and Theory*, 2 (1981), pp. 113–34.

principles that help explain historical change, can, in turn, become a guide for action. History thus generates theory. This theory is not absolute knowledge, not a final revelation or a completeness of rational knowledge about the laws of history. It is a set of viable working hypotheses. It is a form of knowledge that transcends the specific historical epoch, that makes the epoch intelligible in a larger perspective – not the perspective of eternity which stands outside of history, but the perspective of a long sweep of history.[6]

There are special epistemological as well as ontological issues to be resolved in working within an era of structural change. Positivism offers an epistemological approach congenial to periods of relative structural stability. The state of the social whole can be taken as given in order to focus upon those particular variables that frame the specific and limited object of inquiry. Positivism allows for detailed empirical investigation of discrete problems. The observing subject can be thought of as separated from, as not directly involved with, what is investigated. The purpose of inquiry is to bring the aberrant activity that focused attention as an object of study back into a compatible relationship with the relatively stable whole. Although this is not always clearly recognized, in positivism there is an implicit identity between the observer-analyst and the stable social whole. This identity at the level of the whole allows for the fiction of a separation between subject and object at the level of the specific issue.

Positivism is less well adapted to inquiry into complex and comprehensive change. For this we need an epistemology that does not disguise but rather explicitly affirms the dialectical relationship of subject and object in historical process. Intentions and purposes are understood to be embodied within the objectified or institutionalized structures of thought and practice characteristic of an epoch. Where positivism separates the observing subject from the observed object of inquiry, this other historically oriented, interpretative, or hermeneutic epistemology sees subject and object in the historical world as a reciprocally interrelated whole. Such an epistemology is more adequate as a guide to action towards structural change, even though it may not attain the degree of precision expected of positivism. This chapter is an attempt to develop such an approach.

---

[6] This perspective on history as the unifying field of social sciences was pioneered in Western thought by Giambattista Vico, *The New Science*, trans. Thomas Goddard Bergin and Max Harold Fisch (Ithaca, NY: Cornell University Press, 1970), and has perhaps best been explained in a contemporary context by Fernand Braudel, "History and the Social Sciences: The *Longue Durée*," in *On History*, trans. Sarah Matthews (Chicago: University of Chicago Press, 1980), pp. 25–54.

A shift of ontologies is inherent in the very process of historical structural change. The entities that are significant are the emerging structures and the processes through which they emerge. Reflection upon change discredits old ontologies and yields an intimation of a possible new ontology. Use of the new ontology becomes the heuristic for strategies of action in the emerging world order.

One reason to reexamine the thought of Ibn Khaldun is that he confronted this kind of situation. He was aware of living and acting in a period of historical change, a period of decline and disintegration of the social and political structures that had been the underpinnings of past glory and stability; and he wanted to understand the reasons that lay beneath the brute facts of historical events, reasons that, when understood, could become guidelines for action. Following the reasonings of such a mind while appreciating the differences between his fourteenth-century Islamic world and our own time and place in history is one good reason for rethinking his thought.[7] Other reasons will appear in due course.

KNOWLEDGE ABOUT GLOBAL POLITICS

As a preliminary to discussing the writings of a sophisticated fourteenth-century Islamic scholar whose sense of the basic entities and relationships of his world was different from ours, it is necessary to find some categories that can be assumed to be applicable to both our worlds. I have already used some terms – world order, institutions, structures – which, though not common to both Ibn Khaldun and ourselves, may be understood to be of such generality and comprehensiveness that they can be held to apply transhistorically for purposes of comparison.

Hedley Bull defined "order" to mean "that [the constituents of order] are related to one another according to some pattern, that their relationship is not purely haphazard but contains some discernible principle."[8] This suggests a dimension ranging from something just short of the "purely haphazard" to a condition of stasis. Even the notion of the haphazard can be contested, as scientists now perceive orders within chaos,[9] so may some kind of order be perceived in anarchy. Order is thus not to be perceived as a limited range of social situations,

---

[7] R. G. Collingwood, *The Idea of History* (Oxford: Clarendon Press, 1946), influences my approach to rethinking the thought of the past.
[8] Hedley Bull, *The Anarchical Society. A Study of Order in World Politics* (New York: Columbia University Press, 1977), ch. 1.
[9] James Gleick, *Chaos: Making a New Science* (New York: Penguin, 1987).

e.g., those which are free from turbulence or conflict. Order is whatever pattern or regularity of interaction is to be found in any social situation.

Hedley Bull proceeded to introduce a normative element or the promotion of certain goals or values into the concept of order. That is to say, different orders promote different goals or values. This is consistent with the hermeneutic approach. Purpose or intention is inherent in individual and collective human activity and so it is natural to inquire what goals or values inspire or are promoted by any particular order. Bull then goes one step further to maintain that three specific values transcend all differences among orders – security against violence, *pacts sunt servanda*, and relative stability of possessions (or property). In this last step, I think he introduces too much normative specificity. This is not a given but a problem: how to introduce into order the norms of behavior that will come to inform individual and collective conduct.

Hedley Bull also distinguishes usefully between "world order" and "international order." World order is genuinely transhistorical. It refers to the order prevailing in all mankind, without prejudging the manner in which mankind is institutionalized. International order refers to a particular historically limited condition of institutionalization: that of a system of nation-states.[10]

Institutions and institutionalization are the next concepts applicable to a comparative study of world orders. Institutions are the broadly understood and accepted ways of organizing particular spheres of social action – in our own era, for instance, from marriage and the nuclear family, through the state, diplomacy, and the rules of international law, to formal organizations like the United Nations and the International Monetary Fund (IMF). In other eras and in different cultures, the set of institutions has been otherwise. Even where institutions within different orders bear the same names, e.g., family or state, the meanings behind the names have been different.

Institutions are the ways in which social practices, developed in

---

[10] Writing in January 1991, I cannot ignore that the term "world order" has been used by the U.S. administration of President George Bush in one of several justifications of its war against Iraq. Bush's "new world order" would be an order enforced by U.S. power. It is pertinent to recall words written by E. H. Carr almost half a century ago: "To internationalize government in any real sense means to internationalize power; and international government is, in effect, government by that state which supplies the power necessary for the purpose of governing." (*The Twenty Years' Crisis, 1919–1939* [London: Macmilllan, 1946], p. 107.) One might add, at this later date: . . . and which has the power to compel other governments to finance the cost of the use of power. The general category "world order" should not become reduced to one specific and politically manipulative use of the term.

response to particular problems confronting a society, become routinized into specific sets of rules. They may be more or less formally organized, and the sanctions that sustain rules may range from the pressure of opinion to enforcable law. At the global level this includes practices with a conventional backing in the law of nations like diplomacy, those enduring arrangements regulating actions in particular spheres that are now commonly referred to as "regimes," and formal international organizations with explicit rules and enforcement procedures.

Institutions are sustained within something broader called structures. Structures are the product of recurrent patterns of actions and expectations, the *gestes répétées* of Braudel's *longue durée*.[11] Structures exist in language, in the ways we think, in the practices of social and economic and political life. Any particular way of life in time and place, when analyzed, will reveal a certain structure. Any particular sphere of life will have its structure. Structures are then the larger context within which institutions are to be located.

Structures are socially constructed, i.e., they become a part of the objective world by virtue of their existence in the intersubjectivity of relevant groups of people. The objective world of institutions is real because we make it so by sharing a picture of it in our minds quite independently of how we value it, whether we approve or disapprove of it.

Intersubjectively shaped reality, the institutions that structure how material life is organized and produced, is as much a part of the material world and as independent of individual volition as the brute physical material upon which those institutions work. Marx expressed this in terms of the interaction of relations of production (intersubjectively constituted reality) and productive forces.

How this objective world is made and remade through changes in intersubjectivity is the principal question to be answered in any attempt to understand the process of historical change. Such a study will focus upon the relationship between (a) the stock of ideas people have about the nature of the world and (b) the practical problems that challenge them – on the aptitude or inaptitude of ideas to provide an effective and acceptable means of acting on problems that cannot be ignored because they do not go away. Where there appears to be a disjuncture between problems and hitherto accepted mental constructs, we may detect the opening of a crisis of structural transformation. Thus some of us think

---

[11] Fernand Braudel, *Civilisation matérielle, économie et capitalisme, XVe–XVIIIe siècle* (Paris: Armand Colin, 1979).

the erstwhile dominant mental construct of neorealism is inadequate to confront the challenges of global politics today, while others, of course, think it still works.

It is impossible to predict the future; but it may be possible to construct a partial knowledge that can be helpful in making a future, i.e., in channeling the direction of events towards a desired option from among those that appear feasible. Such practical knowledge as a guide to political action is to be derived from an attempt to understand historical change.

To be useful, this knowledge must be specifically relevant to salient practical problems, the handling of which will condition the kind of future to be made. Thus, a first emphasis should be upon identifying the salient problems of the present. Problems are not just *given* as in a positivist epistemology. Problems are *perceived*, that is to say, they arise in the encounter of social being with social consciousness.[12] Thus awareness of new problems makes us sensitive to the inadequacies of conventional mental structures that tend to make us focus on problems other than those of emerging salience.

REVISION OF CONVENTIONAL ONTOLOGIES

Because we cannot know the future, we cannot give a satisfactory name to future structures. We can only depict them in terms of a negation or potential negation of the dominant tendencies we have known. I use "negation" here in the sense of dialectical overcoming – *Aufhebung* in Hegel's usage,[13] i.e., in which the past stage is both annulled and preserved in the succeeding stage. This sense of transition away from known structures towards an as yet unnameable future accounts for the large number of approaches in different fields of study that begin with "post-" – post-industrial, post-modern, post-structural, post-capitalist, post-marxist, etc.

There are three still dominant tendencies of thought that are candidates for negation in the emergence of future world order: hegemony,

---

[12] Marx and Engels, in *The German Ideology* said that social being determines social consciousness. E. P. Thompson formulated the relationship in a more balanced and interactive way which I follow here. See especially, "The Poverty of Theory," in E. P. Thompson, *The Poverty of Theory and Other Essays* (London: Merlin Press, 1978). He writes: "changes take place within social being, which give rise to changed *experience*: and this experience is *determining*, in the sense that it exerts pressures upon existent social consciousness, proposes new questions, and affords much of the material which the more elaborated intellectual exercises are about" (p. 200).

[13] As explicated, e.g., in Charles Taylor, *Hegel and Modern Society* (Cambridge: Cambridge University Press, 1979). p. 49.

the Westphalian state system, and the globalization trend in world political economy. I shall therefore suggest some implications of an order that would become post-hegemonic, post-Westphalian, and post-globalizing.

Post-hegemonic

I do not use "hegemonic" in the conventional international relations meaning of a dominant state's relationship with other less powerful states. "Dominance" will do for that. Nor, consequently, do I use the term "hegemon" which refers to the dominant state in a relationship of dominance. I use "hegemony" to mean a structure of values and understandings about the nature of order that permeates a whole system of states and non-state entities. In a hegemonic order these values and understandings are relatively stable and unquestioned. They appear to most actors as the natural order. Such a structure of meanings is underpinned by a structure of power, in which most probably one state is dominant but that state's dominance in itself is not sufficient to create hegemony. Hegemony derives from the ways of doing and thinking of the dominant social strata of the dominant state or states insofar as these ways of doing and thinking have acquired the acquiescence of the dominant social strata of other states. These social practices and the ideologies that explain and legitimize them constitute the foundation of hegemonic order (Ashley's Archimedean point that is a candidate for deconstruction).[14]

Hegemony expands and is maintained by the success of the dominant social strata's practices and the appeal they exert to other social strata – through the process that Gramsci described as passive revolution. Hegemony frames thought and thereby circumscribes action.

The prospect of a post-hegemonic order implies doubt as to the likelihood that a new hegemony can be constructed to replace a declining hegemony.[15] It suggests doubt as to the existence of an

[14] This point is developed in Robert W. Cox, "Gramsci, Hegemony and International Relations: An Essay in Method," *Millennium. Journal of International Studies*, 12, 2 (Summer 1983), pp. 162–75.

[15] Whether or not the Pax Americana is declining is, of course, a matter of open debate. I am taking here the proposition that it is declining. Susan Strange contests this proposition (see her article "Toward a Theory of Transnational Empire," in Czempiel and Rosenau, eds., *Global Challenges and Theoretical Challenges*, pp. 161–76) but her use of "hegemony" is different from mine, more akin to that of the theorists of hegemonic stability, more like my "dominance." We differ in the use of words, not, I think, in substance. When she points to a tendency towards unilateralism in U.S. behavior as an irresponsible use of U.S. power, that, in my usage, would indicate an abdication of hegemonic leadership. Of course, the tendency is not irreversible. There is a question

Archimedean point around which a new order could be constructed. Previous hegemonic orders have derived their universals from the dominant society, itself the product of a dominant civilization. A post-hegemonic order would have to derive its normative content in a search for common ground among constituent traditions of civilization.

Is there a basis for common ground? The question takes us back to Hedley Bull's concern with the normative content of a world order. We raise it now, not as a matter of prior definition, but as a matter of historical contingency. What common ground is conceivable?[16]

A first condition would be mutual recognition of distinct traditions of civilization, perhaps the most difficult step especially for those who have shared a hegemonic perspective, and who are unprepared to forsake the security of belief in a natural order that is historically based on universalizing from one position of power in one form of civilization. The difficulty is underlined by the way political change outside the West is perceived and reported in the West – the tendency to view everything through Western concepts which can lead to the conclusion that the "end of history" is upon us as the apotheosis of a late Western capitalist civilization. Mutual recognition implies a readiness to try to understand others in their own terms.

Incidentally, speculation concerning Japan as a future hegemonic leader[17] raises implicitly this question of universalizing from a particular form of civilization. Whereas U.S. history and Soviet history have both exhibited a strong tendency to self-universalization, Japan's civilization has been tenaciously particularistic. Japan has the economic power to pursue a hegemonic project, but seems to lack the intent to assimilate the rest of the world to its socio-cultural practices. This self-restraint at the threshold of universalization could give Japan an advantage in showing the way towards a post-hegemonic form of order provided it does not degenerate into a new nationalistic striving for dominance.[18]

A second condition for a post-hegemonic order would be to move

---

whether, if reversed, the new direction would be towards an attempt to reestablish Pax Americana, or towards U.S. adaptation to a post-hegemonic world.

[16] Ibn Khaldun wrote: "We must distinguish the conditions that attach themselves to the essence of civilization as required by its very nature; the things that are accidental and cannot be counted on; and the things that cannot possibly attach themselves to it." *Muqaddimah*, p. 38. This may sound very like Bull's basic normative principles. I prefer to think, not of principles which can be deduced from the nature of civilization, but rather of principles which, in the actuality of the historical encounter of civilizations, can be accepted as common.

[17] For instance, Ezra Vogel, "Pax Nipponica?," *Foreign Affairs*, 64, 4 (Spring 1986).

[18] Robert W. Cox, "Middlepowermanship, Japan, and future world order," *International Journal*, 44 (Autumn 1989), pp. 823–62.

beyond the point of mutual recognition towards a kind of supra-intersubjectivity that would provide a bridge among the distinct and separate subjectivities of the different coexisting traditions of civilization. One can speculate that the grounds for this might be (1) recognition of the requisites for survival and sustained equilibrium in global ecology – though the specific inferences to be drawn from this may remain objects of discord; (2) mutual acceptance of restraint in the use of violence to decide conflicts – not that this would eliminate organized political violence, though it might raise the costs of resort to violence; and (3) common agreement to explore the sources of conflict and to develop procedures for coping with conflict that would take account of distinct coexisting normative perspectives.

For those who have shared a common hegemonic perspective, the search for the common ground for a post-hegemonic order can best begin with an effort to understand those perspectives that have appeared most to challenge the existing hegemonic ways of understanding and acting in world politics. This is another reason for revisiting the thought of Ibn Khaldun. The Islamic tradition is the "other" in relation to the Western tradition which is both the closest and the most difficult for the Western-conditioned mind to understand. A rationalist and historicist Islamic philosopher and historian can be the point of access to empathy with that other.

Post-Westphalian

To foresee a post-Westphalian world order seems initially to contradict the revival of interest in the state that has been common to both liberals and Marxists in recent decades.[19] It is, however, all the more important to give attention to the nature of the state if it is to be assumed that the role of the state and its relationship to non-state forces may be in process of significant change – that the essence of global politics may no longer be conceivable solely in terms of the interstate system (and of the principal powers within it at that).

One indication of a changed position of states is the dramatic increase in the number of state entities. That number seemed to be declining up

---

[19] I refer, e.g., to Marxian theorizing on the state by Nicos Poulantzas, *Pouvoir politique et classes sociales* (Paris: Maspero, 1968), and Ralph Miliband, *The State in Capitalist Society* (London: Weidenfeld and Nicolson, 1969); and to Stephen D. Krasner, *Defending the National Interest: Raw Materials Investments and U.S. Foreign Policy* (Princeton, NJ: Princeton University Press, 1978), and Theda Skocpol, *States and Social Revolutions* (Cambridge: Cambridge University Press, 1979). See in particular the chapter by Mark Zacher in the present volume.

to the early decades of the twentieth century[20] but has greatly expanded in the second half of the twentieth century. The neorealist responds that middle and small states do not matter;[21] they can be ignored in calculating the configuration of effective power relations.

Lesser powers do, however, alter the milieu of interstate relations. They have a collective interest in erecting limits on great power activity; and they encourage norms of international behavior that are anti-colonial and anti-interventionist, and which favor redistribution of global resources. Even as victim, the small state highlights a shift from hegemony to dominance, undermining moral certainties, underlining arbitrariness and departure from rule – consider the undermining of hegemonic beliefs in the cases involving Vietnam, Afghanistan, Grenada, Nicaragua, El Salvador, and Panama.

Territoriality was the defining feature of the Westphalian state. The contemporary state retains this feature, but its importance has diminished in relation to non-territorial power.[22] Even those neorealists who predict a new mercantilist world order do not conceive it on the model of the autarkic territorially defined blocs of the 1930s. The new mercantilism would be a struggle among some territorially located centers of non-territorial political-economic power. It would be a struggle for markets and investment opportunities over the whole globe, including the domestic territories of the rival centers of power. Each of these power centers has a stake within the others. Non-territoriality gives greater scope for action to economic and social organizations of civil society whose activities cross territorial boundaries.

In the last half of the twentieth century, the relationship of states to the world political economy has altered. Formerly, the state's role was conceived as bulwark or buffer protecting the domestic economy from harmful exogenous influences. Latterly, the state's role has been understood more as helping to adjust the domestic economy to the perceived exigencies of the world economy. "Competitiveness" is the key word indicative of this shift in perspective. The state is tributary to

---

[20] Indeed, E. H. Carr, *Conditions of Peace* (London: Macmillan, 1944), assumed that one of the causes of World War II was the breakup of pre-World War I empires into a number of weak states, and that a future peace would depend upon a reconcentration of power into a more limited number of economically and militarily viable states.

[21] I recall Kenneth Waltz saying "Denmark doesn't matter."

[22] See Strange, "Toward a Theory of Transnational Empire," also Richard Rosecrance, *The Rise of the Trading State: Commerce and Conquest in the Modern World* (New York: Basic Books, 1986). I have discussed the dualism of territorial and interdependence principles in "Production and Security," a paper prepared for the Conference on Emerging Trends in Global Security, Montebello, Quebec, October 1990.

something greater than the state. The state has become "international-ized" as a consequence, a transmission belt from world economy to domestic economy. Evidently, the process of adaptation is uneven. Some states use their powers to resist adaptation by attempting to force other states to adjust to their interests. Some states seize the new economic environment as an opportunity to control their own adjust-ment and advance their own economies. Many have adjustment thrust unwillingly upon them. All, however, reason about state policy from the premise of the world economy.

In these changes in the role and capacities of states, it is increasingly meaningless to speak of "the" state as do neorealists, or even (as among Marxists) of "the capitalist" state. It becomes more useful to think in terms of *forms* of state – different forms which condition the ways in which different societies link into the global political economy.[23]

Moreover, the changes taking place in state roles give new oppor-tunity for self-expression by nationalities that have no state of their own, in movements for separation or autonomy; and the same tendencies encourage ethnicities and religiously defined groups that straddle state boundaries to express their identities in global politics. Multinational corporations and transnational banks develop their autonomy, partly exploiting the opportunities of a deregulated inter-national environment, partly falling back upon state support in difficulties. Social movements like environmentalism, feminism, and the peace movement transcend territorial boundaries. Transnational cooperation among indigenous peoples enhances their force within particular states. These various developments lend credibility to Bull's vision of a "new medievalism."[24]

Post-globalization

Some observers have discerned a double movement in the economic and social history of Europe during the nineteenth century. The thrust behind the utopian vision of a self-regulating market was the first phase of movement. The market was conceived as bursting free from the bonds of society, a newly unleashed natural force that would subject society to its laws. Then came, unplanned and unawaited, a second phase of movement – society's response of self-preservation,

---

23 Robert W. Cox, *Production, Power, and World Order: Social Forces in the Making of History* (New York: Columbia University Press, 1987), pp. 105–9.
24 Bull, *The Anarchical Society*, pp. 254–5.

curbing the disintegrating and alienating consequences of market-oriented behavior. Society set about to tame and civilize the market.

In the late twentieth century, we can discern a similar recurrence of the double movement. A powerful globalizing economic trend thrusts toward the achievement of the market utopia on the global scale. At the present moment, the protective response of society appears to be less sure, less coherent. Yet the elements of opposition to the socially disruptive consequences of globalization are visible. The question remains open as to what form these may take, as to whether and how they may become more coherent and more powerful, so that historical thesis and antithesis may lead to a new synthesis. Globalization is not the end of history but the initiation of a new era of conflicts and reconciliations.[25]

The characteristics of the globalization trend include the internationalizing of production, the new international division of labor, new migratory movements from South to North, the new competitive environment that accelerates these processes, and the internationalizing of the state (referred to above) making states into agencies of the globalizing world.

Looking to the future of global politics, it is of the first importance to consider the sources of conflict that may be exacerbated by the globalization trend. Conflicts arising from ecological issues (pollution, waste disposal, preempting of depletable resources, etc.); from migration; from social polarization produced by new structures of production; from vulnerabilities to competition; and from ethnic, gender, and other group differentiations that become identified with and manipulated in the interest of economic and social cleavages. Conflicts from such sources can break out directly within societies and can become extended into the interstate system through the differential responses of particular states and the transnational linkages of social groups.

It is equally important to identify probable sources of opposition to globalization – the relatively disadvantaged who will affirm the right of social forces to make economy and polity serve their own self-determined goals. The confrontation precipitated by globalization presages a new synthesis in which economic efficiency may better serve social goals and buttress the identities of self-defined social groups. The relevant sources of opposition include the new social movements, those

---

[25] I have discussed this in "The Global Political Economy and Social Choice," in Daniel Drache and Meric Gertler, eds., *The New Era of Global Competition: State Policy and Market Power* (Montreal: McGill–Queen's University Press, 1991).

labor movements that have been capable of transcending what Gramsci[26] called the economic-corporative level of consciousness, democratization movements that strive to enhance popular control over those aspects of social organization that directly affect people's lives. Forms of struggle also change, and emerging cleavages become aligned with ideologies in new ways.

IBN KHALDUN: ROOTS OF AN ISLAMIC PERSPECTIVE ON HISTORICAL CHANGE

The foregoing outlines the perspective from which I inquire into the thought of Ibn Khaldun and something of the reasons for choosing this subject of inquiry as part of a collective project of rethinking the contemporary meaning of international relations. Let us now turn more directly to the relevancy of Ibn Khaldun.

Ibn Khaldun was born in May 1332 in Tunis of a distinguished family which had emigrated from Seville to the Maghreb some years previously, before the fall of Seville to the *reconquista*. Both his parents died in the Black Death while he was still a young man. He was educated by some of the best minds of this time, and made a career in the court politics of a turbulent era in the history of North Africa and Andalusia.

As a participant observer of politics, he had excellent opportunity to develop his judgment, with access to many of the prominent personalities of the time, both within the Arabic–Islamic world and beyond it. From another point of view, his political career was tumultuous and on the whole unsuccessful. His political projects failed; and at a certain point he withdrew from active politics in order to pursue an effort at deeper understanding of politics through history. It was during this phase that he composed the *Muqaddimah* or prolegomena to his world history,[27] entitled *Kitab al-'Ibar* which was completed in 1377 while he was living in refuge in a fortress village in the province of Oran.

Soon thereafter he obtained permission to make the pilgrimage to Mecca and travelled as far as Cairo, then the most brilliant remaining center of a contracting Islamic world. He accepted appointment to a prestigious judgeship. Family tragedy struck again when his wife and children died in shipwreck on their way to join him. He continued the

---

26 Antonio Gramsci, *Selections from the Prison Notebooks*, ed. Quintin Hoare and Geoffrey Nowell Smith (New York: International Publishers, 1971), pp. 131–2, 173–5, 181–2.
27 The standard English translation is by Franz Rosenthal (Princeton, NJ: Princeton University Press, 1967).

pilgrimage to Mecca and on his return to Cairo was appointed first to a most eminent academic charge and then again to a judgeship.

The latter part of his career was thus in the judicial sphere, where the first had been in court politics and diplomacy, the two spheres of activity being separated by the phase of reflections on history. He died in Cairo in March 1406.[28]

Why should Ibn Khaldun's thought be of interest to us today? One reason already suggested is that he provides a point of access to the understanding of Islamic civilization; and Islamic civilization is asserting its presence in the shaping of any future world order. There are also some reasons that derive from analogies between Ibn Khaldun's times and our own. He enables us to examine how a differently constituted mind confronted similar problems to those we now face and what factors shaped his understanding of and response to these problems.

He confronted the problem of decline. The *reconquista* had reduced the Islamic hold on Spain to Granada. The North African states were hard pressed by nomadic tribes on one side and the control of Mediterranean seaways by the Christian states to the north on the other. Christians and Jews were the middlemen in international trade. To the east, Mongol invasion shattered the existing structures, even though the invaders ultimately became absorbed into Islamic culture. Major cities were ruined; irrigation systems were disrupted or destroyed; oppressive taxation and the practice of tax farming fragmented power and undermined administrative organization. Although the cultural preeminence of Islam remained, the material foundations of Islamic hegemony were much weakened.

During his own career, Ibn Khaldun had personal encounters with Pedro the Cruel of Castile in Seville, and with the Mongol conqueror Tamerlane outside of Damascus. Both sought his advice and collaboration and both were discreetly refused. The challenge to understand the

---

[28] Currently available works on Ibn Khaldun include Aziz Al-Azmah, *Ibn Khaldun in Modern Scholarship: A Study in Orientalism* (London: Third World Centre for Research and Publishing, 1981), which includes an extensive bibliography; Aziz Al-Azmah, *Ibn Khaldun: An Essay in Reinterpretation* (London: Frank Cass, 1982); Majallat Et-Tarikh, *Actes du colloque international sur Ibn Khaldun*, Algiers, June 21–6, 1978 (Algiers: Société nationale d'édition et de diffusion, 1982); Charles Issawi, *An Arab Philosophy of History* (London: J. Murray, 1950); Yves Lacoste, *Ibn Khaldun: The Birth of History and the Past of the Third World* (London: Verso, 1984); Muhsin Mahdi, *Ibn Khaldun's Philosophy of History: A Study in Philosophical Foundations of the Science of Culture* (London and Chicago: Phoenix Books, University of Chicago Press, 1957); Nathaniel Schmidt, *Ibn Khaldun: Historian, Sociologist, and Philosopher* (New York: AMS Press, 1967); and Heinrich Simon, *Ibn Khaldun's Science of Human Culture*, trans. Fuad Baali (Lahore: Sh. Muhammad Askraf, 1978).

composite nature of decline was a principal incentive for Ibn Khaldun to undertake his studies on the meaning of history.[29]

The state was a focus of his interest; but the state could not be taken by Ibn Khaldun as a given, as the unquestioned basis of world order.[30] The construction and maintenance of states was problematized in his work. He perceived a process of emergence, maturity, and decline of states. States had to be seen and understood in the context of broader-ranging political processes. The *polis* was not, as for the Greeks, the beginning and end of politics. Politics emerged from the tribal community; and it extended to the empire. The state was a critical phase of political process, but only one phase, and that phase one of mutation, not of finality. There is little in common between Ibn Khaldun and our contemporary neorealism. There is much in common with the effort to conceive of a post-Westphalian world.

There is a profoundly material basis to Ibn Khaldun's political thought. He is keenly aware of the relationship of political forms to ecology. The prospects of civilized life are seen by him to be conditioned by matters of climate. The alternation of forms of state depended upon the balance between steppe and sown, nomadic and sedentary life, each generating its specific political culture.

This perspective is more congenial to our present than it would have been to the two centuries that preceded our time. Unique in world history, those two hundred years knew continuous growth. The doctrine of progress, child of material growth, is now challenged by a new awareness of ecological limits and a fear that perhaps that awareness may have come too late. Globalization is the expression of latter-day confidence in material growth. Ibn Khaldun may have something to say to those endeavoring to think in terms of post-globalization.

THE POLITICAL ONTOLOGY OF MEDIEVAL ISLAM

A first problem in approaching Ibn Khaldun's thought is to grasp the intersubjective meanings that would be shared as points of reference among his contemporaries. This is, in other words, to attempt to define the ontological content of his world.

This world would have been understood by contemporaries in terms

---

[29] Mahdi, *Ibn Khaldun's Philosophy of History*, pp. 18–26.

[30] For Ibn Khaldun, the state was not conceived as an abstraction; it was always a concrete historical phenomenon equated with a dynasty. The dynasty created the state and the state ceased to exist with the collapse of the dynasty. The Arabic word for "state" and for "dynasty" was the same (*dawlah*). (Introduction by Franz Rosenthal to the *Muqaddimah*, p. xi.)

of a primary cleavage between Islam and the non-Islamic world. In its origins, Islam connoted a sense of community, of religious fellowship, that transcended narrower communities centered on kinship.[31] Common faith overcame the limitations of blood bonds.

It also drew a line between believers and non-believers outside the pale of Islam. Community within contrasted to war without. Indeed, the identity of religion and politics characteristic of Islam is conditioned by this cleavage. The Prophet had to found a new political community in Medina, following the *hijra*, as a base for the propagation of God's message. The Caliphate, succeeding the rule of the Prophet, upheld the injunction to pursue *jihad*, holy war, through the fusion of the Law with military-political power. This fusion distinguished the Islamic whole from the European-Christian, with the latter's distinction of religious and secular authorities symbolised by the dualism of papacy and empire.

In historical experience, the cleavage between Islam and infidels may not have been quite so extreme. Certainly, Islamic political identity was reinforced by military pressure from Christian Europe and from Asian Mongol invaders. However, diplomatic, trade, and cultural exchanges between Islamic and non-Islamic worlds constituted factors of coexistence. Ibn Khaldun himself participated in such exchanges. Nevertheless, Islam constituted the broadest entity with which a Middle Easterner or North African individual would identify. In much the same manner, a European would identify with the *Respublica Christiana*, a religious-cultural entity to which no specific political institution corresponded, but which was nonetheless intersubjectively real.

In another dimension (the vertical by contrast to the horizontal), Islam expressed the linkage between the conditions of material existence, the forms of human organization, and the realm of the angels and of God. Prophesy consummated this linkage. The Prophet was the messenger of God. God was unity, suffering no separation into distinct persons such as occurred in Christian trinitarianism. The Prophet conveyed the Laws through which human society was to be shaped; and taught how mankind was to cope with the problems of material existence under the Law. In the time of the Prophet, there was an

---

[31] Ira M. Lapidus, *A History of Islamic Societies* (Cambridge: Cambridge University Press, 1988), p. 251, suggests that in the twentieth century the continuing strength of Islam is demonstrated in its ability to give a new social identity to peoples severed from their traditional social structures. Other works I have found useful towards an understanding of the political ontology of Islam are Ernest Gellner, *Muslim Society* (Cambridge: Cambridge University Press, 1981); and R. M. Savory, ed., *Introduction to Islamic Civilization* (Cambridge: Cambridge University Press, 1976).

identity between religion, law, politics, and social organization; and this identity remained the Islamic ideal.

From the time of the Prophet, however, this identity became fragmented in practice. The fragmentation did not destroy the ideal of unity. Rather, it took a dialectical form in which different aspects assumed what today might be called a "relative autonomy," emphasizing some aspects of the whole at the expense of others, but not separating out from the whole. The relationship between these aspects took the form of what Croce called a dialectic of distincts, as contrasted with a dialectic of opposites.[32] These different aspects were constituted by the distinct traditions that were encompassed by Islam as an historical phenomenon.

The basic elements that united in Islam with the religious-political tradition of prophesy, yet remained distinct to constitute its historical dialectic were (1) the sociopolitical organization of the pre-Islamic bedouin Arab clan, (2) the administrative and political structure of the pre-Islamic (notably Sasanian Persian) empires, (3) the Sultanate or emergent states that represented both the transcendence of the clan group and the disintegration of the imperial administration, (4) the social and economic organization of urban society, (5) the intellectual rationalist tradition of classical Greek philosophy, and (6) a mode of production continuous from pre-Islamic times which remained substantially unchanged though permitting an oscillation between the satisfaction of bare necessities and a cyclical appearance of instances of relative luxury. Each of these distinct elements in the Islamic tradition in turn lent itself to contradictory perspectives.

In the Sunni tradition, unity of political and religious authority embodied in the Caliphate remained as an ideal, but the rule of kingship that emerged in independent states succeeding the Caliphate had a relative legitimacy. It was still the higher duty of rulers to uphold the Law, but kingly rule also had rational justification as the means of maintaining order. The state and the Islamic tradition became historicized.

The Shi'ite tradition embodied by contrast an essentially ahistorical eschatological view of politics. The believer awaited the coming of the Mahdi, the Islamic messiah, the hidden Twelfth Imam, who would inaugurate the reign of heaven on earth. In this conception, all states were fundamentally illegitimate with no more than a spurious claim upon the transitory allegiance of the believer.

---

[32] Benedetto Croce, *Ce qui est vivant et ce qui est mort de la philosophie de Hegel*, trans. Henri Buriot (Paris: V. Giard & E. Brière, 1910).

Politicized and non-politicized perceptions of Islam coexisted in distinct social milieu quite apart from the Sunni/Shi'a distinction. The milieu of the kingly courts fostered a politicized form, tending even at times, despite the hostility of the Islamic tradition to any form of organized church, towards a state religion.[33] Popular piety, on the other hand, was more consistently represented by the *ulama*, local elites of religious teachers and judges, respected for their learning and probity. For most people, membership in a universal Islamic fellowship became concretized less in the state than in the local urban community. This localization of identity was further reinforced by the appeal of Sufi mysticism among rural as well as urban populations.

The educated elites had also to wrestle with the rival claims of prophesy, religious revelation, and mysticism, on the one hand, and rationalism, on the other. Islam preserved the classical Greek texts of Plato and Aristotle, and developed the ideas contained in them through the works of Avicenna, Averroes, and others. It was through contact with the higher culture of Islam that the Christian West recovered knowledge of Greek philosophy. Ibn Khaldun's education was in this rationalist tradition. He, along with others of the educated elite, did not regard the rival claims of revelation and rationalism as mutually exclusive. Both had their place in Islamic thought. To some extent it was a question of to whom you were speaking.[34] The discourse of rationalism was appropriate for the educated elite, and the discourse of revealed authority for the masses. Ultimately both discourses ought to be consistent one with the other. The Law, revealed by the Prophet as the guidelines for human life, was the basis for the state. Politics, the construction and maintenance of the state, was a matter for rational scientific inquiry. A prophet, indeed, to be effective, would need to function rationally in being able to communicate and to build the human foundation for the revealed message.[35]

Finally, there is a contradiction inherent in two forms of society, each grounded in a different ecology and economy: the nomadic bedouin culture, and the urban culture. This contradiction became the central theme of the *Muqaddimah*. The bedouin culture is one of blood relations and relative economic equality. All members of such populations are satisfied with a minimum of material necessities. All male members share in the tasks of defense and expansion in relation to other

---

[33] In different historical phases, Shi'ism in Persia was taken over and domesticated by the state as a form of state religion. It did, however, throughout such phases remain a latent subversive force in relation to the state.

[34] Mahdi, *Ibn Khaldun's Philosophy of History*, pp. 103–25.

[35] *Ibid.*, pp. 89–91.

communities. Morals are simple and pure. There is a kind of military equality under patriarchal leadership. The urban culture begins with the division of labor in the development of specialized arts and crafts. It culminates in luxury dissolution, and effeminate decline. Since the mode of production did not admit of cumulative growth, the two cultures were condemned to a continuing oscillation. The limits to growth were quickly reached in urban expansion, precipitating a reversion to the regime of primitive necessity. Urban decadence opened the way to nomadic incursions and a restarting of the cycle.

THE EPISTEMOLOGY OF IBN KHALDUN

Ibn Khaldun entitled his major work *Kitab al-'Ibar* which is usually rendered as "world history." Muhsin Mahdi comments on the meaning of the key word *'Ibar*: it signifies to pass from the outside to the inside of a thing.[36] The concept suggests that Ibn Khaldun's aim is to pass from the immediate world of sensible things, the world of events, to penetrate into the world of rationally intelligible explanation that lies behind events. Ibn Khaldun called what he was doing a "new science." What he envisaged was a critical, scientific knowledge of history. Knowledge of events was a basis for reasoning about underlying causes. The rationally knowable principles conditioning such causes, once demonstrated, could serve as critical standards of the validity of evidence about events.[37]

The inquiry was directed, not to individual historical actions, but to collective human action in history. The object of enquiry was *'umran* or culture. *'Umran* represented the ways in which human communities confronted their specific problems of material existence. These

---

[36] *Ibid.*, pp. 64–71.

[37] The resemblance between Ibn Khaldun's work and that of Giambattista Vico, who composed his *New Science* in Naples in the early years of the eighteenth century, has been contested by some scholars of Ibn Khaldun. The grounds on which they discard the comparison are the ontological positions of the two theorists concerning a cyclical interpretation of history. There are undoubtedly differences between Ibn Khaldun's and Vico's cycles. There is also a similarity in the interpretation of decadence, the problem that most concerned both. More striking to me is their resemblance on epistemological grounds, notably in Vico's joining of certainty (concerning events) with a rational understanding of principles of "ideal eternal history" underlying events and providing a hermeneutical guide for the understanding of events. There is, of course, no evidence that Vico knew Ibn Khaldun's work directly. The intriguing question remains whether he might have, whether at first or second hand. Vico's prudence in avoiding censure by the Inquisition, still active in Naples during his lifetime, would have precluded his acknowledging an Islamic author. But Naples, as a cross-roads of Mediterranean cultures, would also have been in a privileged position in Europe for contact with Islamic literature.

problems varied according to climate and ecology. Culture could only develop in propitious circumstances, where the climate was neither too hard nor too easy. In these temperate zones, different peoples, influenced by their environment, have adopted different modes of association and economic activity, some nomadic and practicing animal husbandry, some sedentary and agricultural.

Prophesy played a critical role of stimulus in bringing about the diverse existing patterns of human organization. The prophet is the legislator and teacher who adjusts human organization to material conditions, showing a people how they should live, instructing them in new attitudes and founding new institutions.

Prophesy is not, however, a sufficient cause. It is inoperative in the absence of 'asabiya. The concept of 'asabiya in Ibn Khaldun is the subject of as much discussion and shades of meaning as the concept of virtù in Machiavelli. It has been roughly but probably inadequately translated as "group feeling" in Franz Rosenthal's standard English translation of the *Muqaddimah*. In Yves Lacoste's[38] reading of Ibn Khaldun's text, 'asabiya arises with the emergence of a *de facto* aristocracy within a tribal community. It is a form of military solidarity congruent with the passage from a classless to a class structure. In the terms I have employed above, 'asabiya is the form of intersubjectivity that pertains to the founding of a state. It is the creative component in this critical phase of human development; and in this respect 'asabiya has (for a Westerner) some relationship to Machiavelli's virtù.

This vital component is, however, subject to decay, and therein lies the dialectical character of the concept. The expansion of the power of the founders of a state leads to their corruption; they become accustomed to urban luxury, abandon their military habits to depend upon mercenaries, resort to tax farming and bribery, and lose touch with their followers. Lacoste writes: " 'Asabiya is the motor of development of the state, and it is destroyed by the emergence of the state."[39]

In Islam, an insistent monotheism, exclusive of any intermediary or distinct theological personalities such as figure in Catholic Christianity, is the mirror of the unity of the faithful. Monotheism transcends tribal or ethnic blood bonds; it becomes the ideological basis for unity in a multi-ethnic world order. The political basis was, however, rooted in

---

[38] Lacoste, *Ibn Khaldun*, pp. 110–17.
[39] *Ibid.*, p. 116. Ibn Khaldun discerned a circulation of 'asabiya among dominant and subordinate groups linked together through political power. A decadent dynasty could be confronted by the gathering strength of a hitherto subordinate group which could overcome and displace it, founding a new dynasty. *Muqaddimah*, p. 108.

tribal society, the 'asabiya of the nomadic bedouin conquerors. The social structure resulting from the fusion of these political and ideological elements was what the Moroccan sociologist Mohammed Al-Jabri,[40] building on Ibn Khaldun's work, called the "invasion economy." The nomadic tribesman extracted surplus from the sedentary agricultural and urban societies to maintain their rule. This relationship became, in turn, the cause of their own decline.

To summarize Ibn Khaldun's epistemology: (1) reason can discern explanatory principles of history that make events intelligible to the retrospective inquirer; (2) human natures, and thus human capacities for understanding, take different forms as human collectivities confront the problems of material existence in different ways; (3) 'asabiya is the necessary intersubjective condition for the creation of a higher form of collective existence, i.e., the state; (4) prophesy superimposed on 'asabiya creates the fullest potentiality for the founding of a world order; (5) the state is the form in relation to which culture is the matter, the state having the capacity to shape a higher culture; (6) the development of a state contains the seeds of its own destruction, from which it may be inferred that the intersubjectivity that was the basis of state power will cease to exist.

Although Ibn Khaldun does not state this explicitly, one must infer that the knowledge comprised in the "new science" could only come about as a consequence of this historical development of human understanding. Knowledge, in other words, must be historically conditioned. In the sequel to decline, the historian-philosopher who knows about the no-longer-existent 'asabiya, is left in a lonely position.[41] He can be neither prophet nor state-builder and is possessed of a knowledge that may not be well received by his contemporaries.

---

[40] Mahmoud Dhaouadi, "Ibn Khaldun: The Founding Father of Eastern Sociology," *International Sociology*, 5, 3 (September 1990), pp. 316–35. Gellner, *Muslim Society*, writes: "the traditional Muslim state is simultaneously and without contradiction both a Robber State, run for the benefit of the dominant group, and a moralistic state, bound to promote good and proscribe evil. It is carried by and identified with a dominant group, yet it also has an inbuilt vocation towards the implementation of a sharply identified divine order on earth" (p. 47). The necessary relationship between these two aspects was clear to Ibn Khaldun when he wrote: "The truth one must know is that no religious or political propaganda can be successful, unless power and group feeling ('asabiya) exist to support the religious and political aspirations and to defend them against those who reject them" (*Muqaddimah*, p. 258).

[41] Mahdi, *Ibn Khaldun's Philosophy of History*, pp. 125–32.

PERCEPTIONS OF WORLD ORDER AND THE
PHILOSOPHER-HISTORIAN'S ROLE

Ibn Khaldun's life story says something about the relationship of the philosopher to world history in an era of decline. His career, as indicated above, encompassed three phases: (1) a period of intense political-diplomatic activity, of involvement in the life of the courts; (2) a phase of withdrawal and reflection during which he composed his major study of history; and (3) a final phase devoted to the piecemeal amelioration of existing society through the application of the Law.

This suggests that he had tested the possibility of achieving a desirable political order through the political process, through the state, and found that wanting. From his own reasoning, the failing could not lie with individuals or miscalculated events. It would have to lie with the inadequacies of the prevailing culture. *'Asabiya* had eroded as an under-pinning of political structures. Thus one could not look to the existing forms of state for the creative force necessary to raising culture to a higher level

In this situation, two possibilities remained. One was the potential of the enlightened individual in an era of decline. This could be exercised through the *ulama*, the role of an educated and devout elite, that persistent element within Islamic society which had acted as a counter-point to the state. The *ulama* could be the voice of the Law, appealing to the source of religious belief for authority. The philosopher would conceal his faculty of reason without abandoning it. Reason would remain as esoteric among initiates. The philosopher would express himself to the public through Plato's noble lie.

The other possibility was a future revival of *'asabiya* under the aegis of a new world force. The new force would not come from among those peripheral semi-barbarous Arab and Berber tribes whose incursions into the diminishing sphere of the North African states had reduced them to an unstable residue of their one-time glory. These tribes were too primitive and undisciplined to found a state.

There was, however, the possibility of a new emerging world power reinstituting order. Muhsin Mahdi writes:

> A Messiah might very well appear at some future time. But if he is to put into effect the expected reforms, he must come at the head of a powerful people with great solidarity. He might even need to bring a new religion to unite and inspire his people. Ibn Khaldun thus intimates that such a Messiah could not appear among the Arabs where he is expected and might not even be a Muslim . . . He will have to possess the qualifications necessary for a leader and must be born

in circumstances conducive to the creation of a powerful state, which in turn must follow the natural course of rise and decline.[42]

Ibn Khaldun analyzed the political role of religion. Under this aspect, the rational science of culture could yield knowledge concerning the circumstances in which prophesy combined with 'asabiya could be politically effective, and the circumstances in which this efficacy ceased. Circumstances of political efficacy, however, could say nothing about the truth of religious revelation. Ibn Khaldun could remain a devout Muslim while being pessimistic about the prospects of the Islamic world. In historical experience, the decay of the institutions of his world system enhanced the importance of moral action at the local level.

Ibn Khaldun's reflections on world history contemplated the "world" that would have been intelligible to him, just as ours contemplate the "world" intelligible to us. Any such reflections are historically conditioned. A first requirement, accordingly, is to become conscious of the nature of that conditioning. One way of achieving this awareness is to rethink the thought of someone who has attempted to do this in the past, and especially in the circumstances of a different tradition of civilization from our own. That is the initial purpose of turning to Ibn Khaldun.

Recent decades have seen a number of works about Ibn Khaldun, and references to his work by contemporary scholars. These various readings of Ibn Khaldun find interesting things in his work; but none of them is concerned directly with the question raised here about how to understand change in world order.[43]

---

42 *Ibid.*, p. 256.
43 Arnold Toynbee praised Ibn Khaldun as a great, perhaps the greatest, philosopher of history. Toynbee certainly borrowed from him some of his leading ideas, including the principle that physical environments must not be either too hard or too lush in order that they stimulate the development of civilization (Arnold Toynbee, *A Study of History*, abridgement of vols. I–IV by D. C. Somervell [Oxford: Geoffrey Cumberledge, 1946], I, chs. 7 and 8; and vol. XII, *Reconsiderations* [London: Oxford University Press, 1961], p. 205). Gellner considers Ibn Khaldun to be the best interpreter of Islamic society and a sociologist whose theoretical insights are comparable to those of Durkheim and Weber. A recent Foucaultian interpretation, on the other hand, finds little in Ibn Khaldun's work that would not have been common knowledge in his time – no paradigmatic unity, no epistemological break, no coherent discourse, but only a cluster of conventional discourses (Aziz Al-Azmeh, *Reinterpretation*, pp. 146–62).

  Some commentators have pictured Ibn Khaldun as the father of sociology, and have emphasized the rationalist, empirical element in his work, perceiving him as continuous with the Aristotelian–Averroist current of Islamic thought and a forerunner of a modernist secular Islam (Simon, *Ibn Khaldun's Science of Human Culture*). Others, by contrast, stress his religious commitment (H. A. R. Gibb, "The Islamic Background of

In this latter perspective, inquiry focuses upon what the constituent elements of world order are (or were at any given time) and how and why the relationships among these elements has changed during critical phases of structural transformation. In the world of Ibn Khaldun, order begins with a unity of message and power, the rule of the Prophet and its succession in the Caliphate. That order is then transformed in a dispersion of power among states, and a separation of political power from the propagation of the message. The message instead becomes embedded in society, while court circles are motivated by the gaining and preservation of power more than by the application of the message.

The status of the state in this process of transformation is worth underlining. The state might have become the focal point of power and the principal object of Ibn Khaldun's inquiry;[44] but the state in Muslim history never attained the absolute claims accorded it in European history. The claims of world order and the image of the Caliphate never completely vanished from the intersubjectivity of Islam despite the prolonged absence of institutional embodiment. This is particularly significant at the present time, when states, though repositories of organized power, are perceived as intermediate between the *telos* of Islamic peoples and the achievement of a reunified Islam.

Much of the fluidity among institutional forms and ideal conceptions in the Islamic political ontology Ibn Khaldun finds to be explainable in terms of how human groups relate to economic conditions of survival (pastoral, agricultural, and urban artisan and commercial forms of social life), and to the formation of rival dominant classes – both political-military-administrative classes linked to the state, and an urban-commercial class outside the state. This decentralization of power has left the message as a thin bond of fellowship with no corresponding institutionalized support, a residue of intersubjectivity

Ibn Khaldun's Political Theory," *Bulletin of the School of Oriental and African Studies*, 7 [1933–5], pp. 23–31).

The revival of Ibn Khaldun has also nourished the revival of Arab and Islamic nationalism. He has been read as showing the means of Arab renaissance through an *'asabiya* capable of creating unity in a modern pan-Arab state. This interpretation has been seen as strengthening both the Ba'ath concept of a secular Islam, and the Qadafist and Muslim Brothers' notion of Islam providing the cohesive force for national restoration on the scale of the whole Islamic world (Olivier Carre, in Majallat Et-Tarikh, *Actes*, pp. 264–5).

One recent study views Ibn Khaldun's analysis of the fourteenth-century Maghreb as probing the underlying causes of underdevelopment and as giving a clue why economic development in Third World conditions has taken a different course from Western capitalism (Lacoste, *Ibn Khaldun*).

44 Aziz Al-Azmeh, *Reinterpretation*, pp. 11–33.

awaiting some future possible but not necessarily probable revival through the coming of the Mahdi.

The above changes can be understood rationally in terms of human thought reflecting upon human behavior. They are not to be interpreted as determined by some extra-human transcendent or immanent force, neither by a Divine Providence nor by a Hegelian Reason. There is thus a science of politics which is in practice the science of history, i.e., the rational understanding of collective human practices. Under distinct circumstances, ideas and material conditions come together to form consistent patterns of action or structures which in their turn are worn out by experience and changing circumstances and replaced by other structures.

What is, then, the relationship of this rational understanding of history to the Law, i.e., to the revealed message about good and evil in human action? By putting together Ibn Khaldun's text with his life, we may reply that the two are distinct but not irreconcilable. A person can have both an understanding of why things are the way they are and a conviction that some things are morally reprehensible and stand to be corrected. One of our contemporaries, Isaiah Berlin, has stated this dilemma succinctly in terms applicable to the late twentieth century:

> In the end, men choose between ultimate values; they choose as they do, because their life and thought are determined by fundamental moral categories and concepts that are as much a part of their being and conscious thought and sense of their identity, as their basic physical structure.
>
> . . . Principles are not less sacred because their duration cannot be guaranteed. Indeed, the very desire for guarantees that our values are eternal and secure in some objective heaven is perhaps only a craving for the certainties of childhood or the absolute values of our primitive past. "To realise the relative validity of one's convictions," said an admirable writer of our time, "and yet stand for them unflinchingly, is what distinguishes a civilised man from a barbarian." To demand more than this is perhaps a deep and incurable metaphysical need; but to allow it to guide one's practice is a symptom of an equally deep, and far more dangerous, moral and political immaturity.[45]

There are certain rules of prudence suggested by Ibn Khaldun in the situation of conflict or inconsistency between moral principles held with conviction and the practical possibilities of politics. His rule is to pursue moral principle within the realm of the feasible. This is not a

---

[45] Isaiah Berlin, *Two Concepts of Liberty* (Oxford: Clarendon Press, 1958), p. 57. The "admirable writer of our time" was, I think, Joseph Schumpeter, but I have not been able to trace the source of the quotation.

counsel of despair. It need not imply passivity or defeatism. Analysis of feasibility may reveal opportunities for a new departure. The moment of prophesy seizes the historical opportunity when the message can become political reality. This is the moment when the rational and the revealed again attain unity. Such moments mark a new beginning in historical process, the founding of a new order; but the new order will, in the rational understanding of the laws of historical change, itself be subject to fruition and decay. It has no eternal guarantee, even though its proponents act as though it should have.

What Ibn Khaldun does not explicitly contemplate is the possibility of alternative intersubjective worlds coexisting without losing, each of them, their internal conviction and dynamism; and without one coming to dominate and absorb the others through its superior 'asabiya. This is the essence of our problem of conceiving a post-hegemonic world on the threshold of the twenty-first century.

Can there be distinct, thriving macro-societies, each with its own solidarity, each pursuing a distinct *telos*, which could coexist through a supra-intersubjectivity? This supra-intersubjectivity would have to embody principles of coexistence without necessarily reconciling differences in goals. It would have to allow for a degree of harmoniz-ation of the trajectories of the different macro-societies.

Or is the only model of the future one in which differences become absorbed into a new unity, a new global hegemony, perhaps the creation of a new global Mahdi? (The global Mahdi could take the form of a collectivity rather than an individual.)[46] Ibn Khaldun does not answer, but perhaps his skepticism concerning the coming of a Mahdi and his apparent preference for action at the level of local societies can give us a clue.

---

[46] Much as Gramsci envisaged the modern Prince not as an individual but as the Party.

6 THE EFFECTIVENESS OF INTERNATIONAL INSTITUTIONS: HARD CASES AND CRITICAL VARIABLES

Oran R. Young

Should we invest scarce resources on a continuing basis in studies of international institutions or, to use a currently fashionable phrase, international regimes? Or will the recent revival of interest in the role of institutional arrangements in international society prove to be no more than a passing fad, interesting as a response to current events but soon to be forgotten by students of international relations in their relentless search for new ideas?

The answers to these questions must surely flow from the conclusions we reach about the role of social institutions in shaping the behavior of individual members of international society as well as collective behavior flowing from interactive processes at the international level. If, as I and many other students of international institutions believe, institutions are driving forces in the sense that it is possible to explain or predict a sizable proportion of the variance in individual and collective behavior in terms of the operation of institutional arrangements, the study of such arrangements will acquire a prominent and lasting place on the agenda of international relations as a field of study.[1] It will not matter much whether analysts choose to treat institutions as independent variables or as intervening variables.[2] In either case, we will find ourselves thinking long and hard about international institutions in a continuing effort to formulate and test a set of (hopefully cumulative) generalizations spelling out the nature of the links between institutional arrangements on the one hand and individual and collective behavior on the other.[3]

---

[1] See also Oran R. Young, *International Cooperation: Building Regimes for Natural Resources and the Environment* (Ithaca, NY: Cornell University Press, 1989), esp. ch. 3.

[2] Stephen D. Krasner, "Structural Causes and Regime Consequences: Regimes as Intervening Variables," in Stephen D. Krasner, ed., *International Regimes* (Ithaca, NY: Cornell University Press, 1983), pp. 1–21.

[3] This chapter focuses throughout on the role of institutions as determinants of behavior in international society. But this is not meant to diminish the importance of thinking concomitantly about institutions as dependent variables whose character is shaped by the operation of a variety of factors, including the impact both of ideas and of material conditions. In international society, the causal links among institutions, ideas, and material conditions ordinarily flow in both directions.

But if, as most realists and some neorealists apparently believe, international institutions are epiphenomena in the sense that powerful actors are able not only to ignore their dictates when they dislike the expected results but also to restructure the arrangements at will, the current interest in international regimes and institutional arrangements more generally will prove to be no more than a passing fad of the sort familiar to all those who have studied international relations in recent times.[4] Though some scholars might still find it convenient to make use of the notion of international regimes for descriptive purposes, those seeking to develop powerful generalizations about international phenomena would have little interest in dwelling on the intricacies of institutional arrangements.

THE PROBLEM OF EFFECTIVENESS

How can we assess the significance of institutions as independent or intervening variables with regard to individual and collective behavior at the international level and, in so doing, resolve the conflict between these divergent points of view?[5] It will help, at the outset, to clarify what is at stake in efforts to come to terms with the problem of effectiveness.

At the most general level, effectiveness is a measure of the role of social institutions in shaping or molding behavior in international society. The idea of effectiveness with regard to the behavior of individual actors is straightforward enough. An institution is effective to the extent that its operation impels actors to behave differently than they would if the institution did not exist or if some other institutional arrangement were put in its place. The only significant complication concerning individual behavior arises from the fact that states, which are the principal members of international society, are collective entities. In assessing the effectiveness of international institutions, therefore, we must look at the behavior of states not only in responding to the dictates of international institutions on their own behalf but also in implementing the provisions of regimes in such a way as to ensure that those operating under their jurisdiction (for example, corporations,

---

4 For a clear expression of this view see Susan Strange, "Cave! Hic Dragones: A Critique of Regime Analysis," in Krasner, ed., *International Regimes*, pp. 337–54.
5 Students of domestic society habitually assume that social institutions are effective, an assumption that accounts for their practice of focusing on specific ways in which institutional arrangements shape collective outcomes. But the force of the realist and neorealist critique makes this practice untenable for students of international society.

non-governmental organizations, and even individuals) comply with institutional requirements as well.

The concept of collective behavior (discussed by some writers under such headings as collective outcomes, social outcomes, or macro-behavior), on the other hand, requires some explication.[6] Collective behavior is not simply a term used to describe the behavior of the members of international society in the aggregate. Rather, it refers to the outcomes of interactive processes involving two or more members of international society. The results of arms races, exchange relationships under conditions approaching perfect competition, unregulated uses of common property resources, and other phenomena that can be treated as reaction or Richardson processes all belong to the category of collective behavior.[7] So also do the results of interactive decision-making, like agreements reached through explicit negotiations or outcomes arrived at through tacit bargaining at the international level. The members of international society can and often do differ in their assessments of collective behavior. In the extreme, some members will regard the net welfare effects of a particular form of collective behavior as highly positive, while others see the same behavior as detrimental to their welfare. But none of this alters the fact that collective behavior is properly understood as a concept referring to the products of interactive processes in contrast to the results of individual behavior alone.

In practice, analysts often find it helpful to approach the problem of effectiveness in more concrete terms, posing a series of focused questions about specific international institutions. Has the operation of the institution solved or alleviated the problem that led to its formation? Have the participants been able and willing to implement the institution's principal provisions with respect to activities taking place within their jurisdictions? Do the members ordinarily comply with the institution's core rights and rules? Is the operation of the institution cost effective? Can the institution adapt to changing circumstances without losing its capacity to handle the problem it was created to solve? Is the institution able to survive intact in a changing social, biological, and physical environment? As social scientists have long observed, the gap between the ideal and the actual with respect to the performance of institutions is sizable in every social setting; reliable implementation and perfect compliance are no more to be expected in international

---

[6] Thomas C. Schelling, *Micromotives and Macrobehavior* (New York: Norton, 1978).

[7] On the generic properties of reaction processes, see Anatol Rapoport, *Fights, Games, and Debates* (Ann Arbor, MI: University of Michigan, 1960), Part I.

society than they are in domestic society. But as this array of questions suggests, the effectiveness of international institutions, like their domestic counterparts, can be measured in terms of their success in the areas of implementation, compliance, and persistence.

Effectiveness, treated in this manner, is a matter of degree rather than an all-or-nothing proposition. Institutions are effective to the extent that their operation accounts for the variance in individual and collective behavior observable across spatial or temporal settings. But a number of other factors, like the distribution of power among the members of international society, prevailing systems of ideas, and the interests of individual parties, ordinarily exert an influence on international behavior at the same time. This suggests that multivariate relationships will constitute the norm rather than the exception in this realm. The relative importance of each factor in determining the content of individual and collective behavior consequently becomes a matter for investigation through the formulation of hypotheses about the relationships in question and the application of these hypotheses to actual cases.[8] Research of this kind may yield powerful generalizations. Conversely, it may eventuate in the conclusion that the effectiveness of institutional arrangements differs from one issue-area to another, one regime type to another, one spatial setting to another, or one time period to another.[9]

[8] The argument of this chapter, in contrast to some of the other contributions to this volume, is rooted in a neopositivist epistemology. It therefore takes issue with the call for an interpretive epistemology in the study of international regimes issued by scholars like Kratochwil and Ruggie: Friedrich Kratochwil and John Gerard Ruggie, "International Organization: A State of the Art or an Art of the State," *International Organization*, 40 (Autumn 1986), pp. 753–75. Still, it is appropriate to be clear at the outset about several problems confronting neopositivist studies of the roles social institutions play as determinants of behavior. Deductive models, as exemplified by the theory of games, ordinarily abstract away institutional considerations, a practice that undoubtedly helps to make them tractable in analytic terms but that, at the same time, constitutes a major source of the poorness of fit between the expectations such models generate and observable behavior at the international level. Conventional inductive procedures, on the other hand, are limited by the fact that universes of cases at the international level are often small. Nor do laboratory experiments offer an easy solution to the resultant limitations. Not only is it difficult to generate realistic incentives under laboratory conditions, but it is also common practice in work of this type to treat much of the institutional setting as given rather than as a set of variables subject to alteration in a controlled fashion in the interests of developing generalizations about the consequences of changes in institutional arrangements. The challenge for those working within the epistemological program of neopositivism is to devise imaginative techniques to overcome or circumvent these limitations.

[9] Some of the other contributions to this volume suggest that the effectiveness of international institutions – and indeed the nature of the institutions themselves – is historically contingent in the sense that it differs from one historical era or epoch to another. For a particularly clear expression of this view, see Chapter 5 by Robert W. Cox in this volume.

These observations lead also to an important distinction between effectiveness as such and the performance of institutions as measured in terms of criteria like efficiency or equity.[10] Judged in terms of Pareto optimality, for example, any situation in which the welfare of at least one participant can be improved without harming any of the others is inefficient because it fails to maximize social welfare. Though there is less consensus about the meaning of the criterion, equity is often employed as a measure of the extent to which collective behavior conforms to some normatively preferred distribution of gains among the members of a group or the extent to which the processes leading to the distribution of gains conform to various procedural norms.[11] With these observations in mind, it is easy to see how the idea of effectiveness differs from these evaluative concerns. Effectiveness is simply a measure of the role that institutions play as determinants of the content of individual and collective behavior. While highly effective institutions may produce outcomes that are efficient or equitable, there is no guarantee that the results will always or even frequently conform to the requirements of efficiency, equity, or any other criterion of evaluation. It is easy to understand, under the circumstances, why those convinced that institutions make a difference soon shift their attention to efforts to assess the performance of alternative institutional arrangements in terms of their contribution to the attainment of efficiency, equity, or any of a number of other social goals.[12]

In the discussion to follow, I address the problem of effectiveness from several vantage points in an effort to resolve the controversy surrounding the question of whether international institutions matter.[13] The next section introduces and makes use of an analytic device designed to lay to rest the doubts of those who question whether institutional arrangements or regimes ever make a difference in

[10] For a clear discussion of a number of performance criteria, see Robert Dorfman and Nancy S. Dorfman, eds., *Economics of the Environment*, 2nd edn. (New York: Norton, 1977), Introduction.

[11] For an influential account focusing on outcome/end state ideas about equity or fairness, see John Rawls, *A Theory of Justice* (Cambridge, MA: Harvard University Press, 1971). A similarly influential account stressing process/procedural ideas about equity is Robert Nozick, *Anarchy, State, and Utopia* (New York: Basic Books, 1974).

[12] In a typical formulation, Alt and North ask "Why do some property rights structures lead to productive activity and underpin economic growth, while others result in waste and unproductive activity?" James Alt and Douglass North, "Series Editors' Preface," in Gary D. Libecap, *Contracting for Property Rights* (New York: Cambridge University Press, 1989), p. ix.

[13] Young, *International Cooperation*, ch. 3, and Peter M. Haas, "Do Regimes Matter? Epistemic Communities and Mediterranean Pollution Control," *International Organization*, 43 (Summer 1989), pp. 377–403.

international society. I focus on situations that are, in effect, similar to what natural scientists think of as critical experiments. In the case of international institutions, this means concentrating on what may be called hard cases or situations in which the circumstances at hand are distinctly unfavorable to the operation of social institutions as determinants of individual or collective behavior. Through an examination of several hard cases in some detail, I show that institutions do make a difference, even under these adverse conditions. This is sufficient, I argue, to license the conclusion that it will not do simply to dismiss international institutions as epiphenomena.

Yet this finding hardly justifies a leap to the opposite conclusion or, in other words, an assertion that institutions are always or even typically critical determinants of individual or collective behavior in international society. What is needed to make further progress at this juncture is an analysis of factors that will either enhance or diminish the impact of institutional arrangements on individual and collective behavior. In the second half of the chapter, I take up this challenge and begin the process of pinpointing factors that control the extent to which institutional arrangements determine behavior at the international level.[14] In the process, I seek to launch a program of research and analysis that transcends the sterile debate between those who contend that international institutions are of central importance and those who assert that they are mere epiphenomena. This program should prove interesting to anyone desiring to broaden and deepen our understanding of the role of institutional arrangements in international society.[15]

HARD CASES

A hard case when it comes to the effectiveness of international institutions is a situation in which participants have both incentives and opportunities to disregard or change institutional requirements.

---

[14] To maximize the prospects for developing powerful generalizations, I focus throughout on international regimes or, in other words, institutional arrangements that deal with specific issue areas. Other contributors to this volume direct attention to international or world orders, a perspective pitched at a much higher level of generality and, therefore, unlikely to yield a sizable universe of cases.

[15] To the extent that institutions are effective, they are central to the idea of governance without government in international society. Given the well-known drawbacks associated with relying on centralized organizations (that is, governments) in domestic society, the more decentralized methods of handling the task of governance in international society may emerge during the foreseeable future as a source of insights of interest to students of governance in other social settings.

Among the factors likely to produce such conditions, the following stand out.

1   One or more of the prominent members of the subject group are predisposed to dislike the outcomes they expect a regime to produce.
2   It is comparatively easy to violate the rules of the regime either without detection or in such a way that incontrovertible evidence of the violation is difficult to obtain.
3   Ongoing changes in the character of international society raise doubts about the sociopolitical or intellectual underpinnings of the regime.

The more of these conditions present at the same time, the harder the case as far as the effectiveness of institutional arrangements is concerned.

A finding that international institutions are often, or even always, ineffective in hard cases would not warrant the conclusion that institutional arrangements are never significant determinants of individual or collective behavior in international society. But the essential point for this analysis arises when we turn this observation around. If international institutions not only survive intact but also play significant roles in shaping behavior in hard cases, we can fairly conclude that they will be influential under more benign conditions as well. It follows that an examination of hard cases can yield results of profound importance to those of us endeavoring to assess the role of institutional arrangements in international society.

To pursue this line of reasoning more systematically, I have chosen three hard cases for consideration in some detail: (i) the regime for the Svalbard Archipelago set forth in the Treaty Relating to Spitsbergen of 1920, (ii) the regime for whaling formalized in the International Convention for the Regulation of Whaling of 1946, and (iii) the regime governing international trade articulated in the General Agreement on Tariffs and Trade (GATT) of 1947. In each case, I will argue, these institutional arrangements have had a substantial and continuing impact on individual and collective behavior, despite the presence of one or more of the conditions identified at the beginning of this section.

Svalbard

The regime outlined in the 1920 Treaty Relating to Spitsbergen, negotiated during the course of the Paris peace conference called to settle a range of issues outstanding in the aftermath of World War I, represents a sharp departure from the terms of the regime for the

Svalbard Archipelago contemplated before the War.[16] In 1914, those interested in Svalbard had been on the verge of an agreement to declare Svalbard *terra nullius* and to establish a three-party directorate composed of Norway, Russia, and Sweden to manage the affairs of the archipelago. The Treaty of 1920, by contrast, awards sovereignty over Svalbard to Norway on the condition that Norway agrees to allow nationals of all the contracting parties access to Svalbard's natural resources on an equal footing, to abide by strict limits on the taxation of commercial enterprises in the Svalbard area, and to maintain the archipelago in a permanently demilitarized state. Shifting conditions on the ground, like the sale of American assets in Svalbard to a Norwegian company in 1916, certainly played a role in bringing about this change. But there is little doubt that the agreement to create the regime articulated in the 1920 Treaty owes much to the facts that the Soviet Union and Germany did not participate in negotiating the terms of the regime and that neither the new Soviet government, preoccupied with a burgeoning civil war, nor the defeated German government was in any position to veto the agreement arrived at in Paris.

Within days after the signing of the 1920 Treaty, however, the Soviet Union lodged a protest against the proposed regime, refusing to recognize the validity of the Spitsbergen Treaty and becoming, in the process, an important dissatisfied player with regard to this arrangement.[17] But the nascent regime for Svalbard had little difficulty surviving this initial Soviet challenge to become a widely accepted institutional arrangement. Though formal adherence on the part of the Soviet Union did not come until 1935 (due to American opposition arising from the general unwillingness of the United States to recognize the Soviet government), the Soviet Union had agreed as early as 1924 to withdraw its protest regarding the Svalbard regime in return for diplomatic recognition by the Norwegian government. In effect, the Soviets concluded early on that acknowledgment of specific international arrangements, like the regime for Svalbard, constituted a reasonable price to pay for the acceptance of the Soviet Union as a member in good standing of the community of nations.

Yet this early success did not eliminate Soviet sensitivities regarding the institutional arrangements pertaining to Svalbard. On the contrary, the growing strategic importance of the area served to heighten Soviet

---

[16] For histories of the formation and early operation of the Svalbard regime see Trygve Mathisen, *Svalbard in International Politics 1871–1925* (Oslo: Broggers Boktrykkeris Forlag, 1954), and Elen C. Singh, *The Spitsbergen (Svalbard) Question: United States Foreign Policy, 1907–1935* (Oslo: Universitetsforlaget, 1980).

[17] Singh, *The Spitsbergen (Svalbard) Question*, pp. 108–9.

interest in efforts to restructure the Svalbard regime. In 1944, with the war in Europe drawing to a close and Soviet troops occupying part of Finnmark, the Soviet Union proposed to the government of Norway (in exile) the abrogation of the 1920 Treaty and its replacement by a joint Norwegian–Soviet arrangement for the defense of the Svalbard Archipelago coupled with the cession of Bear Island by Norway to the Soviet Union.[18] Yet even under these inauspicious circumstances, the Svalbard regime remained intact. Unable to achieve their goals through diplomacy, the Soviets refrained from forcing the issue militarily. The Norwegian government, following the liberation of Norway from German occupation, simply resumed the administration of Svalbard on the terms laid out in the 1920 Treaty.

During the 1980s, a new disagreement arose regarding the applicability of the treaty regime to the continental shelf area adjacent to the Svalbard Archipelago.[19] The Soviet Union, along with several other signatories to the 1920 Treaty, has taken the view that Svalbard has a continental shelf of its own and that the treaty's guarantee of equal access to natural resources should be extended to apply to this shelf area. For its part, Norway maintains that the continental shelf in the area is a natural extension of Norway proper so that there is no Svalbard shelf as such. Not surprisingly, the treaty, which was negotiated before the era of intense interest in the resources of the outer continental shelf, is silent on the matter. Today, the issue remains unresolved, though there is a striking asymmetry in the distribution of power favoring those advocating the more expansive interpretation regarding the application of the treaty to the adjacent shelf areas.

Periodic quarrels have arisen over the application of specific Norwegian mining regulations and certain other rules to the activities of Soviet nationals residing in the Svalbard coal-mining communities of Barentsburg and Pyramiden, exacerbated in some instances perhaps by the difficulty in verifying compliance with such rules on a non-intrusive basis.[20] But it is indisputable that the treaty regime has proven generally effective in governing human activities in and relating to the archipelago since 1920. Svalbard remains demilitarized; the nationals of all the signatories to the 1920 Treaty enjoy access to the resources of the

---

[18] *Ibid.*, Epilogue, and David Scrivener, "The Soviet Union and Northern Waters," in Clive Archer and David Scrivener, eds., *Northern Waters* (London: Croom Helm, 1986), pp. 208–33.

[19] Scrivener, "The Soviet Union and Northern Waters," and Willy Ostreng, "Soviet–Norwegian Relations in the Arctic," *International Journal*, 39 (Autumn 1984), pp. 866–87.

[20] Willy Ostreng, *Politics in High Latitudes: The Svalbard Archipelago* (London: C. Hurst, 1977), esp. ch. 11. These quarrels have shown signs of tapering off in recent years.

archipelago on an equal footing, and Norwegian sovereignty in the area is widely acknowledged. The recurrent discontent of the Soviet Union, by any measure the region's preeminent power, has neither undermined nor severely distorted the regime negotiated in Paris in 1919–20. No doubt, it is fair to observe in explaining this outcome that the Soviets have always concluded that the costs of forcing the issue with regard to the Svalbard regime would exceed any benefits they might reasonably hope to reap from doing so. But this in no way detracts from the striking evidence of the long-term effectiveness of institutional arrangements in this hard case.

Commercial whaling

Faced with incontrovertible evidence regarding the depletion of stocks of most of the great whales, the principal whaling nations negotiated an international regime in 1946 designed to regulate commercial whaling.[21] As initially organized under the terms of the International Convention for the Regulation of Whaling, this regime took the form of a users' club dedicated to the conservationist goal of managing the consumptive use of whales on a maximum sustainable yield basis. During its early years, the performance of the regime was relatively uncontroversial but also generally ineffectual in protecting remaining stocks of great whales. By the 1960s, most of these whales were widely considered to be endangered species.[22]

In 1972, however, the United Nations Conference on the Human Environment "called for a ten-year moratorium on commercial whaling to allow time for more research on whales and the development of a better regulatory system."[23] By the early 1980s, some of the traditional whaling nations (for example, the United States) had gone out of the business of commercial whaling. A sizable number of non-whaling nations had also acceded to the 1946 Convention, acting in many cases with the express intent of using membership to work toward terminating commercial whaling. What had once been a relatively small users' club, therefore, soon evolved into an arrangement the majority of whose members did not engage in whaling

---

[21] For a recent review of the origins and performance of this regime, consult Pat W. Birnie, "International Legal Issues in the Management and Protection of the Whale: A Review of Four Decades of Experience," *Natural Resources Journal*, 29 (Fall 1989), pp. 903–34.

[22] Simon Lyster, *International Wildlife Law* (Cambridge: Grotius Publications, 1985), ch. 2.

[23] Robert Mandel, *Conflict Over The World's Resources* (New York: Greenwood Press, 1988), p. 47.

themselves and strongly favored the cessation of commercial whaling on the part of major whaling nations, like Iceland, Japan, and the Soviet Union. A direct result of this development was the transformation of the group of whaling nations into a beleaguered minority within the whaling regime, a condition that has made this regime a hard case since the early 1980s.[24]

In 1982, the International Whaling Commission, responding to the preferences of the new majority, voted to impose a moratorium (to last at least five years) on commercial whaling from 1985/6 in Antarctica and from 1986 elsewhere.[25] Japan and the Soviet Union immediately filed formal objections to this decision, a procedure recognized under the whaling regime as a means of allowing individual members to exempt themselves from the provisions of specific decisions of the Commission.[26] But what looked like an emerging confrontation with the potential to destroy the whaling regime never materialized. Not only did the whaling nations remain parties to the regime, but they also soon began to alter their behavior in such a way as to bring it into line with the requirements of the moratorium, at least on a *de facto* basis. At the 1985 meeting of the International Whaling Commission, the Soviet Union announced its intention to end commercial whaling; the last Soviet whaling ship ceased operations in 1987. For its part, Japan announced in 1985 that it would end commercial whaling in 1988. Not surprisingly, both countries asserted that their actions were based entirely on domestic considerations and denied that their decisions to terminate commercial whaling could be construed in any way as an acceptance of the will of the majority within the whaling regime. For the most part, however, these explanations are properly construed as face-saving devices. In actual fact, both Japan and the Soviet Union found themselves facing strong pressure emanating from a variety of sources to comply with the International Whaling Commission's moratorium on commercial whaling.

---

[24] For an analysis that focuses on the implications of shifting membership in the whaling regime, see Alf Hakon Hoel, *The International Whaling Commission 1972–1984: New Members, New Concerns* (Oslo: Fridtjof Nansen Institute, 1985).

[25] Certain species of small whales (for example, pilot whales, Baird's beaked whales) are not included in the moratorium. Additionally, the moratorium exempts subsistence whaling on the part of aboriginal peoples (for instance, the Inupiaq of northern Alaska). A particularly sensitive point concerns the treatment of what has come to be known as small-type coastal whaling (STCW) in Japan, Norway, and a few other countries. See Arne Kalland and Brian Moeran, *Endangered Culture: Japanese Whaling in Cultural Perspective* (Copenhagen: Nordic Institute of Asian Studies, 1990).

[26] On the objection procedure, consult Lyster, *International Wildlife Law*, pp. 27–8.

More recently, several countries, including Japan and some of the smaller members of the whaling regime (for example, Iceland, South Korea, and Norway), have sought to exploit a loophole in the whaling regime by taking a sizable number of whales for purposes of "scientific research." But the overwhelming majority of the regime's members have branded this effort to circumvent the moratorium on commercial whaling an unacceptable practice, and pressure has begun to mount on the nations involved to discontinue their "scientific" whaling.[27] Already, South Korea and Iceland have capitulated and agreed to give up the taking of whales for scientific purposes; it seems probable that the Japanese will feel compelled to bow to international pressure on this matter before long.

A remarkable feature of this case is the evidence it provides that a regime can become more effective as a result of changes in its membership and, consequently, in the will of the majority.[28] What began as a users' club imposing few meaningful restrictions on the actions of its members has become an institutional arrangement capable of bringing substantial pressure to bear on nations to comply with its decisions.[29] No doubt, some will point out that a good deal of the pressure flows from the actions of individual states rather than the International Whaling Commission itself (for example, American actions or threats of action involving reductions of catch quotas within its fishery conservation zone and restrictions on imports of fish products from countries unwilling to comply with decisions of the Commission).[30] Additionally, the developments of the 1980s regarding commercial whaling reflect a growing worldwide sentiment in favor of the cessation of commercial

[27] See, for example, Scott Armstrong, "US Makes Few Gains at World Whale Meeting," *Christian Science Monitor*, June 19, 1989, p. 7.

[28] For an account arguing that the whaling regime has become politicized but confirming, in the process, that it is hard for individual participants to ignore the will of the majority in this case, see Milton M. R. Freeman, "A Commentary on Political Issues with Regard to Contemporary Whaling," *North Atlantic Studies*, 2 (1990), pp. 106-16.

[29] Today, there are indications that some of the smaller states that became active in the whaling regime during the 1980s are beginning to lose interest. Needless to say, there is much speculation on how this will affect the actions of the International Whaling Commission.

[30] For a sophisticated account of fisheries issues involving the United States and Japan, see Edward L. Miles, *The U.S./Japan Fisheries Relationship in the Northeast Pacific: From Conflict to Cooperation?* (Seattle, WA: University of Washington School of Fisheries, 1989). More generally, the actions of individual states in circumstances of this sort amount to a form of social pressure. In cases where a single, dominant actor relies heavily on social pressure to elicit compliance with the provisions of an institutional arrangement, it is appropriate to ask whether it makes sense to describe the institution itself as effective. For the most part, however, social pressure is an important basis of compliance with the dictates of institutions in domestic as well as international society.

171

whaling. But there is nothing unusual about the role of such factors as determinants of the effectiveness of international (or, for that matter, domestic) institutions, and these observations do nothing to alter the principal conclusion to be drawn from this case. The whaling regime has clearly played a role as a determinant of behavior in this area, despite the fact that a number of those subject to the regime's provisions, including powerful states like Japan and the Soviet Union, have been openly unhappy about the substantive content of these outcomes.

International trade

Crystalized in the provisions of the General Agreement on Tariffs and Trade of 1947, the postwar regime governing international trade reflects the liberal belief that free trade yields economic benefits for all and, in the process, contributes to a peaceful world by stimulating the development of a dense network of mutually beneficial commercial relationships. To this end, the regime sets forth a series of concrete arrangements (for example, the minimization of discrimination through a generalization of most-favored-nation treatment, the avoidance of non-tariff barriers to trade, the elimination of unfair trade practices, the acceptance of certain safeguards) designed to reduce tariffs and other barriers to trade and to eliminate discriminatory treatment in international commerce.[31]

Though it has become fashionable to dwell on a variety of stresses that have arisen in connection with these arrangements (for example, the rise of bilateral and sectoral approaches to trade, the emergence of voluntary export restraints, the problem of dealing with the rapidly growing trade in services), it is hard to deny that the GATT regime has been remarkably successful over the last forty years. As one prominent commentator puts it, the regime has not only

> successfully avoided trade wars (indeed, even isolated retaliatory measures have been rare and contained), but it also has made possible a large expansion of trade. The liberalizing of international trade under the GATT has resulted in a growth of real exports well in excess of the increase in world production of movable goods. This has meant that a significant part of the growth in the world economy [has been]

[31] For detailed accounts consult Kenneth W. Dam, *The GATT: Law and International Economic Organization* (Chicago: University of Chicago Press, 1970), and Jock A. Finlayson and Mark W. Zacher, "The GATT and the Regulation of Trade Barriers: Regime Dynamics and Functions," in Krasner, ed., *International Regimes*, pp. 273–314.

export-led. Altogether, this is an impressive record for the . . . negotiated order in international trade.[32]

Yet the GATT regime has faced severe challenges that make it an exceptionally hard case in the terms of this analysis. Two of these challenges are particularly relevant to this discussion of the effectiveness of international institutions: the structuralist challenge of the 1970s spearheaded by the Group of 77 on behalf of the world's less developed countries and the protectionist challenge of the 1980s fueled by the dramatic growth of trade imbalances affecting major players like the United States.

The structuralist challenge arose, in part, from a desire for stability or predictability on the part of those heavily dependent on exports of commodities (for example, sugar, coffee, tin) whose world market prices have historically been subject to rapid and severe fluctuations. At a more fundamental level, however, the structuralists have argued that the liberal regime for international trade, with its emphasis on relatively unregulated market transactions, inevitably rewards participants in proportion to their initial resource endowments. Because the distribution of resource endowments is highly skewed in favor of the advanced industrial countries of the first world, the liberal regime will necessarily lead to a situation in which the rich get richer and the poor remain poor. The antidote to this problem, according to the structuralists, is to replace the liberal regime for trade with one in which authoritative interventions are employed to alter the distribution of rewards that would be produced by an unregulated market-oriented regime.[33]

Working through the Group of 77 and articulating their concerns in various United Nations forums (most strikingly, the United Nations Conference on Trade and Development), the structuralists mounted a concerted attack during the 1970s on prevailing international arrangements governing an assortment of economic interactions, including international trade. Treated as an interlocking set of concrete proposals, the institutional vision of the structuralists became known as the new international economic order (NIEO), a program calling for drastic changes in the GATT regime along with a number of other economic

---

[32] Gardner Patterson, "The GATT and the Negotiation of International Trade Rules," in Alan K. Henrikson, ed., *Negotiating World Order: The Artisanship and Architecture of Global Diplomacy* (Wilmington, DE: Scholarly Resources, 1986), p. 184.

[33] For a sophisticated presentation of the argument underlying the structuralist challenge, see Stephen D. Krasner, *Structural Conflict: The Third World against Global Liberalism* (Berkeley, CA: University of California Press, 1985).

institutions.[34] Yet today there are few who would deny that the structuralist challenge has failed to produce significant changes in the trade regime or in other international economic regimes. In effect, the GATT and most of its counterparts maintained their effectiveness in the face of this challenge.

Despite the fact that the agenda of the structuralists attracted the support of the majority of those participating in the relevant regimes and became a source of serious concern in United Nations circles, some observers may well dismiss this episode as an effort on the part of the weak to force changes on the strong. Adopting an interpretation of this sort, in fact, it is possible (though not altogether convincing) to argue that the structuralist challenge never posed a profound threat to the effectiveness of the GATT regime.

In the case of the protectionist challenge, by contrast, such an argument is clearly inappropriate. Everyone acknowledges that the influence of protectionist forces grew rapidly during the 1980s and that these forces now constitute a severe stress on the GATT regime.[35] The problem is particularly serious in the case of the United States, a member of the trade regime that is still one of the giants (along with Japan and the European Community), even though it no longer enjoys hegemonic power with regard to the institutional arrangements governing international trade. Over the last decade, the United States has become increasingly burdened by massive trade imbalances resulting from a combination of declines in the competitiveness of key industries (for example, automobiles), a movement of American-controlled production offshore to benefit from cheap labor, an over-valued currency, and the effects of certain non-tariff barriers (especially in the realm of service industries not presently covered by the GATT).[36] And internal political considerations make it infeasible at this juncture to adopt the traditional prescription of domestic austerity to deal with such problems.

Under the circumstances, the United States (along with a number of other GATT members) has resorted increasingly to devices, like bilateral trade agreements and voluntary export restraints for specific

---

[34] For a succinct introduction to the NIEO see Marvin S. Soroos, *Beyond Sovereignty: The Challenge of Global Policy* (Columbia, SC: University of South Carolina Press, 1986), ch. 6.

[35] See, for example, the essays on trade policy by Richardson, Strauss, Kunihiro, and Pratt in Martin Feldstein, ed., *International Economic Cooperation* (Chicago: University of Chicago Press, 1988), pp. 167–231.

[36] The extension of GATT rules to various service industries is one of the issues on the agenda of the ongoing but deeply troubled Uruguay round of negotiations intended to reach agreement on a package of adjustments in the provisions of the trade regime.

industries, that violate the spirit, if not the letter, of the GATT regime and that could eventually lead to a severe erosion or even the collapse of the GATT. No doubt, these are serious matters. Even so, there is an alternative perspective on the current situation that commands particular attention in the context of this discussion. While the GATT regime is clearly experiencing severe stresses today, no one would argue that the postwar institutional arrangements governing international trade are no longer effective; few would be rash enough to predict confidently the imminent demise of the GATT regime in the face of the protectionist challenge of the 1980s and early 1990s. What we see here, then, is an extremely hard case in which an international institution has already withstood unusual stresses without losing its effectiveness and may well survive the even greater stresses that many analysts now see on the horizon. Under the circumstances, I conclude that the GATT case provides additional testimony to the effectiveness of institutional arrangements as determinants of individual and collective behavior in international society.

What conclusions can we draw from this discussion of hard cases? Certainly, such a brief account does not license the conclusion that institutional arrangements invariably (or even generally) determine the content of behavior in international society. But it does suffice, I believe, to demonstrate that the argument of those who assert that international institutions are mere epiphenomena is wrong. International regimes and, more broadly, international institutions do matter. In the face of this evidence, there is little to be gained from continuing to debate this issue. The important thing, at this stage, is to move on to an examination of factors influencing the degree of effectiveness of specific institutional arrangements in international society.

CRITICAL VARIABLES

Like their domestic counterparts, international institutions vary greatly in terms of effectiveness. Some end up as dead letters that have little or no impact on individual or collective behavior, while others evolve into coercive social practices that even the most influential members of international society can ignore only at their peril. What is needed now, therefore, is a search for those factors that enhance or diminish the role of institutions as determinants of behavior at the international level. In the discussion to follow, I address this concern in a preliminary way, articulating, explaining, and illustrating a set of propositions dealing with the circumstances under which international institutions are likely to prove more or less effective.

The sources of effectiveness are separable, in a rough and ready fashion, into two broad categories. There are, on the one hand, factors that are endogenous in the sense that they involve properties or attributes of the institutional arrangements themselves. The identification of such factors is of obvious practical value, since an understanding of them will yield insights directly relevant to the efforts of those currently responsible for designing international regimes for any number of distinct issue areas. Additionally, there are factors that are exogenous in the sense that they involve broader social or contextual conditions within which specific institutional arrangements operate. Those designing international regimes will find these factors harder to subject to conscious control than the factors in the first category. Even so, a knowledge of these contextual factors can play an important role both in improving decisions about the timing of efforts to launch new institutions and in assisting those responsible for devising the provisions of constitutional contracts to adjust the character of new institutions to the conditions under which they will operate. The factors emphasized in the discussion to follow exemplify both of these sources of effectiveness.[37]

Transparency

The effectiveness of international institutions varies directly with the ease of monitoring or verifying compliance with their principal behavioral prescriptions. It requires no sophisticated analysis to realize that institutions can be effective only when members of the subject group ordinarily comply with the requirements embedded in their rights and rules. But compliance in turn involves at least three distinct sets of considerations: (i) the ease with which violations on the part of subjects can be detected, (ii) the probability that violators will be subject to sanctions of one kind or another, and (iii) the magnitude of the sanctions imposed.[38] The essential insight underlying the proposition under consideration here is that the prospect of being found out is often just as important, and sometimes more important, to the potential violator

[37] Marc Levy has suggested to me that the determinants of effectiveness are likely to vary with regime type or with the character of the underlying problems institutions address. Coordination regimes and institutions that take the form of clubs, for instance, may differ significantly in these terms. I regard this as a promising line of inquiry, whose exploration must nonetheless wait for another occasion.

[38] For more general treatments of compliance see Oran R. Young, *Compliance and Public Authority, A Theory with International Applications* (Baltimore, MD: Johns Hopkins University Press, 1979), and Roger Fisher, *Improving Compliance with International Law* (Charlottesville, VA: University Press of Virginia, 1981).

than the prospect of becoming the target of more or less severe sanctions of a conventional or material sort. There are, in other words, many situations in which those contemplating violations will refrain from breaking the rules if they expect their non-compliant behavior to be exposed, even if they know that the probability that their violations will be met with sanctions is low. Policy-makers, like private individuals, are sensitive to the social opprobrium that accompanies violations of widely accepted behavioral prescriptions. They are, in short, motivated by a desire to avoid the sense of shame or social disgrace that commonly befalls those who break widely accepted rules.[39]

This does not mean, of course, that the prospect of exposure will be sufficient to deter all potential violators of the rights and rules of international regimes. As in domestic social settings, some level of non-compliant behavior is not only expectable, but it also does not pose a serious threat to the viability of most sets of rights and rules or the social practices they embody. Nor does this proposition imply that social opprobrium is the only source of incentives for the members of international society to comply with the dictates of institutional arrangements; far from it. Even so, these observations about the importance of shame or social disgrace as a mechanism of social control should constitute good news for those alarmed by the fact that enforcement is even harder to use effectively (not to mention efficiently) in international society than it is in domestic society. In actuality, the role of enforcement as a basis of compliance is regularly exaggerated by those who worry about the problem of compliance. The social costs of enforcement are high in all social settings; any society compelled to rely on enforcement as the principal means of ensuring compliance would quickly find itself facing both financial and moral bankruptcy. The realization that the prospect of exposure, in contrast to the prospect of becoming a target of conventional sanctions, is a key determinant of compliance in international society is therefore a matter of considerable importance.

The practical implications of this proposition are also significant. Transparency is, at one and the same time, a function of the way in which behavioral prescriptions are formulated and of the technology that can be brought to bear in efforts to monitor or verify compliance with behavioral prescriptions. It makes a difference, for example, whether institutional arrangements require responsible parties (whether they are in charge of weapons systems, bank accounts, or

---

[39] On the distinction between shame and guilt as mechanisms of social control, see Rawls, *A Theory of Justice*, esp. Section 65.

fishing boats) to present positive evidence from time to time proving that they are in compliance with the applicable rules or simply to submit to inspections on the part of knowledgeable observers following allegations of non-compliance. It follows that there is scope for the exercise of skill regarding the issue of transparency on the part of those charged with formulating the terms of provisions to be included in institutional arrangements.

At the same time, the significance of transparency at the international level has increased markedly in recent years with the advent of technologies, like earth-orbiting satellites, capable of verifying compliance with a wide range of behavioral prescriptions without resorting to intrusive and therefore politically unacceptable forms of inspection. Perhaps the most dramatic cases in point involve the prospects for reaching agreement on the terms of arms control regimes; the likelihood that any actor can conduct secret nuclear tests or engage in undetected deployments of proscribed weapons systems in violation of the requirements of an arms control regime is now vanishingly small. But these observations about transparency apply with equal force to institutional arrangements in other issue-areas. As the sophistication of monitoring equipment grows, for example, the prospects of being able to engage in undetected violations of environmental regimes, dealing with such matters as restrictions on emissions of airborne pollutants or actions threatening habitat of importance to endangered species, have all but disappeared. Under the circumstances, it is hard to avoid the conclusion that there is a clear and substantial connection between the growth of opportunities to take advantage of transparency on the one hand and the renewed interest in the role of international institutions on the other.

Robustness

The effectiveness of international institutions is a function of the robustness of the social-choice mechanisms they employ. In addition to interlocking sets of rights and rules governing the behavior of the members of subject groups, institutions ordinarily establish procedures for arriving at social (in contrast to individual) choices.[40] The character of these procedures ranges widely from the relatively lightly managed markets featured in the GATT regime through the voting procedures of

---

[40] For an accessible overview of recent theoretical work on social choice see John Bonner, *Introduction to the Theory of Social Choice* (Baltimore, MD: Johns Hopkins University Press, 1986).

the whaling regime and the consensus decision-making of the regime established under the Antarctic Treaty of 1959 to the first come, first served procedure (also known as the law of capture) associated with traditional regimes governing high seas fishing.

Social-choice mechanisms also vary substantially from one institutional arrangement to another in terms of their robustness. Robustness, in this context, has two distinct dimensions. A social-choice mechanism is robust, in contrast to fragile, to the extent that is it can withstand perturbations or disruptive occurrences arising in conjunction with the activities it governs. Robustness in this sense is akin to the idea of stability in equilibrium models.[41] At the same time, the robustness, in contrast to brittleness, of social-choice mechanisms is a matter of their capacity to adjust to changes or disturbances occurring in the broader social environment without undergoing radical transformation. Because these dimensions of robustness do not always covary, a social-choice mechanism can be fragile without being brittle or vice versa.

The robustness of the social-choice mechanisms embedded in specific international institutions is a matter of considerable complexity. Mechanisms that are highly robust so long as the membership of an institutional arrangement remains fixed, for instance, may prove remarkably fragile in the wake of changes in the composition of the subject group. The experience of the United States in the period preceding the Civil War offers a classic case in point. But similar concerns are prominent in international settings (for example, the International Monetary Fund, the European Community, or the International Seabed Authority proposed under the terms of the 1982 Law of the Sea Convention). Similarly, a practice that is highly robust in one social setting may prove much more brittle under other conditions. This is what underlies the now familiar observation that the robustness of relatively unregulated markets in the realm of international trade has declined as a consequence of the waning ability of domestic policy-makers to deploy traditional policy instruments (for example, deflation, unemployment, and recession) to correct severe imbalances in trade at the international level. Much the same can be said about the consequences of certain technological changes. The law of capture as a social-choice mechanism in regimes for high seas fisheries, for instance, which was robust enough to remain relatively unchanged for several

---

[41] For a straightforward discussion of equilibrium models with reference to international relations see Rapoport, *Fights, Games, and Debates*, Part I.

centuries, collapsed within a few years following the introduction of high endurance stern trawlers.[42]

All this suggests that it is important to avoid embracing simplistic conclusions in thinking about the robustness of the social-choice mechanisms embedded in international institutions. Arrangements that are highly stable in terms of their inner workings may have little capacity to adjust to exogenous changes. And institutions that exhibit a remarkable ability to adjust to some types of contextual change may prove extremely brittle in the face of other types of change. Even so, the argument underlying the proposition under consideration here is relatively straightforward. Robustness is one of the keys to the effectiveness of international institutions. It is apparent that excessively fragile or brittle arrangements cannot be effective at all; they will fall by the wayside under the impact of minor crises or insignificant shifts in the social environment. But beyond this, it is the robust institutional arrangements that play an important, ongoing role as determinants of individual and collective behavior in international society, whether or not we find the outcomes they produce appealing in normative terms. This is surely one of the major lessons to be learned from the discussion of hard cases set forth in the first part of this essay.

Transformation rules

The effectiveness of international institutions varies directly with the stringency of acknowledged rules governing changes in their substantive provisions. International institutions differ markedly in the extent to which they encompass explicit and widely acknowledged procedures for handling efforts to alter their substantive provisions. The Svalbard regime, for example, is silent on the question of amending procedures, and there is no simple method for restructuring the market mechanisms that form the backbone of the institutional arrangements governing international trade. While the regime for polar bears articulated in a five-nation 1973 agreement clearly anticipates the possibility of restructuring, it merely recommends consultations among the signatories in the event that alterations seem desirable. The 1959 treaty that forms the core of the Antarctic Treaty System, by contrast, spells out a clear-cut amending procedure that requires the unanimous consent of the Consultative Parties for the adoption of changes.

---

[42] William W. Warner, *Distant Water: The Fate of the North Atlantic Fisherman* (Boston, MA: Little, Brown & Co., 1983).

Even among institutions encompassing well-defined and widely acknowledged procedures governing change, there is great variation regarding the stringency of the requirements imposed on those endeavoring to bring about alterations. Compare the unanimity rule of the Antarctic Treaty System, for instance, with the requirement of a two-thirds majority of parties "present and voting" incorporated in the regime governing trade in endangered species.[43] Contrast both these cases with the possibility of altering resource regimes by simple majority vote in many domestic legislative arenas (for example, the U.S. Congress). And these are all comparatively straightforward cases. The scope for introducing complexities in specifying requirements to be met in altering the provisions of institutional arrangements is virtually limitless.

Turn now to the argument underlying the proposition under consideration here. International institutions will be resistant to change to the extent that requirements for making changes that are both widely acknowledged and stringent impede the efforts of those advocating alterations. Unless it is easy to violate the dictates of existing institutions with impunity, conditions that make it hard to restructure or replace institutional arrangements will contribute to their effectiveness. Compare, in this context, the relative ease with which the U.S. Congress can amend or even replace the provisions of resource regimes (for example, the arrangements for marine fisheries set forth in the Fishery Conservation and Management Act of 1976 or the regime for offshore hydrocarbon development laid out in the Outer Continental Shelf Lands Act Amendments of 1978) with the difficulty of making adjustments in the international institutions governing Antarctica, whaling, or the trade in various commodities.[44]

When change does come to institutional arrangements that are difficult to alter, however, it is apt to be far-reaching and may give the appearance of occurring suddenly. Witness the fundamental changes in the traditional system of rights and rules governing the use of marine resources (for example, the establishment of exclusive economic zones) introduced in the context of the third United Nations Conference on the Law of the Sea (UNCLOS III). Of course, interested parties

---

[43] The regime for trade in endangered species is set forth in the 1973 Convention on International Trade in Endangered Species of Wild Flora and Fauna. For a detailed account, consult Lyster, *International Wildlife Law*, ch. 12.

[44] See also Oran R. Young, *Resource Regimes: Social Institutions and Natural Resources* (Berkeley, CA: University of California Press, 1982), and Jock A. Finlayson and Mark W. Zacher, *Managing International Markets: Developing Countries and the Commodity Trade Regime* (New York: Columbia University Press, 1988).

are ordinarily aware of this prospect. An understanding of this phenomenon, in fact, is likely to reinforce opposition to opening the floodgates to change, at least among those reasonably satisfied with the *status quo* regarding particular institutional arrangements. Some such reasoning, for instance, may well deter any of the Consultative Parties from calling for the thirty-year review envisioned under the terms of Article XII of the Antarctic Treaty.[45]

As the preceding observations imply, there is a sense in which international institutions can prove more difficult to restructure or replace than domestic institutions. There is no widely acknowledged legislative mechanism operative in international society as a whole, and the members of this social system exhibit a pronounced propensity to insist on stringent requirements for change in connection with specific institutional arrangements. Of course, some regimes establish legislative mechanisms of their own. The United Nations can and sometimes does play a role in this area, even though resolutions of the General Assembly are not legally binding on individual members. Legislative conferences also offer a well-known, though somewhat *ad hoc*, mechanism for adjusting or restructuring institutional arrangements at the international level. In this connection, recent experiences with efforts to protect the ozone layer are distinctly encouraging. The framework convention signed in Vienna in 1985 was supplemented within two years by the 1987 Montreal Protocol, a measure with significant substantive content. And the 1990 annual conference of the members held in London reached agreement on a series of substantive, and, in some cases, far-reaching amendments to the provisions of the Montreal Protocol.

Even so, there is no comparison between these relatively cumbersome mechanisms and the operation of smoothly functioning legislatures in domestic societies when it comes to handling alterations in the provisions of social institutions. Whereas international institutions are typically subject to infrequent but far-reaching changes, then, domestic institutions are more often subject to continuous changes that are incremental in nature. I conclude from this that international institutions may well be more effective than domestic institutions during the normal course of events, though the effectiveness of international institutions is likely to be punctuated by occasional

---

[45] Philip W. Quigg, *A Pole Apart: The Emerging Issue of Antarctica* (New York: McGraw-Hill, 1983), ch. 8.

dramatic breaks arising from the transformation of existing institutional arrangements.[46]

Capacity of governments

The effectiveness of international institutions varies directly with the
capacity of the governments of members to implement their provisions.
Because the members of international society are collective entities, the
effectiveness of international institutions depends on the capacity of
governments to implement institutional arrangements within their
jurisdictions as well as on the willingness of governments acting on
their own behalf to comply with the relevant rules. Those imbued with
modern, Western conceptions of the role of government in society often
assume that governments are competent organizations capable of
implementing the provisions of regimes effectively and inducing
subjects to comply with their dictates. But in actuality, this is a
simplistic assumption. It is possible to identify a number of factors that
can and often do limit the capacity of governments to implement
institutional arrangements, even when those representing the participating states enter into international constitutional contracts in good
faith.

Most governments face severe resource constraints limiting their
ability to apply the provisions of regimes to areas and activities under
their jurisdiction. This is obviously true of the governments of developing countries that must contend with a wide range of pressing
problems, even though they control a comparatively small proportion
of their countries' resources. Consider, for instance, the problems facing
Kenyan officials endeavoring to control poachers whose activities
threaten the provisions of the regime dealing with trade in endangered
species or Columbian officials seeking to implement the terms of
various international agreements relating to the traffic in drugs.[47]
Increasingly, moreover, resource constraints hamper the activities of
the governments of advanced industrial countries as well. The United
States, Canada, and others facing large and persistent public deficits,
for example, now find it difficult to take on the additional obligations
arising in conjunction with the formation of new international regimes.
It will come as no surprise, under the circumstances, that most

---

[46] This last point assumes the relatively stable settings we typically consider in thinking
about domestic society. In actuality, however, sharp breaks occur from time to time in
many domestic systems as well.

[47] Ethan Nadelmann, "Global Prohibition Regimes: The Evolution of Norms in International Society," *International Organization*, 44 (Autumn 1990), pp. 479–526.

members of international society exhibit a strong preference for regimes requiring clear-cut actions on the part of a small number of actors whose behavior is easy to monitor. The attractions of the ozone regime with its emphasis on an across-the-board cut in the use of chlorofluorocarbons produced by a small number of corporations are easy to understand in these terms. The same reasoning helps to explain why most observers believe that it will be much more difficult to devise an effective regime to control emissions of carbon dioxide in the interests of limiting global climate change.[48]

Frequently, the problems go well beyond the matter of resource constraints. Governments in many countries confront severe limitations on their capacity to govern. A variety of factors can and often do contribute to this phenomenon. Ethnic, racial, or class conflicts may cause domestic turmoil that hampers the ability of a government to channel the behavior of individuals and groups nominally under its jurisdiction. Large segments of the population may refuse to acknowledge a government's legitimacy and, consequently, feel little obligation to comply with the requirements of institutional arrangements the government has entered into or endorsed. The deadening effect of an entrenched bureaucracy may severely limit the capacity of a government to translate the terms of international regimes into domestic rules and regulations in a manner likely to elicit compliance on the part of affected individuals and organizations. In short, there is frequently a large gap between the ideal and the actual when it comes to the capacity of governments to apply the terms of international regimes to areas and activities under their jurisdiction. These observations reinforce the argument that effective international regimes are likely to be those that feature clear-cut rules calling for action on the part of a small number of actors whose behavior is easy to monitor.

Beyond this, it is important to bear in mind the role of interest-group politics when it comes to implementing the provisions of international regimes. In the typical case, some domestic interest groups will object to the provisions of specific international regimes, just as others endorse these provisions. As in the more familiar case of domestic policy, those who dislike the provisions of a regime are unlikely to give in and agree to abide by arrangements they dislike just because they have been formalized in an international agreement. Rather, they will simply shift their efforts from the negotiation phase to the implementation phase, deploying the political, legal, and economic resources at

---

[48] Eugene B. Skolnikoff, "The Policy Gridlock on Global Warming," *Foreign Policy*, 79 (Summer 1990), pp. 79–93.

their disposal to block or impede efforts to implement the regime's provisions. This may result in litigation, bureaucratic stonewalling, or efforts to make use of the mass media to arouse public sentiment against an institutional arrangement. In extreme cases, opposition of this sort can transform an international regime into a dead letter, even when governments in the participating states have good intentions of implementing its provisions within their own jurisdictions. In the more typical case, opposition of this kind acts as a drag on the effectiveness of international regimes, accounting for a significant part of the gap between the expectations or hopes of the regimes' architects and actual performance.

What we are dealing with in all these cases are examples of non-market failures, the political counterparts of the more familiar category of market failures.[49] Such failures are facts of life in connection with international regimes, just as they are in the case of purely domestic arrangements. There is no reason to allow this realization to put a damper on efforts to institutionalize international cooperation through the formation and implementation of regimes. But it does suggest that those responsible for designing international regimes should make a concerted effort to extract lessons from experience with non-market failures in other contexts. It seems probable, for example, that the case for channeling behavior through the use of incentive systems in contrast to command-and-control regulations is at least as strong at the international level as it is at the domestic level.

Distribution of power

Sharp asymmetries in the distribution of power (in the material sense) among participants circumscribe the effectiveness of international institutions. There is nothing remarkable about the observation that members of a society who are rich and powerful are less constrained by the dictates of social conventions than those who are relatively powerless. Observers of domestic society have long studied the strategies and tactics that powerful individuals employ to flout behavioral standards (from social norms to legal prescriptions) routinely imposed on others. This has given rise to a sizable body of empirical work describing the actions of various elites, together with a wide range of normative arguments intended either to justify the existence of power elites/

---

[49] Charles Wolf Jr., *Markets or Governments: Choosing between Imperfect Alternatives* (Cambridge, MA: MIT Press, 1988).

ruling classes or to decry their existence and, in some cases, to propose initiatives designed to overthrow them.

Yet the implications of asymmetries in the distribution of power for the effectiveness of social institutions are more complex than these preliminary observations would suggest. Sharp asymmetries typically produce two (or more) class systems which in turn serve to determine the domain of effectiveness of social practices. The weak or powerless are apt to feel, with some justification, not only that institutional arrangements are effective but also that the pressures to comply with the dictates of these arrangements are coercive and even oppressive. As the case of the trade regime articulated in the GATT suggests, they can be expected to struggle (often in vain) to bring about fundamental changes in prevailing institutions as a means of improving their lot. The rich and powerful, by contrast, frequently exhibit little awareness of the operation – or even the existence – of key institutions; they are likely to argue that such arrangements are socially desirable when pushed to justify prevailing institutions. It is consequently incorrect to say that asymmetries in the distribution of power eliminate or even reduce the effectiveness of social institutions. Rather, such asymmetries serve to circumscribe the effectiveness of institutional arrangements, minimizing the force of their dictates as far as some members of society are concerned while reinforcing and on occasion intensifying their impact on others.

It is worth noting also that symmetry with regard to the distribution of power should be thought of as a continuum rather than a dichotomy. The range of this variable extends from perfect symmetry, a condition in which the power of each member of society is exactly the same, to the opposite extreme, a situation in which one member of the social system is all powerful while the rest are powerless.[50] Though neither of these extremes occurs in reality, a consideration of the relationship between movement along this continuum and the effectiveness of social institutions is instructive. Broadly speaking, the more symmetrical the distribution of power, the harder it is to establish institutional arrangements initially but the more effective they are once formed. Symmetry drives up the transaction costs associated with regime formation by making it necessary to reach agreement among numerous members of

[50] On the recent debate about hegemony (in the material as opposed to the Gramscian sense) in international society, consult Paul Kennedy, *The Rise and Fall of the Great Powers: Economic Change and Military Conflict from 1500 to 2000* (New York: Random House, 1987), together with the large literature this book has spawned.

a social system.[51] Yet, at the same time, symmetry ensures that no individual will possess sufficient power to flout the dictates of institutional arrangements with impunity or to instigate a transformation of prevailing arrangements. Asymmetry has the opposite effect. Sharp asymmetries facilitate the formation of institutions by creating a power elite – a dictator in the extreme – capable of imposing institutions on the other members of society. But they also reduce the effectiveness of the institutions formed by allowing some members of the group to ignore their dictates whenever it suits their purposes and by breeding resentments on the part of others that can quickly erode institutional arrangements if the dominant members of the group falter. It seems reasonable to conclude, then, that there is an optimal level of asymmetry in the distribution of power, so far as the effectiveness of social institutions is concerned. Such an optimum would feature enough asymmetry to single out one or more parties able to take the lead in processes of regime formation without reaching the point of creating a power elite able to ignore the dictates of the resultant institutions with impunity.[52]

The application of this line of reasoning to international society is instructive. While the distribution of power is certainly far from symmetrical in this social setting, a marked trend toward the diffusion of power within international society during the last several decades has produced a significant decline in the asymmetry characteristic of the immediate postwar era.[53] This observation helps to resolve some of the disagreements noted earlier in this chapter about the extent to which international institutions are no more than epiphenomena. Institutional arrangements that may have been treated properly as sharply limited in their effectiveness during the heyday of American hegemony have become more effective with the diffusion of power in international society that has occurred over the last two decades. This observation licenses the conclusion that we are entering a period of increasingly effective and, consequently, increasingly important international institutions. But it also introduces a note of caution, suggesting as it does that there is no guarantee that the heightened effectiveness

---

[51] On the role of transaction costs in regime formation see also Robert O. Keohane, *After Hegemony: Cooperation and Discord in the World Political Economy* (Princeton, NJ: Princeton University Press, 1984), chs. 4–6.

[52] On the role of leadership in this context see Charles P. Kindleberger, *The International Economic Order: Essays on Financial Crisis and International Public Goods* (Berkeley, CA: University of California Press, 1988).

[53] As the recent debate about American hegemony has made clear, the issue here concerns relationships of relative power rather than absolute power.

of institutional arrangements in international society will last indefinitely.[54]

Interdependence

The effectiveness of international institutions varies directly with the level of interdependence among the participants. Interdependence is a much debated and notoriously elusive concept in the field of international relations. Yet the essential core of the matter is straightforward enough. Interdependence arises when the actions of individual members of a social system impact (whether materially or perceptually) the welfare of other members of the system.[55] Those who are interdependent are affected by and react in a sensitive manner to each other's behavior; the higher the level of interdependence, the more pronounced these impacts and reactions will be.[56]

A particularly clear-cut way of thinking about interdependence is reflected in the modern literature on interactive decision-making. By definition, interactive decision-making involves situations in which two or more autonomous actors are linked together in the sense that the outcomes associated with the choices of each individual participant are determined, in part, by the choices of each of the others. The greater the effects of the choices of others on the outcomes accruing to each individual, the higher the level of interdependence. This is, of course, a defining characteristic of the class of situations to which the theory of games is applicable. But the resultant processes of strategic interaction have long been of interest to students of international relations, whether or not they employ the theory of games as a means of analyzing them.[57]

---

[54] These comments suggest the importance of asking whether the evolution of international society is fundamentally linear or cyclical, an issue that remains unresolved at this time. But for a discussion of the idea that there are long cycles in international affairs, see Gorge Modelski, ed., *Exploring Long Cycles* (Boulder, CO: Lynne Rienner, 1987).

[55] Oran R. Young, "Interdependencies in World Politics," *International Journal*, 24 (Autumn 1989), pp. 726–50.

[56] See also Robert O. Keohane and Joseph S. Nye, *Power and Interdependence: World Politics in Transition*, 2nd edn. (Glenview, IL: Scott, Foresman, 1989). Keohane and Nye introduce an additional distinction between sensitivity interdependence and vulnerability interdependence. Whatever its utility in other contexts, such a distinction strikes me as unnecessary in connection with this discussion. The heart of the matter is the impact of the actions of individuals on each other's welfare.

[57] For an account of the principal streams of theoretical work dealing with strategic interaction, see Oran R. Young, ed., *Bargaining: Formal Theories of Negotiation* (Urbana, IL: University of Illinois Press, 1975).

Because the members of international society are themselves complex social entities, it is important to consider as well the relationship between interdependencies within individual members of this society (internal interdependencies) and interdependencies among the members of international society (external interdependencies). What matters most, in thinking about the effectiveness of international institutions, is the ratio between these two types of interdependence. When the ratio of internal to external interdependencies is high, the members of international society will be preoccupied with their domestic affairs and, as a result, less concerned about their interactions with others. As the level of external interdependencies rises relative to internal interdependencies, on the other hand, policy-makers find themselves devoting more time and energy to interactions among the members of international society.

Rising levels of external interdependence generate two distinct streams of incentives for actors to establish social institutions and to comply with their requirements once they are in place. In an interdependent world, actors are no longer able to pursue their own goals without adjusting for and (usually) endeavoring to regulate the actions of others. In effect, the behavior of the members of an interdependent system generate reciprocal side-effects or externalities that individual members cannot ignore as they pursue their own interests. As is the case in domestic society, institutional arrangements and the social practices they embody emerge under such conditions as a means of minimizing mutual interference or, at least, allowing individuals to predict the behavior of others and therefore to plan accordingly.

The growth of interdependence also contributes to the effectiveness of institutional arrangements by enhancing the capacity of each member of the social system to retaliate for the infractions of others. The fact that each individual's rewards or payoffs are determined, in part, by the actions of other members of the collectivity in an interdependent system makes them all vulnerable to each other's threats and promises.[58] As the much studied case of deterrence demonstrates, threats and promises may influence behavior even when the relevant actions would prove costly to the initiator as well as to the target.[59] It follows that rising levels of interdependence not only increase the need for institutional arrangements to control mutual interference, but they also provide the members of a social system with forms of social

---

[58] Young, "Interdependencies in World Politics," pp. 746–8.
[59] For a seminal account that emphasizes this point, consult Thomas C. Schelling, *The Strategy of Conflict* (Cambridge, MA: Harvard University Press, 1960).

pressure usable against actual or prospective violators of an institution's rights and rules.

While the debate is far from over, there is a persuasive case to be made for the proposition that levels of interdependence have risen markedly in international society during the postwar era. The fact that the ratio of exports to gross national product (GNP) has increased substantially for many countries is only one striking indicator of this trend. Numerous other developments, including military applications of advanced technologies and the appearance of dramatic transboundary ecological concerns, point in the same direction.[60] One implication of these observations is that the ratio of external to internal interdependencies, which was relatively high in the seventeenth and eighteenth centuries but appears to have declined during the nineteenth century as countries became preoccupied with the domestic transformations brought on by the industrial revolution, is on the rise again as the twentieth century draws to a close. What is more, it would be hard to argue convincingly that we will experience a reversal of this trend during the foreseeable future. To the extent that this is true, the growing interest in international institutions is not an aberration. On the contrary, there is every reason to believe that this newfound concern will flourish as the level of interdependence in international society continues to rise.

Intellectual order

International institutions cannot remain effective for long after the erosion or collapse of their intellectual substructures. There is nothing new about the observation that human affairs are heavily influenced by the power of ideas. Yet it is worth discussing in some detail the relationship between systems of ideas and social institutions.[61] Though there is a tendency to suppress the recognition of their role in undergirding institutional arrangements in the interests of persuading subjects to regard specific arrangements as natural and enduring, there is no escaping the fact that institutions are expressions of cognitive constructs devised and disseminated by human beings. Institutions cannot take root in the absence of a coherent system of ideas, remain effective

---

[60] For an account that stresses a number of these factors see World Commission on Environment and Development, *Our Common Future* (New York: Oxford University Press, 1987).

[61] See also Chapter 5 by Robert W. Cox in this volume. Drawing on Islamic texts for illustrations, Cox provides a subtle and provocative account of the intellectual underpinnings of social institutions.

for long when these generative ideas fail, or resist transforming pressures following the rise of new systems of ideas.

Some simple examples will help to clarify these observations. The states system itself rests on an often unstated but nonetheless firmly entrenched vision of the sovereign state as the basic unit of international society. Interestingly, the idea of the *nation*-state (a phrase in common use among students of international relations) has never achieved similar status, and there are good reasons to anticipate a continuing decline in the influence of this idea during the foreseeable future. Even the idea of the sovereign state shows some signs of losing its grip on thinking about international society during this era of rising interdependencies and the growing influence of non-state actors.

To take another example, the postwar regimes governing international trade and monetary transactions rest squarely on a vision of international economic intercourse that Ruggie and others have characterized as embedded liberalism.[62] The current tug of war over international trade is properly understood, in fact, as a conflict between proponents of embedded liberalism anxious to defend and extend the reach of relatively free trade and those who advocate various forms of protectionism as a means of ensuring the political autonomy of individual states in an era of rising interdependence, which would otherwise force decision-makers to adjust domestic policies in response to irresistible outside pressures.

There is no need to resort to grand theories about the influence of comprehensive worldviews or intellectual hegemony to understand the power of ideas as determinants of the effectiveness of international institutions. It is notoriously difficult to document the rise and fall of worldviews; the idea of intellectual hegemony seems destined to become at least as controversial as the more familiar idea of hegemony in the material sense.[63] What is more, most international institutions take the form of regimes dealing with relatively well-defined regional or functional issues in contrast to broad framework arrangements pertinent to international society as a whole. It is not difficult, for example, to trace the transition in recent decades from regimes for

[62] John Gerard Ruggie, "International Regimes, Transactions, and Change: Embedded Liberalism in the Postwar Economic Order," in Krasner, ed., *International Regimes*, pp. 195–231.

[63] But see Robert W. Cox, "Gramsci, Hegemony and International Relations: An Essay in Method," *Millennium. Journal of International Studies*, 12, 2 (Summer 1983), pp. 162–75, for a thoughtful discussion of intellectual hegemony in the Gramscian sense.

natural resources built on the conservationist ideal of managing resources to achieve maximum sustainable yield from individual species to regimes that reflect what has become known as a whole ecosystems approach. Similar comments are in order regarding monetary regimes. Analysts have made considerable progress, for instance, in documenting twentieth-century transitions from institutional arrangements reflecting the idea of the gold standard to regimes built on the ideal of fixed but adjustable exchange rates or even freely floating exchange rates.[64]

This much said, the point to be stressed in this discussion is that international institutions cannot remain effective for long after the collapse of their intellectual underpinnings. While much more has been written about adjustments in institutional arrangements following shifts in the distribution of structural power in international society, there is a case to be made for the proposition that institutional change follows at least as quickly and decisively in the wake of shifts in prevailing systems of thought. In the face of changes in the distribution of structural power, institutions show a remarkable tendency to remain in place until some new constellation of power becomes clear-cut and widely acknowledged. Consider the institutional arrangements embodied in the provisions of the United Nations Charter dealing with membership on the Security Council as a case in point. When systems of ideas collapse, by contrast, regimes built on the old construct may quickly lose their effectiveness whether or not some new cognitive construct is waiting in the wings to fill the vacuum left by the collapse of the old construct. As the struggle to devise a new and widely accepted system of ideas on which to base regimes to cope with global environmental changes (for example, climate change or the loss of biodiversity) attests, this can lead to a more or less protracted period of ambiguity during which there are no unambiguous rights and rules to guide the actions of the members of international society. But this simply reinforces the proposition under consideration here regarding the power of ideas as a determinant of the effectiveness of international institutions.

One inference to be drawn from this discussion is that the immediate future may well be a period of dramatic alterations in international institutions. A combination of forces, including rising levels of international interdependence, the growing role of non-state actors and the emergence of the global change agenda, is now raising profound questions about some of the intellectual underpinnings of the states

---

[64] Colin D. Campbell and William R. Dougan, eds., *Alternative Monetary Regimes* (Baltimore, MD: Johns Hopkins University Press, 1986).

system.[65] Given the fact that the states system, in one form or another, has dominated international society for several centuries, it is not surprising that there is a certain poverty of ideas regarding alternative forms that international society may take during the foreseeable future and, especially, the driving forces that could energize the transition to one or another alternative.[66] This could well lead to a period of ambiguity during which there are increasing doubts about the effectiveness of some institutional arrangements at the international level whose role in shaping individual and collective behavior has long been taken for granted. But, at the same time, it seems certain to produce a substantial increase in the attention devoted to the design and implementation of new international institutions in many quarters.

CONCLUSION

If I am right, institutional arrangements do matter in international society, and we should acknowledge this by accepting the study of international institutions as a continuing priority for students of international relations. Yet to say that institutions are important is hardly to assert that they invariably or even usually operate as critical determinants of individual or collective behavior at the international level. To ascertain when and to what extent institutions are effective, we must launch a systematic investigation into factors governing their effectiveness. In the second half of this chapter, I have initiated such an analysis, considering the role of variables that are endogenous in the sense that they involve attributes of social institutions themselves as well as variables that are exogenous in the sense that they pertain to aspects of the larger social setting within which institutions operate. This preliminary effort is sufficient, I believe, to demonstrate that this is a fruitful enterprise and that there is much more to be learned from pursuing this line of inquiry.

Even at this early stage, the analysis of factors governing the effectiveness of international institutions suffices to explain why we are currently witnessing a rebirth of interest in international institutions among practitioners and scholars alike. Increased transparency, the

---

[65] For a sophisticated account of the states system see Hedley Bull, *The Anarchical Society: A Study of Order in World Politics* (New York: Columbia University Press, 1977). Mark W. Zacher's Chapter 3 in this volume documents some of the changes that are now raising questions about the future of the states system.

[66] A partial exception to this generalization is the body of work produced under the auspices of the World Order Models Project (WOMP) during the 1970s and 1980s. See, for example, Saul H. Mendlovitz, ed., *On the Creation of a Just World Order* (New York: Free Press, 1975).

diffusion of power, and rising levels of interdependence have all served to heighten the effectiveness of existing international institutions as well as to intensify the need to establish new institutional arrangements in international society. Nonetheless, our understanding of institutional design at this level remains primitive. It is no cause for surprise, therefore, that we have experienced recently a rapid growth of analyses of international regimes or that many thoughtful students of international relations have begun to ask probing questions about the nature of international institutions, the reasons why actors in international society endeavor to create such arrangements, the processes governing the formation of international institutions, and the sources of the effectiveness of the resultant social practices.

Will this surge of interest in international institutions prove to be a flash in the pan? The answer, I now believe, lies in our views concerning the probable evolutionary path of international society. If the current trend toward the diffusion of power does not give way to the emergence of a new hegemon, for example, the heightened role of international institutions is likely to prove lasting. Similarly, if rising levels of interdependence at the international level prove irreversible, the need for effective institutions will continue to grow. There is, of course, room for differences of opinion regarding matters of this sort. But if the premises underlying the vision of "our common future" prove correct,[67] both the effort to strengthen existing international institutions and the need to create new and more effective successors will grow rapidly during the foreseeable future. Inevitably, this will place a premium on the work of those able to offer penetrating insights relating to the formation, operation, and persistence of international institutions.

[67] World Commission on Environment and Development, *Our Common Future*.

7 EXPLAINING THE REGULATION OF TRANSNATIONAL PRACTICES: A STATE-BUILDING APPROACH

Janice E. Thomson

With the decline of the Cold War, the search for new or continuing threats to the West is already well underway.[1] Among the major candidates are international terrorism, the international drug trade, and the turbulent, unstable Third World in general. All of these threats, it is important to emphasize, come principally from the South. So by some accounts, the focus of security concerns will shift from the East–West to the North–South axis.

Interestingly, several centuries ago the situation was largely the reverse, with the Europeans bringing comparable threats to the non-European world. European pirates, privateers, mercantile companies, *conquistadores*, and adventurers of various sorts used violence against civilians and governments outside Europe in the pursuit of their own interests and the interests of their home states. Their actions had devastating consequences for areas beyond the European state system.

The carnage and destruction wrought by the mercantile companies in Asia and by the *conquistadores* in Latin America are well known. Sir Francis Drake extorted large ransoms from two Spanish colonial cities by threatening to burn them to the ground. He actually destroyed three other cities. Individuals in the nineteenth-century United States launched numerous international military expeditions to acquire new territory for the United States, liberate Latin American territories from Spanish rule, or acquire their own "kingdoms." Undoubtedly, the most famous of these was William Walker who invaded Nicaragua, declared himself president and ruled the country for eighteen months.

Similarly, the locus of the international drug trade has shifted considerably over the past century and a half. The contemporary U.S. drug war was preceded by a very different kind of drug war 150 years ago. In the 1840s, the British state made war on China in order to reopen

[1] Funding for this research was provided by the John M. Olin Institute for Strategic Studies at Harvard University. For comments on earlier drafts of this chapter I am grateful to the members of the Olin Institute's National Security Seminar, especially Andrew Moravcsik, Robert Keohane, Joseph Nye, and Christopher Daase, as well as to the other contributors to this volume.

China's markets to the East India Company's opium exports.[2] In the nineteenth century, when Britain was the supplier and China the consumer, the opium trade was treated as an economic issue – an important element in overcoming Britain's trade deficit with China. Today, when the South is the supplier and the North the consumer, the drug trade is treated as a political issue – a matter of national security.

Though these historical and contemporary practices differ in some respects – for example, Sir Francis Drake's activities were not covered by CNN – it is important to recognize the extent to which significant violent or pernicious activities, widely practiced by European states for centuries, are now deemed illegitimate[3] by most states. In pointing to the parallels between these practices my intent is not to pass judgment on them or to suggest that the West is hypocritical in condemning activities in which it once readily engaged. Instead, I draw these analogies in order to highlight the degree to which the legitimacy of some international practices has changed over time, and to examine the processes through which certain practices are delegitimated and subsequently regulated or banned at the international level.

Theorists of international regimes and multilateralism have focused a great deal of attention on how states develop mechanisms for coordinating their policies in particular issue-areas. Yet this literature devotes much less attention to determining what sorts of activities become the objects of interstate coordination efforts and why. The question is: "what is regulated internationally and what is not regulated internationally in the world, and why?"[4] Answering these questions is important for several reasons, not the least of which is to avoid biases which are inherent in an exclusive focus on existing multilateral arrangements.[5] Knowing which activities are and are not amenable to interstate coordination or cooperation is surely as important as understanding how coordination or cooperation is achieved.

---

[2] Peter Ward Fay, *The Opium War 1840–1842* (New York: Norton, 1975).
[3] This chapter uses Tilly's definition of legitimacy which is "the probability that other authorities will act to confirm the decisions of a given authority." Charles Tilly, "War Making and State Making as Organized Crime," in Peter B. Evans, Dietrich Rueschemeyer, and Theda Skocpol, eds., *Bringing the State Back In* (New York: Cambridge University Press, 1985), p. 171.
[4] Brent A. Sutton and Mark W. Zacher, "Mutual Advantage, Imposition, and Regime Formation: Evolution of International Shipping Regulations," paper presented at the 14th World Congress of the International Political Science Association, Washington, DC, Aug. 28–Sept. 1, 1988; cited in Robert O. Keohane, "Multilateralism: An Agenda for Research," *International Journal*, 45 (Autumn, 1990).
[5] See Susan Strange, "Cave! Hic Dragones: A Critique of Regime Analysis," in Stephen D. Krasner, ed., *International Regimes* (Ithaca, NY: Cornell University Press, 1983), pp. 337–54.

The primary focus of this chapter is the politicization or delegit-imation of a practice at the international level or, put differently, the process through which practices are brought to the international political agenda. Explaining why politicization produces international regulation in some cases but not in others is a separate and equally large question which cannot be taken up here in any systematic way. I do argue, however, that there is a third alternative to the international regulation–no regulation dichotomy: the convergence of state prac-tices.[6] This refers to an outcome in which all, many, or most states impose similar controls on an activity. Thus, no international regulation is instituted but the result is the same; namely, universal control or prohibition of the practice.

I attempt to shed some light on the issue of what gets regulated and what does not (and why) through an historical analysis of two practices which have become subject to international control – terrorism and the trade in certain drugs – and a number of comparable practices which have not. Of the former, some were subject to international regimes while others were controlled through a convergence in state practices. Drawing on arguments and concepts derived from theories of state-building, I attempt to illuminate the conditions which support and those which impede the development of international regulation.

As the following case studies will demonstrate, there is no objective, timeless reason for regulating or not regulating any of these activities. On the surface, delegitimation is largely arbitrary. It is highly context-dependent and does not exhibit any obvious logic or rationality. Practices are defined as illegitimate for different reasons and by different kinds of actors. Nevertheless, I argue that state-building theory is a quite powerful tool in explaining delegitimation and therefore provides a promising starting point for theorizing about international regulation.

STATE-BUILDING AND DELEGITIMATION

International regulation can be imposed only if the legitimacy of a practice is successfully challenged at the international level. Put differently, some actor has to bring the practice to the inter-national agenda in the first place. The theoretical puzzle is why the

---

6 On the convergence of practices, see Chapter 4 by Thomas J. Biersteker in this volume. State control or regulation may achieve the status of an international regime, but need not. According to the standard definition, a regime is comprised of principles, norms, rules, and decision-making procedures which implies a highly formal set of arrange-ments. Krasner, "Introduction," in Krasner, ed., *International Regimes*, p. 1.

delegitimation process is initiated. In seeking an explanation for the origin of delegitimation, I will draw on political theories of state-building.[7]

According to this theoretical perspective, state power and state leaders' material interests explain which activities get defined as legitimate or illegitimate. The basic assumption here is that policy will reflect the state's primary interest which is maintaining or building its power relative to both internal and external challengers to its authority.[8] Changes in transnational practices reflect the ongoing processes of state-building, in which the state responds to internal challengers, and of war-making, where the threat is external. In this view a state will support, encourage, and even participate in pernicious activities if those activities contribute to its own power and authority. Conversely, a state will define an activity as illegitimate when that activity empowers others to threaten the state's power, control, or authority.

From this perspective the role of norms is quite different from what many scholars suggest, which is that norms are the weapons of the weak against the strong.[9] Instead, powerful states, which have benefited from participating in a particular practice, ban it when it becomes a threat to themselves. With an international norm in place, new state-builders are denied the opportunity to exploit these activities in developing their state's power.[10]

[7] Especially the work of Charles Tilly, including *The Formation of National States in Western Europe* (Princeton, NJ: Princeton University Press, 1975), "War Making and State Making as Organized Crime," and *Coercion, Capital, and European States* (Cambridge, MA: Basil Blackwell, 1990). The modifier "political" is used to distinguish this approach from economic theories which see state-building as driven by the state's desire to maximize revenue or profits. For the latter view see Margaret Levi, *Of Rule and Revenue* (Berkeley, CA: University of California Press, 1988), and David A. Lake, "The State and the Production of International Security: A Microeconomic Theory of Grand Strategy," paper presented at the Annual Meeting of the American Political Science Association, San Francisco, Aug. 30–Sept. 2, 1990. Krasner's comparative analysis of post-World War II international regimes provides compelling evidence for the political perspective. Third World unhappiness with the global economic order simply cannot be explained in terms of economic interests. In terms of economic growth, the South did as well as or even better than the North. Stephen D. Krasner, *Structural Conflict: The Third-World against Global Liberalism* (Berkeley, CA: University of California Press, 1985).

[8] Stephen D. Krasner, "Approaches to the State," *Comparative Politics*, 16 (January 1984), pp. 223–46.

[9] Robert H. Jackson and Carl G. Rosberg, "Why Africa's Weak States Persist: The Empirical and the Juridical in Statehood," *World Politics*, 35 (October 1982), pp. 1-24.

[10] Krasner's analysis of international regimes is generally confined to issue-areas in which the North had a dominant position. He argues that the Third World sought to move established regimes away from market principles and toward a greater level of state control and make sure that new regimes would be based on (state) authoritative rather than free-market allocations. However, there is no reason to suppose that the Northern states, in areas where they are at a disadvantage, would not opt for

Table 1. *Patterns of regulation*

		International regulation?	
		Yes	No
		1	2
Brought to the international agenda?	Yes	drugs terrorism	alcohol arms
		3	4
	No		mercenarism tobacco

From the argument that the state's interest is to maintain or augment its power relative to other states and its own society, we can deduce the following hypothesis about the origins of delegitimation: a transnational practice will be delegitimated when strong states perceive it as an internal or external threat to their power and control. With this hypothesis about the sources of delegitimation, I now turn to a comparative historical analysis of a number of transnational practices.

TESTING THE ARGUMENT

This section presents historical case studies of the six practices listed in Table 1. Analyzing the evolution of cases within a particular category will serve to identify the common conditions which lead to a particular outcome. These can then be compared with conditions found in the other two categories to explain the variation in outcomes across categories.

Case selection was based on several criteria. Most importantly, hard cases[11] for the state-building hypothesis are included. Two of the cases (drugs and terrorism) are, according to Nadelmann,[12] explained by morality or normative ideas and, therefore, constitute hard cases for the state-building approach. Arms and mercenarism are directly related to

authoritative regimes as well. In other words, they want to maximize their authority and control when threatened. They are simply threatened by different things. See Krasner, *Structural Conflict*.

[11] See Chapter 6 by Oran R. Young in this volume for a description of hard cases.

[12] Ethan A. Nadelmann, "Global Prohibition Regimes: The Evolution of Norms in International Society," *International Organization*, 44 (Autumn 1990). I must emphasize that Nadelmann does not claim to explain terrorism *per se*, but only piracy and privateering. I am including piracy and privateering in the category of terrorism.

state power and war so should be hard cases for alternative arguments. Three of the cases (arms, mercenarism, and terrorism) are related to the exercise of violence and war, while the rest are commodities whose use and trade are or have been regarded as particularly pernicious.

Another aim of the selection process was to include the time dimension by examining cases from different centuries. This will provide some indication of whether the patterns of control reflect changes in the international system such as the balance of power. Finally, these cases were selected, in part, because they are timely. Each is the object of contemporary international concern and is expected to continue to be a major focus of international politics.

CASE 1: INTERNATIONAL REGULATION

Drugs

The call for international control of the opium trade came from the United States in 1908. Before 1915 there were no restrictions on the import of opium to the United States, other than a small tariff, and the United States did not export manufactured opiates because its products were not price-competitive with Europe's. At the same time, U.S. per capita import of opium was declining, having peaked in 1896.[13] Since the U.S. central state had no domestic restrictions on opium, its call for an international conference on opium requires some explanation.

U.S. concerns about opium stemmed from its economic and political interests in China. While the United States had an intense desire to "open" China to its commercial and financial interests, its brutal treatment of Chinese immigrants and travelers was a source of tension between the two states. The Chinese had even organized a voluntary boycott of U.S. products in protest.[14] So despite the decline in U.S. opium consumption, the United States took the lead in organizing the conference to "help" China with its opium problem.[15]

Meanwhile, in 1906 Britain and China had reached an agreement phasing out the opium trade between India and China. A British report issued in 1895 had argued that "opium was more like the Westerner's

---

[13] David F. Musto, *The American Disease: Origins of Narcotic Control*, expanded edn. (New York: Oxford University Press, 1987), p. 2. The extent to which this decline was due to market saturation or to the proliferation of regulations at the individual state level is unclear.

[14] *Ibid.*, p. 30.

[15] *Ibid.*, p. 4. This action was also related to the U.S. need to develop an opium policy for the newly acquired Philippines. See *ibid.*, pp. 26–8.

liquor than a substance to be feared and abhorred."[16] Nevertheless, Britain and China agreed that India's opium production and China's opium consumption would be reduced by 10 percent per year. The latter would prevent Turkey, Persia, or domestic producers from stepping in to replace the reduced Indian (British) supply.[17]

Still, it was the United States which took the lead in organizing the Shanghai Opium Commission[18] which met in 1909. At the time the United States had no federal laws proscribing the opium traffic nor any reliable statistics on its own opium "problem." In order to have something in hand for the conference, but to avoid offending the medical community and drug manufacturers, the United States instituted in 1909 a ban on the import of opium for smoking. This act was clearly intended for international effect as the State Department admitted "that banning itself was not so essential as the enactment of specific anti-opium legislation to prove the nation's sincerity in Shanghai."[19]

The legislation was passed while U.S. representatives were attending the 1909 conference, and "the American delegation proudly and with dramatic flourish announced the victory to the commission, then in session."[20] However, the United States attended two subsequent conferences with no domestic legislation other than the ban on importing opium for smoking.

The 1909 conference produced a number of resolutions. Among them was a call for all governments to suppress opium smoking; the ban (U.S. position) or careful regulation (British position) of opium use; and a halt to the export of opium to countries which had prohibited its importation.[21] These reflected fundamental disagreements, especially between the United States and Britain. There simply was no consensus "that the use of opium for other than medicinal purposes was evil and immoral."[22]

If this is how opium was placed on the international agenda, the case of cocaine is equally interesting. The next meeting dealing with opium (the Hague Conference) was held in 1911, again at the behest of the United States, which was now preparing its list of demands on China (e.g. currency reform) in repayment for all the help the United States

---

[16] *Ibid.*, p. 29.
[17] *Ibid.*, pp. 28–9.
[18] This commission was empowered only to do fact-finding and make recommendations. *Ibid.*, p. 35.
[19] Quoted in *ibid.*, pp. 34–5.
[20] *Ibid.*, p. 34.
[21] Kettil Bruun, Lynn Pan, and Ingemar Rexed, *The Gentlemen's Club: International Control of Drugs and Alcohol* (Chicago: University of Chicago Press, 1975), p. 11.
[22] Musto, *American Disease*, p. 36.

had provided on the opium issue.[23] This time Britain, which was averse to international control, demanded that cocaine and morphine be included in the convention expecting that the need to compile detailed statistics on these drugs for the meeting would delay the conference.[24] This British action produced conflict with Germany which, as "the leading country in drug manufacture at the time, was opposed to the control of cocaine." While it was not able to remove cocaine from the convention, Germany did engineer a "peculiar ratification procedure" which required unanimous ratification by all forty-six states in the system.[25] Thus, the implementation of control was successfully delayed until after World War I when countries which ratified the Versailles Treaty automatically became parties to the Hague Convention.[26]

These two cases suggest that the state's geopolitical and economic interests are the key to the delegitimation of a practice. The United States pressed for an international ban on opium before it had domestic controls, much less a ban, in place. And its reasons for desiring the prohibition had little to do with morality and much to do with its political and economic interests in China. Moreover, Britain was careful to ensure that a reduction in its opium exports to China would not benefit economically other producer states. Finally, Britain's introduction of cocaine to the international agenda reflected its interest, not in curbing cocaine use, but in delaying international control over opium.

Terrorism[27]

Terrorism is not new to the international system; it was a common European practice up to the mid-nineteenth century. If we define international terrorism as politically motivated acts of violence

23 *Ibid.*, p. 40. The Shanghai meeting was apparently the first in which China was treated as an equal (*ibid.*, p. 36), for which the United States may have anticipated some gratitude.
24 Bruun *et al.*, *Gentlemen's Club*, pp. 11, 28.
25 *Ibid.*, p. 12.
26 The League of Nations was given "general supervision over agreements with regard to the traffic in opium and other dangerous drugs." Its Advisory Committee, set up to do just that, was dominated by the colonial powers, which had opium monopolies in their Far Eastern colonies, and the drug manufacturing countries. The committee was nicknamed "the old Opium Bloc." See *ibid.*, p. 13.
27 "Terrorism" is such an ideological term that I hesitate to use it. It is interesting to note that the term was apparently first applied to state practices. It referred to "government by intimidation as directed and carried out by the party in power in France during the Revolution of 1789–94." *Oxford English Dictionary*, 2nd edn. (1989). Nowadays,

committed by non-state actors outside their home state's territory, then the practices mentioned at the outset of this chapter merit the label. Clearly, modern technology provides today's "terrorist" with both enhanced capabilities and a world stage. Theoretically, however, the real issue is not the means employed but who can legitimately use violence and to what end. My argument is that these issues were resolved by European states in the nineteenth century.

The English invented one form of state-sponsored terrorism in the thirteenth century when Henry III ordered privately owned English vessels to attack France and turn over half the loot, if any, to him. Thus began the practice of privateering which flourished for the next 600 years. Initially, authorizing individuals to engage in "legalized piracy" was surely viewed as an expedient or necessity of war. In retrospect, however, international law legitimated the practice on the basis that it was employed in the public interest and authorized by the state. Piracy, in contrast, was the use of violence for private ends. In short, privateering was an act of war while piracy was a crime.

In the real world of interstate relations, however, three factors blurred these boundaries between the legitimate and illegitimate. First, for strictly military reasons, states not only allowed but encouraged their people to engage in piracy. Interwar piracy provided sailors with the experience and training they needed to perform effectively as privateers during war. Moreover, to raise a naval force very quickly, states offered pardons to pirates who would accept privateering commissions. So there were no strong incentives to eliminate piracy.

Second, and most importantly, states were unable to resist the temptation of "plausible deniability." They permitted or even secretly supported non-state violence directed abroad without officially authorizing it. If the operation were successful, state leaders could claim a share of the gains and, if not, could deny any responsibility for the consequences. This led to numerous arguments, for example, between England and Spain over whether various English adventurers in the Americas were privateers or pirates. It also produced the third factor which blurred distinctions between piracy and privateering. Individuals understood the game the state was playing and exploited it to their own ends. Raleigh, for example, continued his depredations in the Spanish empire even after England and Spain had made peace

---

however, the term is applied less to the state's violence against its domestic population and more to non-state violence directed against a state – either the home state or other states. Indeed, many forms of state violence today are legitimated as counter-terrorism, more or less turning the term's original meaning on its head.

because he assumed his king "would secretly connive at violations of the treaty with Spain."[28]

So the boundary between legitimate and illegitimate non-state violence was more theoretical than real. But even the nice legal distinctions mask deep ambiguities in these practices, most importantly, in the interests they served.

For one thing, the individual privateer was generally motivated by economic interests. Privateering was a legally sanctioned way for individuals to engage in the piratical seizure of other's property. Financing privateering expeditions was a popular and lucrative venture, especially among the British upper classes.[29] Privateering was an investment opportunity for the wealthy. The fact that whenever states demanded a larger share of prize money a reduction in privateering quickly ensued underscores the priority of economic over political interests in this practice.

At the same time, pirates were not simply criminals preying on property for individual economic gain. Piracy, which was eventually criminalized, was in many instances a highly political practice. What is often overlooked is that criminalizing a practice may serve to delegitimate particular forms of resistance to state control or social conformity. "Pirate commonwealths" were formed by people who shunned European society, national identities, and enmities, and were viewed by the developing national states as both a political and military threat. Late seventeenth-century pirates "were more loyal to each other than they were to their country of origin or to their religion or even to their own race."[30] With the criminalization of piracy, state leaders not only quashed a threat to property but also one form of resistance to the consolidation of the national state system.

All of this real-world ambiguity and confusion was resolved in the nineteenth century when European states gave up the right to commission privateers.[31] Great Britain brought privateering to the international agenda because it regarded the practice as the only real threat to its naval supremacy and because its global trade networks made it

---

[28] Francis R. Stark, "The Abolition of Privateering and the Declaration of Paris," *Studies in History, Economics and Public Law*, ed. Faculty of Political Science of Columbia University, 8, 3 (1897), p. 23.

[29] Pat O'Malley, "The Discipline of Violence: State, Capital and the Regulation of Naval Warfare," *Sociology*, 22, 2 (May 1988), p. 258.

[30] Frank Sherry, *Raiders and Rebels: The Golden Age of Piracy* (New York: Hearst Marine Books, 1986), pp. 94–5.

[31] For greater detail, see Janice E. Thomson, "The State, Sovereignty and International Violence: The Institutional and Normative Basis of State Control Over External Violence," unpublished doctoral dissertation, Stanford University, 1988.

most vulnerable to privateering attacks. With the European powers' adoption of the "Maritime Law in time of War" in 1856, Britain achieved an international agreement banning privateering in exchange for Britain's yielding its right to search neutral ships for enemy goods. If states did not lend their authority to non-state violence beyond their borders, such violence would automatically be defined as piracy. State-sponsored terrorism was abolished and terrorism was criminalized. All the subsequent international agreements and conventions dealing with terrorism and piracy[32] represent attempts to enforce these norms in a new global state system.

CASE 2: BROUGHT TO THE AGENDA/NO INTERNATIONAL REGULATION

Alcohol

The first international agreement to limit alcohol consumption was the Brussels General Act of 1889–90 which provided for the prohibition on manufacturing or importing "distilled liquors" in Africa.[33] Under the League of Nations' mandate system, the "advanced nations" were required to prohibit abuses, including "the liquor traffic." In 1919 the Convention on the Liquor Traffic in Africa, which replaced the Brussels General Act, tightened the restrictions on alcoholic beverages, apparently in response to the rise in illegal trafficking sparked by earlier measures.[34]

Then the United States "went dry" on June 30, 1919 when the Wartime Prohibition Act took effect. The immediate purpose of this act was to save resources (particularly grain and coal), and to enhance the efficiency of the working class in the war effort.[35] Six months later, the 18th amendment took effect and prohibition became permanent.

The United States was not alone in its anti-alcohol campaign. In the aftermath of World War I came an "emotional outburst against alcohol"

---

[32] Piracy was formally defined as an international crime only in 1962 when the 1958 Convention on the High Seas entered into force. M. Cherif Bassiouni, "Introduction," in *idem*, ed., *International Criminal Law* (Dobbs Ferry, NY: Transnational Publishers, 1986), pp. 151–2.

[33] One notable exception to this rule was for the benefit of the "nonnative population based on the belief that it was not the liquor as such but the characteristics of the African people which accounted for the dangerous results of drinking" (Bruun *et al.*, *Gentlemen's Club*, p. 165).

[34] *Ibid.*, p. 166.

[35] K. Kerr, *Organized for Prohibition* (New Haven, CT: Yale University Press, 1985), pp. 202–7.

leading to "suppressive steps" being taken by most European states.[36] Apparently, wartime alcohol restrictions introduced by all belligerents provided a springboard for temperance advocates. Nevertheless, only the United States, Finland, and Iceland adopted prohibition, with Canada and Norway opting for partial prohibition.[37]

The mystery is why Finland sought international control while the United States chose only to enlist the cooperation of other states in enforcing its own laws.[38] Perhaps the answer is that the United States viewed the liquor trade as largely a U.S.–British issue.

A thriving smuggling operation had developed in the Bahamas, with British distillers shipping their product to this crown colony from whence it was shipped to just outside U.S. territorial waters. There, small boats ferried it to the U.S. mainland. The Bahamian government benefited substantially from this "illegal" trade as its revenues from the liquor duty rose about twentyfold between 1918 and 1921.[39]

By 1921, "the smuggling fleet in the Caribbean now was sailing from a British Crown colony, with a cargo of liquor from London, under the protection of Great Britain's flag. The British connection was complete."[40] Thus, rum-running became a diplomatic problem for the U.S. and British states. "By the summer of 1923, prohibition enforcement was the most visible, unsettled source of Anglo-American postwar disagreement."[41]

Britain's interests were two. First and foremost was the state's interest in preserving the 3-mile territorial limit. The United States was threatening to expand this limit to 12 miles in the interest of seizing the smugglers' ships. The second principal British interest was to achieve an exemption from U.S. prohibition for liquor carried on British ships for use by their crew or passengers. Europeans traditionally supplied their sailors with a daily liquor ration, so in banning liquor from its ports the United States would violate international comity.[42] Indeed, French seamen went on strike to demand the preservation of their right to a 2-liter daily wine ration when they perceived that U.S. law

[36] John Koren, "Drink Reform in Europe," *Atlantic* (December 1915), pp. 739–50.

[37] Bruun *et al.*, *Gentlemen's Club*, pp. 12–13.

[38] One might also ask why Saudi Arabia, for example, which strictly forbids the importation of alcohol, has not sought an international prohibition.

[39] Lawrence Spinelli, *Dry Diplomacy* (Wilmington, DE: Scholarly Resources, 1989), p. xiv.

[40] *Ibid.*, p. 4.

[41] *Ibid.*, p. 59.

[42] Customarily, national laws applied on ships and another state interfered (e.g., imposed its own national laws) only when public order was threatened. See Robert L. Jones, *The Eighteenth Amendment and Our Foreign Relations* (New York: Thomas Y. Crowell, 1933), pp. 26, 29.

threatened it.[43] So the principal aim of the other European powers was to receive an exemption for liquor carried in their ships for use by passengers and crew.[44]

In June of 1923 the United States made treaty proposals to Britain, France, Italy, Spain, and Japan. Since the U.S. Justice Department determined that more than 90 percent of the smuggling vessels were British, the Anglo-American negotiations were the most important.[45]

These negotiations produced the Anglo-American Liquor Treaty of 1924. The treaty's two major provisions allowed the United States to board and search ships, not out to 12 miles, but not beyond "a greater distance from the coast of the United States its territories or possessions than can be traversed in one hour" by the suspect ship, and the British to bring sealed liquor into U.S. waters.[46] This treaty provided a model for U.S. agreements with the other major maritime powers which were signed later in 1924.[47]

The United States and Britain continued their cooperation right up to World War II, which put an effective end to smuggling.[48] Through all of this, the United States apparently did nothing to spread prohibition to other countries but was content with enlisting the cooperation of other states in enforcing its own law.

In 1925, eleven Baltic-area governments adopted a convention which was an attempt to regulate the liquor trade in light of Finland's prohibition. When this effort failed Finland, along with Poland and Sweden, requested that the League of Nations produce an international convention on the illicit alcohol trade and investigate the whole alcohol question. Later Belgium, Denmark, and Czechoslovakia joined these three in asking for a conference to draw up an international convention on the liquor traffic and for a committee on alcohol similar to the one set up for narcotics control.[49]

---

[43] Ibid., p. 101.
[44] In April of 1923 the U.S. Supreme Court ruled that prohibition did not apply to U.S. ships beyond the 3-mile limit but did apply to foreign ships in U.S. territorial waters. When word of this decision reached Britain, some Conservatives introduced legislation "to require all foreign ships to carry liquor in British waters." See Spinelli, Dry Diplomacy: 46.
[45] Jones, Eighteenth Amendment: 6, 18, 44.
[46] Spinelli, Dry Diplomacy: 81.
[47] Ibid.: 94, 103 (fn 22) and Jones, Eighteenth Amendment: 18. In fact, the French exploited the exemption for liquor carried for medicinal and dietary purposes by applying it to all liquor. The United States was well aware of this practice, but did nothing. The French were the slowest to reach an accord with the United States, taking 32 months to ratify the treaty after its signing in 1924 (ibid.: 110–12).
[48] Spinelli, Dry Diplomacy, pp. 141–2.
[49] Bruun et al., Gentlemen's Club, p. 169.

In the League's debate on this question in 1927, France took the lead in opposing the expansion of League activities concerning alcohol. Belgium's delegate noted the irony here when he said that while the League was attempting to control the use of "dangerous drugs used in certain distant countries . . . some of its Members seemed hardly inclined to fight with the same energy against the abuses and dangers resulting from the use of dangerous drugs in Europe."[50] Ultimately the Finns withdrew their request. After 1932, the League's commission responsible for oversight showed "very little interest . . . in either the liquor traffic or in any other aspect of the alcohol problem."[51]

So international cooperation in controlling alcoholic beverages was limited to the forty years of the African mandate period. "International cooperation was even lacking in controlling the illegal trafficking in alcohol"[52] as the United States pursued bilateral and Finland, regional agreements on this subject. The League was not involved in either case and neither it nor the UN took action to foster any international control efforts.[53]

Arms trade

In the 1930s, people in the United States and much of the rest of the world became convinced that the private manufacture of armaments was a major contributor to international conflict. In their quest for profits, the private manufacturers of armaments were said to engage in a broad range of nefarious activities (see below) in an attempt to spur the demand for their products. This contributed to the international arms race which, in turn, was a major cause of war. Based on this "merchants-of-death" thesis, people argued that armaments production should be nationalized[54] and the export of arms be controlled by the state.

---

50 Quoted in *ibid.*, p. 170.
51 *Ibid.*, p. 167.
52 *Ibid.*, p. 180.
53 With the advent of the UN, alcohol abuse came under the jurisdiction of WHO. One indication of its bias against alcohol control is the very different treatment WHO gave to two NGOs. The International Federation of Pharmaceutical Manufacturers Association, "essentially a lobby for drug industry interests," was founded in 1968 and granted NGO status three years later. The pro-alcohol control International Council on Alcohol and Addictions applied for NGO status in 1947 which it was granted twenty years later in 1968. During that period, "there had been no change in WHO qualifications for admission" (*ibid.*, pp. 178–9).
54 "The issue of nationalization erupted in all of the major Western nations" in the mid-1930s. Robert E. Harkavy, *The Arms Trade and International Systems* (Cambridge, MA: Ballinger, 1975), p. 36.

League of Nations' efforts to regulate the arms trade were ineffective as the United States refused to ratify its conventions. Even the League's 1921 report, which charged that arms manufacturers "had inspired war scares, bribed officials, exaggerated reports of military and naval programs, organized international munitions combines, and sought to influence public opinion through the press," failed to generate support in the United States for state control of the arms trade.[55]

The 1930s saw publication of a number of books which attempted to document the arms merchants' trading with the enemy, bribery of foreign officials, and efforts to sabotage arms control agreements.[56] But the purveyors of the merchants-of-death thesis were not limited to a few muck-rakers and pacifists. As Wiltz puts it:

> If such allegations had been country store or main street gossip that would have been one thing. They were something else when echoed by the President of the United States, the Premier of France, two former Secretaries of State, the League of Nations, *Fortune* magazine, the *Christian Science Monitor*, members of Congress, the peace movement, leaders of religion, and even the *Wall Street Journal* and the *Chicago Journal of Commerce*. Who could blame people in the mid-thirties for taking seriously this heady business about merchants of death?[57]

In 1931, peace organizations in the United States began a campaign to eliminate the private manufacture of arms. One of their tactics was to distribute Alexander Hamilton's "Report on Manufactures" which

---

[55] *Ibid.*, p. 6.

[56] Among these were H. C. Engelbrecht and F. C. Hanighen's *Merchants of Death: A Study of the International Armaments Industry* (New York: Dodd, Mead, 1934), George Seldes' book, *Iron, Blood and Profits: An Expose of the Worldwide Munitions Racket* (New York: Hapres, 1934) and Phillip Noel-Baker's *The Private Manufacture of Armaments* (London: V. Gollancz, 1936). Also appearing in the spring of 1934 was an article in, of all places, *Fortune* magazine, which argued that "detail upon detail, incident upon incident, illustrate how well the armament makers apply the two axioms of their business: when there are wars, prolong them; when there is peace, disturb it" (quoted in John Edward Wiltz, *In Search of Peace: The Senate Munitions Inquiry, 1934–1936* [Baton Rouge, LA: LSU Press, 1963], p. 20). It was placed in the *Congressional Record* and a condensed version was published by the *Readers Digest* in May of 1934.

[57] Wiltz, *In Search of Peace*, p. 23. The United States had come a long way from the laissez-faire attitude expressed by Thomas Jefferson (1793): "Our citizens have always been free to make, vend, and export arms. It is the constant occupation and livelihood of some of them. To suppress their callings, the only means perhaps of their subsistence, because a war exists in foreign and distant countries, in which we have no concern, would scarcely be expected. It would be hard in principle and impossible in practice." Quoted in William C. Morey, "The Sale of Munitions of War," *American Journal of International Law*, 10, 3 (1916), p. 474.

called for a nationalized arms industry.[58] Clearly, the idea that the state should monopolize arms production was not a new one, but had been around since the very beginning of the United States.

In 1932 the U.S. section of the Women's International League for Peace and Freedom (WILPF) called for a Senate investigation into the arms trade and persuaded Senator Nye of North Dakota to sponsor the investigation. The Senate passed Nye's resolution and on September 4, 1934 the Senate Committee Investigating the Munitions Industry held the first of ninety-three hearings which concluded in early 1936.[59]

Meanwhile, the British section of the WILPF worked with other peace organizations to administer the League of Nations' national "Peace Ballot" in Britain. About 40 percent of the electorate was polled and 90 percent of the respondents agreed that "the manufacture and sale of armaments for private profit [should] be prohibited by international agreement."[60] By late 1934, "there was a considerable demand in Britain for a public inquiry into the arms industry and the case for its nationalization." In February of 1935 the Prime Minister appointed a Royal Commission to conduct such an inquiry and on May 1 the commission held the first of twenty-two hearings.[61]

In 1935, the United States, France,[62] the Netherlands, and Sweden implemented new controls on the arms trade by requiring the licensing of arms production or foreign sales, or both. Great Britain retained the licensing system it had adopted during World War I.[63]

---

[58] In his report Hamilton wrote that "it might hereafter deserve legislative consideration, whether manufactories of all the necessary weapons of war ought not to be established, on account of the Government itself . . . As a general rule, manufactories on the immediate account of the Government are to be avoided; but this seems to be one of the few exceptions which that rule admits, depending on very special reasons." Alexander Hamilton, "Report on the Subject of Manufactures," in Harold C. Syrett, ed., *The Papers of Alexander Hamilton*, X (New York: Columbia University Press, 1966), p. 317.

[59] Wiltz, *In Search of Peace*, pp. 73, 208.

[60] Gertrude C. Bussey and Margaret Tims, *Pioneers for Peace: Women's International League for Peace and Freedom, 1915–1965* (London: WILPF, British section, 1965), p. 144.

[61] Basil Collier, *Arms and the Men: The Arms Trade and Governments* (London: Hamish Hamilton, 1980), pp. 179–81.

[62] Elected in 1936, the Popular Front government in France nationalized key sectors of the arms industry. While some justified this action in terms of the merchants-of-death thesis, others argued that state-owned production facilities would be more efficient as production would be geared toward meeting the security interests of the nation rather than the economic interests of individuals. Edward Kolodziej, *Making and Marketing Arms: The French Experience and its Implications for the International System* (Princeton, NJ: Princeton University Press, 1987), p. 28.

[63] Wiltz, *In Search of Peace*, pp. 160, 183; Elton Atwater, "British Control over the Export of War Materials," *American Journal of International Law*, 33, 2 (April 1939), p. 297. It should be noted that, while Great Britain and other European states could refuse to license arms exports for foreign policy reasons, the U.S. state could do so only if the

Demand for expanded state control over the arms business was based on two beliefs – one causal and one normative.[64] New "knowledge" about the behind-the-scenes machinations of the arms dealers revealed the profit motive to be an important "cause" of international conflict. But there was also an argument which had to do with fairness or even morality:

> For giving aid or comfort to the enemy in time of war the penalty is death. Both civilians and soldiers share this punishment. If an American or a British or a French soldier in No Man's Land had ever been caught giving a rifle or a grenade to a German, he would have been shot on the battlefield. But the Allied armament-makers who not only before the war, but during the war, gave rifles and grenades and the comfort of food to the enemy, received baronetcies and the ribbons of the Legion of Honour while making a profit of millions of dollars.[65]

It was simply unfair to compel citizen-soldiers to face death on the battlefield while their fellow citizens made money by selling weapons to the very people the soldiers confronted in the trenches.

Political and moral entrepreneurs[66] placed the arms trade on the international agenda. Beliefs about the causes of war and the unequal demands placed on citizens led to investigations into the practices of the arms industry. While U.S. failure to join the League doomed efforts to achieve international control, these entrepreneurs did succeed in generating tighter state, and therefore democratic, control over the arms trade.

CASE 4: NOT BROUGHT TO AGENDA/NO INTERNATIONAL REGULATION

Mercenarism

As I have demonstrated elsewhere,[67] mercenarism was a legitimate and near-universal practice in the European state system for

---

sale would violate a U.S. law or treaty obligation (Atwater, "British Control," p. 315, and *idem, American Regulation of Arms Exports* [New York: Carnegie Endowment for International Peace, 1941], p. 212).

[64] This distinction between causal and normative ideas is drawn from discussions at the SSRC Conference on Politics and Ideas held at Stanford University in January 1990 and from the attendant memos prepared by Judith Goldstein and Robert Keohane.

[65] Seldes, *Iron, Blood and Profits*, p. 1.

[66] This is derived from Nadelmann who, in "Prohibition Regimes," uses the term "transnational moral entrepreneurs."

[67] Janice E. Thomson, "State Practices, International Norms, and the Decline of Mercenarism," *International Studies Quarterly*, 34 (1990), pp. 23–47. Mercenarism refers to the practices of recruiting for and enlisting in a foreign army.

three centuries. It was delegitimated during the Napoleonic War when Britain objected to U.S. citizens accepting commissions from France to attack British shipping. It should be emphasized, however, that Britain was challenging a particular instance of the practice, and not attempting to delegitimate mercenarism as an institution. Indeed, Britain itself continued to hire mercenaries up through the Crimean War.

The United States responded to British pressure by passing neutrality laws which made it a high misdemeanor for a U.S. citizen to accept and exercise a commission to serve another state engaged in war with a state friendly to the United States. These laws served as a model for other states which, in the course of the next century, voluntarily adopted similar measures in their own municipal law. Mercenarism is subject to universal, though not international, regulation. In other words, state practices converged around the U.S. approach to controlling mercenarism.

Like most laws, the neutrality laws contain loopholes and are not always enforced so mercenary activity persists, mostly in the Third World. African states, which have been especially vulnerable to it, have recently placed mercenarism on the international agenda. In 1976 Nigeria submitted to the UN a proposal for an international ban on mercenarism. So far, however, the Western industrialized states have blocked the imposition of a ban, claiming that it would violate their citizens' rights to free speech and movement. So while mercenarism has lately been placed on the international agenda, it was actually delegitimated and subjected to state control nearly 200 years ago.

Tobacco[68]

Smoking tobacco for personal enjoyment was introduced to Europe with Spain's conquest of America. Spanish and Portuguese sailors took up the practice, spreading it to both Europe and Asia. Smoking was introduced to Central Europe by English and Spanish soldiers during the Thirty Years War. European slave traders introduced it to Africa, and Portugal brought it to Japan which then spread it to Korea and Manchuria. It took only about 100 years for smoking, which originated in Central America, to become a worldwide practice.

In almost every instance, the state's immediate response was to prohibit smoking. King James I of England, in 1603, described smoking as "a custom loathsome to the eye, hateful to the nose, harmful to the

---

[68] Except where noted, the following account is taken from Count Corti, *A History of Smoking*, trans. Paul England (London: George G. Harrap, 1931).

brain, dangerous to the lungs," and tried to tax it out of existence. Germany, Switzerland, Austria, Turkey, Russia, Japan, and China all attempted to ban it. The Sultan even imposed the death penalty for smoking.

During the seventeenth century, there was no consensus on the health effects of smoking. Many physicians believed that smoking reduced the chances of contracting the plague and some even saw tobacco as a cure for cancer. Opponents of smoking made some pretty weak arguments. They charged that smoking was barbaric and complained that tobacco smoke was terribly annoying to non-smokers. More persuasively, some suggested that tobacco might crowd out cultivation of food crops and that smoking was an extreme fire danger.

Fairly early on, however, states found that tobacco was a potentially lucrative revenue source and adopted the Italian model of making the tobacco business a state monopoly. This naturally provided states with an incentive to encourage tobacco-use, though taxation of tobacco often was rationalized as an anti-smoking measure.

During the course of the seventeenth century, smoking with pipes declined as the upper classes took the lead in shifting to the use of snuff. This trend away from smoking was interrupted by the Napoleonic wars which introduced European soldiers to the American practice of cigar smoking. By the mid-eighteenth century, cigarette smoking had made its way from South America to Europe which, in turn, introduced it to the United States. The practice increased dramatically in Europe with the Crimean War and in the United States with the Civil War. Smoking tobacco became popular in the United States during the Civil War when Yankee soldiers were introduced to the practice in the South.[69] The habit became widespread during World War I when tobacco rations were provided to the troops. The military viewed smoking as an antidote to fear, stress, and boredom. From France General Pershing cabled that "Tobacco is as indispensable as the daily ration; we must have thousands of tons of it without delay."[70] World War I led to a three to fourfold increase in smoking by Europeans and North Americans.

Tobacco has never been placed on the international agenda. Nadelmann argues that the reason for this is that tobacco and alcohol were too integrated into too many societies by the time "global society had advanced to the point of being able to construct an international prohibition regime."[71] I would offer a different explanation. After all,

---

[69] Peter Taylor, *The Smoke Ring: The Politics of Tobacco* (London: Bodley Head, 1984), p. 23.
[70] *Ibid.*, p. 1.
[71] Nadelmann, "Prohibition Regimes," p. 511.

several states did in fact prohibit alcohol and some did attempt to develop international controls. Moreover, most states attempted to ban tobacco use almost immediately following its introduction. The real problem was that tobacco-use was globalized at a time when states were weak and unable to enforce restrictions much less prohibition. At the same time, each of the major forms of tobacco-use was tied up with war and conquest. It was the state's own agents – soldiers and sailors – who spread it, and it was the army's use of it as a morale-booster which encouraged it. For these reasons, states treated tobacco as a revenue source rather than a social evil. Tobacco was never introduced onto the international agenda because by the time states had developed the capability to regulate it, it provided too much revenue to too many states. They had an institutionalized economic interest in tobacco-use.

SUMMARY OF FINDINGS

The results of this analysis, summarized in Table 2, lead me to draw several conclusions about the power of the state-building hypothesis.

First, the state-building hypothesis is confirmed by half the cases (terrorism, alcohol, and tobacco) and partially supported by the mercenarism case. Mercenarism's demise is consistent with the hypothesis in that a strong state (Britain) "imposed" the ban on the United States. However, Britain was not threatened by the weak United States but by another strong state, France. Because the French state was strong, Britain simply attacked the weaker, supply-side of the practice of mercenarism – the United States. Yet the recent failure of Third World states to institutionalize an international regime banning the practice is consistent with what a state-building perspective would predict.

In contrast, opium was prohibited at the urging of the United States, which was not a strong state; nor was it facing domestic or international threats. The strong states of Europe were among those most resistant to international prohibition of the drug trade. Finally, the case of the arms trade is entirely inconsistent with the hypothesis as the impetus for control came from non-state actors. Moreover, the threat to strong states came, not from the weak, but from other strong states in World War I.

Second, the delegitimation of a practice is most likely to occur in the context of strategic interaction among states. This suggests that it is not societal beliefs about the morality of a practice, but its impact on state material interests which calls its legitimacy into question.

214

Table 2. *Summary of findings*

Case	Delegitimation context	Initiator	Form of control
opium	strategic interaction	United States	international regime
terrorism	strategic interaction	Britain	international regime
mercenarism	war	none	convergence
arms trade	interwar	moral entrepreneurs	convergence
alcohol	war	Finland	N.A.
tobacco	N.A.	N.A.	N.A.

Third, power provides only a partial explanation for the ultimate fate of a practice. Convergence or no control tends to correspond with weak advocates of control (Finland, moral entrepreneurs). Britain did take the lead in prohibiting terrorism. Yet, none of the other international regulation or even the convergence cases was the result of hegemonic leadership. The British sparked the decline in mercenarism, but only inadvertently, and U.S. laws became the model for Britain and other states.

Finally, time, as a surrogate for change in the international context, provides little help in explaining the outcomes displayed in Table 2. It would account for the anomalous tobacco case because at the time tobacco-use was introduced to Europe, states were too weak to impose control. Though most of them attempted to ban the practice, states lacked the organized policing, surveillance, and other coercive capabilities to enforce their restrictions. But because tobacco-use was suspect, states were able to tax tobacco.

Various aspects of violence came under state control in the nineteenth century, but the form of regulation differed with, for example, convergence in the case of mercenarism and an international regime for privateering. In addition, control of trade in the means of violence – arms – did not make it to the international agenda until the twentieth century. Finally, recreational drugs other than tobacco came to the agenda in the twentieth century, but ended up being treated quite differently. Opium and cocaine were subjected to international regulation while alcohol was not.[72]

---

[72] New knowledge also does not explain the pattern of substance prohibitions. According to the National Institute on Drug Abuse, the annual deaths in the United States from various drugs are as follows: Tobacco, 346,000; alcohol, 125,000; alcohol and drugs, 4,000; heroin/morphine, 4,000; cocaine, 2,000; marijuana, 75. See Thomas J. Crowley, "Learning and Unlearning Drug Abuse in the Real World: Clinical

CONCLUSIONS

It hardly bears stating that this chapter provides no definitive answer to the questions of what does and does not get regulated internationally and why. The results of this analysis suggest that patterns of delegitimation and regulation are largely arbitrary, random, or non-rational.[73] Practices are delegitimated in a variety of circumstances, for different reasons, and by both weak and strong states and by non-state actors. The state-building approach is of little help in predicting whether delegitimation will result in no control, convergence, or international regulation.

Still, the historical record in these cases is largely consistent with state-building theory. The analysis demonstrates quite clearly that the powerful determine both the legitimacy of practices and the form regulation – if any – will take. It was the powerful states of the West, though not particular hegemonic states, which were responsible for the outcome in all these cases. In the one case (mercenarism) in which Third World states attempted to generate an international ban, the North blocked the effort. That the powerful make the rules comes as no great surprise to a student of politics. Nevertheless, it should serve to remind us that world order and governance rest upon a highly institutionalized set of practices developed in the course of several centuries of predominantly Western interstate relations. Moreover, while norms of contemporary international practice are a product of the West, they do not reflect the imposition of a hegemonic vision, but the unintended consequences of a long history of state-building and interstate relations.

Treatment and Public Policy," in Barbara A. Ray, ed., *NIDA Research Monograph 84* (1988), pp. 101–5. If public health were the determinant, alcohol and tobacco (and perhaps automobiles) should be banned alongside other drugs. If the pattern of prohibitions makes little sense from a public health perspective, from an economic perspective, the ban on drugs is positively irrational. A recent analysis suggests that "the drug war will cost (U.S.) government at all levels $30 billion a year," while legalizing and taxing drugs could yield $10 billion in state revenue. See Richard J. Dennis, "The Economics of Legalizing Drugs," *Atlantic* (November 1990), p. 129. The question is: why has the United States persisted in this economically irrational strategy of prohibition for nearly 100 years? An economic argument can, however, account for the lack of control on tobacco. For example, in Britain "revenue from cigarettes brings the Treasury over £4 billion a year; cigarette related diseases cost the National Health Service a tiny fraction of that in direct costs – £165 million a year." (Taylor, *Smoke Ring*, p. xix). Even if the broader social costs of smoking, such as lost working days, are included, "the total cost of cigarettes to the nation is estimated to be considerably less than half the £4 billion revenue which tobacco brings in" (*ibid.*, p. 73).

73 Herein lies the appeal of the moral progress argument; if an outcome does not appear rational, then it must be due to something non-rational like morality.

This research also provides evidence which is inconsistent with arguments – stated or implied – that the proliferation of norms represents moral progress in the international system.[74] The findings of this chapter suggest that we should be very cautious in invoking terms like morality, civilization, or justice.

First, it is unclear just how much "civilizing" has actually occurred. Skeptics can point to the continued existence of various forms of slavery, neocolonialism, and proxy armies (neomercenarism) as indications that the elimination of many pernicious activities has merely resulted in the turn to new forms of the old practices. Defining slaves as persons who are unable voluntarily to withdraw their labor, anti-slavery groups estimate there are at least 200 million "slaves" in the world today.[75] Piracy not only continues on the high seas but has moved to the skies. Mercenaries have been replaced by proxy armies.

The problem here, it seems to me, stems from the tension which arises from banning individual participation in a practice while reserving the state's right to engage in it. With the institution of sovereignty the state can legitimately choose to behave in ways which non-state actors cannot. The history of the state's symbiotic relationship with organized crime, its involvement in the "illicit" drug trade, and its covert operations (which often employ terrorist tactics) all suggest that morality has little to do with international norms. Instead of eliminating certain practices, states simply monopolize them. The widespread belief among people that the practice is evil is a bonus; it simply reduces the state's costs of enforcing its monopoly.

Second, a moral progress argument, by accepting the inherent evil of a practice, obscures the political nature of many of these practices. Nadelmann does note the political motives of U.S. abolitionists who sought to repress minorities. Alcohol was associated with Catholics and Jews; opium with Chinese immigrants, cocaine with Southern blacks, and marijuana with Mexicans. He neglects to mention the linking of heroin use to revolutionaries in New York in 1919.[76] But the political nature of the practice itself is not examined. Moreover, in many instances, including slavery and piracy, the practices were already in decline before they were legally proscribed. The question is why states

---

[74] James L. Ray, in "The Abolition of Slavery and the End of International War," *International Organization*, 43, 3 (Summer 1989), p. 439, is most explicit in making this argument. However, Nadelmann writes of "the civilizing of international society" which suggests that the spread of Western ideas or morality has eliminated barbaric practices. "Prohibition Regimes," p. 488.

[75] See *The Economist*, January 6, 1990, p. 42.

[76] Musto, *American Disease*, p. 134.

217

expend the effort and resources to implement an international ban on a practice which is dying a natural death. Perhaps what these types of international regulations or prohibitions represent is the triumph, not of morality, but of state efforts to narrow the possibilities for resistance to its projects.

8 "AND STILL IT MOVES!" STATE INTERESTS AND SOCIAL FORCES IN THE EUROPEAN COMMUNITY

Linda Cornett and James A. Caporaso

Over the last several years, world politics has entered into a period of transition that rivals in depth and scope the changes of the immediate postwar era. These changes intrigue many observers all the more since they materialized from orderly and otherwise unexceptional processes rather than among the convulsive aftershocks of war. Nowhere do the effects of these changes stand out more clearly than in Europe.

Brief years after a United States president reaffirmed the Cold War commitment to combat the Soviet Union's "evil empire," the bipolar division of the European continent is rapidly disappearing. The strident and divisive themes suffusing Cold War rhetoric find little support in emerging visions of world governance and order. After having spent the last four decades trying to undermine the Soviet Union's position in Eastern Europe, the West now encourages Gorbachev's tenure of power in the interest of European stability, as one-party regimes in Eastern Europe topple to be replaced by more competitive political systems. Suddenly, DeGaulle's ambitious call for a Europe "from the Atlantic to the Urals" is upstaged by the possibility of "a unified Europe stretching from Cork to Kamchatka."[1] While the dismantling of the Soviet bloc and the uniting of the two Germanies serve as striking symbols of the powerful forces of change sweeping Europe, a more subdued revolution continues in Western Europe centering on the European Community (EC).[2]

The causes and consequences of changes across the continent undoubtedly interconnect on a number of points. Nevertheless, the integrationist ambitions of the European Community predate, and remain largely distinct from, developments in Eastern Europe and the Soviet Union. Quite apart from the ultimate outcomes of these latter

---

[1] Malcolm Chalmers, "Beyond the Alliance System: The Case for a European Security Organization," *World Policy Journal*, 7, 2 (Spring 1990), p. 235.

[2] Sometimes the Common Market is referred to as the EEC and at other times the EC. Technically, the proper abbreviation depends on the period of time in question. In 1968 the European Coal and Steel Community and European Atomic Energy Agency merged with the EEC. After 1968 the EEC was commonly referred to as the EC.

reforms, debates concerning the scope, depth, and potential significance of the Community's cooperative achievements will continue to challenge international relations theorists in the decades to come. Although the long-term portent of the Community's course toward economic and political "union" remains a much-debated issue, theorists of all persuasions have taken an interest in the EC as they continue to search for models of peaceful change. The profound uncertainty concerning the future of East Europe and the Soviet Union lends particular urgency to inquiries about "governance without government." Most observers agree that, at the very least, the Community represents a novel experiment in regional cooperation. Some believe that it may provide the foundations for an alternative form of international organization, one less divided by the boundaries of states and "dictates" of anarchy.

In attempting to understand the relaunching of West European integration and its potential significance for international order, we employ several contrasting theoretical perspectives: neoclassical economic theory, neorealism, neoliberal institutionalism, and functionalism and neofunctionalism. We attempt less to test these four bodies of thought than to illustrate the strengths and limitations of each in the context of European integration. How, we ask, do each of these theories help or hinder us from understanding the broad changes taking place in Western Europe? And what vision do they offer for the future? In the remainder of the chapter, we will provide a brief overview of the European integration process, offer an examination of this process in light of our four theories, and draw tentative conclusions on the basis of this comparative theoretical exploration.

BACKGROUND

In 1958 the Treaty of Rome brought into force the European Economic Community, a grouping of six countries (France, West Germany, Italy, Belgium, the Netherlands, and Luxembourg) pursuing the goal of economic integration. The EEC grew out of earlier, more narrow integrative efforts institutionalized in the Coal and Steel Community (1952) and shared with the European Atomic Energy Community (1958). Although related to these two prior experiments, the more ambitious objectives of the EEC gained separate organizational and legal status in 1958. The formation of the EEC combined a pragmatic emphasis on solving concrete problems with dramatic ideas about how to tame or transcend the nation-state.

The first years of the EEC's existence stimulated remarkable progress toward the Community's self-defined goals. From 1958 to 1961 the EEC prepared the foundations for advances in agriculture, common pricing policies, and the customs union. Between 1962 and 1965 a series of important decisions substantially altered and even reorganized European agriculture. According to Lindberg and Scheingold,

> By the end of 1963 approximately 300 regulations, directly binding in all six countries, had been adopted by the Council on the proposal of the Commission. They set up a uniform system governing trade and the marketing of agricultural products both within the Community and with outside countries . . . In setting up the common levy system the member states in effect relinquished autonomous control of one of the prime elements of national agricultural policy – the option of closing borders or restricting access to the domestic market in order to maintain internal price levels and sustain the income of farmers.[3]

Significantly, however, these decisions had ramifications which extended well beyond agricultural policy.

Once in effect, agricultural integration stimulated activity on other fronts. If there were to be common grain prices, there would have to be common national policies on tariff and non-tariff barriers, taxes, national food subsidies, etc., in order to protect the initial benefits of integration. For example, to enjoy the advantages accruing from reduced tariffs, participants would be pressed to regulate jointly exchange rates. Otherwise states could effectively offset tariff reductions by devaluing their currencies by an equivalent amount. To help combat these perceived dangers, the Commission's supporters sought to enhance Community influence and resources in related issue-areas.

As part of the agreement on common grain prices, the Council of Ministers asked the Commission to prepare proposals on financing the common agricultural policy (CAP). The Commission developed and submitted the appropriate proposals, but exceeded its mandate by appending provisions for independent Community resources under the budgetary control of the European Parliament. If accepted, these proposals would have provided for a Community budget not directly subject to national control and would have contributed to an expansion of a political Europe.

The proposals were not accepted. Instead, the French representative walked out of the Council of Ministers, and the EEC was deadlocked from June 1965 to January 1966. The infamous Luxembourg

---

[3] Leon N. Lindberg and Stuart A. Scheingold, *Europe's Would-Be Polity* (Englewood Cliffs, NJ: Prentice-Hall, 1970), pp. 146–7.

Compromise effectively arrested the institutional development of the EC. Proposals to institute majority voting, establish independent revenues, and increase powers for the European Parliament suffered an abrupt setback.[4]

The record of the EC since the Luxembourg Compromise appears mixed at best. The EC continued to make modest progress in several issue- areas, including monetary policy and industrial policy. However the broad significance and transformative potential of European integration seemed to dissolve. State leaders emerged stronger than ever. The policies and institutions of Brussels were seen more and more as instances of delegated power – not rival centers of political control. This description of the EC remained salient throughout the seventies and at least halfway through the eighties.

RECOVERY AND PROGRESS

Predictions of the European Community's demise appear to have been premature, however. The Community's dramatic recovery in 1985–6, following years of paralysis, startled politicians and scholars alike and prompted a reevaluation of the context surrounding "1992." Some scholars attribute the EC's astonishing turnaround to France's succession to the Community's rotating presidency in January 1984 and Mitterand's personal commitment to a regional solution to Western Europe's economic problems.[5] Under the expert guidance of the new Commission president, Jacques Delors, an emerging consensus for liberalization among Britain, France, and West Germany was codified in Lord Cockfield's 1985 White Paper. The White Paper included 300 measures (later reduced to 279) designed to facilitate progress toward completion of the internal market by 1992. Although it contained no directive for procedural reform, Delors' public statements stressed that liberalization implied and presupposed majority voting.[6]

Despite the decidedly reluctant support of the British, the 1992 Single Act instituted several procedural reforms to complement the substantive legislation promoting the internal market. The principles of

---

[4] For an extended discussion of the EC crisis (called the Constitutional Crisis), see John Lambert, "The Constitutional Crisis: 1965–66," *Journal of Common Market Studies*, 4, 3 (1966).

[5] Much of the following history draws from Moravcsik's detailed account of events culminating in the White Paper and Single Act. Andrew Moravcsik, "Negotiating the Single European Act: National Interests and Conventional Statecraft in the European Community," *International Organization*, 45, 1 (Winter 1991), pp. 19–56.

[6] *Ibid.*, p. 40.

qualified majority voting and mutual recognition[7] gained jurisdiction over internal market issues, with several notable exceptions.[8]

Although safeguard clauses allow states to claim exemption from treaty obligations under certain extenuating circumstances, the Court and Commission, not the states, now act as final arbiters. Community offices, not member states, "ultimately determine what constitutes proper justification for exempting a state from a Community decision."[9] The Court's power of arbitration, along with its elevation of Community over national law, involves an important shift of power and responsibility to Community institutions and represents one of the potentially more important reforms to emerge in 1985. Consequently, while the Single Act merely reiterates many of the common-market objectives already articulated in the 1957 Treaty of Rome, it also contains enabling procedural and institutional reforms to support the White Paper's substantive design. In fact, significant advances toward the single market objectives followed upon these accomplishments.

In the aftermath of the substantive and procedural reforms of 1985 and 1986, the momentum toward "1992" quickened. By the summer of 1990, 60 percent of the White Paper directives enjoy Euro-law status and bind member states.[10] Further progress toward the internal market proceeds unevenly, however, varying from sector to sector. While technical barriers to the movement of goods, services, and capital continue to topple at a steady pace, the Council more reluctantly tackles some of the thorniest issues, including joint policies for taxation and social welfare. Nonetheless, Community leaders have pledged to multiply their efforts even in the more contentious issue-areas.

The remainder of this chapter will explore the Community's recovery and further development from the vantage point of four international relations theories. In particular, we will adopt the analytical tools and insights offered by neoclassical economic theory, neorealism, neoliberal institutionalism, and functionalism and neofunctionalism to account for the Community's evolution over the last several years. As stated

---

[7] Mutual recognition ensures that after minimal standards gain acceptance by delegates, goods and services produced in compliance with the regulations of any member state automatically earn access to the markets of any other. This principle acknowledges diversity of members' needs and releases delegates from the onerous task of negotiating each detail of legislation.

[8] Moravcsik, "Negotiating the Single European Act," p. 42; Albert Bressand, "Beyond Interdependence: 1992 as a Global Challenge," *International Affairs*, 66 (1990), p. 48. Exceptions include fiscal harmonization, taxation, emigration and workers' rights, social policy, and agricultural regulations.

[9] Moravcsik, "Negotiating the Single European Act," p. 43.

[10] *The Economist* (July 7, 1990), p. 5.

earlier, our attempt is not to test these theories. Instead, we apply them with the hope that they shed some light on the unexpected acceleration of European integration, in particular, and the possibilities for "governance without government" more generally.

NEOCLASSICAL ECONOMICS AND PERFECTION OF THE EUROPEAN MARKET

Concern about the broad purposes and goals of the EC are bound to be important to the 1992 process. To those who are interested in a stronger "political Europe," the institutional aspects of the transition, especially those aspects having to do with the democratic deficit, are central. To others, perfection of the internal market represents the key social purpose of 1992. Deregulation, privatization, and broadening the scope of market exchange assume centrality. From this perspective, "EC '92" is first and foremost about the elimination of obstacles to a larger, unified market, the creation of a more rational economic structure, a more efficient regional division of labor, and enhanced competitiveness in the global arena.

As a body of theory, neoclassical economics explains the potential gains from trade or, more broadly, from exchange. However, the theory is not all of one cloth. Neoclassical economics has spawned three separate but related branches of inquiry. First, the theory of market exchange focuses on the allocative behavior attendant to competition and free exchange. Second, the theory of games and strategic interaction analyzes the behavior of actors (usually firms) in imperfect markets. And finally, the economics of organization or institutions identifies institutional arrangements most suitable for economic transactions. We will comment briefly on the first and the third branches.

Since Adam Smith, neoclassical economists have attempted to refine, perfect, and extend the fundamental principle of economic exchange. In neoclassical theory, the market refers to the realm of voluntary exchange. In this sense, the market need not refer to the economy as conventionally described but can be thought of as characterizing the behavior of individuals within governments, universities, and firms insofar as that behavior involves choice and exchange. The limits of the market are defined by the boundaries of mutually improving exchange. Thus, the market ends where exchange is inappropriate or impossible in principle (compliments, friendship, love), where it brings loss to at least one party (as in "power-over"), or where there are political bans on exchanges that would otherwise be possible (voting rights, minimum wage laws).

Within these boundaries, the scope of the market may vary. Indeed, attempts to expand the market domain are central to the goals of the "1992" process. Neoclassical economics provides a theory which claims to demonstrate that, once the problem is cast in terms of utility-maximization on the basis of individual preferences, resources, and a given technology, the market will produce the maximum wealth (benefits) for its members. As Wolff and Resnick state, "In neoclassical theory, there is a precise and necessary correspondence between a fully cooperative private property economy and an optimally efficient one."[11]

The EC involves more than exchange and markets, however. It also contains institutions, which constitute a framework for contracting and bargaining, as well as mechanisms to foster cooperation and preserve independence. Both neorealist and functionalist integration theory point out that the types of institutions that enhance efficiency and those that preserve national autonomy (not to mention the relative power positions of individual states), often contravene. Although space limitations prevent a detailed analysis of institutional issues, a brief sketch follows, examining the rudiments of a neoclassical theory of institutions as it applies to the 1992 initiative.

While the theory of market exchange can inform us about the comparative economic incentive structure facing member states, it says little about institutions. Why, in an interstate environment littered with Pareto-inferior results, do states sometimes construct institutions to overcome them and more often not? Part of the answer lies in the theoretical baseline established by market exchange – a world of cost-free transactions. In such a world, where property rights are perfectly specified, agents engage in contracting costlessly. As North argues, such a world presumes that we can go directly from calculations of utility to outcomes with no intervening variables, such as institutions.[12]

While economics organized along lines of the Walrasian model of exchange (unidimensional goods, no transaction costs, instantaneous market transactions) provides no account of institutions, another

[11] Richard D. Wolff and Stephen A. Resnick, *Economics: Marxian versus Neoclassical* (Baltimore, MD: Johns Hopkins University Press, 1987), p. 88. Seen in this light, the task of the EC is to expand the scope of the market.
[12] Douglass C. North, "Institutions and a Transaction-Cost Theory of Exchange," in James E. Alt and Kenneth A. Shepsle, eds., *Perspectives on Positive Political Economy* (Cambridge: Cambridge University Press, 1990), p. 182.

branch of economics deals with institutions explicitly.[13] In 1937 Coase turned our attention to transaction costs and their implications for economic organization. In the real world, he suggests, huge costs routinely accompany exchange. These include information costs, the costs of identifying the relevant partners and opportunities, bargaining and influence costs, and costs associated with implementation and monitoring.

While these costs may remain limited under ideal circumstances – within countries, enjoying common legal structures, language, and close physical proximity – they are likely to be more pronounced across the borders of different countries. The EC's twelve member states, while similar in some respects, support a wide array of governmental structures, domestic law, economic organizations, state–society relations, national goals, and habits of communication. Even if the distribution of interests across states revealed potential gains from exchange, many opportunities would be missed due to poor information, lack of trust, incentives to defect, uncertainty regarding the duration of contact, and ease of escaping detection if contracts are broken.

Given that the EC member states potentially face all of these obstacles to exchange, there would be strong pressures for institutions to respond. Neoclassical economists argue that the EC's institutional structure accomplishes several things. First, it provides greater visibility to transactions, making it more difficult and costly to hide uncooperative actions behind obscure national regulations. Second, the EC cuts down on the negotiating costs associated with bargaining over outcomes. Multilateral negotiations among twelve representatives in Brussels is certainly more efficient than bargaining bilaterally. Third, the EC contributes to a diminution of coordination failures, i.e., to a failure to find a mutually satisfactory solution when several exist.[14] Finally, the existence of regional institutions enhances the value of reputation, by bringing participants back into the same setting and by "lengthening the game" for these participants.

The above interpretation of Europe 1992 represents a continuation of the Rome Treaty, the central goal of which was to create a unified market. In broad terms, this Treaty did lay out a timetable for movement

---

[13] See Ronald H. Coase, "The Problem of Social Cost," *Journal of Law and Economics*, 3 (October 1960), pp. 1–44; Oliver Williamson, *The Economic Institutions of Capitalism* (New York: Free Press, 1985); and Paul Milgrom and John Roberts, "Bargaining Costs, Influence Costs, and the Organization of Economic Activity," in Alt and Shepsle, eds., *Positive Political Economy*.

[14] Milgrom and Roberts include coordination failures among bargaining costs. See *ibid.*, p. 74.

from free trade area to customs union to a common market in which goods, services, and productive factors flowed freely. The free trade area and customs union developed smoothly and were completed ahead of schedule. But after 1968, movement toward a more liberalized market slowed.

The Commission's 1985 White Paper attempted to renew the EC's original resolve to move toward completion of the market. The White Paper classified extant barriers to exchange under three headings: physical, technical, and fiscal.[15] The Commission attempted to deal with the numerous specific obstacles subsumed under these headings by adopting some 300 legislative proposals. The obstacles identified by the White Paper included a broad range of non-tariff barriers (ntbs), subsidies, health and safety standards, border controls, unnecessary transportation costs, and discriminatory practices.

The Cecchini Report[16] provides the detailed statistical analysis to support the White Paper. This report identifies three important areas where costs could be decreased and efficiency enhanced: static gains from trade (buying from the cheapest suppliers), competition improvements (causing price reductions), and the restructuring effect due to the reorganization of industry and economies of scale. The estimate of total gain resulting from the White Paper's implementation amounts to about 200 billion European currency units (ECUs) or between 4.3 percent and 6.4 percent of the EC's domestic product in 1988.[17] This is the economic cost of "non-Europe."

While the White Paper and the Cecchini Report present themselves primarily as technical documents, some of the broader implications of the internal market are recognized. The social dimension, even though important for Jacques Delors, is not something the report seems anxious to emphasize. Not only would a strong social policy invite stern opposition from several member states, it also fits uneasily with the basic liberalization thrust of EC '92. As Garrett points out, one view of the 1992 goals is that it involves deregulation, liberalization, and de-institutionalization of the European economy.[18] From this perspective, Europe's social dimension and the monetary union, and

[15] Gary Clyde Hufbauer, ed., "An Overview," in *Europe 1992: An American Perspective* (Washington, DC: The Brookings Institution, 1990), p. 8.
[16] Paolo Cecchini, Michael Catinat, and Alexis Jacquemin, *The European Challenge, 1992* (England: Wildwood Press, 1988).
[17] *Ibid.*, p. 17.
[18] Geoff Garrett, "Explaining '1992': Economic Functionalism, Neofunctionalist Spillover, or Political Bargain?" (Stanford, CA: Stanford University, mimeo, 1990), p. 6.

the institutional development necessary to sustain both, appear inconsistent with the liberal slant to 1992 since they are interventionist and involve ceding sovereignty.[19]

Finally, Western Europe's position in the world in terms of competitiveness, market shares, and regional comparative advantages occupies a central position in the cost-benefit calculations behind the 1992 project. The Cecchini Report posits a direct and positive relationship between the adoption of the White Paper's recommendations and Europe's standing in the international political economy:

> if they [Europeans] respond robustly, the continent's citizens, companies, and governments will do more than realize their collective economic potential as Europeans. They will propel Europe onto the blustery world stage of the 1990's in a position of competitive strength and on an upward trajectory of economic growth lasting into the next century.[20]

Although the projected costs and benefits of the Community's internal-market project are often calculated at the state or regional level, neoclassical economic theory allows supporters to make claims about individual welfare on the basis of aggregate numbers.

Neoclassical economics has followed in Adam Smith's footsteps by attempting to link individual self-interest and the good of society. This identity holds most reliably when individuals freely pursue their own goals with minimal interference. Advocates of this theory predict inevitable social benefits resulting from efforts to liberate the market from political obstacles to exchange. Theoretically, "EC 1992" will lower transaction costs, enhance efficiency, and ultimately enrich the entire population. Consequently, although the White Paper and Single Act attempt to harmonize – not eliminate – standards, the distinct deregulatory accent of EC 1992 represents a continuation of the classical and neoclassical designs. The enabling legislation for 1992 focuses on measures for removing barriers to exchange and improving efficiency, even if hues of neomercantilism accompany these goals at the global level.[21] Indeed, the 1992 project can be seen as a combination of domestic deregulation and international mercantilism.

---

[19] *Ibid.*, p. 7.
[20] Cecchini, Catinat, and Jacquemin, *The European Challenge*, p. xvii.
[21] For an account emphasizing the neorealist aspects of contemporary European integration, see Wayne Sandholtz and John Zysman, "1992: Recasting the European Bargain," *World Politics*, 52, 1 (October 1989), pp. 95–128.

NEOREALISM

Neorealism is a theory of international conflict, alliances, balance of power, war, and peace. It may seem an odd candidate for explaining regional integration in Western Europe. The "two track" treatment of security and economic issues assigned security concerns to the North Atlantic Treaty Organization (NATO) and economic issues to the EC. Functionalism and neofunctionalism were designed to explain economic and social processes, realism and neorealism were fashioned with security in mind.

However, realism always expressed theoretical interest in European cooperation and integration,[22] especially in reference to the background factors necessary for integration to take off. Recent versions of neorealism, exemplified by the work of Kenneth Waltz and Joseph Grieco,[23] have developed the theory to specify the conditions under which relative gains (hence rivalry) become less salient. Neorealism leads us to emphasize state interests and bargaining behavior. These interests, neorealists caution, do not dissipate or become submerged when states interact within international organizations; they merely take different forms. In this context two topics take on particular importance in the neorealist explanation of 1992: one, the background conditions shaped by anarchy and changes in the global distribution of power; two, the importance of particular EC states, their interests and their bargaining behavior. In Waltz's theory, both anarchy and the distribution of capabilities establish the permissive conditions for cooperation as well as the limits.

Neorealist theory holds that the lack of global authority motivates states to pursue power in a relentless effort to secure themselves against other like-animated units. All states are compelled by insecurity to build and strengthen their capabilities against the contingency of war. In this environment, states face strong disincentives to cooperation. First, they worry that the division of possible gains arising from cooperation may benefit others more than themselves so that "even the

---

22 Stanley Hoffmann provides a good case in point in "Obstinate or Obsolete: The Fate of the Nation-State and the Case of Western Europe," *Daedalus*, 95, 3 (Summer 1966), pp. 862–915. We do not mean to categorize Hoffmann as a neorealist. However, his work (particularly his earlier work) emphasized the role of anarchy, power, and the distribution of capabilities. He has also dealt extensively with international law, morality, human rights, and international institutions.

23 Kenneth N. Waltz, *Theory of International Politics* (Reading, MA: Addison-Wesley, 1979); Joseph M. Grieco, "Anarchy and the Limits of Cooperation: A Realist Critique of the Newest Liberal Institutionalism," *International Organization*, 42, 3 (Summer 1988), pp. 485–507.

prospect of large absolute gains for both parties does not elicit their cooperation so long as each fears how the other will use its increased capabilities."[24] Second, states resist cooperation lest their interactions lead to increased vulnerability. The more deeply involved a country becomes in the international division of labor, and the more it profits from specialization along comparative cost lines, the more vulnerable it is. The gains from trade, the very *raison d'être* for specialization in liberal economic theory, become – perversely – a source of political insecurity.

In an anarchic environment, even differential economic gains may be seen as threats to security. Yet anarchy does not determine uncooperative outcomes. Power may be distributed among states in such a way that security concerns may become either more or less salient.

In its account of European integration, neorealism emphasizes the importance of shifts in the global distribution of power. Two changes in the power distribution are critical: one, from multipolarity to bipolarity; two, from Europe as the center of great power activity to the United States and the Soviet Union. These changes are important in the permissive sense; they allow, they do not determine the specific course of events.

Waltz argues that as long as Europe was the center of gravity, changes in power relations were accompanied by the usual fears among relatively weaker states. As a result, the benefits of economic cooperation were severely limited by the fear that economic superiority might be turned to political advantage. While the success of European integration was by no means guaranteed by the structural changes, the project at least became possible.[25]

Contrary to neofunctionalism, which stresses supranational actors and private groups, neorealism highlights states – especially powerful states – and state interests as the keys to understanding the process of integration. In a recent article in *International Organization*, Andrew Moravcsik identifies the enabling source of the 1985–6 reform package in the interstate bargaining process among the Community's three predominant members – France, West Germany, and Britain. In his estimation, the convergence of political and economic interests among the Community's major actors represented the "essential preconditions

---

[24] Waltz, *Theory of International Politics*, p. 105; also see Grieco, "Anarchy and the Limits of Cooperation," p. 498.
[25] Waltz, *Theory of International Politics*, p. 70.

for reform."[26] The convergence of interests was made possible by the election of a Conservative government in Britain in 1979, the French disappointment with Keynesian policies and consequent "turnaround" in 1983, and the existence of a sympathetic Kohl government in the Federal Republic of Germany. From this perspective, the political bargains leading to "1992" were based on: (1) the coincidence of national interest in developing the internal market; and (2) West Germany's and France's ability to convince Britain that its own interests would best be served by further compromise and cooperation.[27] Moravcsik presents his findings as an explicit "challenge [to] the prominent view that institutional reform resulted from an elite alliance between EC officials and pan-European business interest groups."[28]

Moravcsik and other neorealists show less interest in the specific origins of these phenomena, however, than in their permissive effects. In his estimation, the convergence of political and economic interests among the Community's predominant members "represented the essential preconditions for reform."[29] Moravcsik adopts the view that the reforms of the mid-80s, like each prior junction in the Community's evolution, "rested on interstate bargains between [the most powerful member states –] Britain, France, and Germany."[30]

There can be little doubt that state leaders made the crucial decisions to go ahead with the Single Act and the 1992 initiatives. This is more or less a matter of observation. However, this interpretation of the "facts" is but one among several possibilities. While recognizing the role of states and interstate bargains, neofunctionalists can still claim theoretical priority if they can demonstrate that socioeconomic processes structure the incentives in theoretically determinate ways. Proponents of functionalism and neofunctionalism do not claim that task-expansion occurs automatically. Politicians are always deemed important in that they are "part of the loop," one link in a circular, self-reinforcing set of causal processes – not a first-mover with independent leverage, as is implied by exogenous interests.

At least one version of the spillover hypothesis reasons as follows: initial cooperative successes "run their course" and encounter obstacles that produce stagnation unless fresh political action is taken. Neorealist accounts reject this proposition since, it is argued, no causal chain can be demonstrated between initial policy successes and the options and obstacles of the mid-1980s. Instead, as Moravcsik argues, "For the

---

[26] Moravcsik, "Negotiating the Single European Act," p. 21.
[27] *Ibid.*, pp. 21–2 and 27–32.
[28] *Ibid.*, p. 20.   [29] *Ibid.*, p. 21.   [30] *Ibid.*, p. 21.

source of state interests . . . scholars must turn away from structural theories and toward domestic politics."[31] Keohane and Hoffmann present a similar view, although they do not write under the neorealist label and both authors differ significantly from neorealism. However, they argue that the spillover hypothesis as an explanation for the Single Act is implausible since, if the relevant processes had been at work, the results would have taken place earlier.[32]

NEOLIBERAL INSTITUTIONALISM

Neoliberal institutionalism accepts neorealism's emphasis on anarchy, state interests, and power, but seeks to introduce an institutional component to systemic-level analyses. In particular, scholars in this tradition explore how international institutions mitigate the most divisive and stressful effects of anarchy. Without questioning the anarchic character of international relations, they seek to understand and explain how the spread of information, norms, and rules may change states' options and influence the order, if not the ordering principle, of international relations. Advocates of this approach maintain that variations in global institutions provide incremental explanatory power for understanding interstate behavior.

Robert Keohane defines institutions as "persistent and connected sets of rules (formal and informal) that prescribe behavioral roles, constrain activity, and shape expectations."[33] In one sense, this definition subsumes and expands upon Krasner's definition of a regime.[34] For Keohane, a regime is one form of international institution, one where there is significant convergence among states regarding norms, beliefs, rules, and procedures, but not necessarily a formal organization.[35] Rules are human artifacts used to proscribe, prescribe, and encourage particular actions. The United Nations Charter rules out the use of international violence except in self-defense. The General Agreement on Tariffs and Trade (GATT) prescribes open trade regimes and most favored nation status as organizing principles to guide international

---

[31] *Ibid.*, p. 21.
[32] See Robert O. Keohane and Stanley Hoffmann, "Conclusions: Community Politics and Institutional Change," in William Wallace, ed., *The Dynamics of European Integration* (London and New York: Pintner Publications, 1990), p. 287.
[33] Robert O. Keohane, "Neoliberal Institutionalism: A Perspective on World Politics," in Robert O. Keohane, *International Institutions and State Power* (Boulder, CO: Westview Press, 1989), p. 3.
[34] Stephen D. Krasner, "Structural Causes and Regime Consequences: Regimes as Intervening Variables," *International Organization*, 36, 2 (1982), pp. 185–205.
[35] Keohane, "Neoliberal Institutionalism," p. 4.

232

exchange. The Montreal Convention targets limits for the emission of chlorofluorocarbons into the atmosphere.

The decisive difference between neorealism and neoliberal institutionalism has to do with the relative significance each attributes to international institutions. In Waltz's estimation, international organizations "are barely once-removed" from the wishes and capacities of the predominant powers.[36] They merely reflect power distributions at best, and add to the power of the powerful at worst. By contrast, neoliberal institutionalism claims that rules provide a determinant of behavior lying outside capabilities (excluding organizational capabilities) and preferences. In saying this, they do not imply that the power and interests of the major actors are irrelevant to the creation of rules and institutions. They do suggest, however, that once formed, the "rules of the game" rarely mirror the pattern of interests and capabilities from which they originated.

The institutional approach provisionally accepts neorealism as a baseline for inquiry. Both understand international politics as a result of states (the actors) pursuing given interests (the motivation) within anarchy (the environment) as their capabilities permit (the means).[37] Neoliberal institutionalism seeks to add (or, more precisely, integrate) institutions into this explanatory equation. By this account, states pursue their interests within an anarchic environment, but one notably modified by the presence of institutions. Institutions not only constrain and empower states in systematic ways but may also shape the perception of self-interests. Additionally, they may significantly transform the means through which states pursue their interests. States' power is defined increasingly in terms of the ability to work with, not against, numerous rival sources of power and influence in world politics.

Consequently, institutions are not merely added, but integrated, into the neorealist explanatory equation. Indeed, they importantly qualify some of the fundamental concepts defining neorealist theory, including interest, power, and anarchy. Neoliberal institutionalists seek to explain how international institutions may temper the effects of anarchy by independently altering the costs and benefits of cooperation.

Western Europe today little resembles the United States of Europe

---

[36] Waltz, *Theory of International Politics*, p. 88.
[37] Power can also be the goal within realist and neorealist theory. Either way, the overall structure of the theory is very much the same, though not identical, since power-as-goal may define a purely positional good, hence one for which cooperation is impossible. In addition, institutionalists relax the assumptions of anarchy. By allowing for rules, external political constraints are brought to bear on states.

that some early enthusiasts envisioned. Nevertheless, the contrast with pre-World War II relations on the continent is instructive. William Wallace observes that in 1938 when Chamberlain discussed the Czechoslovak crisis with Hitler in Munich, it was only his second visit to Germany and his first visit abroad as Prime Minister to meet a foreign head of government. By 1983, Thatcher had made six visits to West European countries each year, including extensive meetings with the European Council as well as a series of bilateral summits.[38] These top-level meetings took place on a foundation of daily contacts and exchanges among governmental functionaries and private groups. The contact is so pervasive that it makes more sense to talk of a transnational and transgovernmental presence rather than discrete, time-bounded exchanges. Predictability, trust, and the value of reputation are fostered by such contacts. What happened in the intervening forty-five years to account for this dramatic transformation of Western European politics?

Several important variables shifted in the tumult created by World War II. Because bipolarity, nuclear weapons, and extensive institutional development emerged almost simultaneously, no clear causal inferences can be drawn directly relating any one to the specific international order that followed. Neoliberal institutionalists provisionally accept that the bipolar division of power significantly influences the range of choices leaders confront and the possibilities for action. They also focus, however, on the constraining and empowering consequences which accompany various kinds and degrees of institutional development at the systemic level.

Neoliberal institutionalism eschews neorealism's Hobbesian conception of anarchy and the corollary interpretations of institutions as reflections of power distributions. At the same time, however, theorists who adopt this approach often view advocates of centralized political institutions with suspicion. The descriptions and prescriptions of neoliberal institutionalism are congenial to a decentralized environment where states, power, and absence of central government are theoretically recognized but fail to evoke the same conclusions associated with stronger versions of neorealism.

In the context of the European Community since 1985, neoliberal institutionalists investigate how the Community's institutional framework facilitates cooperation. First, it brings together leaders of the member states, representatives of parties, and interest groups in

---

[38] William Wallace, *Britain's Bilateral Links within Western Europe*, Chatham Papers, no. 23 (London: Routledge and Kegan Paul, 1984), p. 4.

continuous contact and collaboration. The periodic meetings of the Commission, Council of Ministers, and European Parliament promote a permanent dialogue among parties and provide a means to learn more about the preferences of their counterparts. The incentive to disguise true preferences for public goods recedes in an environment where not only state leaders but interest-group representatives (who bear or enjoy the costs and benefits) are present. The CAP is a case in point. The structural reform policy reduces the number of small, inefficient holdings. Revenues from agricultural levies are used in part to compensate losers (e.g., small farmers). Rather large revenues move across national and class lines, facilitated by the European Commission and its General Directorate for Agriculture.

Repeated interactions enhance the possibility for further cooperation in a second, and closely related, way – by lengthening the time-horizon of participants. In a chaotic environment characterized by one-shot transactions, it is difficult to monitor defections. Indeed, the very idea of defection is hard to grasp in an environment lacking a solid contractual foundation. The EC provides an environment of stability and predictability in which the incentive and capacity to cheat decreases. The interpenetration of the national bureaucracies and interest groups, operating in tandem with Brussels, makes for a more transparent system where actions (cooperative and defective) can be detected, rewarded, and punished. The value of reputation is enhanced by a permanent institutional structure which assures repeated interactions. Leaders tempted to renege on commitments know that they will have to face their partners and risk retaliation in future interactions. As the visibility of actions increases, monitoring and detection become easier, and the prospects for cooperation improve.

Finally, while EC institutions do not harmonize all interests indeed, they create some conflicts), they may unwittingly contribute to cooperation by raising the costs of defection. Many of their policies increase the cost of non-participation for reluctant members. To withhold free trade privileges from a set of countries who have no free trade area and customs union amongst themselves is one thing. It is quite another matter to stay on the outside once others consolidate. Prime Minister Thatcher was often reminded that, whatever differences she may have had with her EC partners, she could not afford to withdraw from the Community since increasing costs were associated with being on the outside.

Neoliberal institutionalists attribute the timing of the White Paper and Single European Act largely to the changing interests of the dominant actors in Western Europe. In this view, the emergent liberal economic consensus at the foundation of 1992 arose from several sources. First, "objective" changes in the international political economy made cooperation more attractive and non-cooperation more costly in terms of Western Europe's steadily eroding competitive base. The unique domestic experiences of France and the United Kingdom also contributed to this consensus. They locate the requisites for the 1985–6 reforms in France's "conversion" to liberal economic principles following its unsuccessful Keynesian experiment of the early 1980s, combined with Britain's recognition that the anticipated benefits of deregulation presupposed some institutional changes. Finally, Community officials themselves, particularly Delors, actively promoted "regional solutions" to states' competitiveness problems under the EC's existing institutional framework.

FUNCTIONALISM AND NEOFUNCTIONALISM

Functionalism offers a very different account of the integration process, even while observing the same data. Moreover, it provides an implicit critique of neorealism's theoretical assumptions. Specifically, functionalism problematizes the state-centric approach characteristic of neorealism and seeks to introduce alternative actors both above and below the state. From this perspective the key actors in international relations increasingly are found not among diplomats and politicians, but either among supranational officials and multinational interest groups or among domestic interest groups and political parties. Mitrany's formulation of functionalism gives analytical primacy to subnational actors and processes at the root of international change in Western Europe.[39] This approach builds from the premise that the contemporary state is inadequate to satisfy the socioeconomic needs of its constituencies. To overcome this deficiency, subnational groups, largely operating outside the purview of governmental control, are said to establish spontaneous networks which effectively, if not legally, bind societies together in complex and multilayered relationships. Mitrany argues that the development of cross-national activities, commitments, expectations, and eventually loyalties will engender numerous international organizations in both public and private sectors.

Functionalists believe that the road to European unity must be built

[39] See David Mitrany, *A Working Peace System* (Chicago: Quadrangle Books, 1966); and David Mitrany, *The Progress of International Government* (New Haven, CT: Yale University Press, 1933).

upon a firm foundation rooted in societal needs and interests. A European political construction could not be established without first bringing together people from various aspects of life and engaging them in practical joint endeavors. Once a wide variety of groups begins to realize the practical benefits of cooperation, the grand debates centering on sovereignty and political prerogative lose force. Functionalists focus on social forces, private actors, and learning. Unlike neorealism, questions of power and international structure (particularly anarchy) are not focal. Unlike versions of liberal economics, the primary concerns lie with learning and the transformation of interests, not with allocative efficiency given a certain distribution of preferences and resources.

Functionalist advocates like Mitrany and Monnet[40] recognize the importance of politics. No strategy to unite Europe could remain apolitical. Nevertheless, with respect to the practical question of what to emphasize first, functionalists single out the social and economic aspects of society. Political considerations (sovereignty, representation, voting arrangements) are best handled by sensitive avoidance. They must be addressed in due time but preferably after the cement of society (economic exchange, shared attitudes, common beliefs) has had a chance to take hold. Only then will states stop talking about sovereignty and see that they "are creating a common sovereignty."[41]

As a theory of action, functionalism deemphasizes state actors, highlights social and economic forces, and devises a strategy by which initial (cooperative) efforts gradually expand into more politically controversial areas. Functionalism's systems-transforming theory is based on two simple propositions: first, societies are composed of sectors that can be separated from one another for initial cooperative purposes; and second, intersectoral linkages ensure that initial cooperative successes can be transmitted to related sectors. These two propositions imply an action strategy: (1) identify areas of society where people can cooperate; (2) arrange cooperative behavior functionally – not along territorial lines; and (3) take advantage of intersectoral imbalances to extend cooperative arrangements into related areas once initial cooperation has taken root. The final stages of integration involve cooperation on many different fronts along with appropriate political institutions. In this way the dramatic "shoot-out"

---

[40] Jean Monnet was primarily an activist who sought to construct Europe through his work on the "Action Committee." He did not influence European integration through his writings so much as through his daily (political and economic) activities.

[41] R. C. Mowat, *Creating the European Community* (London, Blandford Press, 1973), p. 59.

that many anticipated between technocrats and politicians will not take place as state representatives recognize the benefits of integration.

The key to the process-level component of functionalist theory lies in the concept of spillover. This refers to the purported self-expansive tendency of integration within pluralistic socioeconomic environments. Mitrany argues that integration in one sector necessitates further integration, either as a way of generalizing success or, more typically, as a way of overcoming obstacles and imbalances in the achievement of the original goals. Governments, singly or in combination, often enter these processes in a reactive capacity, i.e., in an attempt to gain control over already established integrative activity. Two types of spillover appear in functionalist theory. In the first version, integration is transmitted from sector to sector (e.g., tariff reductions increase the pressure to deal with exchange rate policy). In the other it moves from economic issues to political ones (e.g., "private" cooperation becomes institutionalized).

While functionalism draws our attention to actors and processes neglected by neorealism, by itself it provides a weak account of power and institutions. Mitrany and Monnet tend to see questions of power and institutions as inextricably bound up with sovereignty, national prestige, and high politics. This leads them to downplay the extent to which even the most technical integrative experiments rest on a prior (unstated) political consensus and to misunderstand the ways in which efforts to deepen or expand integration require political struggle. Neofunctionalists attempt to avoid these mistakes while retaining functionalist insights about the importance of social and economic cooperation.[42] In the following pages we briefly examine attempts by Haas and Nye to enrich functionalism's insights by blending them with an institutional perspective.

To see the importance of neofunctionalism, we contrast it with neorealism. Neorealism's explanation of change relies on power and structure, with goals (preferences, interests) remaining constant. By this account, states pursue their goals within an environment of anarchy and uneven (and varying) capabilities. Since anarchy is fundamentally a given and the goal of survival is to a large extent implied by anarchy, the distribution of capabilities becomes focal. Variations in power (capabilities) do most of the theoretical work. Neorealist theory offers a

---

[42] See the essays by Leon N. Lindberg, Philippe C. Schmitter, Ernst B. Haas, and Joseph S. Nye in Leon N. Lindberg and Stuart A. Scheingold, eds., "Regional Integration: Theory and Research," special issue of *International Organization*, 24, 4 (Autumn 1970).

structural explanation of why things change, at least in the limited sense that the distribution of capabilities identifies a component of structure.

What neorealism takes as given, neofunctionalism makes problematic. What neorealism accepts as constant, neofunctionalism attempts to make variable. The work of Haas and Nye is exemplary for its effort to think about how goals and beliefs may change. The attempt to endogenize goals and beliefs lays the basis for a very different theory of change. Explanatory leverage derives not from changes in the distribution of power but from variations in consensual knowledge and perceptions of interest. If the structure of interests is zero-sum, no amount of knowledge will inspire cooperation. Parties will simply become more perfectly informed of their mutual incompatibility. But short of this, increases in knowledge can point to areas of agreement, enable mutually beneficial exchanges, help to identify areas where conflict might lead to damaging results, and even encourage states to transcend (by redefining) old differences.

Haas examines the role of institutions in shaping national definitions of "interest" over time. Institutions may decisively contribute to integration either by acting directly to alter the ideas, expectations, and inclinations of state representatives or by engaging influential segments of society that, in turn, express expectations for government support. Integration becomes self-perpetuating to the extent that it modifies the interests, expectations, and ideas of domestic actors in ways that precondition further integration. Many functionalists fault neorealism for treating the "interests" and beliefs of national leaders exogenously.

In a 1988 article for *World Politics*, Joseph Nye suggests that one of the most valuable neofunctionalist contributions to international relations theory derives from its central focus on how states and social actors perceive their changing interests. Although neorealism contains a theory of learning, it is an impoverished one, in his view. Nye explains that:

> Realist theories maintain that states learn by responding to structural changes in their environment; to put it in game-theory terms, they adjust their behavior to changes in the payoff matrix . . . [But] "change" [or learning] is reduced to merely a change in the means unless we have an account of how such interests are perceived and redefined.[43]

---

[43] Joseph S. Nye Jr., "Neorealism and Neoliberalism," *World Politics*, 40 (January 1988), pp. 238–9.

Neofunctionalists seek to locate such an account of states' changing definitions of interest in the intersection of domestic and international processes. This approach, pioneered by Ernst Haas, offers an initial entrée into the relationship between "process-level" interactions on the one side and the social and self-understandings of international actors on the other.[44]

Whereas Waltz's preoccupation with international anarchy leads him to deemphasize the relevance of beliefs and norms for actors' behavior, Haas' focus on the elements of "society" or "community" at the systemic level encourages a closer examination of the actors' self-defined motives and purposes. Haas argues that "in Functional terms, there really is no state of nature at all. Functionalism calls attention to the variety of motives and relationships that flow from a technologically, economically, and socially diverse environment."[45]

Haas may agree with neorealists who argue that states act on the basis of individual national interests and collaborate to the extent that their interests coincide. But at least part of what he and others want to examine are the ways in which many-sided and continuing interactions among states systematically lead them to redefine their interests. Haas does not mean to suggest that a harmony of interests emerges, only that actors perceive their interests in light of or bound up with the interests of other participants, even as the substantive content of those interests continues to differ or even conflict. The more sophisticated variants of functionalism avoid specious conceptions concerning states' capabilities to surmount all differences. The more important achievements follow to the extent that conflicts can be managed in constructive ways. Haas explains: "There is no common good other than that perceived through the interest-tinted lenses worn by the international actors. But international interest politics causes the tinting to fall into converging patterns, and Functionalism sensitizes us to spotting the tasks responsible for the pattern."[46] Haas conceptualizes international integration as a consequence of interest politics, carried out within existing national and international institutions.[47] He indicates that conflicts of interest persist even as Community members attempt to contain these conflicts within a common normative and institutional order.

Specifically, scholars in this tradition commonly examine the ways in which increased transactions and multiple levels of contact influence

---

[44] Ernst B. Haas, *Beyond the Nation-State: Functionalism and International Organization* (Stanford, CA: Stanford University Press, 1964).
[45] *Ibid.*, p. 71. [46] *Ibid.*, p. 35. [47] *Ibid.*, p. 35.

states' definitions of self-interest, as well as expand opportunities for transnational coalitions. The role of international institutions in fostering such interactions claims a central position in this literature. "In short, [neofunctionalists] emphasize the political process of learning and redefining national interests, as encouraged by institutional frameworks and regimes."[48]

In terms of the European Community, functionalism and neofunctionalism direct our attention to the changing character of the Community's interactions just prior to, during, and after the 1985–6 reforms. Successive periods witnessed a minor "revolution" in terms of the relative importance of various state and non-state actors, the Community's decision-making style, and evidence of spillover.

Functionalists must begin their explanation by noting the proliferation of subnational and supranational actors supporting the 1992 project. Unlike previous attempts at closer cooperation, business leaders have offered their active support to "EC 1992." Surveys suggest that most business planners share the optimistic expectations sweeping the continent.[49] The spate of mergers and acquisitions across the Community forecasts the dramatic change of perspective brought about by the prospect of 1992. Unionized workers also seem more optimistic about the future in an integrated Europe, albeit hesitantly and with qualifications.[50] Clearly "integration" will also create losers, who may organize in opposition. Consequently, functionalists need to specify if and how these actors will be able to combine and press their claims with national and international authorities.

The influential role of the Commission in the Community's sudden reawakening requires some attention. Keohane and Hoffmann note that the Commission's lead in designing the White Paper and Delors' personal efforts on behalf of the procedural reforms embodied in the Single Act were "crucial in defining the agenda which governments had to decide."[51] Delors' efforts to link the anticipated economic benefits associated with the White Paper to the procedural compromise expressed in the Single Act finally paid off. The European Council endorsed the White Paper at Milan in June 1985 and agreed in principle to majority voting covering a wide range of internal market issues. The breakthrough followed Britain's decision to ratify the Single Act despite Thatcher's reluctance to cede further authority to Community

---

[48] Nye, "Neorealism and Neoliberalism," p. 239.
[49] *The Financial Times of London*, May 10, 1988, p. 4.
[50] Peter Holmes, "1992," *Fabian News*, 101, 3 (May/June 1989), p. 7.
[51] Keohane and Hoffmann, "Conclusions," p. 287.

institutions. Keohane and Hoffmann reveal the rationale behind Ms. Thatcher's decision:

> When Margaret Thatcher was asked in May 1989 why she agreed to ratify the Single European Act, she replied simply that "we wished to have many of the directives under majority voting because things which we wanted were being stopped by others using a single vote. For instance, we have not yet got insurance freely in Germany as we wished."[52]

This response is frequently invoked to demonstrate the continuing strength of nationalist self-interest over the nebulous ideal of Community. In fact, Keohane and Hoffmann point out that the genius of the spillover mechanism is that it "does not presume continued enthusiasm on the part of elites; indeed, its significance is most evident in the continuation of regional integration even as *elan* declines."[53] From this perspective, the fact that Ms. Thatcher was persuaded to keep pace with her more ambitious partners, seemingly against her will, presents evidence for a spillover effect.

Britain's decision to join the European Monetary System (EMS), reversing Thatcher's prior resolve to avoid monetary entanglements represents a second supporting case. Despite her continued and vociferous objections to monetary union and a single currency, Community leaders hope to establish a central European bank by early 1994 to sustain and complement the anticipated benefits of the common market.[54] Functionalists recognize that Thatcher's, and now Prime Minister Major's, willingness to continue on this path is in no way assured. Spillover was never assumed to be automatic. It works best, however, when cooperative arrangements approximate Haas' conception of supranationality.

Supranationality denotes a style of decision-making which encourages "a cumulative pattern of accommodation in which participants refrain from unconditionally vetoing proposals and instead seek to attain agreement by means of compromises upgrading common interests."[55] Participants are said to learn "when the bargaining positions of the parties are tied to consensual goals, and when concessions . . . are perceived as instrumental toward the realization of

---

[52] *Ibid.*, p. 287.
[53] *Ibid.*, p. 285.
[54] *New York Times*, October 29, 1990, C1.
[55] Ernst B. Haas, "Technocracy, Pluralism and the New Europe," in Stephen R. Graubard, ed., *A New Europe?* (Boston, MA: Houghton Mifflin, 1964), p. 64.

joint gains."[56] Ms. Thatcher's decision to support majority voting and commit Britain to the EMS after all fits well into this definition of learning. Further, since 1985–6, neofunctionalists might plausibly argue that "supranationality" characterizes most Community interactions.

The anticipated economic benefits clearly occupied a central position in the revival of the internal market project. However, the process of articulating, negotiating, and implementing shared economic ambitions also entailed more overtly political consequences and goals. If the Single Act compromised state sovereignty more than some government leaders like, the realization of the internal market presupposes acceptance of procedural reform.[57] The construction of the single market required certain powers of governance and the tasks of governance proved incompatible with the retention of the veto. Pinder articulates the (largely unintended) institutional consequences of members' commitment to the internal market:

> The internal market programme may have been seen as a framework in which to deal with the urgent problem of competitiveness . . . filling the liberal trend of the times as well as the governmental resistance to sharing sovereignty. But it brought with it pressures for . . . institutional reform that could prove more important than the single market itself.[58]

Additionally, the institutional reform resulting from the Single European Act opened the way for a transfer of power from states to Community institutions.

While observers generally agree that the European Community is no surrogate for national government, Community institutions have assumed several important functions usually reserved for state actors, from legislating industrial standards and regulating business mergers to negotiating trade agreements with third parties, coordinating monetary arrangements, and articulating joint positions on foreign policy. The Single Act created no new institutions to speak of, but those already in existence became more effective and gained broader jurisdiction.

---

[56] Ernst B. Haas, "Why Collaborate? Issue Linkage and International Regimes," *World Politics*, 32, 3 (1980), p. 393.

[57] Keohane and Hoffmann, "Conclusions," p. 20.

[58] John Pinder, "Economic Integration vs. National Sovereignty: Differences between Eastern and Western Europe," *Government and Opposition*, 24, 3 (1989), pp. 320–1.

CONCLUDING REMARKS

Each of the preceding theories offers a different account of the European Community's development since the early 1980s. Together they capture the complexities and contradictions of Europe 1992, and provide a fuller understanding of the processes behind European integration. Comparing them in the context of the emerging European order may also enable international relations scholars to develop a more sophisticated understanding of each theory's respective strengths and weaknesses. The final section of this chapter will explore points of intersection and divergence among neoclassical economic, neorealist, neoliberal institutional, and functionalist approaches with reference to the EC.

Although substantial theoretical disagreements separate these four approaches, they do share important commonalities or linkages. Each approach presented in this chapter (like each of the chapters in this book) tries to make theoretical sense of perceived changes in the levels and types of international "governance." Change, however, can be meaningfully discussed only in reference to some theoretically determined baseline. Successive evaluations of the European Community, therefore, derive from more or less explicit theories of order which define the essential characteristics of a system, its primitive units, and identifies changes that are both possible and significant at the various levels.

Neorealism is largely a theory about constraint. Based on Waltz's restrictive understanding of anarchy and the distribution of capabilities, neorealists seek to explain why particular and recurrent patterns of state behavior emerge in international relations, despite the great diversity of actors with disparate intentions and preferences. Waltz's structural (or neo) realist model identifies the conditions which encourage patterns of international cooperation by the same logic that illuminates the permissive causes of war.[59] In this view, anarchy and the distribution of capabilities (by shaping the security of states) determine the permissive cause of both armed conflict and cooperation.

International relations take place within an anarchic environment which powerfully conditions outcomes by circumscribing the choices

[59] "Permissive cause" is used by Waltz in contrast to the "immediate cause" of an outcome. Immediate causes were to be found at the individual and state levels of analysis, in Waltz's view. The system determines the conditions which allow or permit a certain outcome, however, by shaping the conditions for action in which individuals and state leaders perform. Cf. Kenneth N. Waltz, *Man, the State, and War: A Theoretical Analysis* (New York: Columbia University Press, 1959).

available to leaders. The bipolar configuration of power that emerged after World War II presented an optimal environment for cooperation among Western European states, in this view, since these states were liberated from the responsibility of providing for their own protection. To the extent that the superpowers continue to define their own security partly in terms of stability in Europe, the European countries are uniquely positioned to reap the benefits of extensive cooperation without excessive concerns about distributional consequences.

Inquiries as to how Western European states have managed to recognize and realize common interests in this context fall outside the field of vision offered by Waltz's structural model. Neorealists who undertake to apprehend particular outcomes supplement Waltz's model with additional information about the independently given interests and bargaining powers of the major actors in the region. Knowledge of states' second-order interests requires unit-level analyses. The domestic experiences of states, as well as interactions among them, contribute to more detailed accounts of the "immediate causes" underlying "1992."

Moravcsik and others in this tradition explain various advances and lapses in the process of European integration based on the interests of the major actors and their ability to fashion outcomes in line with those interests. These scholars explain the dramatic reforms of 1985–6 by reference to Germany and France's ability to convince Britain that the interests of each would be better served by closer cooperation in developing the internal market. Given anarchy (the ever-present background), bipolarity (the permissive cause in this case), the bargaining power among the EC participants (somewhat variable), and the convergence of interest in economic liberalization among France, Germany, and Britain (exogenous variable), a compelling explanation of the European Community's evolution follows.

While this approach often provides clear and powerful explanations, neorealism is criticized for its static quality. Changes come from outside the purview of the theory, especially changes in the interests of major actors. Consequently, neorealists in the Waltzian tradition are forced to argue that, despite the seemingly fundamental transformation taking place in Western Europe, all of the insecurities associated with the interwar period threaten to resurface with the dissolution of the liberal consensus, significant changes in the regional distribution of power, or the disintegration of bipolarity. John Mearsheimer's nostalgia for the Cold War in a recent edition of *Atlantic Monthly* replicates the logic of Waltz's structural-realist theory of international relations in the specific terms given by current events among the major powers in

Europe.[60] This approach contains no mechanism through which either the system or the constitutive units may themselves change (and change outcomes) either as a consequence of particular system-level processes or as the result of purposive (although still perhaps unintended) activities of the interacting units.[61]

Even scholars sympathetic to Waltz's theory find it necessary to rethink his ontology of the international structure. Waltz's international structure provides an inadequate baseline from which to explore the significance of Western Europe's experiment with integration, specifically, and the possibilities for peaceful international change more generally.

To extend usefully Waltz's "truncated" conception of the international system, some scholars have begun to theorize about the social character of international relations and the systemic effects attendant to various patterns of interactions.[62] David Dessler uncovers the social dimension of international relations, implied but untheorized in neorealism's structural ontology. He contends that

> clearly, anarchy and power distribution cannot alone and in themselves lead to any behavior. Some link between this environment and the realm of action is needed . . . [International relations] would not make sense – and Waltz's central explanatory claims would not stand – were it not for the existence of rules that are constitutive of "the political game" nations find so compelling and through which rational behavior becomes possible.[63]

Dessler promotes a transformational ontology in which rules and institutions represent not "fixed parameters of action, unintentionally reproduced, which constrain and dispose behavior so as to preserve the rule structure . . . [but rather] the material conditions of action which agents appropriate and through action reproduce or transform, possibly intentionally."[64]

Redefining the essential characteristics of the structure and the relationships among actors transforms the realm of possible changes. Efforts to integrate these conventional as well as more fixed aspects into

---

[60] John Mearsheimer, "Why We Will Soon Miss the Cold War," *Atlantic Monthly*, 266, 2 (August 1990), pp. 37–48.

[61] This point and the following comments are importantly influenced by David Dessler's compelling critique of neorealism's "positional ontology." See David Dessler, "What's at Stake in the Agent–Structure Debate?," *International Organization*, 43 (Summer 1989), pp. 440–73.

[62] David Dessler's provocative and illuminating critique of Waltz's "truncated ontology of structure" (*ibid.*, p. 462) and suggestions for an alternative ontology which includes intentional rules very heavily influenced our thinking on this subject.

[63] *Ibid.*, pp. 459, 460.   [64] *Ibid.*, pp. 460–1.

the conception of international structure enables scholars to ask interesting questions about the systemic effects of various possible institutional arrangements. Although seemingly innocuous, this line of questioning leads theorists to challenge neorealism's core assumptions about anarchy, the state, and their purported relationship. For example, even if the formal systemic qualities and the constituent units remain stable, might not certain configurations of units, and the rules governing their interactions, have different meanings for participants and therefore prompt different outcomes? Further, might not the units themselves be transformed in important ways by their interactions?

The neoliberal institutionalist approach speaks directly to the first question by focusing attention on the consequence of anarchy for state action rather than on the formal ordering principle denoted by the term. Neoliberal institutionalism accepts many of the foundational assumptions of neorealism but "assum[es] that the Hobbesian condition can be mitigated by an institutional structure that provides legitimate and effective channels for reconciling . . . [states'] interests."[65]

Neoliberal institutionalists associate the developing order in Western Europe with the growth of multilateral institutions. In this view, order and mutually beneficial cooperation obtain to the degree that organizations (broadly defined) help states identify common interests, foster information flows, facilitate monitoring, and provide effective procedures for settling grievances.[66] Neoliberal institutionalists attribute less causal significance to anarchy *per se*, but focus instead on the destabilizing effects of high uncertainty and risk commonly associated with anarchy but presumably distinct from it. They explore how institutionalized interactions may transform the costs and benefits associated with cooperation in the pursuit of exogenously specified goals – i.e., coordination of separate policies, cooperation on common interests, overcoming collective action problems, etc.

Functionalism and neofunctionalism take the investigation a step further by seeking systematic explanations for how goals and interests may change, and eventually, perhaps, redefine the units themselves. Functionalists and neofunctionalists study not only how given interests are realized through international institutions, but also how participation in institutions – irrespective of substantive content – may, in turn, influence actors' perception and articulation of self-interests.

To explain the European Community's dramatic resurgence in recent

---

[65] Jack Snyder, "Averting Anarchy in the New Europe," *International Security*, 14, 4 (Spring 1990), p. 15.
[66] *Ibid.*, p. 5.

years, both of these approaches highlight the efficacy of Community institutions, although with different emphases. They suggest that, while it is probably true that the major changes punctuating the EC's history could not have taken place over the firm opposition of France, West Germany, and Britain, it appears equally plausible that in the absence of established Community institutions, decision-making procedures, and habits the convergence of interests among the EC's major participants probably would have produced very different outcomes or, more strongly, might not have taken place at all. The convergence of interest among France, West Germany, and Britain no more automatically produced extensive cooperation among them than did the recognized potential for mutual gains from liberalization automatically generate institutional reform. Furthermore, the reluctant cooperation of the British government, despite reservations on Thatcher's part, lends support to the functionalist suggestion that participation in Community institutions may in itself inhibit the kind of firm opposition necessary to arrest integration once initiated.

The events associated with "EC 1992" provide anything but clear evidence for a single theoretical position. Neoclassical economics rivets our attention on the economic gains to be reaped by lowering barriers to exchange. Neorealism highlights state interests and interstate bargains against the backdrop of anarchy. Neoliberal institutionalism focuses attention on the importance of political structures and rules in taming anarchy and, instead, promoting the "permissive causes" of cooperation. Finally, functionalism and neofunctionalism tell a story about the way interests change as the result of flourishing cross-border interactions among governmental and non-governmental elites.

The spirit of our undertaking has not been to demonstrate theoretical superiority of one or another approach. Rather, we hoped to show that each theory offers a different "cut" or "angle of vision." Thus, it cannot be said that "each approach addresses one piece of the puzzle." The same subject matter is addressed by all four theories, yet different parts are highlighted, others are allowed to recede. Much depends on what one chooses to treat as exogenous. If interests are not themselves the products of forces in the theory, they acquire greater leverage in explanation. Neorealism tends to treat interests as unexplained data; neofunctionalism interprets interests as the product of social and economic interactions. For neorealism, states acting on their interests are facts that acquire great theoretical weight. They have the status of "first movers." For neofunctionalists it is precisely the perceived interests of states and non-state actors that needs to be explained. These same facts are treated endogenously.

248

A clearer understanding of these theories – their strengths and their weaknesses, intersections and differences – presents us with a richer and fuller understanding of the changes overtaking Western Europe. Hopefully, international relations scholars may also gain a sharper appreciation of the theoretical and practical challenges precipitated by global change.

9 GOVERNANCE AND DEMOCRATIZATION

Ernst-Otto Czempiel

I understand "governance" to mean the capacity to get things done without the legal competence to command that they be done. Where governments, in the Eastonian sense, can distribute values authoritatively, governance can distribute them in a way which is not authoritative but equally effective. Governments exercise rule, governance uses power. From this point of view the international system is a system of governance. Conflicts are systems of governance with each party trying to induce, or to force, the other party to do certain things it otherwise would not have done. Mutual deterrence, then, was a system of governance par excellence, as was the East–West conflict as a whole. With that conflict having ended, it is instructive to ask how it was sustained. A twofold question is involved. First, how do theories of international relations treat such conflicts and how did the strategy of the North Atlantic Treaty Organization (NATO) fit these theoretical considerations? Second, viewed from the end of the Cold War, did NATO's strategy amount to successful governance? Did the West behave in such a way that its actions together with reactions of the Warsaw Pact produce an interaction favorable to the West's goals in the conflict?

These are very complex questions which cannot be answered exhaustively in this brief chapter. But in times of profound historical change it is important to look for the right questions. Our discipline simply cannot afford to let the end of the East–West conflict occur without confronting the theoretical and strategic implications of such an event.

For more than forty years the conflict dominated the relationship between the United States and the Soviet Union, between NATO and the Warsaw Pact. More than 600 million people were involved, they produced armaments worth about $20 trillions. East and West confronted each other in the center of Europe with piles of deadly and sophisticated nuclear and conventional weapons. Both sides deterred each other by behaving in such a way that only a limited number of strategic options remained for the enemy. Mutual deterrence was the preferred system of governance, regulating the interaction.

In history, conflicts of comparable magnitude and mutual attitude mostly ended in war. This one did not. Not only did the East–West conflict come to a soft landing, the inimical relationship was totally reversed into a cooperative one. This has never happened before in history. Wars have been won or avoided, alliances have been changed. But the disappearance and reversal of such a deep-seated and comprehensive antagonism without resort to war is new in history.

Two explanations are available for this remarkable turn of events. It is easy, but erroneous, to argue that NATO won the conflict, that it steered deterrence as a system of governance to an outcome favorable to the West, that the NATO alliance defeated the Warsaw Pact without firing a single round, so to speak. If this interpretation were true, mutual deterrence could be viewed as a system of governance where one side exercised unyielding military pressure which finally produced the intended result.

Unfortunately, the empirical evidence, as far as it is available, does not bear out such an interpretation. The Warsaw Pact remained a strong military alliance until the very end. It was in many respects superior to NATO.[1] No, a proper explanation lies elsewhere. It is more accurate to view the end of the East–West conflict as having been produced not by the military defeat of the Warsaw Pact, but by the political revolutions and reforms in Eastern Europe and the U.S.S.R. First these developments toppled communism as the prevailing system of government and then dissolved the Warsaw Pact as the prevailing instrument of Soviet imperialism. The Warsaw Pact and its military threat were eliminated from within, not defeated from outside.

This interpretation, if sustained, poses two provocative questions. First, in retrospect, what were the real causes of this conflict? What lessons are to be drawn for theories of conflict and international relations? Second, since deterrence obviously was not responsible for this beneficial outcome, what kind of strategic interaction would have been more effective? Are defense, armaments, the deterrence, and military pressure still the best, and the only, way of governance over the

---

[1] See the assessment by U.S. Secretary of Defense Richard B. Cheney, *Soviet Military Power. Prospects for Change 1989* (Washington: GPO, 1989), pp. 85, 89, 96. See also Thomas J. McCormick, *America's Half-Century: United States Foreign Policy in the Cold War* (Baltimore, MD: Johns Hopkins University Press, 1989); Thomas G. Paterson, *Meeting the Communist Threat: Truman to Reagan* (New York: Oxford University Press, 1988). For the decisive relevance attributed to arms and strategic advantages, see William G. Hyland, *Mortal Rivals: Superpower Relations from Nixon to Reagan* (New York: Random House, 1987).

251

enemy? Is security the only, or the most important, issue-area around which conflicts between industrialized societies evolve and develop? If not, are there other, more comprehensive strategies that can produce systems of governance which are capable of influencing the sources as well as the conduct of such conflicts?

STRATEGIC PERSPECTIVES

Up to 1985 the East–West conflict met exactly the criteria developed by the theory of neorealism. After 1946 the wartime cooperation between the allies was not guaranteed; each side had to look after its interests itself. The explanations differed, but the reasons were the same. Within the anarchical structure of the international system, self-help was the only pertinent behavior. What Hans J. Morgenthau had described in his opus magnum, *Power among Nations*, was developed by Kenneth N. Waltz into a scientific theory.[2] Waltz argued that the behavior of states is determined by the structure of the international system in the same way as the behavior of corporations is shaped by the structure of the market. Whatever the properties of the units, they all obey the same laws. The only dimension of difference is the range of capabilities. Large and strong states can afford more than small and weak ones. Otherwise all states pursue the same goal, their own preservation as a minimum and world domination as a maximum.[3] It is the anarchical structure of the international system which dominates the behavior of all states, leading them unavoidably to a balance of power policy.

Waltz has been criticized for not explaining the fact that different states can behave differently.[4] In the American–Canadian relationship, the famous example used by Nye and Keohane, the structure of the international system was not effective, whereas Germany and France in the 30s, to cite only one example, although similar in the socioeconomic dimension, pursued a totally different foreign policy. Germany became aggressive, France remained defensive. Waltz was forced to admit that "structures affect units even as units affect structures."[5] But he never

---

[2] Kenneth N. Waltz, *Theory of International Politics* (Reading, MA: Addison-Wesley, 1979), pp. 102ff.

[3] Robert O. Keohane, "Realism, Neorealism, and the Study of World Politics," in Robert O. Keohane, ed., *Neorealism and its Critics* (New York: Columbia University Press, 1986), p. 15.

[4] Joseph S. Nye Jr., "Neorealism and Neoliberalism," *World Politics*, 40 (January 1988), p. 243.

[5] Kenneth N. Waltz, "Realist Thought and Neorealist Theory," *Journal of International Affairs*, 44 (Spring 1990), p. 37.

abandoned the fundamental premise of his theory that "wars, hot and cold, originate in the structure of the international political system."[6]

As proof for his theory, Waltz referred to the East–West conflict, and correctly so. In this conflict states as different as the United States and the Soviet Union behaved more or less in the same way. In spite of their profound domestic dissimilarities Western and Eastern states acted similarly. They relied upon a policy of balance of power in order to secure their security. They used deterrence to influence the behavior of the other side and arms control to fine-tune it. After the 60s, they moved beyond the ideological reasons for the conflict and concentrated everything upon armaments and military strategies.[7]

Even within a more sophisticated, four-layered analysis of the East–West conflict, the theory of neorealism holds. The bottom layer consisted of the original conflict, the difference between liberalism and communism as organizing concepts for the society and the state. This conflict stemmed from 1917 and permitted several, and different, political relationships.[8] Seen from the 1990s, it is questionable whether the original conflict between societal organizations ever was of this kind. The revolutions in Eastern Europe since 1989, the reform movements in the U.S.S.R., and the breakdown of socialism as a societal concept worldwide seem to indicate that from the beginning socialism was enforced upon, not inaugurated by, the respective societies. This is certainly true for the time after 1945, to which I shall come shortly.

It cannot be excluded from a comprehensive analysis of the East–West conflict that there was some early societal consensus around socialism and communism, producing the first, the original, layer of the conflict between East and West. After 1946 when the wartime cooperation broke down, a new layer was added: the security dilemma.

---

[6] Kenneth N. Waltz, "The Origins of War in Neorealist Theory," in Robert I. Rotenberg and Theodore K. Rabb, eds., *The Origin and Prevention of Major Wars* (Cambridge: Cambridge University Press, 1988), p. 51.

[7] This is particularly true for the West which, under the leadership of the U.S., interpreted the strategy of containment predominantly in military terms. See for the early periods, John L. Gaddis, *Strategies of Containment* (New York: Oxford University Press, 1982); Martin Beglinger, *Containment im Wandel der amerikanischen Aussen- und Sicherheitspolitik von Truman zu Eisenhower* (Stuttgart: Steiner, 1988). For the Reagan years, see Ernst-Otto Czempiel, *Machtprobe. Die USA und die Sowjetunion in den achtziger Jahren* (Munich: Beck, 1989). For the Soviet Union in the 1970s, see Raymond L. Garthoff, *Détente and Confrontation: American–Soviet Relations from Nixon to Reagan* (Washington: Brookings Institution, 1985), pp. 67 and *passim*.

[8] This fourfold analysis of the East–West conflict is extensively discussed in Ernst-Otto Czempiel, "Nachruestung und Systemwandel. Ein Beitrag zur Diskussion um den Doppelbeschluss der NATO," *Aus Politik und Zeitgeschichte B 5/82* (February 6, 1982), pp. 22–46.

It was a consequence of the anarchical structure of the international system, the basis of neorealistic theory. This security dilemma properly explains that the East–West conflict developed out of insecurity about the behavior of the other side. It was not necessary to assume the existence of aggressive intentions on the part of the enemy. It was sufficient to state that the ongoing cooperation of the opposite side could not be taken for granted. Accordingly, each side tried self-help as prescribed by neorealistic theory.

It was not long before the insecurity in Europe spilled over into the rest of the world. It started with Turkey and Greece in 1947 and found its first climax in the Korean War. Thus the third layer of the East–West conflict was created, · the power struggle outside Europe which expanded during the 1950s into a global rivalry between the Soviet Union and the United States.

In Europe a fourth layer was added in the 60s: the arms race. Starting with the rearmament of the Soviet Union subsequent to the early 1960s, the arms race soon dominated the conflict relationship between East and West. Everybody talked about balances, or imbalances, of power, about military options and strategies.[9] Each side tried to behave in such a way as to oblige the enemy to follow a certain policy. The original conflict became overlapped by the military competition. Nobody discussed any more the antagonism between liberalism and communism, the divergencies of the respective systems of government. In 1982 President Ronald Reagan created "Project Democracy." But it was more a strategic device than a political program. Congress replaced it with its National Endowment for Democracy which pointed in the right direction but remained crucially underfinanced.[10] Ronald Reagan's preferred alternative in the field of politics was, characteristically, the strategy of low-intensity warfare.[11]

---

[9] See the heated discussions within the U.S. Intelligence Community with regard to the nature and dimension of the Soviet threat in United States Congress, Joint Economic Committee, Allocations of Resources in the Soviet Union and China, Hearings (Washington: GPO, 1975–84), Parts 1–10. In 1985 the Congressional Research Service put it as a "question of the greatest significance for all mankind" whether "Russians and Americans can shift their rivalry in the Third World from its increasingly conflictual and militarized direction back toward less confrontational and more political and economic competition." United States Congress 99/1, House Committee on Foreign Affairs, The Soviet Union in the Third World, 1908–85: An Imperial Burden or Political Asset?, Report by the Congressional Research Service (Washington: GPO, 1985), p. xxxiii.

[10] Joel M. Woldman, The National Endowment for Democracy: Project Democracy (Washington: Congressional Research Service, 1984), pp. 2ff.

[11] Michael T. Klare and Peter Kornbluh, eds., Low-Intensity Warfare: Counterinsurgency, Proinsurgency, and Antiterrorism in the Eighties (New York: Pantheon Books, 1987).

The conflict behavior of both sides was thus dominated by the security dilemma enhanced by the arms race of the 1960s. Waltz seemed confirmed in his thesis that the East–West conflict was "firmly rooted in the structure of postwar international politics, and will last as long as that structure endures."[12]

The NATO states defined their policies toward the East predominantly in the issue-area of military security, neglecting the issue-area of economic well-being[13] and disregarding the issue-area of rule. The main argument was that it was impossible and unnecessary to try to influence the political situation within those two other issue-areas. The discussion emphasized arms and military strategies with which to influence the behavior of the East. Both the West and the East tried a system of governance by interaction with arms races, arms control proposals, and military strategies. Whether called Flexible Response, Follow-On-Forces-Attack or Zero-Options, all this was meant to prescribe a certain behavior for the Soviet Union and the states of the Warsaw Pact. Both sides tried to influence each other by acting out of a military posture and thereby silently requiring comparable reactions by the other side. Mutual Assured Destruction really was the prevailing system of governance. The "Logic of Anarchy" dominated the conflict behavior. But was it the right logic?

ECONOMIC PERSPECTIVES

Globalists and transnationalists started to argue in the early 1970s that the issue-area of economic well-being had become as important as that of security.[14] They stressed that not only governments but also societal actors, predominantly transnational corporations, were active in world politics. Regime theory noted that not only governmental but also societal actors used organized cooperation in order to settle controversial issues.[15] Keohane and Nye had already argued that, in addition to military power and governments, world politics was pervaded by transgovernmental and transnational actors, by economic interdependence and the pursuit of economic goals.[16]

---

12 Waltz, "Origins," p. 52.
13 For the reluctant and ambivalent treatment of economic relations with the East, see Abraham S. Becker, ed., *Economic Relations with the USSR: Issues for the Western Alliance* (Lexington, MA: D. C. Heath, 1983).
14 Waltz, "Realist Thought," p. 37.
15 Beate Kohler-Koch, *Regime in den Internationalen Beziehungen* (Baden-Baden: Nomos, 1989).
16 Robert O. Keohane and Joseph S. Nye Jr., *Power and Interdependence: World Politics in Transition* (Boston, MA: Little, Brown & Co., 1977).

Beitz criticized the theory of neorealism for continuing to see in the world only states acting in favor of security and military predominance.[17]

For globalists and transnationalists alike the world was not a world of states any more; it had become a world society. For them the issue-area of security, with its built-in antagonisms, still exists, but the issue-area of economic well-being acquired salience, strengthening the processes of cooperation, compromise, and even integration.

The neorealists answered by emphasizing that the new theories simply chose different examples and asked different questions. This criticism is not unjustified. It is true that globalists and transnationalists have evaded the issue-area of security and concentrated upon that of economic well-being. The U.S.–Canadian relationship and relations between the U.S. and Japan have been of a different type than those between NATO and the Warsaw Pact. It is also true that economic development and progress, the promotion of human rights and democracy are not necessarily related to international security. Globalists and transnationalists did not alter, or leave, the traditional model of the world as a world of states.[18] They added – and emphasized – the new issue-area of economic well-being. They did not discuss the relationship between the two issue-areas but believed that the two could be kept separate, that it was possible to portray the world with different views. The globalist model, then, would fit the Organization for Economic Cooperation and Development (OECD) world, the realist model the relationship between OECD and the Council for Mutual Economic Assistance (COMECON).[19]

What seemed to be an elegant solution missed, in effect, the problem. Two or three different worlds between which states can move freely and independently do not exist. These worlds are interconnected. Somewhere in the space of politics the OECD world meets the NATO world. To put it differently: the three issue-areas of security, well-being, and rule are related to each other. What happens in one is not independent from what is happening in the others. The three worlds intermingle, so to speak. If in the economic well-being issue-area societal actors matter, if in the issue-area of rule the system of governments

---

[17] Charles R. Beitz, *Political Theory and Institutional Relations* (Princeton, NJ: Princeton University Press, 1979).
[18] Donald J. Puchala and Stuart I. Fagan, "International Politics in the 1970s: The Search for a Perspective," in Ray Maghroori and Bennett Ramberg, eds., *Globalism Versus Realism* (Boulder, CO: Westview Press, 1982), pp. 41ff.
[19] Maghroori and Ramberg, "Globalism Versus Realism: A Reconciliation," in Maghroori and Ramberg, eds., *Globalism Versus Realism*, pp. 225ff.

plays an important role, then both are relevant for the security issue-area as well.

It was the neorealists themselves who realized these important consequences. Gilpin admitted that their original theory had neglected the importance of the economy and the capabilities of societal actors to influence world politics.[20] The concession had grave theoretical conse-quences. It was reductionist, combined the analytical level of the state with the level of the system. This Kenneth Waltz had always rejected. But now it became more and more evident that a theory of the state had to be included into the theory of international relations,[21] that the behavior and properties of a state contributed considerably to its foreign policy and to interactions within the international system.

STATE PERSPECTIVES

Although this argument discounts the realist model of the world as a world of states, of course the world is populated by states. But they can no longer be treated as billiard balls without internal content. Because of their domestic structure, states act differently in the international system. They are microcosms within which the configur-ation of actors and their movements are decisive for their "foreign policy." By not recognizing these microcosms the realist theory of international relations misses the large picture[22] and four of the five causes of violence. Waltz saw this an advantage: "a theory can be writ-ten only by leaving out most matters that are of practical interest."[23] In the eyes of his critics, this was a weakness. If a theory explains only a small part of the variance, it is "academic" in the polemic sense of the word.

Wendt is right in asking for a theory of the state in order to develop a theory of international relations. He would have been even more right had he related the theory of the state to that of foreign policy. Waltz is correct in stating that a theory of international relations belongs to the third level of analysis, where only relations, not actions or interactions, are considered. This is the highest stage of any academic discipline. It is, at the same time, the most difficult one, particularly in the field of

---

[20] Robert Gilpin, "The Richness of the Tradition of Political Realism," in Keohane, ed., *Neorealism and its Critics*, pp. 303ff, 313.
[21] Alexander E. Wendt, "The Agent–Structure Problem in International Relations Theory," *International Organization*, 41 (Summer 1987), p. 365.
[22] David Dessler, "What's at Stake in the Agent–Structure Debate?," *International Organization*, 43 (Summer 1989), p. 466.
[23] Waltz, "Realist Thought," p. 31.

international relations. Here a theory at the third level would amount to a theory of contemporary world history in real time. This dimension of the task explains why it has not been fulfilled yet, why it is possible that the void created by sheer impossibility produces so many frameworks and even invites other disciplines, e.g., philosophy or epistemology, to use the empty space.[24]

A theory of foreign policy is complex, and so is a theory of the state. But both can be tackled with some hope for success. If there is no theory of the state available, it is at least possible to have a model of the state showing the three political issue-areas and their interaction. This would be a first step in replacing one-dimensional neorealist thinking with liberal theorizing which reflects the importance of societies and of societal demands.

RULE PERSPECTIVES

In addition to the security issue-area emphasized by neorealism and the economic well-being issue-area added by transnationalists and globalists, there is a third issue-area, that of rule (*Herrschaft*) and participation. This issue-area encompasses the relationship between the society and its political system. It is the overarching structure containing what is often called the state. The main differences among states can be found along this dimension. The system of rule (*Herrschaft*) not only decides upon the distribution of property rights,[25] but also upon the distribution of all politically relevant values, beginning with security, including property rights and opportunities of economic well-being and its permanent enhancement, and culminating in civil rights and possibilities for participation in ruling through elections and codetermination.

Seen from this angle, the system of rule is the most important issue-area of the three. It relates and integrates the security and economic well-being issue-areas. This is the link which is being missed by transnationalists and globalists (not to speak of neorealists). The issue-area of economic well-being is not independent from that of security. The two are closely related, as the old alternative between "Guns or

---

[24] Pauline Rosenau, "Once Again into the Fray: International Relations Confronts the Humanities," *Millennium. Journal of International Studies,* 19, 1 (Spring 1990), pp. 83–110. For the impact of critical philosophy, see Jim George and David Campbell, "Patterns of Dissent and the Celebration of Difference: Critical Social Theory and International Relations," *International Studies Quarterly,* 34 (September 1990), pp. 269–94.

[25] Gilpin, "The Richness of the Tradition of Political Realism," pp. 317ff.

Butter" indicates; the relation/distribution is decided upon by the political system. It is the political system which links the two and defines priorities between security and economic well-being.

Thus the political rule issue-area must not be neglected. It is the political system which defines whether – and to what degree – national security is endangered. It is the political system which prescribes and distributes the sacrifices that the society has to make in order to meet external threats. This threat is never, or in very rare cases only, an independent, objective element. It is a perceived one, the perception of which depends to a very large degree on political interests. To magnify external threats is a common instrument of political leaders for stirring and securing domestic consensus. Autocratic rulers love the "Primacy of Foreign Policy."[26] Democratic elites use it, as did Ronald Reagan when he enlarged the defense budget in order to cut the social welfare expenditures.[27] Even the anarchical structure of the international system is not an independent objectivity. Of course, the structure is anarchical. But the effects of this structure are being defined by political systems which, in turn, are influenced by their relationship to their societal environment. It is interesting to note that democracies have never waged war against one another.[28] The anarchical structure is weakened if the system is composed of democracies. Against non-democracies, however, democracies have been no less warlike than non-democracies. This implies that the system of government is not the only variable which explains foreign policy behavior. It is, however, the most important one.

CHANGE PERSPECTIVES

A change in the system of rule may produce a very different foreign policy. The East–West conflict came to an end because Gorbachev reformed the Soviet governmental system by introducing Perestroika and Glasnost and because the societies in Poland, Hungary, and the German Democratic Republic (G.D.R.) replaced their communist governments with pluralistic ones. The change of the system of rule changed the conflict, transforming it from confrontation to cooperation.

---

[26] For this aspect, mostly neglected within the scientific discussion, see Ernst-Otto Czempiel, "Der Primat der auswaertigen Politik," *Politische Vierteljahresschrift*, 4 (September 1963), pp. 266ff.

[27] Czempiel, *Machtprobe*, pp. 203ff.

[28] Michael W. Doyle, "Kant, Liberal Legacies, and Foreign Affairs," *Philosophy and Public Affairs*, 12 (Part 1, Summer 1983), pp. 205–35 (Part 2, Fall 1983), pp. 323–53.

This change was not induced by the Western military alliance. When Gorbachev came to power in 1985, President Reagan, for reasons of American domestic pressure, had already changed the course of his Soviet policy by focusing on the idea of arms control and détente. By introducing his domestic reforms Gorbachev intended to strengthen communism.[29] By pressing for the Intermediate Nuclear Forces (INF) treaty Gorbachev intended to denuclearize Europe. Among the unintended consequences were the delegitimation of communism by the supreme communist and a substantial reduction of international tensions. Both changed profoundly the political context of Eastern European states. With communism abrogated and tensions lowered, the civil-rights movements gained a freedom of maneuver which enabled them finally to topple their communist governments. This, in turn, reinforced the reform movements in the U.S.S.R. to the degree of ultimately dissolving the Union.[30] Of course, President Reagan's confrontational politics and military build-up have to be taken into consideration as the international context when Gorbachev came to power. His reforms and the revolutions in Eastern Europe occurred, as indicated, when, and after, American military pressure was lowered. The Warsaw Pact had been able to face the military threat by NATO. It was unable to compete with the economic and political achievements of the West that surfaced after the INF treaty had lowered the degree of military tensions.

This course of events corresponds exactly with certain theoretical assumptions. According to Seeley's law, the degree of freedom within a country is inverse to the degree of external pressure against its frontiers.[31] For reasons of theory as well as reality, it can be said that by its unyielding balance of power politics (the Harmel formula remaining declaratory in the eighties) NATO for many years stabilized the decaying communist governments of the Warsaw Pact.

By following the "logic of anarchy"[32] NATO became the victim of a strategy which isolated, exaggerated, and misinterpreted the reality. The end of the East–West conflict indicates that the theory of neorealism is as incomplete as its offspring, the strategy of power

29 United States Congress, Senate Committee on Foreign Relations, *Soviet Imperatives for the 1990's: Hearing*, 99th Congress, 2nd sess. (Washington: GPO, 1986), Statement Richard F. Kaufman, pp. 21ff.
30 Michael R. Gordon, "INF: A Hollow Victory?," *Foreign Policy*, 65 (Winter 1986/7), pp. 159ff.
31 Quoted in Otto Hintze, *Staat und Verfassung. Gesammelte Abhandlungen zur Allgemeinen Verfassungsgeschichte*, ed. Gerhard Oestreich (Göttingen: Vandenhoeck und Ruprecht, 1962), p. 411.
32 Waltz, "Realist Thought," p. 37.

balancing and deterrence. Both introduced and pursued a system of interaction which was detrimental to the interests of the West (and of the democrats in Eastern Europe). It took many years, many endeavors, and the incidence of Glasnost and the INF treaty to overcome this peculiar kind of governance and to start the successful revolutions in Eastern Europe.

To put it differently and back into the realm of theory: the most crucial variable for dealing with military violence in modern industrialized societies is the system of rule. Defense, of course, is necessary against a military threat. But it should not exhaust the strategy by confining inquiry to the military security issue-area; it should also aim at the system of rule. If this can be changed toward more democracy, toward the production of values for economic well-being and a better, more equal, distribution of those values, "Victory" is at hand.

MULTIDIMENSIONAL PERSPECTIVES

To concentrate upon the "Second Image of the World," upon the state, foreign policy, and international politics, does not negate Waltz's perspective on military violence, the anarchical structure of the international system. It is, and remains, one cause of violence. But the second image suggests four more sources for the use of organized military violence: the system of rule, the existence and demands of partial societal groups with special access to the government, the interaction between two or more actors/states, and the strategic competence of the actors. I shall deal with all of them briefly because only the comprehensive view upon all five causes offers the perspective of a comprehensive, multidimensional theory of foreign policy and international politics. This view at the same time reveals what actions in what direction should be undertaken in order to create a system of governance which is pertinent and successful under the conditions of modern industrialized societies.

The most important cause of violence/war is the system of rule organizing and practicing the distribution of values in the security, economic well-being, and rule issue-areas. They are not independent. As indicated, the definition of security depends on the governmental needs of the system of rule and of the distributive interests within the economic well-being issue-area. Whether military violence is asked for to protect the units against any kind of external threat or to protect a certain economic interest depends fundamentally on the prevailing system of rule. Governing the relations between the political system and its societal environment, the system of rule is the most important of the five causes of violence which theory must address.

Theoretical considerations reveal that democratic systems of rule tend to refrain from using military violence in their foreign policies for three reasons. First, they do not have the tradition of violence because in their domestic context they work by compromise and consensus. Second, for this lack of use they do not have the military means at hand. Democracies usually have command over only residual military forces, as was the case in the United States in the 30s and as it was preparing to do again before the outbreak of the Gulf war. Third, because of high degrees of domestic consensus, democracies do not depend on external tensions and military pressures to produce artificially the necessary consensus. This consensus does exist because political values are being distributed equally. Everybody is content with what she/he gets. Power is not concentrated but decentralized; its benefits can be consumed generally.

By contrast, autocratic systems of rule are familiar with the use of violence for producing domestic consensus. If the distribution of values is fundamentally unjust, only violence can subdue the protest and make the society accept this kind of distribution. Such is the history of the communist regimes in Eastern Europe and the Soviet Union. Since those regimes failed for many decades to produce the necessary values, and since they distributed an insufficient number of values in a very unfair manner, they had to use violent means to keep their societies down. The G.D.R., for instance, depended upon the wall and a fence around its frontiers because otherwise the inhabitants would have fled. The need for violence was the greater the less those regimes could afford to have their societies participate in the distribution of values. The elections were a deception, as human rights and political rights were suppressed, the freedom of the individual was severely restrained as many Helsinki Groups have documented.

The argument is not that autocratic systems of rule are externally aggressive *per se*. The Franco regime in Spain during the 1930s demonstrated that dictatorships can behave peacefully in the international environment. But this is an exception. Since those dictatorships habitually use violence in the relationship with their domestic societies, they will not hesitate, if necessary, to use violence also in foreign policy. There is no institutional and/or traditional barrier which would keep them from doing so. Without being able to instrumentalize a "Primacy of Foreign Policy," they might not be able to survive. Therefore, they are bound to have external conflicts with at least a threat of military violence. The East–West conflict demonstrates that communist regimes nourished the military confrontation in order to consolidate and to protect their rule over their societies. Communist governments in the East obviously never tried to gain the consensus of their societies but preferred to rule them autocratically and to cover this system of rule with an external conflict. When this conflict was weakened, those societies revolted and won. After their victory the conflict evaporated. With (more or less) democratic governments at the helm, the East European countries and the Soviet Union found that their relationship with the West was a friendly, and not an inimical, one.

This conclusion indicates that the East–West conflict was not between divergent organizations of societies, not between liberalism and communism as competing principles of societal organization; rather it was a conflict between autocratic systems of rule in the East and liberal systems in the West.

To put it more generally, autocratic systems of rule (*Herrschafts-systeme*) are the main causes of threat and military violence in the international system. This result must be reflected in a liberal theory of international relations. The most important causes for violence are non-democratic systems of rule. The anarchical structure of the international system is also an important source of violence. But the system of rule, the governmental structure of societies, is much more important. As relations within the OECD world demonstrate, democracies can live under the conditions of international anarchy without using violence. But as demonstrated by the history of communism in the Eastern part of Europe, or by Feudalism in the Middle East and probably in Africa, autocratic governments cannot.

EMPIRICAL PERSPECTIVES

The thesis that the democratization of systems of rule eliminates the most important cause of war collides with many empirical findings. From Wilkenfeld[33] to Chan,[34] there is a long chain of articles denying a relationship between democracy and non-violence. Rummel[35] is the significant exception. The reasons for this discrepancy cannot be discussed exhaustively here, but it is possible and necessary to name two. The empirical research so far suffers from

---

[33] J. Wilkenfeld, "Domestic and Foreign Conflict Behavior of Nations," *Journal of Peace Research*, 5 (1968), pp. 56–9.

[34] Steve Chan, "Mirror, Mirror on the Wall . . . Are the Freer Countries more Pacific?," *Journal of Conflict Resolution*, 28 (December 1984), pp. 617–48.

[35] R. J. Rummel, "Libertarianism and International Violence," *Journal of Conflict Resolution*, 27 (March 1983), pp. 27–71.

problems of data and theory, and from the one-dimensionality of its approach.

The problem with the data is that they are either too small, spanning only two to four years, or too large covering the period from 1815 to 1965.[36] Some of them include domestic violence, some use dyadic, others multidyadic relationships. Most importantly, the data are imperfect reflections of democracy. Numerous divergent indicators are used to measure democracy, from the absence of strikes and domestic violence to regular elections and the existence of parliament.[37] Admittedly, it is extremely difficult to operationalize democracy. But long ago Kant pointed to the crucial element: codetermination. If all those, he wrote in 1795,[38] who suffer from and pay for war can decide whether there shall be war or not, war would disappear.

We know from social psychology that this connection is not easily made, but we also know from the experience of the British appeasement policies in the thirties and from the American reluctance to join in World War II that the Kantian relationship is basically right, as Doyle has pointed out.[39] Theoretically, it is convincing. With the exception of defending themselves against attack, people will not make war if they have nothing to gain and everything to lose. Thus, the crucial element in defining democracy involves the society's codetermination of whether to go to war or not.

Obviously, democracies which offer a high degree of codetermination do not exist today. No wonder there is no correlation. No wonder there is no correlation whatever in the nineteenth century and outside the Western industrialized countries in general. Thus, why look for the effects of a condition which definitively was not, and is not, there?[40] The emphasis should be on the theoretical task of formulating what is being meant by democracy in the Kantian sense. The next step

[36] This is the time span chosen by Melvin Small and J. David Singer, "The War Proneness of Democratic Regimes, 1816–1965," *Jerusalem Journal of International Relations*, 1 (Summer 1976), pp. 51–69.

[37] For a general discussion, see Kenneth A. Bollen, "Issues in the Comparative Measurement of Political Democracy," *American Sociological Review*, 45 (June 1980), pp. 370–90.

[38] Immanuel Kant, *Zum Ewigen Frieden. Ein philosophischer Entwurf*, Werke in sechs Baenden, ed. Wilhelm Weischedel, VI (Darmstadt: Wissenschaftliche Buchgesellschaft, 1964), pp. 205–6. For an extended discussion of the consequences for the organization of democratic systems of rule, see Ernst-Otto Czempiel, *Friedensstrategien. Systemwandel durch internationale Organisationen. Demokratisierung und Wirtschaft* (Paderborn: Schoeningh, 1986), pp. 110–43.

[39] Doyle, "Kant."

[40] Chan, "Mirror," p. 630, looked into the nineteenth century although he knew, and stated, that the criteria for democracy were absent in this period.

would then be to look into history to test the hypothesis. Even this will not offer unambiguous results. The system of rule is only one, albeit the most important, cause of violence. To exclude the other four easily leads to the attribution to democracy what in reality has been caused by other factors.

The third cause, the interests of societal actors, is narrowly connected to the system of rule. A perfect democracy would not privilege certain groups; instead it would distribute the values equally to all. Obviously, democracies of this degree of perfection do not exist today. Even Western democracies are still in the process of developing. As James Mill noted, partial interests do exist and the interests of "the few" often prevail over those of "the many." As long as this remains the case, democracies will not be free from using violence in their external relations. Access to resources and raw materials induce social actors to ask the political system for military intervention, for violence. Allende's fall is a case in point. The number of cases have declined, but the cause as such has not been eliminated.

The revisionist school of American historians points to the economic interests of U.S. corporations or to the strategic and military interest of power groups.[41] The theorem of the military-bureaucratic complex highlights the interests the American military and parts of the business community had (and have) in pursuing the arms race.[42] Oil certainly was a decisive factor in Washington's decision to liberate Kuwait and to punish Iraq.

There is no denying that Western democracies have not matured to such a degree that partial interests do not influence the course of foreign policy. Progress is necessary. But in order to eliminate special interests as a cause of violent foreign policies, it is not necessary to eliminate these groups. They are an essential element of society. What is necessary is to deny them privileged access to government. They should not be able to stimulate their government and society into

[41] See the interesting collection of contradictory views, in David Carlton and Herbert M. Levine, eds., *The Cold War Debate* (New York: McGraw-Hill, 1988). Particularly revisionist, Joyce and Gabriel Kolko, *The Limits of Power: The World and United States Foreign Policy, 1945–1954* (New York: Harper & Row, 1972). Walter LaFeber, ed., *The Origins of the Cold War, 1941–1947: A Historical Problem with Interpretations and Documents* (New York: John Wiley & Sons, 1971). More recent and more comprehensive, Walter LaFeber, *The American Age: United States Foreign Policy at Home and Abroad since 1750* (New York: Norton, 1989).

[42] Gordon Adams and Randal Humm, "The U.S. Military-Industrial Complex and National Strategy," in Carl G. Jacobsen, ed., *Strategic Power USA/USSR* (Houndmills: Macmillan, 1990), pp. 286–97. Richard A. Stubbing with Richard A. Mendel, *The Defense Game: An Insider Explores the Astonishing Realities of America's Defense Establishment* (New York: Harper & Row, 1985).

violent actions in the international environment for their particular purposes.

INTERACTION PERSPECTIVES

Interaction dynamics are a fourth set of factors that often conduce to the use of violence, although unintentionally. It can be assumed that about 40 percent of all wars derive from the unintended outcomes.[43] World War I is the most conspicuous example. But it is not the only one. The more numerous the actors, the more complex the relationship, the more difficult it is to steer the relationship successfully to a non-violent course.

Closely connected with this fourth cause of violence is a fifth one: the strategic competence of actors. Certainly, politicians and diplomats do their utmost to be successful. For this they have to rely upon their personal ingenuity or the generalized experiences of their peers. There is no systematic education for international politicians, as there is for international lawyers or economists. This was already detrimental under the conditions of the nineteenth century, when it was no longer possible to tackle international relations with so-called "common sense." The lack of systematic education in international relations can be no less fatal under the conditions of the second half of the twentieth century. When announcing his doctrine in March 1947, for example, President Truman certainly exaggerated the Soviet threat and the American response, thereby pushing the development of the East–West conflict.[44] Nikita Khrushchev made a great mistake by deploying Soviet missiles on Cuban soil, thus bringing the world to the brink of a nuclear war.[45] Secretary of State Dean Rusk revealed after the end of the Vietnam war that it probably had been a great mistake to start it. Events do not happen in international politics because of historical necessity, although politicians like to portray it that way. They happen as a result of human decisions, which may be right, but which very often have been wrong. In the foregoing cases incompetence, not democracy or the lack thereof, underlay the use of violence.

The comprehensive understanding of the causes of violent conflict

---

[43] Dieter Ruloff, *Wie Kriege beginnen* (Munich: Beck, 1987).
[44] Richard M. Freeland, *The Truman Doctrine and the Origins of McCarthyism, Foreign Policy, Domestic Policy and International Security, 1946–48* (New York: New York University Press, 1972, 1985).
[45] Ray S. Cline, "The Cuban Missile Crisis," *Foreign Affairs*, 68 (Fall 1989), pp. 190–7. McGeorge Bundy, transcriber, James G. Blight, ed., "October 27, 1962: Transcripts of the Meetings of the ExCom," *International Security*, 12 (Winter 1987/8), pp. 30–92.

behavior and of democratization as an historical process, which in the West has begun and reached an important stage but not its optimal point, explains why empirical research has failed to find an important relation between democracy and non-violence. That is, the relationship has not been falsified. It is still reasonable to hypothesize on the basis of theoretical considerations that democratic systems of rule tend toward non-violent solutions of conflict. There is one exception: defense. When attacked, democracies will fight back. For this reason, it is necessary that all members of international systems have democratic systems of rule. Then aggression could originate only in the anarchical structure of the system – which could be weakened by an international organization – or in the strategic incompetence of the actors, rendering them unable to steer the interaction continuously in the direction of non-violence.

The end of the Cold War is, although it possesses tremendous historical weight, not enough to confirm the theory. But it lends strong support for the theory developed here and it teaches important lessons for the praxeology of foreign policy and the steering of international politics. When the system of governance sustained by NATO during the Cold War did not bring an end to East–West conflict, deterrence might have been necessary, but it certainly was not sufficient. The foregoing analysis suggests a different behavior would have been much more successful.

DEMOCRATIC STRATEGIES

If security and peace depend on a democratic system of rule for all members of an international system, democratization becomes the most important strategy. Governance through the balance of power obliged all parties to the East–West conflict to prepare for defense and deterrence. Armaments produced interactions marked by arms races and, in the best case, by the balance of power. What behavior would have produced interactions leading to the democratization of all member states involved? In other words, how can interactions be guided in order to become a system of governance within which all conflicts are being solved without violence?

It is easy to give an abstract answer: interactions must lead to the elimination of all five causes of international violence. Since it is impossible here to translate this principle into five pertinent strategies, I shall concentrate upon the strategy of democratization. It is the most important and the most difficult.

What strategies are available in order to democratize the societies of Eastern Europe, let alone the world? At first glance there are none.

Systems of rule cannot be changed from the outside. They are protected by the law of non-intervention and by the fact that penetration[46] is the exception and not the rule.

A closer scrutiny reveals quite a number of indirect and direct strategies. For instance, deterrence and balances of power influenced the systems of governance in the countries of the Warsaw Pact. They stabilized the autocratic systems of rule. Whether this outcome was intended or not, known or not, does not matter. The relationship existed, the behavior of the international environment influenced the domestic context.

This relation can be used in support of democratization. If deterrence as governance strengthens dictatorship and autocratic rule, then a system of governance centered around détente and arms control would also have consequences, this time in favor of the democratic elites. The first social revolution in Poland occurred after Bundeskanzler Brandt concluded the Warsaw Treaty with Poland in 1972, lowering the Polish–West German tensions considerably. To frame an international context in which little pressure is placed upon your enemy's frontiers is the best, and indirect, strategy of strengthening the democratic opposition. Under those circumstances non-pressure might be much more rewarding than relentless military pressure.

In other words, if threatened, defense is necessary, but is not enough, and should be completed with initiatives for détente and disarmament. Only this mix, the practical implementation of which has been discussed within the strategy of gradualism,[47] produces the right system of governance. It protects its own side and at the same time organizes the system in such a way that the forces of liberal democracy, which are on the opposite side by definition, are expressed and gain more leeway. In sum, the framing of systems of governance favorable to the process of democratization within all members of the international system is the best indirect method of steering the system into non-violent modes of conflict resolution.

Direct means are also available. Any interaction is in itself some kind of intervention. Private investments strengthen the basis of a market economy. Cultural exchanges transfer the values of liberty and self-determination. Cooperation among private organizations establishes the patterns of a pluralistic society. These effects could be enhanced if

---

46 James N. Rosenau, *The Scientific Study of Foreign Policy* (New York: Free Press, 1971), pp. 116ff.

47 For an interesting and comprehensive discussion of gradualism, see Oliver Thraenert, *Ruestungssteuerung und Gradualismus: Moeglichkeiten und Grenzen einer alternativen Sicherheitspolitik* (Munich: Tuduv, 1986).

such interactions were aimed explicitly at societal democratization. Diamond has laid out the riches of strategies for global democratization.[48]

These strategies are non-interventionist in the classical sense of the term, but they nevertheless intervene effectively in the relationship between the political system and the social environment. Modern strategies of democratization do not involve making "the world safe for democracy." They do not use covert actions, as the Central Intelligence Agency (CIA) did in its Project Democracy. Democratization is what the National Endowment for Democracy does: to use all kind of interactions to transfer the concept and practice of individual liberty, self-determination, and practical codetermination. Their implementation will vary according to culture, history, and economic development. The principle, however, is worldwide in scope. To promote its implementation by non-interventionist strategies means to intervene in favor of the society and the individual. The greater the interaction, the greater the effects.

Societal interaction should become a normal ingredient of foreign policy. Up to now the foreign policies of Western democracies are organized along the traditional monarchical lines. Governments deal with governments, international relations are being pursued as intergovernmental relations. Again, balance of power gives a striking example. This kind of interaction was invented by governments which kept their societies from interacting. In the feudal age intervention from the outside was forbidden by the law of non-intervention. Authoritarian governments still evoke it to protect their rule. During the East–West conflict even Western governments severed societal contacts with the East. The end of this conflict indicates that this was exactly the wrong strategy; it would have been much better to strengthen the democratic aspirations of the opposition in the East by interacting with them. The Conference on Security and Cooperation in Europe (CSCE) was, by contrast, the right strategy, even though a rather weak one.

The general rule should be: let the society participate in that which is called foreign policy. Societal contacts should be promoted, maybe even institutionalized. Societal regimes could fill the space between nations. This, then, would be the liberal alternative to the still monarchical praxis of foreign policy. It would contribute tremendously to democratization by strengthening the societal forces through interaction.

---

[48] Larry Diamond, "Strategies for Democratization," *The Washington Quarterly*, 1 (Winter 1983), pp. 141ff.

If interaction could be guided in this way, a system of governance would prevail which by promoting democratization would help to eliminate the most important source of violence: autocratic systems of rule. Included in the remedy would be the decentralization of power and the control of partial interests.

CONCLUSION

Conflicts between industrialized societies should be understood as highly complex systems of governance. To interpret them still as military conflicts confined to the security issue-area means to use an outmoded model of the world as a world of states and to fall into the trap of the two meanings of realism: realism as a strategy recommends a behavior the implementation of which then serves to confirm realism as a theory.

This trap became obsolete with the ending of the East–West conflict. the revolutions in Eastern Europe demonstrated how much NATO, by concentrating upon deterrence and neglecting the other two issue-areas, had damaged its own interests. By organizing the context of the conflict, its system of governance, in such a way that it would have promoted the democratization of the states of the Warsaw Pact, the West would have gained much more much earlier. Instead, by concentrating on the anarchical structure of the international system as the only cause of violence and the state as the only actor, neorealism kept its identity and stringency but missed the reality. By stepping down to the second image of the world, by opening up, and looking into the state, neorealism would have learned that it is not unrealistic to consider the three issue-areas and to emphasize the third one, the system of rule.

This is what a modern theory of foreign policy and international politics should do. It is not idealistic but highly realistic to consider that in modern industrialized societies (as a matter of fact, in all societies) the three issue-areas are closely connected and in this interrelatedness produce the conflict behavior. To influence the enemy successfully means to develop pertinent insights into this connection and to use it to steer the conflict behavior. There are many more strategies to be applied because there are more causes of conflict. But the authoritarian system of rule is the most important cause and the strategies of democratization are therefore especially relevant.

To understand modern conflicts as systems of governance is to grasp the growing importance of societies and the degree of interdependence between them. The industrialized world is no longer a world of states and not yet a world society. It is a societal world, still divided up into states within which, however, societies play the important role. For this reason the economic well-being issue-area and that of rule have become as important as that of security. The theory of foreign policy must come to grips with this new reality and foreign policy as praxis must be in tune with the societies and their systems of rule. This is not a return to the famous "crusade for Liberty" or to a so-called liberal policy of intervention. It is only the consequence of the fact that conflict and international politics are systems of governance which influence the societies and their systems of rule. Such a perspective focuses on the need to organize and steer this system of governance in such a way that the most effective causes of violence, dictatorships and the unjust distribution of values, are being affected and diminished.

Understanding international systems as systems of governance also leads to the insight that the object (and subject) of foreign policy is not the state but the individual. While the strategy of deterrence and neo-realism neglected the individual, the strategy of democratization, and liberal theory, center around it. Since governance means to allocate values, not in the same but in a similar manner as within states, under-standing conflicts as systems of governance makes it evident that every foreign policy behavior on the other side of a conflict affects not an anonymous entity, but human beings with their aspirations for economic well-being and democratic codetermination.

It is impossible to indicate the many, profound consequences flowing from this understanding of international politics and conflicts. Much remains to be done to fashion a liberal theory of foreign policy that avoids all the pitfalls and contradictions and that delineates the construction of those systems of governance which eliminate rather than contest the causes of violence.

10 CITIZENSHIP IN A CHANGING GLOBAL ORDER

James N. Rosenau

If world politics is presently marked by the emergence of new forms of governance without government, what does this imply for the world's citizens who have long been accustomed to governance being sustained by governments? How do they respond to authorities who are not created by constitutions, who are not located in formal governmental structures, and whose legitimacy may be in flux? And whatever may be their responses, can there be profound transformations in the nature of global governance without alterations in the skills and orientations of citizens? That is, if new dimensions of citizenship are likely to evolve in response to the emergent global order, how will they in turn shape the way in which the new institutions of governance develop?

Such are the questions addressed by this concluding chapter. It explores possible relationships between the emergence of a new global order – the foundations of which were laid well before the end of the Cold War[1] – and the changing competence of people throughout the world. In so doing it seeks to demonstrate that such vast transformations as the emergence of a new order at the macro level of politics cannot occur without corresponding, or at least compatible, changes taking place among citizens at the micro level.[2] It further undertakes to show that the causal processes move in both directions, that the macro changes impact significantly upon micro actors and, conversely, the changes in the latter feed back to sustain or enlarge the dynamics unfolding at the macro level. And, not least, the discussion also probes the kind of choices and responsibilities that seem increasingly likely to confront citizens everywhere as the world shrinks and its parts become both more interdependent and less coherent.

[1] For an analysis which locates the emergence of a new order in the 1950s, see James N. Rosenau, *Turbulence in World Politics: A Theory of Change and Continuity* (Princeton, NJ: Princeton University Press, 1990), pp. 107–12.

[2] Although most inquiries treat the distinction between the macro and micro levels as that between a system and its subsystems, here the micro level is confined to individuals and face-to-face groups, while all more encompassing aggregations are regarded as located at the macro level. For a discussion of the reasons for drawing the distinction in this way, see Rosenau, *Turbulence in World Politics*, ch. 6.

Finally, by joining the micro analysis that follows with the macro formulations of the preceding chapters, the chapter concludes with a brief assessment of the new global order that may be emerging as the Cold War recedes into history. The assessment proceeds from the assumption that while much research into the dynamics of global governance and order remains to be done, it is not too soon to speculate about the implications of our inquiries for the immediate future of world politics.

These efforts are founded on a theoretical rather than a factual understanding of the transformations currently at work in world politics. Since the transformations are still very much in an early stage and have yet to display the mark – well-established and clearly recognizable patterns – of an emerged rather than an emerging order, the centrality of changing micro actors cannot be empirically proven. One can only show how the course of events is consistent with a theoretical and functional explanation that locates individuals at the core of the transformation processes.

To proceed in this fashion is, of course, to be controversial. Conceptions of global order and large-scale governance normally treat macro collectivities and institutions as the bases for whatever form the order may take. Many analysts, perhaps especially those who conceptualize world politics in terms of the realist and neorealist paradigms, tend to treat the micro level as composed of constants, of citizens who comply with the directives and requirements of the macro collectivities. Viewed from this micro-as-constants perspective, global order is the order which international organizations, states, multinational corporations, and a host of other large and complex organizations evolve for managing their affairs. These macro actors are the ones whose decisions and policies, capabilities and conflicts, are conceived to frame and sustain whatever form of order prevails, and any micro-as-variables formulation which accords causal consequences to citizens is regarded as erroneous and far-fetched.

Controversial as it may be, however, rejection of the micro-as-constants approach seems inescapable in an era of rapid and profound transformations. Since macro structures and processes are by their very nature aggregates of numerous individuals, their transformation is bound to be experienced at all levels. Put empirically, too many of the squares of the world's cities have lately been filled with large crowds who make a wide variety of demands, who return again and again even in the face of brutal governmental efforts to repress them, who thus escalate conflicts and solidify stalemates with a frequency indicating contagion effects that are transforming problems of domestic order into

273

processes of global order – to note only the more obvious dynamics – to ignore the possibility that the micro level is a source as well as a consequence of global change. Stated in still another way, the micro level of individuals has to be integrated into the analysis because structures at the macro level seem increasingly vulnerable to shifts in the skills and orientations of the publics they encompass.

As implied, on the other hand, this is neither to minimize the causal consequences of macro collectivities and institutions nor to overstate the impact of citizens. The course of events is sustained by the policies and activities of collectivities as well as by the talents and attitudes of their constituent parts. Indeed, it is in the nature of collectivities that they normally develop a life of their own as individuals become accepting of and habituated to the macro policies. Not each and every policy and practice pursued at the macro level, in other words, is a function of immediate micro inputs and dynamics. On a day-to-day basis micro phenomena can often be treated as constants. From a long-term perspective and at specific historic junctures, however, basic transformations at the micro level can have substantial macro consequences. The present is one such juncture, thus heightening the need for a conceptual understanding which posits the causal flow as a two-way process, for what amounts to a macro-and-micro-as-variables framework.

MICRO BASES OF MACRO GLOBAL ORDER

Yet, some might dismiss this theoretical understanding on empirical grounds. One does not have to adhere to the realist perspective to quarrel with the premise that citizens have become important variables rather than remaining constants in global politics. Noting the foregoing concession that the centrality of micro actors is subject to conflicting interpretations, one could highlight data suggesting that in fact they continue to be peripheral to the course of world affairs, that the crowding of the squares of the world's cities with citizens demanding change in the late 1980s was a transitory phenomenon, that history is pervaded with such upheavals, and that therefore there is no reason to view micro variables as any more powerful today than they were in earlier times. While it may not be possible to generate proof that this reaffirmation of the constancy of micro actors is flawed, at least five reasons can be cited for presuming that it is unfounded and for proceeding as if citizens at the micro level are variables relevant to the emergent global order:

1   The erosion and dispersion of state and governmental power and the progressive weakening of other societal institutions (such as trade unions or political parties) have resulted in corresponding accretions to the potential roles that individuals can play through collective action.

2   The advent of global television, the widening use of computers in the workplace, the growth of foreign travel and the mushrooming migrations of peoples, the spread of educational institutions at the primary, secondary, and university levels, and many other features of the post-industrial era has enhanced the analytic skills of individuals.

3   The crowding onto the global agenda of new, interdependence issues (such as environmental pollution, currency crises, the drug trade, AIDS, and terrorism) has made more salient the processes whereby global dynamics affect the welfare and pocketbooks of individuals.

4   The revolution in information technologies has made it possible for citizens and politicians literally to "see" the aggregation of micro actions into macro outcomes. People can now observe support gather momentum as street rallies, the pronouncements of officials, the responses of adversaries, the comments of protesters, the flight of refugees, and a variety of other events get portrayed and interpreted on television screens throughout the world, thus conducing to swift and fluctuating consensuses as to how much support exists and how solid it may be. Unlike earlier times, when the communication of words and images was less instantaneous and consensuses were thus relatively slow to form and change, today the processes of aggregation are fast-moving, easily observable cascades, a fragile set of competing estimates that can readily shift direction and convey the impression of citizens sustaining an unfolding, restless momentum which leaders can ignore only at great peril.

5   This new-found capacity of citizens to "see" their role in the dynamics of aggregation has profoundly altered, possibly even reduced, the extent to which organization and leadership are factors in the mobilization of publics. As indicated by the increasing role in world affairs played by inchoate social movements such as the environmental, feminist, and peace movements,[3] spontaneous word-of-mouth processes can

---

[3] Cf. R. B. J. Walker, *One World, Many Worlds: Struggles for a Just World Peace* (Boulder, CO: Lynne Rienner, 1988).

precede and give direction to organizational efforts. In some important sense, leaders are increasingly becoming followers because individuals are becoming increasingly aware that their actions can have consequences.

Although more anecdotal than systematic, a few accounts of recent moments when citizens converged to initiate macro consequences serve to indicate the dynamism underlying these five bases for presuming that causality attaches to the conduct of individuals. Consider, for example, these on-the-scene descriptions of recent events in Burma, China, Germany, and Poland:

[Within a matter of weeks the people of Rangoon] learned public defiance . . . It is a population that has tasted political power, through street demonstrations, for the first time since U Ne Win took power 26 years ago, that has exulted in its defiance and that has seen a hated Government in retreat. At first tentatively, then, flinging their masks away, more boldly, the people learned the satisfaction of voicing their grievances openly.[4] [Indeed, this learning led to] one of the few examples of a pure popular revolution that we are seeing anywhere in the world. There are no leaders, there is no organization and there is no international movement outside the country pushing the people one way or the other.[5]

[Despite the fact that the coalescence of pro-democracy forces in Tiananmen Square] happened with startling, and seemingly inexplicable swiftness,[6] [the flow of people into the center of Beijing was the product not of organizational skills and infrastructures but of separate decisions made by hundreds of thousands of individuals. In the words of one observer, these events were] unlike anything I've ever seen before. No American student demonstration or mass civil-rights actions can begin to compare with it. From our central square, Tiananmen, "People Power" (a slogan deliberately borrowed from the Philippine Revolution of 1986) has radiated out to control almost every Beijing intersection and, at last report, streets in forty other Chinese cities as well. This youth rebellion may not be able to hold out much longer, but . . . without weapons, without communications other than *xiaodao xiaoxi*, or grapevine, without transportation other than bicycles, and trucks borrowed from farmers and work units, without even any agreement on what they were demonstrating for – except the right to demonstrate – the students and those protecting them are blocking a modern, well-equipped army . . . The sight of [Tiananmen

---

4 Seth Mydans, "Brute Force in Burma," *New York Times*, September 23, 1988, p. A17.
5 Robert Pear, "Burmese Revolt Seen as Spontaneous," *New York Times*, September 10, 1988, p. 3.
6 Nicholas D. Kristof, "China Erupts . . . The Reasons Why," *New York Times Magazine*, June 4, 1989, p. 28.

Square] covered by more than a million young people, most of them not angry but, rather, good-naturedly eager to match their collective strength against the limits of state power . . . is, quite simply, the most awesome thing I have ever seen.[7]

The Government's liberalized travel regulations . . . were an act of desperation by a Communist regime left with little alternative after the mass demonstrations that swept over East Germany. Largely leaderless and entirely peaceful, the marchers pressed the regime inexorably, forcing it first to shed its aging leaders, then to loosen restrictions on news organizations and finally to promise free elections and economic reforms. During that time, New Forum developed from a small group of veteran dissidents branded "hostile to the state" into a movement with more than 100,000 supporters.[8]

For a moment, [the leaders were caught by surprise. They] were not so much leaders as followers of a process of social combustion that raced forward spontaneously and uncontrollably: first came the mass movement; then came the demands and the negotiations . . . Suddenly, there was a power in society where none was supposed to be . . . Right in the heart of a totalitarian system, under which people are supposed to be at their most helpless, Solidarity gave the world one of the most startling demonstrations of the power of the people that it has ever seen.[9]

In short, powerful forces at work today are rendering citizens and the circumstances in which they conduct themselves very different from earlier eras. The relatively stable conditions that enabled the Concert of Europe to function in the nineteenth century (see Chapter 2 above) are a far cry from the speedy, restless pace that marks public affairs in the current era. Upheavals sparked by micro actions mark both the past and the present, but those of the current era unfold with a rapidity, spontaneity, scope, and durability that is so much greater as to make them different in kind rather than degree. Micro variables may not be sufficient as causes of the bases and forms of global order, but they certainly appear to be necessary sources.

Of course, to attribute additional causal strength to individuals and their collective endeavors is not to account for their variability. This variability occurs in two prime ways. One has already been alluded to, namely, a progressive process of learning wherein the skills of people expand and thereby enable them to perform better the tasks of group membership and to engage more effectively in varying kinds of

---

[7] Fred C. Shapiro, "Letter from Beijing," *The New Yorker*, June 5, 1989, p. 73.
[8] Serge Schmemann, "Opposition Sees Blessing and Threat," *New York Times*, November 13, 1989, p. A12.
[9] "Notes and Comments," *The New Yorker*, October 20, 1986, p. 35.

citizenship behavior. The learning may occur in fits and starts, reaching new heights in acute crises and subsiding to a steady state in "normal" periods, but across time it varies and thereby differentially impacts on the course of events.

Furthermore, the learning consists of both intellectual and emotional development. In the former case the circumstances and technologies of a globalizing world appear to have enlarged the analytic skills of individuals everywhere, enabling them to become substantially more capable of constructing complex scenarios wherein the processes of world politics culminate at their doorstep or in their pocketbook than was the case for earlier generations.[10] This skill revolution is not as surprising as it may seem at first glance. A five million-year history of human evolution (Table 1) demonstrates a clear pattern of continual growth in "metabolic memory systems" and "the symbolic energy system of the human" as a result of ever greater social complexity.[11] Although the developmental pattern is less striking with respect to cathectic skills – those capacities which enable people to recognize and focus their emotionality – the fact that huge crowds can today engage in collective actions by spontaneously converging in city squares without prior organizational effort suggests that the ability to use and channel emotions has also undergone a worldwide expansion. As one observer puts it,

> the actual structures of the social world, especially as centered on the networks upholding property and authority, involve continuous monitoring by individuals of each other's group loyalties. Since the social world can involve quite a few lines of authority and sets of coalitions, the task of monitoring them can be extremely complex. How is this possible, given people's inherently limited cognitive capacities?
>
> The solution must be that negotiations are carried out implicitly, on a different level than the use of consciously manipulated verbal symbols. I propose that the mechanism is *emotional* rather than cognitive. Individuals monitor others' attitudes toward social coalitions, and hence toward the degree of support for routines, by feeling the amount of confidence and enthusiasm there is toward certain leaders and activities, or the amount of fear of being attacked by a strong coalition, or the amount of contempt for a weak one. These

---

[10] For an extended discussion of the expansion of analytic skills among citizens in all parts of the world, see Rosenau, *Turbulence in World Politics*, ch. 13.
[11] Both Table 1 and a discussion of how systems of metabolic memory and symbolic energy have grown across millennia can be found in Esmond S. Ferguson, "Biological Memory Systems and the Human Species," *Journal of Social Biological Structures*, 11 (1988), pp. 409–14.

Table 1. *Stages in the evolution of the human*

Stage	Characteristic	Period (years ago)
I. Animistic	(1) *Australopithecus*	5,000,000–1,300,000
	(2) *Homo erectus*	1,300,000–300,000
	(3) *Homo sapiens* Neanderthal	300,000–50,000
	(4) *Homo sapiens sapiens* Acquisition of speech Lack of self-awareness Possessing symbolic memory ("consciousness") Environmental interpretation: totemism	50,000–10,000
II. Magical	*Homo sapiens sapiens* Acquisition of "self" and language Rise of god-kings claiming miraculous powers All forces personalized, under human control	10,000–0
III. Normative	Breakdown of dual class societies Rise of craftsmen Awareness of "self" in populace Awakening of "conscience"	4,000–0
IV. Rational	Discovery of nature of language Creation of "faculty" of reason Mathematical generalization	3,000–0
V. Critical	Integration of perceptual and conceptual functions	
	(1) Cosmic energy interpreted	500–0
	(2) Biological energy probed	150–0
	(3) Human energy system – "consciousness"	Interpretation dawning

emotional energies are transmitted by contagion among members of a group, in flows which operate very much like the set of negotiations which produce prices within a market.[12]

The second form of micro variability involves the way in which people tip the macro–micro balance by altering their support for the collectivities that constitute the macro level. As will be seen, the turbulence of world politics presents citizens with continuing choices as to which of the conflicting demands upon them they give highest priority as the tensions between centralizing and decentralizing dynamics sustain the shifting loci of authority. The interaction of macro- and micro-level phenomena, in other words, is anything but constant. In different eras of history the macro–micro balance can tip in

[12] Randall Collins, "On the Micro Foundations of Macrosociology," *American Journal of Sociology*, 86 (March 1981), p. 944 (italics in original).

279

either direction to varying degrees. In periods when states and their international system predominate, it tips in a macro or centralizing direction and global stability is likely to be enhanced. On the other hand, when the balance shifts in a micro or decentralizing direction (as this chapter argues is presently occurring), the probability of greater global instability increases as the locus of authority moves down to subgroup and individual levels. Due to the greater analytic skills of citizens, moreover, the shifting macro–micro balance stems in part from a greater capacity of individuals to appreciate that their collective actions can result in a counterproductive lurch in a decentralizing direction, that macro collectivities and macro institutions may need to be shored up so that goals can be realized through a modicum of order.

TERRITORIAL AND GLOBALIZING TENDENCIES

To be persuaded that micro-level variables are relevant to world politics is not, of course, to delineate how their influence operates at macro levels or to suggest the kinds of choices and responsibilities with which citizens are likely to be confronted in an era where governance without government is more pervasive. To do this we need also to set forth some initial premises as to the central tendencies at work on the macro level, those changes in the distribution of power within and among macro actors and in the institutions they evolve to manage their affairs that open up new opportunities for and impose new limitations on citizens and their collective actions.

To be sure, the nature of the emergent post-Cold War global order remains obscure and is doubtless still capable of unfolding in diverse directions. Yet, while it is not possible to assert with confidence what direction is most likely to prove dominant, several central tendencies can be discerned and posited as the underlying conditions that are shaping and being shaped by the world's citizens. Stated more cautiously, even if these tendencies turn out to be misleading and exaggerated, it is instructive for analytic purposes to posit them as operative and thereby to develop some understanding of how macro and micro dynamics may be linked to each other.

One useful way to conceive of the underlying dynamics moving world politics on to new global structures it to focus on the tensions that arise out of the clash of centralizing and decentralizing tendencies that are unfolding in all parts of the world and on every level of organized activity, from the local organization to the international system. As technologies continue to shrink the world and render it more interdependent, that is, so do they initiate forces which lead to division within and among groups. At one and the same time, in effect, the world is thus becoming more and more integrated and more fragmented. Governments, corporations, churches, unions, and virtually every other type of enterprise founded on coordinated action are seeking both to expand and contract their reach, to coordinate more extensively with counterparts elsewhere even as they subdivide their tasks and break up into smaller and more local units. And the processes are mutually reinforcing: the more a collectivity gets enmeshed in the expanding interdependence, the more do some of its parts seek greater autonomy and independence, just as the greater fragmentation then stirs desires for more cohesion and centralization. Thus it is, for example, that even as Western Europe is evolving an economy and polity that encompasses the states of the region, so are some of these states undergoing privatization and fragmentation in response to demands for more local control or to pressures from ethnic, linguistic, and other minorities.

A more empirical way of describing these dialectic dynamics is to conceive of them as based on contradictory principles of world order, on a territorial principle and a globalizing principle.[13] While the former is discernible in activities intended to upgrade the state and other organizations which promote the well-being of a territorially proscribed area, the latter is manifest in a large array of activities that extend across territorial jurisdictions in response to the world's greater interdependence. The incorporation of national economies into the world economy is perhaps the most conspicuous example of the globalizing principle, but many other instances of territorial commitments yielding to broader horizons could also be cited. Even as the globalizing principle appears to be increasingly pervasive, however, so are states and other entities bounded by geography serving the territorial principle by seeking to reinforce and extend their influence.

Still another, more elaborate conception of the fundamental changes at work in the world involves a simultaneous breakdown of three basic parameters that have long served as the boundaries within which international politics have been conducted.[14] One of the parameters operates at the macro level as the boundary for the overall structure of the global

---

[13] The distinction between the globalizing and territorial principles has been developed by Robert W. Cox. See, for example, his Chapter 5 in this volume and also his paper, "Production and Security," presented at the Conference on Emerging Trends in Global Security, sponsored by the Canadian Institute for International Peace and Security (Montebello, Quebec, October 17–19, 1990).

[14] The ensuing discussion of parametric transformations is derived from Rosenau, *Turbulence in World Politics*, ch. 5.

system, which is considered to be undergoing a transformation from the long-standing state-centric, anarchical system to a new set of bifurcated arrangements wherein a multi-centric world composed of diverse "sovereignty-free" collectivities has evolved apart from and in competition with the state-centric world of "sovereignty-bound" actors. Both of these two worlds of world politics are pervaded with turbulence as some of the authority of states is regarded as undergoing relocation to proliferating actors in the multi-centric world – either "outwards" to supranational and transnational collectivities or "inwards" to subnational actors, all of whom thereby further secure their autonomy in the multi-centric world.

As previously noted, in other words, a central tendency on the present world scene involves a diminution of state authority. In their own world, of course, states still predominate as their interests, conflicts, bargains, and institutions shape the course of events in the realms of political, military, and economic diplomacy. But this predominance has lessened as transportational and electronic technologies have extended the autonomy of the diverse collectivities in the multi-centric world and thus multiplied the number and kind of transactions that occur across national boundaries in which states neither participate nor exercise influence.

Contemporaneous with the slippage in state authority, and in part fostered by it, has been a mounting sense of cohesion and common purpose within the memberships of collectivities in the multi-centric world. Today this phenomenon is most visible among ethnic and national minorities. But since it can also be discerned in all kinds of other groups, the dynamism of this phenomenon is not adequately captured by the notion of "nationalism." Rather, to emphasize the diversity of groups whose sense of cohesion is mushrooming, it seems best labeled as "subgroupism," a generic term which encompasses the drive for autonomy that is not necessarily associated with the aspiration for statehood.

The bifurcation of global structures and the spread of intense subgroupism is coincident with the transformation of a second prime parameter of world politics, namely, the macro–micro parameter which consists of the authority relationships whereby macro collectivities achieve the compliance of the micro actors who comprise their memberships. Today this parameter is undergoing a turbulence that amounts to a global authority crisis as the sources of governance within and between societies become increasingly obscure, as crowds gather in city squares, as majorities give way to coalitions, as stalemates persist or cabinets fall, as transnational organizations tap the energies of individuals, and as long-standing social movements (such as the New Left or the Labor movement) with homogeneous memberships and clear-cut organizational structures give way to new movements (such as the women's and the ecological movements) that are less hierarchical and more local, disorganized, and fragmented. In short, with the advent of a vast "network of waxing and waning groups and strategies,"[15] authority has today become problematic where it once was given in world politics.

The third global parameter undergoing change operates at the micro level of individuals. As already indicated, due to the complexity of post-industrial dynamics, the ever-expanding interdependence of economies, the impact of the microelectronic revolution, more extensive education, the travel of immigrants, refugees, and tourists, and a variety of other sources, people in every corner of the world can be viewed as having acquired more analytic skills and cathectic capacities than their forebears, talents that better enable them to discern where they fit in the course of distant events, to appreciate the virtues of collective action, and thus to be present in the squares of the world's cities at those times when the aggregation of micro actions into macro outcomes can have significant consequences. To be sure, huge differences still persist in the analytic skills of people in different regions of the world. Those in the industrialized West continue to be more skillful than citizens in the Third World, but nevertheless the transformation of the micro parameter is global in the sense that the enhancement of analytic capabilities has occurred everywhere. Hence, whatever the differences in skills may be, their enhancement is sufficient to have resulted in a worldwide alteration of the criteria of political legitimacy and authority: where people once complied habitually and automatically with the directives of authorities, today they are much more inclined to assess the performance of the authorities before attaching legitimacy to and complying with directives.

Table 2 presents an overview of the three global parameters and their transformations. It does not indicate, however, the large extent to which simultaneity marks the several transformations. This is another way of saying that they are interactive, that the change in each parameter intensifies the transformation of the other two, thus fostering a turbulent pace and scope of change that is pervaded with uncertainty and susceptible to sudden shifts in direction. The processes of structural

---

15 Heinz-Gunter Vester, "Collective Behavior and Social Movements under Postmodern Conditions," a paper presented at the International Sociological Association Congress (Madrid, July 10, 1990), p. 4.

Table 2. *Transformation of three global parameters*

	From	To
Macro parameter	Anarchic system of nation-states	Bifurcation into state-centric and multi-centric systems
Micro parameter	Individuals less analytically skillful and cathectically competent	Individuals more analytically skillful and cathectically competent
Macro–micro parameter	Authority structures in place as people rely on traditional and/or constitutional sources of legitimacy to comply with directives emanating from macro institutions	Authority structures in crisis as people evolve performance criteria for legitimacy and comply with directives viewed as associated with appropriate conduct by macro officials

bifurcation encourage subgroup formation which, in turn, stimulates further autonomy in the multicentric world that, in turn, expands the complexity to which individuals adapt by enlarging their capabilities, just as the greater skills of citizens weakens states, strengthens subgroups, and thereby extends the divide between the state- and multicentric worlds.

While it is not possible to discern the overall global structure that may evolve out of the tensions between the centralizing and decentralizing tendencies, the contradictions between the territorial and globalizing principles, and the basic parameter transformations, a generalized concept that encompasses all these dynamics and that serves as an apt characterization of the prevailing global arrangements in this interim period of change is available. That is the concept of polyarchy, a perspective that is most often applied to domestic political systems,[16] but that has also been used to describe the present state of world politics:

> The forces now ascendant appear to be leaning toward a global society without a dominant structure of cooperation and conflict – a *polyarchy* in which nation-states, subnational groups, and

[16] See, for example, Robert A. Dahl, *Democracy and its Critics* (New Haven, CT: Yale University Press, 1989), chs. 16–20.

transnational special interests and communities are all vying for the support and loyalty of individuals and conflicts need to be resolved primarily on the basis of ad hoc bargaining among combinations of these groups that vary from issue to issue. In the polyarchic system, world politics is no longer essentially "international" politics, where who gets what, when and how is determined on the basis of bargaining and fighting among the nation-states; rather, the international system is now seen as one of the *sub*systems of a larger and more complex field of relationships.[17]

Such is the nature of the emergent post-Cold War world to which citizens everywhere must now respond. It is a bifurcated world marked by new choices and old options, by many opportunities and heavy responsibilities, by persistent tensions between demands for order and pressures for equity, by a potential for new heights of cooperation and a capacity for intensified conflict. More relevant for present purposes, it is a world in which governance is increasingly pervasive and governments decreasingly effective. What this polyarchical world requires of individuals, both as citizens and as leaders, and how they can seize the opportunities to prosper in it, is the focus of the remainder of this chapter.

CITIZENSHIP UNDER POLYARCHY

Viewed from the perspective of individuals anywhere in the world, the emergent polyarchical structure not only conduces to much higher degrees of uncertainty; it has also generated possibilities for fulfillment and obligations to shoulder with which most people have had no previous experience. Equipped with greater capacities to fashion scenarios that link them into distant developments, and thus more acutely aware of how micro actions might aggregate to collective outcomes, citizens now have many more avenues along which to pursue their interests. The bifurcation of global structures, the advent of new criteria of legitimacy and authority, and the accompanying evolution of governance mechanisms not linked to formal governments affords them a multitude of new points of access to the course of events. They can join social movements, contest their own leaders, protest in support of counterparts abroad seen on television to be enmeshed in struggles relevant to their own, engage in cooperative ventures designed to deepen their foreign links, and otherwise undertake a host

---

[17] Seyom Brown, *New Forces, Old Forces, and the Future of World Politics* (Glenview, IL: Scott Foresman, 1988), p. 245 (italics in the original).

of diverse activities that tie them into the dynamics of an ever more interdependent world.

Clearly the proliferation of governance without government, of access points in a polyarchical world, poses huge new challenges to citizenship in the emergent global order. Increasingly people will have to make unfamiliar choices as to whether they channel their loyalties in systemic or subsystemic directions, as to how they resolve conflicting loyalties, as to the bases on which they attach legitimacy to leaders and institutions at the macro level, as to whether they dwell on the uncertainties or the opportunities inherent in the tensions of a bifurcated world, as to whether they opt for order over change or vice versa, as to whether they become involved in more encompassing non-territorial networks or retreat to more close-at-hand outlets for their needs and wants, and so on through a wide range of persistent and (given the world's vast tilt in micro directions) awesome dilemmas.

While an extensive essay could be developed around each of these dilemmas, here it is possible to explore only some of their main implications. Perhaps the most relentless set of choices pertains to the endless tensions between the desirabilities of systemic order and the satisfactions that flow from subsystemic coherence. Given a bifurcated world marked by pervasive authority crises, intense subgroupism, and ambiguous foci of legitimacy, people are likely to become increasingly sensitive to the potential for pervasive disorder within and among communities even as they simultaneously get caught up by a sense that their subgroups can prosper at the expense of their more encompassing systemic structures. Under these circumstances they are likely to become increasingly aware of their own leverage, of their ability, through joining in collective action, to tip the balance toward either systemic order or subsystemic autonomy. Such an awareness, in turn, will surely heighten for them the question of where their self-interest lies, whether they are best served through the collective goals of their larger territorial community or through the more narrowly defined preoccupations of their globalizing subgroups. And if their inclinations and loyalties run in favor of the former, there is the further question of which territorial community, the existing nation-state, the historic nation or ethnic minority, the regional community, or the local jurisdiction, should be the focus of their support.

This dilemma is acutely present today in the Soviet Union, Yugoslavia, Israel, India, China, and a host of other countries undergoing severe authority crises that may tear them apart. If one is a Serb, does one yield to one's historic nationalist impulses and support leaders who would bring an end to Yugoslavia by pressing Serbian goals? Or does one opt for those who would limit Serbian aspirations in the interests of Yugoslavian unity? If one is a Georgian who subscribes to greater independence for the republic of Georgia in the Soviet Union, does one also support the right of the 100,000 people in South Ossetia to assert their independence of the republic of Georgia? These are not academic questions. Virtually everywhere in the world today citizens are confronting them in the form of conflicting appeals for their loyalty and compliance, for joining or abstaining from a variety of forms of collective action.

Closely linked to the choice between systemic order and subsystemic coherence, between sustaining the historic nation-state and extending subgroup autonomy, is a series of questions involving the use of coercion. Under what conditions does the citizen lend support to subsystemic causes that are sought through resort to armed action or to systemic causes that are pursued through the use of force to maintain public order? Are there occasions, in other words, where one does not join in collective action on behalf of preferred goals because the means employed to achieve them are noxious?

Some might argue that choices such as the foregoing exist only in the mind of analysts, that citizens caught up in the passions of subgroupism are not likely to think twice about where their loyalties lie, where to channel their support, or whether the breakdown of systemic order poses problems no less serious than those which inhibit subsystemic autonomy. Certainly history offers countless instances in support of this argument, a wide array of situations in which people give vent to their subsystemic passions without regard for systemic consequences or a concern for the limits to coercion. One need only point to the most recent outbreaks of violent conflict in parts of the Soviet Union or India – to mention only the more obvious examples of many that could be cited – to demonstrate that the emotional attachments of people can overwhelm their readiness to think twice before lending support to subsystemic goals. Virulent patriotism and nationalism, in short, have surely so scarred the twentieth century that it is difficult to imagine large numbers of individuals heeding appeals for restraint and opting for the patient and peaceful rebuilding of large community ties.

Yet, to repeat, these historic patterns may no longer tell the whole story. Citizenship in a globalizing world is not the same as citizenship in a world that venerated the territorial principle. Notwithstanding the incidents of violent nationalist outbreaks in the Soviet Union and elsewhere, more and more people possess the analytic skills to juggle the conflicting claims on their loyalties and alternative views of the propriety of coercive action. For every example of a breakdown in public order one could probably cite a case where thoughtfulness and patience prevailed to sustain dialogues, contain protests within peaceful bounds, to form coalitions, and to maintain efforts at compromise. Consider, for instance, this account of the mass restraint exercised in Lithuania during a key period of its drive for independence from the Soviet Union:

> In Vilnius, the public's self-control has been phenomenal . . . Television suggested that the people were constantly on the streets, chanting national songs and weeping with joy under their tricolor. Lithuanians, however, are economical with political gestures. When the moment is right, they will turn out by the hundreds of thousands, but for the most part they have behaved as if an attempt to break out of the Soviet Union was a monthly routine.[18]

The possibility of citizens having opposing reactions – retreating either to emotional demands for subsystemic autonomy or to thoughtful preferences for systemic coherence – when change is rapid, uncertainty high, and authority structures in crisis, highlights the necessity of assessing what determines whether people assess their self-interests as best linked to their more encompassing collectivities or to their subgroups. Leaving aside personality factors (which presumably are distributed randomly through any population and thus do not operate systematically), two prime determinants are especially noteworthy. One involves perceptions of how others are making such choices. It is difficult to opt for systemic values, for paying taxes, not hoarding, or otherwise playing by the rules, when one's fellow citizens are pressing a narrow view of their interests and setting their own rules. Put differently, clinging to the middle of the road and championing the virtues of both systemic and subsystemic values requires deep conviction and heroic fortitude when most people are angrily demanding that the road be confined to subsystemic needs and wants. Much the same can be said when the herd instinct runs in the other direction and people are trouncing the values of equity and liberty on behalf of the system's greater glory.

The way in which people perceive how others are according scope to their self-interests is inextricably linked to the second determinant of how they respond to the requirements of citizenship in a fast-changing, bifurcated world, namely, how the leaders of the various collectivities to which they are linked conduct themselves in response to conflicting

---

[18] Neal Ascherson, "The Trial of Lithuania," *The New York Review*, April 26, 1990, p. 3.

systemic and subsystemic challenges. Do leaders acknowledge the need for systemic integrity as they press their subsystemic demands? Or do they argue that preserving systemic integrity is too high a price to pay for limiting their demands? Do they appeal to their followers as thoughtful and fair-minded or as excessively emotional and easily manipulated? Do they call attention to the necessity of adhering to the middle of the road, to finding a balance between systemic coherence and subsystemic progress? Or do they exploit the emotionality of their followers and portray the system and its subsystems as locked into an adversarial relationship?

There is, of course, no general answer to such questions. Much depends on the historic precedents of any system and the kind of people it thrusts into leadership positions. It is easy to cite innumerable cases of leaders who led their collectivity down narrow subsystemic paths, sometimes to its detriment and sometimes to its benefit, just as leaders who focused energy on systemic coherence and integrity can readily be culled from the pages of the past. In recent times, for example, four subsystemic leaders stand out by virtue of having championed systemic integrity at the very moment that they led their subsystem to a triumphant victory over the repressive system in which it was located: just as Vaclav Havel called on the U.S. to aid the Soviet Union within days after successfully leading Czechoslovakia's independence from the Soviet Union, so did Andrei Sakharov, Lech Walesa, and Nelson Mandela initially seek to preserve the coherence of the system that had imprisoned them or otherwise negated their long-standing efforts to achieve freedom, dignity, and equity for the members of their subsystem.

Like their followers, leaders are susceptible to framing their tasks in highly charged contexts. History is strewn with demagogues who appealed to narrow self-interests rather than alerting their audiences to the complexity of situations and the negative systemic consequences of their excessive subsystemic pressures. Great as the temptations to resort to demagoguery may be, however, today's leaders are well situated to resist succumbing to them. The complexities of a globalizing world, the inextricableness of the links between the short run and the long term, the overlap of systemic and subsystemic institutions, and the skills which enable them to construct alternative scenarios that depict their well-being in the future – to mention only a few dynamics that have enhanced effective leadership[19] – are too great for those who

---

[19] For an analysis of how leadership skills have been enhanced in recent years, see Rosenau, *Turbulence in World Politics*, ch. 12.

head collectivities to readily ignore the constraints which limit their legitimacy and their leeway to pursue emotionally satisfying but empirically unrealistic goals. Leaders know, moreover, that the half-life of demagogues is increasingly short, that simplistic solutions do not work for long in complex environments, and that brutal techniques of coercion are normally not sufficient to break through the densities and interdependencies of ever more complex systems and subsystems.

The conception of citizens and their leaders as increasingly skillful is not to assume that in the present era we are witness to the triumph of democracy. To be sure, the skill revolution can be discerned in the worldwide demand for democratic freedoms and institutions. But this is not to assert, as some have, that the end of history has arrived because people everywhere have become imbued with democratic values.[20] On the contrary, and to repeat, commitments and orientations at the micro level are best seen as variables, as subject to evolution and change in response to developments at the macro level. What may seem like the end of history is thus best viewed as a reversal in course which may, in turn, undergo further reversals. Put differently, the central argument here is not that aspirations for democracy are driving the winds of change. These aspirations are seen, rather, as a consequence of the skill revolution that has transformed the competencies of citizens. In another historical era the enlarged skills might result in non-democratic tendencies if people assess their well-being to be served through, say, religious fundamentalism, authoritarian rule, or any other forms of governance not founded on democratic procedures. In short, nothing in the preceding formulation posits a direct causal relationship between the skill revolution and democratic political forms.

Nor should the conception of citizens and their leaders as increasingly skillful be viewed as implying that they have become rational actors. To be able better to locate oneself in complex scenarios or to focus emotions more surely on perceived threats is not necessarily to be more competent in assessing goals, accumulating relevant information, estimating costs and benefits, choosing the most efficacious course of action, or otherwise engaging in the diverse calculations on which rational action is founded. For all their analytic and cathectic advances, people are still subject to abiding by tradition, clinging to habits, yielding to unreasoned passion, screening out unwanted information, and otherwise engaging in the diverse practices through which non-rational conduct is sustained.

---

[20] See, for example, Francis Fukuyama, "The End of History?," *National Interest*, 16 (Summer 1989), pp. 3–18.

There is, however, much room for change within the continuum that locates rational actors at one extreme and habit-driven actors at the other. And this is what the foregoing discussion presumes: that in a transforming, globalizing world pervaded by enormous tensions between continuity and change, people are adapting rather than remaining constant, that the task of coping with complexity is inducing them to alter their habitual responses and perfect their analytic skills even as they remain bound to their cultures and prone to adhere to long-standing patterns. Given a world where governance is increasingly operative without government, where lines of authority are increasingly more informal than formal, where legitimacy is increasingly marked by ambiguity, citizens are increasingly capable of holding their own by knowing when, where, and how to engage in collective action.

THE EMERGENT ORDER

Given more competent and active citizenries as well as a host of other reasons noted in previous chapters, new global orders are not likely to emerge quickly with full-blown clarity. Politicians may announce the arrival of a new order, but such pronouncements stem less from close theoretical/empirical analysis and more from aspirations to break with the past and justify the adoption of new policies. Hence, they are unlikely to appreciate the delicate and complex processes out of which new orders emerge or to acknowledge that old habits and institutions have to be discarded and new ones formed, processes that are halting and disjointed. It may well require decades for historians to pronounce such processes as having run their course.

Viewed in this way, it is hardly surprising that the global order which may be emerging out of the rubble of the Cold War is still obscure, that the arrangements which will constitute governance without government in the future remain unclear and still very much subject to the choices which leaders and publics will make in the years ahead. Some of the dimensions on which the new order will be founded, however, can be dimly discerned and are worthy of notation.

Perhaps the clearest signs of an emergent order are to be found at the behavioral and institutional levels. A series of events since the end of the Cold War and the collapse of the Soviet empire point to a set of arrangements that will be marked by a continuing tension between centralizing and decentralizing dynamics, between pressures for the coordination of transnational efforts to meet the challenges of ever-greater interdependence and those seeking to satisfy subnational demands for autonomy and independence. Expressive of the former pressures are the moves toward unification in Europe, the new missions assigned to the North Atlantic Treaty Organization (NATO), the steps toward resolving old conflicts in Korea, Cambodia, and the Middle East, and the multistate institutions designed to reduce the ozone gap and the dangers of global warming. Indicative of the decentralizing dynamics are the nationalistic pressures for autonomy in Quebec, in all the republics of the Soviet Union, in Yugoslavia, and in a variety of other multiethnic situations. Whether the future global order will encompass persistent tensions between these contradictory transnational and subnational pressures, or whether one or the other will eventually become the dominant set of arrangements, is difficult to estimate. From the vantage point of the early 1990s, it is hard to envision one prevailing over the other, but much will depend on what transpires at the ideational level, on whether intersubjective rationales develop that will allow for the concurrent pressure of powerful transnational and subnational tendencies.

Stated differently, the decentralizing dynamics seem sufficiently strong to block the emergence of a centralized authority in global politics. Or at least there are no signs that the breakup of the Cold War order portends the emergence of an international society with a government capable of exercising authority over national actors. Pockets of such authority may evolve, as seems to be happening in Europe, but the evidence of a reversion to local and subnational values is too extensive to attach significance to a vision in which some form of world government evolves out of the disarray that has accompanied the breakdown of the Cold War order.

Hardly less manifest in recent developments is the likelihood that the future global order will not be dominated by a hegemonic power. Although the relative influence of the great powers has been the focus of extensive debate, with some contending that the U.S. still retains its hegemonic status and others arguing that Japan and Europe are likely successors to the U.S.'s leadership role,[21] it can reasonably be asserted that the growing complexity of global life is too great for any single

---

[21] See, for example, Samuel P. Huntington, "The U.S. – Decline or Renewal?," *Foreign Affairs*, 67 (Winter 1988/9), pp. 76–96; Paul Kennedy, *The Rise and Fall of the Great Powers: Economic Change and Military Conflict from 1500 to 2000* (New York: Random House, 1987); Henry R. Nau, *The Myth of America's Decline: Leading the World Economy into the 1990s* (New York: Oxford University Press, 1990); and Susan Strange, "The Persistent Myth of Lost Hegemony," *International Organization*, 41 (Autumn 1987), pp. 551–74.

country, or any condominium of countries, to acquire a hegemonic status comparable to those once held by the U.S. and Great Britain. To be sure, the United States demonstrated military superiority in the war against Saddam Hussein's Iraq, but its subsequent role in fashioning a peace for the Middle East was more an expression of collaborative than hegemonic leadership. Similarly, while regional centers of power might well evolve, with the common market countries and the Soviet world coalescing enough to create a dominant role in Europe and the U.S. and Japan doing the same for the Western Hemisphere and the Pacific rim, but such arrangements will be far different from those that have prevailed during prior periods of hegemonic leadership.

Still another trend that may well come to be central in the emergent global order concerns the capacity of publics to express their demands by converging on public squares. If this pattern continues, and there are good reasons to believe that it will,[22] it will surely introduce considerable volatility into the arrangements through which world politics move through time. That is, if the pattern is expressive of a spreading global intersubjectivity that values democratic procedures, it will be increasingly hazardous for leaders to ignore the demands of publics, all of which can intrude a measure of uncertainty into the conduct of world affairs.[23] It will mean, in effect, that the arrangements underlying the prevailing order are endlessly subject to revision, to fluctuating somewhat erratically as new issues and challenges surface on the global agenda and arrest the attention of mobilized publics.

Whatever may be the volatility of the future order, however, it seems unlikely to be dominated by the unrelenting threat of nuclear holocaust that shaped the Cold War order. For the end of superpower rivalry, not to mention the widespread realization that the global economy may have replaced the battlefield as the site of competition among international actors, suggests that the emergent global order will be relatively free of strategic underpinnings. To be sure, it will not be free of weapons and an arms trade supportive of localized, low-intensity conflicts, but the likelihood of a pervasive preoccupation with military options and actions does not seem very great.

While the foregoing outline of the emergent global order seems reasonably accurate, it offers little guidance on the complex of perceptions, values, and beliefs that is likely to evolve at the ideational level.

---

[22] See the discussion of how the analytic and coalescing skills of publics have expanded in Rosenau, *Turbulence in World Politics*, ch. 13, and James N. Rosenau, "The Relocation of Authority in a Shrinking World," *Comparative Politics* (April 1992).

[23] As indicated above, however, this is not to imply that the involvement of publics necessarily renders the conduct of world affairs volatile.

The absence of a hegemon, the centralizing–decentralizing tensions, the greater involvement of publics, and the shift from military to economic competition do not, taken together, lend themselves to simplified ideational perspectives. In contrast to prior periods in international history, the emergent order seems likely to be marked by complexities and contradictions that may inhibit the evolution of a widespread ideational consensus. It may be, in fact, that the prime premise of whatever intersubjective understanding of global order lies ahead will be one in which a tolerance of pluralistic tendencies and an acceptance of complexity is considered sufficient to enable world politics to move intact through time.

Does this portend a diminution of governance in the continued absence of a centralized authority? Not at all. It simply means that the arrangements through which governance without government occurs may be more informal, varied, and elaborate than those to which the world became accustomed during the Cold War period. A pluralist order tends to disaggregate the centers of decision, but it too requires a measure of governance if it is to endure.

Furthermore, the centralizing tendencies inherent in the possibility of worsening environmental conditions in the years ahead ought not be underestimated. It is not inconceivable that if the processes of global warming and the widening of the ozone gap – to cite only the more conspicuous of the many environmental threats that may gather momentum – continue to unfold at their current pace, the tendencies toward a pluralist order will be substantially offset by the evolution of shared norms that attach even greater value to forms of governance without government which reinforce a cooperative global order.

294

INDEX

AIDS, 3, 33, 79–80, 275
Abbé de Saint Pierre, 35
Abdoladli, Narsin, 94n
abolitionists, 217
Abrahamson, Dean Edwin, 78n
acid rain, 76
actors, 266, 282
Adams, Gordon, 265n
adaptation, 108, 144
Adler, Emmanuel, 68n, 75, 75n, 121n
Afghanistan, 143
Africa, 43, 46, 50, 79, 94, 106, 116, 116n, 119, 121, 122, 126, 129, 205, 208, 212, 263
aggregation, 21, 275
agriculture, 109, 221
Al-Azmah, Aziz, 147n, 157n
Al-Jabri, Mohammed, 154
Albania, 52
alcohol regime, 205–8, 213–17
Alexander I, 35, 36, 37, 42, 43, 52
Alexander, Yonah, 75n
Algeciras crisis (1906), 50
alliances, 17, 55, 91
Allied Powers, 36, 40
Alt, James, 164n, 225n, 226n
Amnesty International, 5, 6
anarchy, 7–8, 30, 32, 36, 47, 53, 60, 103, 136, 229, 230, 232, 233, 238, 240, 244, 245, 247, 248, 282; principles of, 42, 48, 56, 234, 255, 260
Anderson, Matthew, 43n
Anglo-American negotiations, 206–7
Antarctica, 9, 76, 170; treaties on, 169, 180–2

Apollo mission (1968), 101
Arab, 146, 155, 155n, 157n
Archer, Clive, 168n
areopagus, 36, 38, 39
Argentina, 113, 127
Aristotle, 151
armaments, 53, 199, 200
arms control, 9, 74, 178, 253, 255, 260, 268
arms races, 17, 53, 54, 162, 208, 254, 255, 265, 267
arms trade, 208–11, 214, 215, 293
Armstrong, David, 58n
Armstrong Neil, 89
Armstrong, Scott, 171n
Aronson, Jonathan D., 91n
Artis, Michael, 88n
'asabiya, 153, 153n, 154, 155, 156, 159
Ascherson, Neal, 288n
Ashley, Richard K., 7n, 133, 140
Asia, 94, 106, 122, 149, 212
Atwater, Elton, 210n
Austria, 34, 38, 39, 43, 44, 50, 52, 121n, 213
Austria-Hungary, 25, 47, 51, 52
Austrian Netherlands, 39
autarky, 83, 113
authoritarian regimes, 62, 63, 114, 131, 262, 263, 268–70, 290
authority, 5, 32, 44–6, 50, 81, 103, 150, 198; crises in, 286, 288; relocation of, 2–3, 279–80, 282, 285
autonomy, 71, 281, 282, 284, 292; of the state, 90, 91; vs. order, 286–91
Ayres, Robert, 118n
Azimov, Isaac, 89

295